PARENT-TEACHER COLLECTION

THE

Homeschooling

Book of Answers

REVISED

The 101 Most Important Questions Answered by
Homeschooling's Most Respected Voices

PRIMA PUBLISHING

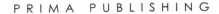

To the memory of Grandma Lind, who took the time
to share the world with a wide-eyed little girl

And to the memory of Janie Levine Hellyer, whose helping
hands will be sorely missed by the homeschooling community

Published by Prima Publishing, Roseville, California. Member of the Crown Publishing Group, a division of Random House, Inc. An earlier edition of this work was published by Prima Publishing, a member of the Crown Publishing Group, a division of Random House, Inc., New York, in 1998.

PRIMA PUBLISHING and colophon are trademarks of Random House, Inc., registered with the United States Patent and Trademark Office.

Photograph of Katharine Houk by Sandy McNay; photograph of Donna Nichols-White by Jill Sabella; photograph of Rebeccca Kochenderfer by Sirlin Photography; photograph of Janie Levine Hellyer by S. Vento; photograph of Marsha J. Ransom by Friesen Photography; and photograph of Pat Montgomery by Terri Wheeler.

Library of Congress Cataloging-in-Publication Data on file
ISBN 0-7615-3570-5

02 03 04 05 BB 10 9 8 7 6 5 4 3 2 1
Printed in the United States of America

Second Edition

Visit us online at www.primapublishing.com

CONTENTS

1

Now That Homeschooling Is Legal and Safe . . .   3

2

Homeschool May Be Cheaper Than You Think   25

5

"Educationese" You Can Understand   95

6

Okay, the Kids Are Home—*Now* What?   113

7

It's Effective! Assessing Your Child's Growth   159

8

You Mean I Don't Need to Know Algebra?! The Teen Years   171

9

Kids Say the Darnedest Things—About Homeschooling 191

10

The Home in Homeschool 211

11
Personally Speaking   225

12
Twenty-First Century Homeschooling   239

13

Lifeboats: Final Inspiration   261

ACKNOWLEDGMENTS

Writing a book would always be twice as difficult without the encouragement given me by my cousin, Louise Pohlman, the big sister I never had. Love you, "Weesie!"

In a project involving as many people as this book has, there are countless more folks behind the scenes, like husbands and wives and children whose lives with the contributors inspire them and whose support gives them time and opportunity to write. There are people like Mary E. Shannon who acted as e-mail go-between for Michelle Barone and me before Michelle got herself "wired," and Christine Webb who kindly became a contact person when I needed to get a message to her son, contributor Adam Grimm. Joan Harriss shared her specialized knowledge to help Rebecca Kochenderfer answer the question about sports, and Pat Lines and Laura Derrick kindly contributed the results of their research as appendices that make this book all the more valuable to its readers. Heartfelt appreciation to all. Your benevolent contributions were necessary pieces that helped make this book whole.

Many thanks, also, to the folks at Prima Publishing, from editors to legal staff, from Ben, wise enough to see the need for this book, to the sales staff who will make sure families have an opportunity to learn more about homeschooling through their work.

There remain only the contributors . . . and how to find the words to share with you how very much your support of this book has meant to me. Over the years as I've met most of you I've been touched by the depth of your understanding, the fire of your enthusiasm, and the warmth of your spirits. I still feel as if I know the few of you I haven't met in person from the way you sprinkle your writing with the same qualities.

We saw. We believed. We did it, gang! (And they say gathering homeschoolers is like trying to herd cats!) You shared the vision. You gave of yourselves—yet again—to the ideal of educational freedom we believe from the deepest parts of our Selves can serve this world's children well. And you did it all with joy in your hearts and smiles in your writing voices.

I've always thought a person fortunate if she discovers just a few kindred spirits while traveling through life. I have found *dozens*, and know life is that much sweeter because we call each other friend.

In as many ways as there are to "homeschool," I thank you all, contributors old and new.

INTRODUCTION

Another letter arrived today:

> Last September I was agonizing over the decision of whether or not to remove my two grade-school age children from public school. After reading your book, *The Art of Education,* I was inspired to give it a try. We've been homeschooling (unschooling, actually!) for almost four months and we all love it. I've seen great changes in my kids already—more creativity, curiosity, less stress. I . . . look at a lot of things differently now, including how we're socialized by institutions. I have a feeling this is just the beginning of a very interesting journey! Thank you so much for your inspiration and information. It changed our lives.

This sentiment is echoing across our nation and, increasingly, around the world: *Homeschooling changed our lives.*

It seems to give a lot of credit to what nonpractitioners see as merely an odd educational choice. Could it be there's something more to it than that?

Looking at homeschooling as an odd educational choice, or even as a valid educational choice, for that matter, places it in a very narrow context. This narrow context is unfortunate because it abruptly ends just where homeschooling begins. Considering homeschooling this way is like looking at someone's finger as it points toward a beautiful sunset. You will better understand the letter writer's enthusiasm when you look past the finger at this: *Homeschooling is a grass-roots educational alternative that originates with the seed of parental love and commitment and blossoms into a lush garden of personal empowerment for child and parent.*

Herein lies the secret of the success of homeschooling as a national movement *and* the personal success of homeschoolers. The life-changing personal empowerment that results is still a secret after all these years, even though home education gets lots of media coverage. It's still a secret, even though just about everybody knows someone who homeschools these days. But it won't be a secret after you read this book.

To read *The Homeschooling Book of Answers* is to realize you can't separate homeschooling from the person practicing it. Homeschooling moves beyond a way to learn toward a way to live. This way of living necessitates well-thought-out, free choices within the framework of complete responsibility. There likely is nothing else you could do with your family that can so profoundly impact who you and your children become.

Since you can't separate home-schooling from the person doing it, this book gives you just that—more than four dozen people whose lives have been forever touched by this act. *The Home-schooling Book of Answers* reaps a bountiful harvest of personal empowerment. Collected for your easy reference is wisdom from parents with *over 400 years of homeschooling experience.* The dozen young contributors add *more than another 100 years' experience.* Additional contributors who have not practiced homeschooling themselves, but who have spent decades researching, writing, and speaking about it, lend their respected voices as well.

Be forewarned. These are voices that frankly express strong opinions. You won't agree with everyone; some may even make you grit your teeth. Hopefully, they'll all help you *think*—about what we as a society call education and what we do to our children in the name of that education. Hopefully, they'll all help you *feel*—what education can really be and what it's like to experience the promise of educational freedom fulfilled.

Who Should Read *The Homeschooling Book of Answers?*

Both the questions and respondents for *The Homeschooling Book of Answers* were carefully chosen to provide you with candid, informative, and entertaining answers to important questions about homeschooling. The questions cover the wide-ranging interests of those who repeatedly ask them. This book will be most helpful to:

- Parents who are considering or new to homeschooling
- Current homeschoolers looking for the ideas and inspiration usually found at homeschooling conferences
- Teachers, school board members, and school administrators
- Reporters, journalists, and political commentators
- Educational and social researchers
- Local, county, state, and national legislators

How to Use *The Homeschooling Book of Answers*

Please read the biographies first. Remember, you can't separate homeschooling from the person doing it. Get to know the people; that's what this book is all about. You'll discover they're very much like your neighbors, your friends, and your favorite aunt, just a lot more knowledgeable about how children learn, since they chose to accept complete responsibility for it. Before you read an answer, refer back to the biographies to see who wrote it. (Of course, if you have a photographic memory, you can skip this step.) Additionally, all contributors who listed contact information within their biographies are willing to be contacted for the legitimate needs of reporters, journalists, researchers, legislators, and so on.

Note the chapter titles. The titles reflect the broad topic areas into which the questions are divided. This way you can easily locate the topic you're most interested in at any particular reading. A quick scan of the questions within that topic in the table of contents will lead you to your particular question.

I hope you'll read *all* the answers to each question. This way you'll have a much broader understanding of the answer, and also begin to understand how many people—geographically, economically, politically, culturally, and religiously diverse—all came to similar conclusions while walking what are oftentimes very dissimilar paths.

The homeschooling books mentioned or recommended throughout this book are all included in appendix A so you may easily find the titles in your bookstore or library.

Sit back, put up your feet, and relax! While the education of our nation's youth is an important, serious issue, let these homeschoolers show you how to have your education and enjoy it, too!

The Bright Idea, or How *The Homeschooling Book of Answers* Came to Be

At the time I was in consultation with Prima Publishing acquisition editor Jamie Miller, I was in the midst of a summer spent speaking and giving workshops at homeschooling conferences. I met new friends and caught up with business and personal relationships with old friends, all of whom are some of the most interesting, educationally well-informed people I know. And I realized it was the collective energy and knowledge of all these people that made working at these conferences the enlightening, exciting, and personally rewarding experience it was. That's when it hit: The Bright Idea.

Not everyone can get to these conferences, I thought. Certainly those who are merely *considering* the idea of home education don't necessarily spend time to even search out a conference. Those with a professional interest in homeschooling often find themselves attending enough out-of-town conferences and events without adding more. Yet these are some of the people with the most important, most urgent questions about homeschooling, and the ones this collective energy and knowledge would most benefit.

So I proposed to Jamie The Bright Idea: a book of the most important and frequently asked questions about home-schooling answered by a few dozen or so of the most dedicated, most practiced, most knowledgeable, most commonsensical voices on homeschooling. Soon, the same mind that got The Bright Idea began spinning with the practical aspects of such a project. Did I just tell an editor I could get three dozen people, three dozen extremely active, busy people, to contribute to a book—without having asked any of them beforehand?

I told my husband what happened. "You must be crazy," he said.

"They'll do it," I said. "I just *know* they will." As I waited for acceptance of the idea, one day I hoped the publisher would like it and the next I hoped he would hate it and I wouldn't have to put what I *knew* to the ultimate test. I mean, what if most of them said no?

"It's a go," Jamie told me by phone. The publisher liked the idea, was excited about it, in fact.

Gulp.

Time to finalize the list of potential contributors. Time to create an invitation to contributors. Time to formulate the list of perfect questions. Time to decide which questions should go to whom. Time to send The Bright Idea out into the homeschooling community and see if it had wings.

I snail-mailed a few invitations, faxed one, and e-mailed the rest. I held my breath. The day is etched in my heart and mind forever.

Within an hour I nervously opened a return e-mail message which read, "I'm honored. Of course I will help in any way I can. Thank you for asking. Good luck! Rebecca (Kochenderfer)."

Two hours after sending the fax, I read the reply: "Hi, Linda. OK. Where are the questions; I'm not *here* very often! Love, John [Gatto]." I had actually found John, a favorite of the talk circuit, at home in his New York City apartment.

Lillian Jones wrote from California a couple of hours later: "This is so exciting—a dream come true! There are lots of good books around, but I can't point people to just one with certainty that they're going to 'get it.' This sounds like the closest thing to that dream book! . . . So yes, yes—please deal me in. Wonderful idea! Thank you!"

The next few days were delightful as acceptances reached my computer via cyberspace. I could picture Deb Shell at the computer in her Vermont home responding, "This is such a timely project—so much of what you've said rings true; what's been nagging me since the [Growing Without Schooling] conference in August is the feeling that many long-time homeschoolers have accrued so much experience, yet there hasn't been an easily accessible means of communicating what we know. I embrace this project—yes, I would love to participate. Best regards, Deb." Two of Deb's daughters ultimately became contributors, too!

Did I forget to mention I asked these folks to contribute as the holiday season rapidly approached—and that I only gave them one month to complete their work?

"You can count me in!" wrote Janie Levine Hellyer from far-away Washington state. "Of course you just HAD to choose the busiest time of the year! Seriously, bring on the questions, and I'll clear some time on my calendar to work on them." My eyes—again—swelled with tears of gratitude.

"OK. You're on!" came the answer from Michigan's Clonlara School e-mail address. "But I give you fair warning that you will have to nudge me at least once, and possibly twice before I complete it. If you're game, I am. Pat (Montgomery)" But Pat surprised herself and me by meeting the deadline, just like *almost* all the other contributors. (Don't worry, gang, I'm not going to reveal any names here!)

Still others were sentimental about the project, like Katharine Houk. "The new book project sounds exciting," she wrote, "and I would be very happy to be part of it. Now that we are coming out at the other end of homeschooling, it would be an excellent time for synthesis and reflection on what this grand adventure has been about."

And then there was Donna Nichols-White. Not wanting any of the recipients to miss my e-mail message, I "shouted" the subject in all capital letters, in the fashion of the junk e-mail so many re-

ceive. "Good thing I noticed your screen name was ldobson," she wrote. "I thought you were selling girlie mags or something. I almost deleted your e-mail. I most definitely am willing to contribute to this book. It sounds great!" You'll soon be as glad as I was that Donna saved her invitation from a quick trip to the trash.

The responses from "the gang" were everything I'd hoped they would be—and more. As acceptances piled up, the scope of what we as a team were about to attempt began to sink in, and yet again I wondered if I'd bitten off more than I could chew. I made and hung huge wall charts containing both the questions and contributors' names to ensure even distribution. I stuck dozens of index cards containing chapters and questions on the wall and constantly shuffled them around in search of the perfect order. Soon my makeshift office looked like a command post for . . . homeschool wisdom. After I gave the question distribution a tenth or twelfth "final" review, I scattered the questions across the United States and Canada.

You now hold the results in your hand: 500 collective years—half a millennium—of thoughts, observations, philosophies, tips, and personal stories that can lead you to the personal empowerment of homeschooling.

Thanks to this personal empowerment, growing numbers of children are today living and learning in the real world, donating time to community volunteer organizations, getting wooed by college admissions officers, and learning to get along with, enjoy, and appreciate people of all ages. The contributors have discovered that children growing free of the educational institution sprout up and learn naturally, following schedules suited to their unique interests and abilities.

Homeschooling brought learning, family life, values, and ideals of freedom into sharp focus for all of us. It allowed us to create this "dream" book. And, yes, homeschooling changed our lives. We hope this book and homeschooling can change yours, too.

Introduction to the Second Edition

2002. It's been four years already? Well, thank goodness, much of what is best and brightest about homeschooling has remained the same. As a flexible educational approach, though, homeschooling continues to evolve, ever led to new and different challenges and opportunities. Its entrance into the twenty-first century proved no exception, so throughout the pages, courtesy of six wonderful new contributors, you'll find updates addressing the most important issues, including an entirely new chapter that helps you think about current events exploding onto the educational landscape. You'll find answers to new questions for your consideration, such as these: Do new cries for "accountability" affect homeschoolers? If you live in a town with a daytime curfew, how can you use

the community as your classroom? There's up-to-date information on the growing use of distance-learning tools, homeschool charter schools, the record number of homeschoolers entering colleges and universities, the increase in families homeschooling children with special needs, and more. Don't forget to check out the important thoughts and resources collected in easy-to-read-and-use lists you'll refer to again and again.

A plethora of homeschooling materials, a favorite of many readers, is not just revised but expanded.

But mostly, remember to enjoy what you're doing as you put all this information to work for your family. Children are children but once; let homeschooling help build childhood memories that will last a lifetime.

CONTRIBUTORS

MICHELLE BARONE is a single homeschooling parent to two children and has been home-schooling for twelve years. She is a credentialed teacher in California. She is also a licensed marriage, family, and child counselor, and has a private counseling practice specializing in attachment-style parenting, alternative education, and personal growth issues. She also facilitates parent support and education groups. She is currently writing a book and lecturing on the topic of homeschooling as healing.

Phone: (818) 951-7744
E-mail: mebarone@earthlink.net

CHRIS CARDIFF, a homeschooling father of three girls, has over twelve years experience. He is the founding president of the California Homeschool Network and the former executive director of the Separation of School and State Alliance. With his two eldest daughters, he edits *AWL News,* the monthly newsletter of All Ways Learning of San Jose, California. A homeschooling crusader by night, during the day he's a mild-mannered director of engineering at Netscape Communications Corporation.

California Homeschool Network
Phone: (800) 327-5339
E-mail: tifchris@aol.com
Web site:
http://people.netscape.com/ccardiff

CAFI COHEN homeschooled her two children for eight years, from about ages ten to eighteen. She cohosts the Web-based Kaleidoscapes Homeschooling Bulletin Boards and presents workshops at homeschooling conferences across the nation. She wrote *And What About College? How Homeschooling Leads to Admissions to the Best Colleges and Universities.* Her Web site addresses the challenges of homeschooling teenagers. She and her husband live on California's central coast.

375 Plancha Way
Arroyo Grande, CA 93420
Phone: (805) 473-4963
E-mail: cfcohen@pacbell.net

DAVID COLFAX is a fourth-term at-large trustee of his county's board of education, and until recently hosted a weekly public radio public affairs program. A former professor of sociology, he has served as a social research and forensic consultant to public and private, local, state, and national agencies such as the National Institutes of Health and the U.S. Department of Education. With his wife, Micki, he coauthored *Homeschooling for Excellence* and *Hard Times in Paradise.*

Colfax Associates
246 Redwood Ridge Road
Boonville, CA 95415

For book information:
Mountain House Press
Box 353
Philo, CA 95466

MICKI COLFAX is a graduate of Penn State who attended the London School of Economics. She has taught in the United States, Canada, and England, and has served as director of field operations for many educational survey research projects. Micki and David are proud grandparents of Bailey, frequently speak at educational conferences, and together survived an onslaught of media attention when the first of their three sons was homeschooled into Harvard in the early 1980s. Their fourth son is now married and works with developmentally disabled people in Sacramento.

(See David Colfax for contact information.)

ADAM DOBSON, born in 1983, lives in the Adirondack mountains of New York and has homeschooled his entire life. He enjoys playing and listening to music, participating in various sports, working with computers, and spending time with his niece. He is currently employed as a prepared foods manager for a large chain supermarket, and is studying psychology and sociology.

LINDA DOBSON is the author of *The Art of Education* (Holt Associates), author of several books published by Prima Publishing, and editor of the Prima Home Learning Library. Linda is a popular conference speaker, workshop presenter, and *Home Education Maga-*

zine columnist. She has learned at home with three children since 1985.

368 Trudeau Road
Saranac Lake, NY 12983
Phone/Fax: (518) 891-4714
E-mail: ldobson@northnet.org
Web site:
www.geocities.com/homeschoolers
    _success_stories

KIRBY DODD, fourteen, has never been to school, but nobody can tell without asking. His reading primers were *Nintendo Players' Guides* and *Nintendo Power Magazine,* and he has an orange belt in karate from the local Shorin Ryu dojo. He is named after his grandfather, not a Nintendo character or a vacuum cleaner (honest).

MARTY DODD (at the time of this writing) was an eight-year-old (now eleven), ice-hockey-playing, unschooled kid in Albuquerque, New Mexico. He has an older brother and a younger sister. He wears his hair short to bald, sings funny songs, makes up characters and draws them. Marty's specialty is putting things together without the directions, a manly art that drives moms crazy (especially when the little men are good at it).

SANDRA DODD lives in Albuquerque, New Mexico, with her husband, Keith, and their three children—Kirby, Marty, and Holly—who have never been to school. Kirby was born in 1986, and Sandra's responses were made when he would have been in sixth grade (had he attended school). Sandra has a degree in English, and taught junior high school for six years. For fun she writes, plays music, and sings, and amazes her kids with things and ideas.

2905 Tahiti Court, NE
Albuquerque, NM 87110
Phone: (505) 299-2476
E-mail: SandraDodd@aol.com
Web site: Http://expage.com
/RadicalUnschooling

SUSAN EVANS and her family, including four children (Luke, born in 1977; Jesse, in 1979; Margaret, in 1982; and Kathryn, in 1986), live in southeastern Michigan. She has volunteered over the years for several family-centered organizations: counseling breastfeeding mothers in La Leche League, planning homeschooling conferences for Clonlara School, coordinating the office for the National Homeschool Association, leading workshops at the Family Empowerment Institute's retreats, and representing Holt Associates at midwestern homeschooling conferences.

ANN FISHER homeschooled her daughters Erin and Alice for more than twenty years. A founder of Oregon Home Education Network and several other homeschooling organizations, Ann is the author of *Homeschooling in Oregon,* a model state handbook; has contributed several chapters to *Creating Learning Communities;* and is putting the final touches on her forthcoming book, *Foundations for Homeschooling.* Ann and Don have recently put down roots near the Columbia River gorge.

PO Box 1279
Carson, WA 98610
E-mail: Ann@nettlepatch.net
Web site: www.nettlepatch.net
/homeschool

JOHN TAYLOR GATTO was a public school teacher in New York for thirty-five years, including five at the university level. He was named New York State Teacher of the Year twice and New York City Teacher of the Year three times by various organizations. He has spoken at NASA, the White House, United Technologies, Omega Institute, and for over 500 other organizations in forty-nine states and seven foreign countries. He is the author of *Dumbing Us Down, The Exhausted School,* and *The Empty Child* (forthcoming), and is listed in *Who's Who.*

The Odysseus Group
295 E. 8th Street
New York, NY 10009
Phone: (212) 529-9327
Fax: (212) 721-6124 (Rarely able to
respond to personal correspondence)

NANCY AND BILLY GREER met and became friends while attending colleges near each other. A crucial kiss in front of the library marked a turning point in the relationship and a shared passion for books that led to marriage in 1982. Involvement in homeschooling began in 1988 with the birth of their son. "In trying to decide if we should start saving for a private school education or rely on public education, we visited several schools and read about many educational philosophies. No one program offered everything we were interested in, and we saw that parental involvement seemed the most important factor in learning success. Homeschooling allowed us to tailor a program that suited our family and maximized parental involvement." In 1992 Nancy and Billy and two other people started North County Home Educators, a Maryland support group open to anyone interested in home learning. They created the Family Unschoolers Network in 1994, which offers support via *F.U.N. News,* a quarterly newsletter, and discounted books through F.U.N. Books.

> Family Unschoolers Network
> 1688 Belhaven Woods Court
> Pasadena, MD 21122-3727
> Fax/Voice Mail: (410) 360-7330
> E-mail: FUN@FUN-Books.com
> Web site: www.fun-book.com

MARY GRIFFITH is the author of *The Unschooling Handbook: How to Make the World Your Classroom* and *The Homeschooling Handbook: From Preschool to High School, a Parent's Guide,* both from Prima Publishing. She is past editor of *California HomeSchooler* and a longtime activist with the Homeschool Association of California. For the past ten years, she's spent the bulk of her nonwriting time unschooling with her two daughters.

> 18 Madison Ct.
> Roseville, CA 95678
> E-mail: mgriff@ns.net

ADAM GRIMM was named Oregon's only homeschooled National Merit Scholar in 1997. Adam earned a perfect 800 on the verbal portion of both his PSAT and SAT exams. Primarily an unschooler, as a teen-ager Adam chose to plot his own educational course, which included lots of exploring, travel, reading, video watching, lectures, museum visits, games, computer work, and some community college classes. He was also awarded a Type 1 Air Force ROTC scholarship, which he used at Rensselaer Polytechnic Institute (RPI). Adam graduated in 2001, and reported for active duty in the U.S. Air Force.

> E-mail: grimma@alum.rpi.edu

MARK AND HELEN HEGENER are the parents of five children: John, Jim, Jody Ellen, Christopher, and Michael. All their children have always been homeschooled. The Hegener family has published *Home Education Magazine* since 1983, and they have appeared as featured speakers at homeschooling conferences across the nation. They live in Washington.

> *Home Education Magazine*
> PO Box 1083
> Tonasket, WA 98855
> Phone: (509) 486-1351
> E-mail: HEM@home-ed-magazine
>   .com
> Web site: www.home-ed-magazine.com

SHARI HENRY and her husband, Tim Jones, live in Huntsville, Alabama. They have always homeschooled their three children: TJ, Bekah, and Phoebe. Shari is a columnist and senior editor for *Homeschooling Today* magazine, and otherwise likes to read, cook, 'blade, bike, and laugh with her family.

> E-mail: ShariHenry@aol.com

LORETTA HEUER is mom to Tad and Jed, eclectic homeschoolers who combined unschooling, traditional coursework, internships, and travel. Tad, with a public policy degree from Brown University, is a graduate student at the London School of Economics, while Jed is an art direction major at Pratt Institute in New York City. Loretta has served as legislative liaison for the Massachusetts Home Learning Association, and is the author of *The Homeschooler's Guide to Portfolios and Transcripts*.

MaHmLearn@aol.com

DORIS HOHENSEE is the mother of six children who learn at home. When the New Hampshire legislature enacted a home education law in 1990, she found it necessary to become politically active while openly refusing to comply with the demands of the new law. In 1993, she started discussing politics on the Internet to try to hold back the tide of regulatory homeschooling laws.

> 15 Swart Terrace
> Nashua, NH 03060
> Phone: (603) 881-8323
> E-mail: doris@mainstream.net

MICHAEL HOHENSEE was born in 1980. He is a science and engineering enthusiast who also fences epée. He acquired anarchistic attitudes primarily from the works of L. Neil Smith and Robert Heinlein. Since the age of four, he has been homeschooled, unschooled, high schooled ("briefly, thank heaven"), and college schooled, in that order. He prefers unschooling to homeschooling, and college to high school. Next fall he hopes to attend a university with like-minded technogeeks. He resides in Nashua, New Hampshire, with five younger siblings and nine pet cockatiels.

> 15 Swart Terrace
> Nashua, NH 03060
> Phone: (603) 881-8323
> E-mail: michael@mainstream.net

KATHARINE HOUK, homeschooling since 1983, brings people together in groups, learning centers, and educational events. She believes that by learning together, we can each become spirited inventors of our lives. She is cofounder/director of the Alliance for Parental Involvement in Education (AllPIE), works as an artist in Chatham, New York, and attended divinity school. Katharine's husband, Seth Rockmuller, and their children—Tahra, Ben, and Emily—have been a vital part of her life and work.

> Alliance for Parental Involvement in
>   Education
> PO Box 59
> East Chatham, NY 12060-0059
> Phone/Fax: (518) 392-6900
> E-mail: allpie@taconic.net
> Web site: http://www.croton.com/allpie

THERESA HYLAND, seventeen, has been homeschooled for six years, and began attending Paul Smith's College in fall of 2001. Since this book was first published, Theresa's interests have evolved to include Celtic music, anthropology, history, and anything Celtic or Japanese. She still loves Star Wars. She is a member of Phi Theta Kappa, and hopes to eventually have a career in anthropology, music, or ethnomusicology.

LINDSEY JOHNSON has been unschooled her whole life. ("My parents discovered John Holt when I was three.") She has three brothers and two sisters who are also unschooled. Lindsey is writing a book about the dangers of compulsory education, a result of her new-found interest in why our current educational system is failing us. She plans to continue writing, pursue an acting career, and carry her autodidactic lifestyle as she gets older.

LILLIAN JONES earned a degree in anthropology, trained to be an elementary teacher, substituted in schools, but never felt comfortable with what she found there. She feels from firsthand experience that teaching credentials (and college degrees) are highly overrated as measures of competence in the real world. Along with her other interests, she is a homeschool advocate and a volunteer with the HomeSchool Association of California. She and her husband, Ed, have a teenage son, Ethan.

> E-mail: wrensong@monitor.net
> Web site: www.besthomeschooling.org

TJ JONES has been homeschooling all his life and plans to stay home through high school. He enjoys all types of sports, especially hockey (ice and roller) and competitive swimming.

LARRY AND SUSAN KASEMAN have been learning through homeschooling with their four children since 1979. They are very active in the Wisconsin Parents Association, a statewide inclusive grassroots homeschooling organization of which Larry is executive director. They are the authors of *Taking Charge Through Homeschooling: Personal and Political Empowerment* and columnists for *Home Education Magazine.* Together they hike, sing, garden, work with families, and spend time with their children.

MEGAN KASEMAN is delighted to be making her debut as a published writer. She's been homeschooling forever and acting for twelve years. Her favorite roles include Ophelia in *Hamlet,* title roles in *Othello* and *Romeo and Juliet* (Romeo), and Rebecca Gibbs in *Our Town.* Other activities include singing, listening to music, and spending time with her family and her cat, Katza. She dedicates her writing to directors Richard and Anne with a heart full of thanks and love.

REBECCA KOCHENDERFER is editor and cofounder of Homeschool.com. In addition to receiving the *Forbes* Favorite Best of the Web award, Homeschool.com has been featured on Oprah.com, WorldNetDaily, and others, and on television programs *Web TV* and *Internet Tonight.* Embracing the diversity of the homeschooling community, Homeschool.com holds exclusive licenses with ChildU and the JASON Project.

> Homeschool.com
> 3751 Bolsa Court
> Sacramento, CA 95864
> Phone: (916) 488-6589
> E-mail: Rebecca@Homeschool.com
> Web site: www.Homeschool.com

JANIE LEVINE HELLYER was active in the homeschool community for many years and developed and taught a course on homeschooling at Evergreen State College in Olympia, Washington. She was the mother of three grown homeschoolers.

PATRICIA LINES has been writing on homeschooling for over twenty years, tracking the movement practically from its infancy. She is the proud mom of a twenty-eight-year-old computer genius who was never formally homeschooled, but who learned quite a lot on his own outside of school. She is currently on sabbatical from her position with the National Institute on Student Achievement, Curriculum and Assessment, and is writing a dissertation for Catholic University of America on the idea of education as a private affair, as articulated by thinkers from John Locke to the Antifederalists. She is also a senior fellow at Discovery Institute in Seattle.

Discovery Institute
1402 Third Avenue, Suite 400
Seattle, WA 98101
Phone: (206) 292-0401
patlines@earthlink.net

ISABEL (IZZY) LYMAN is the daughter of Costa Rican immigrants. She is proud of her heritage and proud to be a homeschooling American. Her columns on home education have appeared in the *Wall Street Journal, Investor's Business Daily, Dallas Morning News, Boston Herald, Los Angeles Daily Journal,* and *National Review.* She is author of *The Homeschooling Revolution* and mother of two teenaged sons, one of whom is currently taught by her husband; the other is a college freshman.

Web site:
www.homeschoolingrevolution.com

MARY H. MCCARTHY and family have been homeschooling since 1981, after hearing John Holt speak. They live in Washington, where Mary occasionally writes for *Home Education Magazine* when she isn't searching the house for her sanity.

E-mail: HSLRAwa@sandwich.net

DR. PAT MONTGOMERY is an energetic, indefatigable advocate for home-based educators and the mother of two adult "children." In 1967, she started an innovative private day school for her children in Ann Arbor, Michigan. They taught her a great deal about the natural development of children, and she's been sharing it with anyone who will listen ever since. She extended the philosophy and practices of her school to home educators the world over through the Clonlara School Home-Based Education Program, founded in 1979.

DR. RAYMOND MOORE is an author, researcher, former city school superintendent, and college, university, and consortium head: Chicago, Johns Hopkins, Stanford, Tulane, and Wisconsin. He is noted for upgrading and making colleges and universities debt-free. While graduate research and programs officer for the U.S. Department of Education, he wrote books and articles pioneering interinstitutional cooperation in higher education. He is also internationally known for creative work-study plans at all educational levels here and abroad, and international research on school entrance age. Moore is considered by many to be the "grandfather" of modern homeschooling, America's largest successful education movement.

The Moore Foundation
Box 1
Camas, WA 98607
Phone: (360) 835-5500
Fax: (360) 835-5392
E-mail: moorefnd@pacifier.com
Web site: www.moorefoundation.com

DOROTHY MOORE is an internationally known author, consultant, editor, and child specialist in curricula, reading, and remedial education, and a university teacher honored by school systems, colleges, and universities. She is also the founding head of a medical school cerebral palsy center. She's known by many as "grandmother" of the modern homeschool movement, which she has been involved in since 1944. She is the co-author of the scholarship-winning Moore Formula, a customized low-cost, low-stress, readiness-oriented plan for achievement, behavior, and sociability through a study-work-service balance.

(See Raymond Moore for contact information.)

DONNA NICHOLS-WHITE is the mother of three homeschoolers, the owner and publisher of *The Drinking Gourd Multicultural Home Education Magazine, The Catalog for Independent Learning*, a public speaker, and a writer. She is a contributing author to several books, including *500 Great Books by Women: A Reader's Guide, Freedom Challenge: African-American Homeschoolers*, and *Deschooling Our Lives*.

NANCY PLENT was a school hater who married another school hater. They traded horror stories for years and were determined to find a way out for their son. John Holt and GWS (Growing Without Schooling) came along at just the right time. "I got caught up in the movement. For the last twenty-plus years I have been publishing a New Jersey newsletter, doing seminars, writing 'unschool' curriculum, and finished *An "A" in Life*, a book about famous homeschoolers."

Unschoolers Network
2 Smith Street
Farmingdale, NJ 07727
Phone: (732) 938-2473
E-mail: UnNet@aol.com

WENDY PRIESNITZ is a Canadian homeschooling pioneer. With her husband, Rolf, she helped their two daughters, Heidi and Melanie, learn at home when it was almost unheard of in Canada. In 1979, she founded the Canadian Alliance of Home Schoolers, which provides guidance, support, and information to families across Canada. She continues to share her experience and long-term perspective through workshops, speeches, articles and books, research, and consulting to individuals and governments. Among the eight books she has written is *School Free*, a Canadian bestseller about home-based education. As owner of The Alternate Press, a twenty-two-year-old periodical and book publishing company, Wendy edits *Natural Life*, a newsmagazine focusing on personal and grassroots efforts that integrate economic, political, and social issues. She is an established investigative journalist, writes a weekly small business newspaper column, hosts a daily radio program, and is featured in *Who's Who of Canadian Women*.

Natural Life
Box 340
St. George, Ontario N0E 1N0
Canada
Phone: (519) 442-1404 or
     (800) 215-9574
Fax: (519) 448-4411
E-mail: natural@life.ca
Web site: www.life.ca

ANNAQUISTA PYKOSZ is an unschooler who lives on a homestead in central Vermont with her mother, father, and younger brother. Over the years her interests have included theater, horses, piano, cooking, and antiques. Presently, she enjoys attending flea markets, making discoveries on the computer, sewing, hiking, reading, traveling, gardening, and watching movies. Annaquista is editor of a newsletter for adolescent unschoolers. She plans to own her own business by the age of sixteen and is already saving for her first car.

MARSHA RANSOM, freelance writer, home-school speaker, and author of *The Complete Idiot's Guide to Homeschooling*, has been homeschooling for thirteen years. Residing with her husband, Dwight, and their four children in southwest Michigan, she edits the local homeschooling support group's newsletter and is a state liaison for the National Home Education Network.

South Haven, Michigan
Phone: (616) 637-3748
E-mail: mransom@usa.com

JEAN REED was raised in Winnetka, Illinois. She studied music and dance; won trampo-line medals; was a nationally certified ski instructor; loved to sail and play her guitar; and was pretty much a goof-off until she met Donn in 1962. She is publisher of *The Home School Source Book*, Third Edition.

Brook Farm Books
PO Box 246
Bridgewater, ME 04735
Alternate address:
Box 101
Glassville, New Brunswick E7L 4T4
Canada
Phone Orders: (877) 375-4680
E-mail: jean@brookfarmbooks.com

DONN REED worked as a carpenter, radio announcer, truck driver, dishwasher, librarian, teacher, foundry worker, peace marcher, psychiatric aide, tax assessor, sawmill edgerman, migrant field worker, reporter, columnist, newspaper editor, and publisher. He's been listed in *Who's Who in American Education*. He served three years in jail as a conscientious objector, where he received a Meritorious Service Award from the U.S. Bureau of Prisons for work with adult illiterates. Married thirty-two years, the Reeds homesteaded in Vermont and Canada, birthed four children at home, and spent twenty-four years homeschooling. Donn wrote and published *The First Home School Catalogue* in 1981, the very first of the homeschooling catalogs. He wrote *The Home School Source Book* in 1991 (second edition, 1994). Since Donn's death in 1995, Jean has taken over as manager of Brook Farm Books and has completed the third edition of *The Home School Source Book*.

BECKY AND RANDY RUPP, both cell biologists, have three sons—Josh, Ethan, and Caleb. They live in very rural Vermont, where they garden, stargaze, skate, read, cross-country ski, juggle, and plow snow. Becky has written several books, including *Everything You Never Learned About Birds* (Storey Communications, 1995), *Good Stuff* (Holt Associates, 1997), *Committed to Memory: How We Remember and Why We Forget* (Crown, 1998), *The Dragon of Lonely Island* (Candlewick, 1998), *The Home Learning Source Book* (Crown, 1998), and *Getting Started in Homeschooling* (Crown, 1998). The boys, who have always been homeschooled, are all strong, good-looking, and above average.

WILL AND MARGARET SHAW have been homeschooling for sixteen years in rural Louisa County, Virginia. Their two younger children are still being homeschooled; the older two are in college. Will is employed as a physical plant superintendent at the University of Virginia in Charlottesville. Will and Margaret were both trained to teach in public schools, but they overcame this handicap to become successful homeschoolers. Will has been a lobbyist for homeschool interests and is vice-president of Virginia Home Education Association.

> Virginia Home Education Association
> PO Box 5131
> Charlottesville, VA 22905
> Phone: (540) 832-3578
> E-mail: willfshaw@juno.com

SUSANNAH SHEFFER was the former editor of *Growing Without Schooling* magazine. She is editor of *A Life Worth Living: Selected Letters of John Holt,* and of Heinemann's *Innovators in Education* series, which brings radical education classics back into print. Her own books include *Writing Because We Love To: Homeschoolers at Work* and *A Sense of Self: Listening to Homeschooled Adolescent Girls.* She is married to Aaron Falbel, who also writes about issues in education.

> Holt Associates/Growing Without
>   Schooling
> 2380 Massachusetts Avenue, Suite 104
> Cambridge, MA 02140
> Phone: (617) 864-3100
> Fax: (617) 864-9235
> E-mail: info@holtgws.com
> Web site: www.holtgws.com

DEB SHELL has been unschooling since her oldest daughter was born in 1976. She is currently working as a licensed psychotherapist with a specialty in attachment therapy. Former director of the Resource Center for Homeschooling, in her spare time she is also a potter, and enjoys quilting, gardening, and exploring Lake Champlain with her boat-builder husband, Fred.

> E-mail: debshell_vt@yahoo.com
> Phone/Fax: (802) 524-9645

MAE SHELL has been an unschooler her whole life. She worked at a small public library, and is currently exploring different career paths, including journalism and computer database design. In her spare time, she enjoys reading, writing, and surfing the Web.

> E-mail: mae@maeshell.com

SCARLET SARA SHELL grew up in Vermont as a lifelong homeschooler. She started dancing at the age of eleven and hasn't stopped since, a love which brought her to Tisch School of the Arts at New York University. She currently attends UC San Diego where she will earn her Ph.D. in molecular biology.

(See Deb Shell for contact information.)

LUZ SHOSIE taught fifth grade in a public school for two years, and that's when she decided to homeschool. Now she grows food and flowers, studies and teaches t'ai chi, runs a support group, and publishes a newsletter for unschoolers. "I enjoy holding people's hands as they take the leap into self-directed learning."

Guilford University
22 Wild Rose Avenue
Guilford, CT 06437
Phone/Fax: (203) 458-7402
E-mail: nedvare@ntplx.net

NED VARE has been homeschooling since 1980. He has enjoyed various occupations, usually with no connection to his "education." Ned adds, "I consider my schooling (private) and college (Ivy League) a waste of time—an expensive warehousing and even damaging experience because so much of it had to be unlearned, and also because it gave me an inappropriate or unrealistic world view. Like most people, almost all my valuable learning was done outside school and after my schooling ended."

(See Luz Shosie for contact information.)

CINDY WADE is an artist and homeschool advocate currently residing on a Vermont homestead with husband Todd and children Annaquista and Zebhdiyah. Cindy founded and directs Gnarly Birch Press, a mail-order company specializing in homeschool materials, and she publishes *Right at Home* newsletter. She is author of *The Vermont Homeschoolers' Directory,* among other publications, and speaks and presents workshops on homeschooling.

Gnarly Birch Press
RR 2, Box 145
E. Wallingford, VT 05742
Phone: (802) 259-2394
E-mail: cwade@vermontel.com

JUDITH WAITE ALLEE, co-author of *Homeschooling on a Shoestring* and *Educational Travel on a Shoestring,* started homeschooling in 1984 so her foster son could escape from "Special Ed." She presents workshops on homeschooling, adoption, and "Parenting Without Losing Your Cool." Judith, her husband John, and their daughter Nancy (now twenty) have visited homeschoolers in fifteen states, while traveling to photograph reunions and conferences.

Web site:
www.DreamsOnAShoestring.com

ANN ZEISE has been a homeschool parent since 1993, and an onliner since 1984. *A to Z Home's Cool Homeschooling* has been her online support for homeschoolers on the Internet since 1996. You may contact her through the site: http://www.gomilpitas.com/homeschooling.

THE
Homeschooling
Book of Answers

REVISED

CHAPTER ONE

Now That Homeschooling Is Legal and Safe . . .

ONCE UPON a time, the most frequently asked question about home-schooling was, "Is that *legal?*" I always thought it a strange one. If I say I'm taking responsibility for my own children's need for food, no one questions if that's legal. If I say I'm taking responsibility for my children's need to be healthy, again, no questions asked. In fact, I could be hauled off to jail if I *didn't* take care of those responsibilities.

Since taking responsibility for my children's need for education isn't very different than taking care of their need for food and health, I find this turn-around interesting. When it comes to "which books they read" instead of "which vegetables they eat for dinner," all of a sudden it's a legal issue. Please allow this book to help you ponder the significance of this.

That the question, "Is that legal?" is not today included in a book of the most important and most often asked questions about homeschooling says a lot about the growth and acceptance of this educational phenomenon. Homeschooling's legality is today a given, in many respects a tribute to the countless families who fought to maintain—or reclaim—parental responsibility for children's education.

That something as personal as the art of education is tied to a series of legal hoops one must jump through in order to practice it is a fact worthy of deep—

possibly life-altering—consideration, particularly to those who cherish the ideal of a free people living in a free country. That a question-and-answer book on homeschooling still needs a chapter on legal issues, and that those questions are important enough to be addressed in the first chapter of this book, says a lot about how much farther we have yet to go along the path toward *assuming*, instead of *allowing*, family responsibility for our own children.

I like to imagine a day when the art of education may be widely viewed as the private family affair it is, a day when those charged with the weighty task of educating future generations *en masse* let loose the reins they've held so tightly for the relatively brief, 150-year-long educational experiment known as public schooling.

Until that day, however, anyone contemplating homeschooling her own children; anyone who has a hand in running, regulating, or in any way supporting the business of schooling—indeed, anyone who would benefit from a microcosmic look at the effects of government influence in our personal lives—needs to know (1) what the hoops are and (2) the most effective way to jump through them. *You* are capable of grabbing those reins, allowing your children to move in a different direction more in keeping with your family's values, dreams, and hopes.

When it comes to "which books they read" instead of "which vegetables they eat for dinner," all of a sudden it's a legal issue. Please allow this book to help you ponder the significance of this.

Why does a thirty-year veteran school teacher tell you you're lucky if you *don't* have teacher training before homeschooling your children? Would you like to know just what the legal requirements in your state are? And where to find the most accurate information about them?

If you've always tiptoed gingerly about your school administrators, or have never had any dealings with them in the past, could you use a few tips on how to approach them? Can you stand to learn that they see your child much differently than you do? And that you can learn just as much if not more about your child's education than they in a very brief time?

Now that homeschooling is legal and safe, welcome to what you need to know about remaining legal issues to fully understand which legal hoops are still real, and which have fallen by the wayside. After addressing these necessary evils, we'll move on to the ideas directly relevant to truly educating children.

1

Can I teach my own children if I don't have any teacher training?

BILLY AND NANCY GREER ◆ Yes! In fact, teacher training can be a disadvantage in the home environment. Traditional teaching methods still tend to break up learning into several separate categories or subjects that are taught independently of each other. This may work well when groups of students are moved from class to class for each subject. In theory, this allows teachers to specialize in a particular subject so that the student gets a teacher with expertise in the subject. This is one of the key ideas in mass production—break a process into separate components and let a specialist handle each component.

In real life, there is no artificial segregation of subjects and there is often an amazing integration. Reading and writing are involved in every subject area; science involves history, foreign languages, math, art, and social studies. It is much more effective to integrate all of these items and treat them as part of a whole. In a home environment, it is easier to take this kind of approach. The payoff is that it is easier to relate what is learned to real life, and to make the material more interesting.

And guess what? Companies are finding that multidisciplinary team approaches work better than traditional mass production. When marketing, engineering, production, and finance work on a project simultaneously, the quantity and quality of work increase. The better and more innovative companies are already moving away from traditional mass-production models.

If you see that you have more freedom and flexibility to use techniques that would not be effective in a classroom setting, but are still worried about your own knowledge, just remember that your children are not limited to what you know. You do not teach your children; you help them learn. Coaches are not the best athletes. They help motivate, and provide resources and support.

NED VARE ◆ Teacher training—the kind of training given to public school teachers—is one of the main reasons for the failure of the schools in the first place. You are not expected to be a classroom teacher overseeing two dozen diverse strangers, anyway. Your job is to be a tutor, on a part-time basis only, for one or maybe a few of your own children—whom you know intimately. You are well qualified to do that; you've already been doing it for years. Children don't need schooling; they want to learn, and they know how to do it. If they have questions, answer them. If you can't answer them, find the answers together. The process is called life. It's not separate from education.

JOHN TAYLOR GATTO ◆ Let me reverse that question. Can you teach your own children if you *do* have teacher training, did well in it, and believe its precepts of scientific pedagogy, its psychological principles of child development, its habits of time management, behavioral control, text selection, sequencing, assessment, and guidance? I don't think so.

Teacher training is not about assisting a mind and character to develop according to the principles of its own internal genius. It is not about education at all, but about successful *schooling,* which is a much different thing. Schooling is a comprehensive indoctrination process, designed—by Plato, Hobbes, Rousseau, and others—to isolate children from their natural sources of personal power, which accrue from family identity and experience, self-discovery, freedom to experiment in a safe and familiar setting, early guidance in metaphysical speculation and participation (what we call religion), access to highly personalized and particularized text and experience matchings (what is called elsewhere in this guide "interest initiated" learning, knowledgeable mentors drawn from the ranks of the talented, not merely from the cohort of "certified" state agents), and much more.

Isolation, followed by controlled abstractions of reality and controlled "sim-

Children don't need schooling; they want to learn, and they know how to do it.

ulation" games, a controlled diet of materials, a highly tense setting (even in the very best of schools) in which authorities are essential for protection—all this is the stuff of schooling. And you know that in your bones because you have been schooled yourself. This is the reason the science of schooling is called "pedagogy" and teachers (sometimes with a secret, innocent pride) hear themselves referred to as "pedagogues."

The word has an ancient and very specific lineage. The *paidagogos* was a form of slave in ancient Greece who drilled children according to instructions issued by a master. He had no latitude, doing as he was told. What Comenius and Rousseau and Pestalozzi and Froebel—those wildly inappropriate saints of holistic/progressive schooling—all taught in the nineteenth century, which gave us mass forced schooling for the first time in human history, was how to do *pedagogy* efficiently. You study each child very closely, embed them in an unending context of undifferentiated "affection," stifle their intellect aborning by parceling out the stuff of experience (the only reliable foundation of character) relentlessly, all the while *wooing* the little charges from home, tradition, church, culture, and so on, bit by bit.

Once the child is fatally narcotized, and that job is largely done by third grade, the real schoolmasters—whoever they may be—have in theory an empty child to fill, a plastic substance to mold. Sounds creepy, right? Aren't you glad to have missed formal teacher training? The trouble is you didn't miss informal teacher training, or you wouldn't have asked this understandable but very dumb question!

Nature, God, common sense, history, or whatever other principle guides the best part of your intelligence should tell you that *you* are the only indispensable teacher your children need besides themselves. (Read Ben Franklin's autobiography for inspiration.) You may believe that you can *purchase* someone else's concern for your children through taxpayer-supported schooling or private-fee schooling, but then you may believe in the tooth fairy, too.

Don't.

2

I know that homeschooling is now legal in every state, but doesn't each state have its own requirements? Do some states allow more educational freedom than others?

DORIS HOHENSEE ◆ Homeschooling laws vary tremendously from state to state. There are three basic categories for homeschooling laws: private school laws, equivalency laws, and home education laws.

The best situation is when home schools are legally recognized to be private schools. Intrusive regulations cannot be imposed upon private schools. Private schools have fought long and hard to protect their curricula from state censorship and to protect their teachers from certification requirements. Numerous court opinions stand in defense of the right of private schools to be free from state regulation. Homeschoolers are fortunate, indeed, if they live in Alabama, Alaska, California, Iowa, Illinois, Kentucky, Michigan, Nebraska, Oklahoma, or Texas, all of which enjoy private school status.

Equivalency laws are those which exempt children from compulsory attendance laws if they are receiving "equivalent instruction" elsewhere. While these laws may vary somewhat from state to state, it's difficult to define "equivalent" and the burden of proof is on the state. For the most part, these states have little by way of regulation, as the vagueness in the law works in favor of parents. Homeschoolers in Connecticut, Delaware, Idaho, Indiana, Kansas, Massachusetts, New Jersey, and South Dakota have equivalency laws.

The most variable laws are the home education laws. Having been classified separately from the rest of the private school community, home education in many of these states is quite regulated. Though the requirements are enumerated, there is still considerable vagueness in these laws. However, many times the vagueness now works in favor of the state, not the parent. What's more, there is little restriction on the amount of regulation that is possible should the legislature decide that more regulation is necessary. Homeschoolers need to be constantly vigilant lest their rights erode still further in these states.

The following states have home education laws: Arizona, Arkansas, Colorado, Florida, Georgia, Hawaii, Louisiana, Maine, Maryland, Michigan (has both private school status and home education laws), Minnesota, Missouri, Mississippi, Montana, Nevada, New Hampshire, New Mexico, New York, North Carolina, North Dakota, Ohio, Oregon, Pennsylvania, Rhode Island, South Carolina, Tennessee, Utah, Vermont, Virginia, Washington, West Virginia, Wisconsin, and Wyoming.

SUSAN AND LARRY KASEMAN ◆ Yes to both questions. Education, including homeschooling, is governed basically by state laws rather than federal laws. Requirements vary widely. Some states have no explicit requirements. Some require that parents notify public school officials that they will be homeschooling. In some states, parents must submit curriculum plans; in others, periodic reports. Some states require testing. Some states require several of these.

However, homeschooling laws are not as hard and fast as may first appear. As homeschoolers, we can influence the amount of educational freedom we have. We have the right and responsibility to read and interpret laws. We know more about homeschooling than most officials and have incentive to find reasonable interpretations that support children and families. Determined homeschoolers have increased our freedom by devising inventive ways to comply with laws. For example, homeschoolers are often required to have a curriculum. However, people, including professional educators, do not agree about what specific curriculum is best. In fact, conventional schools keep changing their curricula. As homeschoolers, we can give the widest interpretation possible within the law and choose or develop an approach to learning that meets our family's needs, whether this be a purchased curriculum, unit studies, or unschooling. (See Question 5.)

We can also refuse to comply with demands from officials that exceed their statutory authority, even though it is often tempting to just give officials what they request. For example, when we receive an official letter demanding more than the law requires, we may want to simply supply it and avoid any hassles. When school officials appear at our door, it may be tempting to give them as much material as we have in hopes that we will then be left alone. Or when filing required reports, it may seem like a good idea to include extra information to show school officials how well our children are doing or to educate them about homeschooling. However, in all these cases, doing more than the law requires sets precedents that may be difficult for us and other homeschoolers to follow in the future. It also increases the authority officials have over homeschoolers.

Standing firm in the face of excessive demands from officials requires a thorough knowledge of the law and constant vigilance.

Standing firm in the face of excessive demands from officials requires a thorough knowledge of the law and constant vigilance. School officials often request more from homeschoolers than is required by law because they have inaccurate information about the law, or are convinced that homeschoolers need their expertise, or are trying to increase their power and authority. Fortunately, when homeschoolers challenge them with accurate information, officials generally back down.

Informing other homeschoolers about the law is also important. Inclusive state-wide grassroots homeschooling organizations encourage homeschoolers to work together to protect everyone's rights.

For more ideas about ways to increase and protect homeschooling freedoms, see Question 98.

For information on homeschooling requirements in a given state, contact homeschoolers who live there. (The NationalHome Education Network, Holt Associates, and *Home Education Magazine* provide lists of contacts. See the resources in appendix A.) Contacting school officials is not a good idea; they often have misleading or inaccurate information. Similarly, contacting lawyers outside the state, including homeschooling lawyers, often results in misleading information.

CHRIS CARDIFF ◆ Generally speaking, statutory homeschool states (that is, states with laws specifically defining and regulating homeschools) are much more restrictive than states that consider homeschools as private schools. Failure to comply with the restrictive regulations within statutory homeschool states results in parents forced to place their children in government schools. These restrictions usually take the form of:

• mandatory curriculum approval by government officials (school district superintendent) or their designate.

- mandatory testing, where permission to homeschool is contingent on the child scoring above a certain percentage.
- education requirements for the parents (college degree or high school diploma, depending on the state) before the state allows them to homeschool their children.

In contrast to the direct regulation of homeschools, states that treat homeschools as private schools have fewer restrictions. In California, for example, private schools are subject to the same general curriculum guidelines and attendance laws as government schools. However, there is no government oversight of these general statutes and, more importantly, none of the harsher restrictions found in those states where homeschooling is regulated directly.

Because of this increased relative educational freedom, you will find homeschoolers in these states actively working to preserve their status quo as private schools. For example, the legislative policy of the California Homeschool Network explicitly states that "California Homeschool Network believes that current state law provides for the legal practice of homeschooling as private schools. We stand opposed to any legislation which would: define 'homeschool,' 'home education,' or related terms; add to or change the definition of 'private school,' as it now exists in law."

While the private school option is much less intrusive than direct regulation, underlying both approaches is the assumption that government has the right to compel the education of children. True educational freedom will be achieved when this assumption has been successfully refuted by the repeal of compulsory attendance and mandatory curriculum laws.

3

How do I find out what is legally required of homeschoolers in my state?

MARY GRIFFITH ◆ You've got several options and it's always best to choose several of them. You can ask your local school district, county office of education, or state department of education. Depending on where you live, the odds of getting accurate information from any of these may be fairly low. You might get lucky and run into a school official who is knowledgeable and forthcoming about the homeschooling regulations; but some school officials often are not familiar with the laws regulating homeschooling (and some may tell you what they think the law ought to be instead of what it is). Some officials may have the additional problem of knowing that more homeschoolers in their jurisdiction may mean less average daily attendance (ADA) funding for their own programs.

You can go to the library and look up the applicable education statutes and administrative regulations for yourself. Sometimes you'll need to try a regional branch or a community college library. Be sure to check the updates in the pocket parts in the backs of the statute books to make sure you've got the very latest version of the laws. You might also want to check into any relevant case law that affects the ways those laws are actually enforced. You may find that some of the language is less than transparent, and you may have to do a bit of digging around to find out exactly how all the different rules interact to learn what exactly they mean for the everyday lives of homeschoolers.

Best of all, you can ask homeschooling organizations in your state. The best first choice would be a statewide homeschool association that maintains a legal and legislative watch and publishes a regular newsletter to keep its members informed. If the group seems to rely on other organizations to do this work for them, or provides only sketchy information about bills and hearings that concern them, watch out. You want a group that will help you help yourself, not one that takes over for you completely. If there are no statewide groups in your state, check with local or regional groups in the larger cities. At least one of them

will probably be performing some of the same functions.

New homeschoolers are often leery of relying on information supplied by other homeschoolers as being somehow suspect or less reliable than information from other sources. But homeschoolers have a vested interest in getting the legal information right: If they are wrong, they are jeopardizing their children's education.

Get information from as many sources as you can. You may be confused by all the variations at first, but you'll sort it out eventually—and, by doing so, you'll know your rights and responsibilities thoroughly. The peace of mind you'll get that way is well worth the trouble.

PAT LINES ◆ Every state recognizes homeschooling as a legal way to meet state compulsory attendance requirements. Many state laws provide for options for qualifying your homeschooling program. All states require the family to file basic information with either the state or local education agency (SEA or LEA). Some states have additional requirements, such as the submission of a curricular plan, testing

Pat Lines

of students or, in a few cases, education or testing requirements for parents.

The basic rules are in the state's compulsory education law. It's a good idea to get a copy and keep it on hand in case there are questions about some particular of the law and your situation. In most states a few sections will specifically apply to homeschooling, but pay attention to other sections. If the age of compulsory education does not begin until eight, for example, you do not have to worry about compliance until your child reaches that age. In those states where there is no specific mention of homeschooling, a court, an attorney general, or the state board of education has ruled that private schools may meet in a home. In these states you must meet the rules for a private school to be "legal."

The law may also give the state board of education authority to make regulations regarding homeschooling. This authority is limited to filling in the details of the law, not to changing it. Most state education agencies have assigned an individual to serve as homeschooling liaison and to provide assistance on understanding the state law and regulations. As a practical matter, I would recommend first checking with your local or state homeschooling organization for tips and help on compliance. There may be some surprises in the way a state or local official reads the law. If there is a dispute over interpretation or a need for a new law, a homeschooling organization run by experienced homeschoolers is your best source for understanding the issues, and for advocating your best interests.

4

Since I don't have much experience dealing and communicating with school administrators, what's the best way to approach them about homeschooling?

PAT MONTGOMERY ◆ Do your homework:

1. Determine first of all whether your state regulations require any interaction between home educators and school officials. In most of the United States, no contact is required, so parents need not approach the school administrators at all.

However, if your child has already been in attendance at a conventional school, it is merely an act of courtesy to inform the officials at the previous school. A brief note to the teacher or principal will do. It ought to state, very simply, that your child "is no longer enrolled in the school." A written note is preferable to a phone call for many reasons, the chief of which is that a note can be placed in the file folder.

> **Every state recognizes homeschooling as a legal way to meet state compulsory attendance requirements.**

The school officials then remove the student's cumulative file folder (school records) from the active files. If another school or program requests the records, the school personnel send the originals or copies of the originals to the next school. If no school requests them, the records are placed in the inactive files. This means they are, for all intents and purposes, "dead" files.

2. If you reside in a state where contact between home-educating parents and school administrators is required by the regulations, ask other home-based educating parents how they dealt with the matter. Or you may choose to hand this task to someone else, like Clonlara School officials, who have a long and successful history with it.

Remember, you are engaged in a political activity: a parent, the primary teacher of her child, is approaching a school official who has, very likely, grown accustomed to believing that he or she bears that primary responsibility. Remember, too, that many school officials are sincere when they state they take their roles seriously.

Know for certain what the regulations require; use those as the yardstick. This coin has two sides: Parents are expected to obey the law; school officials must also obey the law. *Only* what is stated in the regulations need be provided; nothing more. Home education is enough of a job without restrictions and requests being hoisted by (perhaps) well-meaning officials.

Don't hesitate to point out to school administrators that both you, as parent, and they must obey what is written in the regulations. Don't hesitate to point out that when a school official asks for more than is required, this reveals underlying doubts and fears. Ask what prompts these fears. Most parents, after all, graduated from public schools. Is the official implying that the education given was riddled with error?

You are not approaching school officials with hat in hand asking for permission. You are in a position of power and status. You are notifying the officials, not begging or usurping or stealing what is theirs. Politeness, firmness, and humor are excellent tools to employ. Enter with a confident air. The lesson will not be lost on your ever-watching children.

MARY McCARTHY ◆ When you make the decision to educate your children yourself at home, you also accept legal responsibility for your actions. The best way to approach local school administrators is with knowledge. Go to the library, look up your state's truancy and/or homeschooling law, and copy it. Talk with a local support group and buy its legal packet. Compare the two and analyze whether it all makes sense and is complete. When you are sure of the law, follow it. Some states require notification, others do not. If your state's laws do not require notification, do not notify. If they do require notification, follow the instructions you have assembled and comply. Give them only what they ask for and what you are legally required to provide.

Always send your correspondence registered with a "return receipt requested"; that way you establish that on a specific date you notified a specific individual. Always "get it in writing."

If someone from your district contacts you and requests information you did not provide, and which you do not think is legally required, write and ask for the specific law, statute, or regulation that impels you to provide this information. If it's by telephone, request the person write out the questions and send them to you. Always be polite but firm. Understand that the actions of your school district personnel may be nothing more than a test of your resolve to homeschool or a display of their ignorance of the law and your rights.

If you have complied with the law as written, and the school personnel continue to harass you, then you have to take the offensive. Always try to keep the ball in someone else's court. Sometimes a letter to the individual's employer, the board of education, will solve the problem.

You can hire your own attorney or wait until the school district begins legal action and then respond. The best attor-

ney to speak with is a local one who may know the individuals involved as well as the local law, and be able to negotiate a settlement. Some attorneys now specialize in education law. But even if you cannot afford an attorney, you still have all your research and your written record that you are complying with your state's law. Don't be afraid if you are in compliance with your law.

Some homeschoolers choose not to comply with their law for one reason or another. That is your choice. And another question!

LILLIAN JONES ✦ A solid sense of self-confidence goes a long way in dealing with potential conflict—that and the effort to understand the point of view of the other side. Those of us who have been homeschooling for some time know that we are on the cutting edge of education and personal growth. The schools are also very serious about the mission they face. They feel that they hold the hope for the future and, whether we like it or not, they are raising more children than we homeschoolers are. The children they're raising are going to be right out there building tomorrow's world with our own. This is the overview I think is best to keep in mind when dealing with school authorities. Confidence with compassion.

Beyond a good knowledge of the laws, it helps to be comfortable with homeschooling itself. Prospective home-schoolers often ask where they can get "the books." It's a question that seems perfectly reasonable to someone who hasn't entered the territory yet. We're all products of a long-standing system that seemed to materialize the books, the knowledge, the plan, the wisdom, the whole golden enchilada from some mysterious temple of higher education somewhere out there . . .

Those of us who once actually embarked on a journey to that holy temple, expecting to come away as "teachers," found that it was an illusion. There's no one out there in the school system handing out infallible wisdom about how to educate kids, but there are lots of administrative bureaucrats making their livings by pretending to be, or hoping to become, the ultimate authorities on that elusive body of knowledge.

In the homeschooling world, meanwhile, we have thousands of parents who are working full time on the commitment dearest to their hearts—providing their children with a good life and bright future. We network—we communicate in books, in newsletters, in magazines, on electronic bulletin boards, on the Internet, in national and state organizations, and in state and local support groups.

We don't have to settle for textbooks and policies that have filtered down from intellectual discussions in upper-echelon board rooms, to middle board rooms, and through local school boards. We investigate on our own and take in ideas we hear about from one another, ideas for encouraging our children to love life and learning.

Longtime homeschooling families offer many excellent catalog resources that make school texts and methods look pathetic in comparison. Some are specialized to various religious orientations, but many others are relevant for anyone. A company called Pennsylvania Homeschoolers sells, among other offerings, the deliciously well-written math books by Harold Jacobs. Rebecca Rupp's *The Complete Home Learning Source Book,* and Jean and Donn Reed's book, *The Home School Source Book,* describe hundreds of interesting resources for enjoyable learning, very few of which can be found inside a school.

Ironically, as rich as we are in resources, the longer people homeschool the less we tend to buy. We urge new homeschoolers not to make investments in the beginning because we find, to our

> **We're all products of a long-standing system that seemed to materialize the books, the knowledge, the plan, the wisdom, the whole golden enchilada from some mysterious temple of higher education somewhere out there . . .**

surprise, that tremendous learning takes place with very little in the way of specialized resources.

The school systems, on the other hand, are not yet set up in a way to understand and explore the nature of education in the way we do. They face other challenges. Keeping all this in mind can help you avoid feeling intimidated and hold a feeling of compassion for what they're trying to do as you approach them about homeschooling. We can help in the long run. I hope we can eventually be mentors of a sort, people who have explored some very radical and successful ways of thinking that can help the school community become a better place for the kids who are there.

5

Am I required to teach the same curriculum as the local public school?

REBECCA KOCHENDERFER ◆ Although not required to, some of my homeschooling friends follow the public school curriculum when teaching their children. They like this method because they are comforted knowing that their children are learning the same things as their peers.

I don't use this method because I feel it doesn't take advantage of one of homeschooling's strengths—its flexibility. Whereas curricula are developed to fit the masses, homeschooling can be developed to fit the child. You can design your children's education to take advantage of their interests, their pace, and their learning style. For example, California's curriculum requires children to learn about missions in the fourth grade—whether or not they are interested in missions. With homeschooling, you can wait until your child *is* interested in missions, or perhaps even decide not to learn about missions at all.

Another reason our family has chosen not to use a curriculum is because we think it is too teacher-directed. We prefer learning activities that are more student-directed. For example, we have set up learning centers throughout our house. We have an art center, a science center, and a woodworking center. We set up these obvious learning areas because we want the children to initiate their own activities. We want that microscope out in the open where it can beckon to the kids to "come and explore."

The bottom line is: You are not *required* to teach the same curriculum as the local public school. Whether or not you choose to use that curriculum is up to you.

DAVID AND MICKI COLFAX ◆ Yes and no. In some jurisdictions the education code requires that homeschoolers conform to a state-mandated curriculum, while in others there are few if any requirements. But even in states in which the code specifies what must be taught and when, homeschoolers have been quite successful in interpreting the law in the broadest possible of terms, with the result that parents have considerable latitude in what they teach and when. In states in which the work of homeschooled children is closely monitored, most parents can creatively conform

David and Micki Colfax

with the spirit of the law, if not its bureaucratic intent to exercise control. Who is to say that a brisk walk in the park does not qualify as physical education, or that an hour spent watching a television documentary on the Civil War cannot be construed as an American history lesson?

The task homeschoolers face under these conditions is to fit authentic educational experiences into conventionally defined categories in such a way that the authorities can accept them. It may take a bit of imagination and some creativity, but most homeschooling parents shouldn't have too much trouble completing the pedagogically meaningless forms that educrats and politicians, in their wisdom, have deemed such an important part of the educational process.

SUSAN AND LARRY KASEMAN ◆ No. One reason homeschooling works so well is that homeschoolers can choose curricula that meet their needs, sometimes using different approaches for different children and modifying their approach as their needs change. (Some states do require that homeschoolers submit their curriculum plans to officials.)

Some families follow curricula that are similar to those used in public schools, often purchasing them from a curriculum supplier and changing them to suit their own purposes. They spend as much or as little time as they need on specific topics, add subjects, change schedules, and take breaks from subjects that temporarily are not going well.

Other families develop their own curricula. Some use unit studies (see Question 35). Others base their curricula on the children's and parents' special interests and learn the basics while exploring their interests. Another approach is to do real-life projects and learn from building a garage or raising goats or gardening or cooking or whatever. (See Question 33.)

It makes sense for homeschools to use different curricula from public schools. Public school curricula were developed for a classroom, a very limited space where large numbers of children of the same age are all supposed to be learning the same thing at the same time under the guidance of one older person who does not know any of the children well. Curricula have been developed to make this unrealistic, contrived setting somewhat manageable and to reassure taxpayers that they are getting their money's worth from public schools. They were not developed primarily to meet children's needs. By contrast, home-schools have a few children of different ages; one or more adults who know them well, love them, and can give them lots of individual attention, the whole world to explore, and no taxpayers or administrators to keep happy.

Public officials sometimes try to make homeschoolers adopt curricula similar to public school curricula, either by requiring that homeschoolers submit curriculum plans to school officials or that homeschoolers take standardized tests, which means homeschoolers have to adopt a curriculum similar to a conventional curriculum to prepare for the tests. Homeschoolers can use the points below to counter both these requirements. When we homeschoolers understand them, we understand more clearly why we can and should choose our own curricula. We are also better prepared to defend our rights and freedoms when we talk with school officials, legislators, friends and relatives, and members of the general public.

- Homeschools, in many instances, are private schools. Under both state law and historical tradition, private schools choose their curricula. For example, parochial schools can teach religious beliefs. Therefore, home-schoolers have the right to choose their curricula.

- Parents have the right to secure for their children an education consistent with their principles and beliefs. The state may not have a monopoly in education and may not demand a uniform education for all. This right is guaranteed by the First, Fourth, Fifth, Ninth, and Fourteenth Amendments to the U.S. Constitution. It has been upheld by U.S. Supreme Court cases such as *Pierce* v. *Society of Sisters* and *Farrington* v. *Tokushige.*

- Laws require compulsory school attendance but not compulsory education. Compulsory school attendance laws are enforceable; it is not difficult to check attendance for young people enrolled in public and private schools, including homeschools. However, laws that required compulsory education would give the state control over education. The state would have to develop a clear set of definitions and criteria for what it means to be educated and a series of tests to determine whether people have acquired the knowledge, skills, and attitudes that the definitions require. This would cost us our freedom of education and learning, and even our freedom of thought.

6

I've heard some families purchase legal insurance in case of future problems. How many families do this, and is this necessary?

Susan and Larry Kaseman ◆ Legal insurance is not only unnecessary; it is unwise. Few families buy it, a reasonable estimate is less than 10 percent of homeschoolers.

Legal insurance is unnecessary because families are almost never taken to court just because they are homeschooling. (Court appearances by homeschoolers are almost always the result of a larger dispute, such as a custody battle.) Ironically, homeschooling insurance often excludes the people who are most likely to be involved in legal proceedings, such as families whose children were truant or in difficulty with a public school before they began homeschooling.

- Purchasing legal insurance undermines the most valuable asset we have—our willingness and ability to take responsibility ourselves. Just as no one else cares as much about our children's educations as we do, no one else is as motivated to maintain our homeschooling rights and responsibilities as we are. Legal insurance makes us dependent on experts and less inclined to act on our own behalf.

- Homeschoolers working through state-wide inclusive grassroots organizations are more effective than legal insurance in preventing and solving problems faced by individuals and by the homeschooling community as a whole. For one thing, there is a fundamental conflict of interest between us homeschoolers and providers of insurance. We homeschoolers want and need as little government regulation as possible. In states like Illinois, this means living without a specific homeschooling law that says, "Homeschooling is legal as long as homeschoolers do such and such."

However, it is in the best interest of insurance providers to have laws that are clear-cut (although these laws reduce homeschooling freedoms), so homeschoolers who comply with them are easy to defend in court. For example, insurance providers often favor testing requirements. It is easy to defend homeschoolers who have scored well on the tests.

But as homeschoolers, we ask, what about families who don't comply with the law? Those who don't want their children tested, either because they object to the content of the tests, or because they do not want the state to have that much control over their children's educations, or for other reasons? Or families whose children do not score well? Insurance providers can simply refuse to cover these families. This means that a substantial number of homeschoolers are stuck with a law with which they cannot or do not want to comply, and they are more likely to be taken to court than they would be with a less clear-cut, less lawyer-friendly law.

- National organizations that provide legal insurance pose a particular problem. Residents of a state understand the political climate, and have more at stake and stronger incentive than outside experts and will have to live with the resulting law or court decision.
- Legal insurance focuses on laws that sometimes undermine common sense. For example, it is obvious that our homes remain homes and are not school buildings. We do not need laws that say that we do not have to comply with regulations intended for conventional school buildings. We do not need school bus turnarounds.

Reducing fundamental parents' rights to a set of legal rights would cost us a great deal. We have important rights and responsibilities because we are parents. These rights do not originate with the government, and we reduce them significantly if we ask the government to "protect" them through laws. Then the government is seen as the source of basic rights and responsibilities which it can change or reduce.

- Legal insurance is also unwise because people are willing to pay a fairly substantial sum for it. This gives an organization that provides insurance a large budget. Inevitably, such an organization will put a great deal of emphasis on the legal aspects of homeschooling. Also, if the organization has an agenda in addition to homeschooling, perhaps even more important to it than homeschooling, it may be willing to sacrifice our homeschooling freedoms for the benefit of its larger agenda.

Our greatest protection comes from working together through grassroots organizations and responsible individual actions rather than purchasing legal insurance.

WILL SHAW ◆ Many years ago, when the resurgence of home education was in its infancy, it was not unusual for a homeschool family to be harassed by public education authorities or others. Homeschooling was not clearly legal in all states, and the public education industry always wants to protect and strengthen its near-monopoly over the training of children. There really were people out to make life difficult for homeschoolers by using truancy and child neglect processes. Legal insurance for homeschoolers was desired by a minority of homeschoolers.

However, though there are still some nasty local officials, home education is legal everywhere in the United States, and any need for legal insurance is even further reduced. Most homeschoolers don't feel the need. The parents just examine and abide by their applicable laws, network with other homeschoolers and homeschool organizations, and keep abreast of events and practices.

Homeschool legal insurance is a big business, and scary stories increase demand. In my experience in recent years, the very few problems that homeschoolers have had with local authorities are usually due to genuine mistakes or bad judgment that is not motivated by ill will. You need to be familiar with the requirements for homeschooling in your state. You do not need to be an attorney to teach your own kids,

> **You do not need to be an attorney to teach your own kids, and you are not likely to ever need any homeschool-related legal representation.**

and you are not likely to ever need any homeschool-related legal representation.

Realize, too, that the unelected leadership of an insurance provider has a political, social, religious, economic, and home education agenda that goes beyond providing legal insurance, whether or not you need such insurance.

7

Why should I homeschool my children when I'm paying taxes for the same public schools I attended?

JOHN TAYLOR GATTO ◆ First, they *aren't* the same public schools you attended, regardless of appearances. In every decade since the end of World War II, a complex, comprehensive social agenda has unfolded through the agency of public schooling. Each succeeding generation is much more "schooled" than its predecessor, making the movement of this agenda "progressive" through a process of simple addition. Each generation of parents knows less than the generation before it, and hence is less able to counteract the training of schools.

It's impossible to fully analyze this agenda and track it to its source in 500 words or even 5 million, but all of us can see the visible effects it produces in our children: short attention spans; a dramatic inability to spin out satisfactory lines of meaning in their own lives; a profound weakening of family bonds; an indifference to concepts of duty, loyalty, sustained commitment, principle; a substitution of law for morality; and a massive stupidity, even among the bright with specialized competencies, about the great historical, philosophical, religious, political, and narrative contexts that give the details of everyday life their place in a tapestry of meaning.

What does it *mean* (do you know?) that 100,000 retreating Iraqi soldiers were instantly incinerated by the explosion of simple gasoline over their heads, dropped by an air fleet with full intelligence in hand that the war was over? What is the theory of human life that allows such a thing? Unless you know how unique and almost unprecedented such an action was in the history of warfare, you would be left with the notion such things happened every day.

The agenda of public schooling has been, for the entire twentieth century, to remove the power of most people to think for themselves. The methods by which this has been done were developed first in the north German states of Prussia, Saxony, and Hanover, the latter principality the source of the British kings our American revolution overthrew. A full analysis is impossible here; but you need to realize that because of the systematic, hierarchical nature of schooling, your local teachers, principals, superintendents, and the like have almost no say in this—they are *pedagogues,* which means practically that they administer routines made elsewhere far

> **The agenda of public schooling has been, for the entire twentieth century, to remove the power of most people to think for themselves.**

away. Whatever the facts of the case, the results are progressive, following closely a discipline created by the philosophical movement called Positivism.

If you cannot find ways to counteract what amounts to a mechanization of your children's minds and characters, and a low-grade mechanization at that, they will surely cease to be fully human. They might even become people who think it a day's work to burn 100,000 men to death. Break their marriage vows. Put you in an old age home.

Those are some reasons you should homeschool.

NED VARE ◆ Just because we pay for the public schools doesn't mean we have to consume their services. We pay for parks, roads, libraries, and many other things we never use. Taxes pay for the salaries of thousands of people whose services we don't use, from police and secretaries to architects and lawyers.

Children are homeschooled as an alternative to public and private schools because parents believe those schools will not provide what they want for their children. The problem of paying taxes to support the government schools, whether we use them or approve of them, is a political problem and should not cloud the issue. Parents, being legally and morally responsible for the education of their children, have a decision to make: How can I provide my children the best education possible? That question does not go away when parents choose a school or home-schooling. It is a choice that can always change because of circumstances and/or events.

Ned Vare

Government schools have now become so expensive for us all that they have reduced our ability to pay for alternative schooling—and that is part of their strategy of forcing everyone into their system.

Nevertheless, parents need to realize that no matter how much money we give the government, it will not produce the kind of schools we want. After we remove our children, we need to vote against tax increases whenever possible, and be outspoken about the failings and deceit and corruption that are part and parcel of the public school system. A specific step available is to join the Separation of School and State Alliance, an organization whose goal is to disconnect education from government. That will produce huge local tax cuts and leave parents the funds to choose the kind and amount of education they want for their own children.

DAVID AND MICKI COLFAX ◆ If you feel that the public schools can give you a good return on your coerced investment, then perhaps you shouldn't homeschool your children. But if you are suggesting that you should get at least *something* in return for your tax dollars—even if it is a bad education for your children—your interest in economic justice is probably misplaced. To send children to public school simply because you (like most of us) are compelled under penalty of law to support them is rather akin to taking public transportation to places you don't want or need to go simply because your tax dollars subsidize the transit system. Clearly, there are many things our tax dollars are spent on that don't benefit and sometimes even harm us. Too few of us realize that most public schools fall into the latter category.

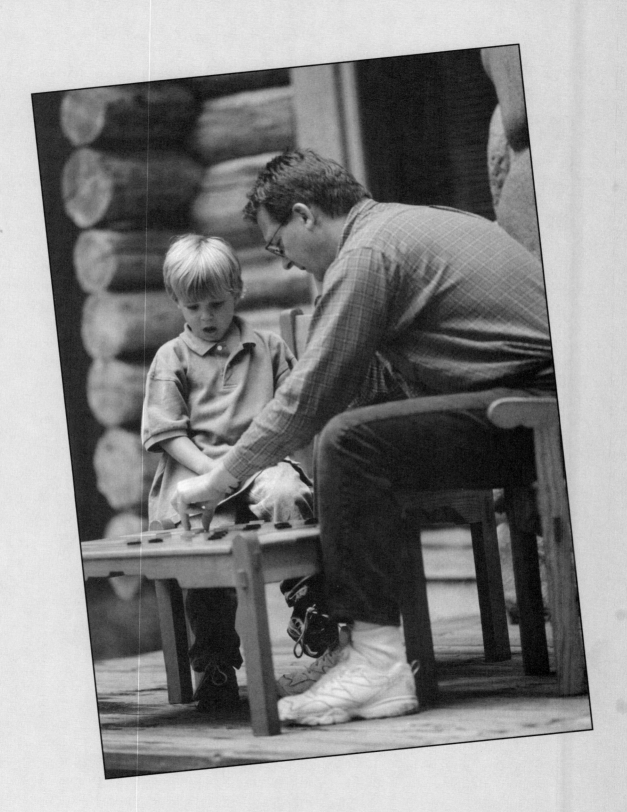

CHAPTER TWO

Homeschool May Be Cheaper Than You Think

H AVE YOU ever thought about how much money you wouldn't spend, and therefore wouldn't need, if you stayed home to educate and enjoy your children? Across the nation families are realizing the cost of a paycheck—in terms of taxes, time, and worth when compared to their children's futures—is too steep. It just might pay—literally—to take a close look at the answers to Questions 8 and 9. Your job could be more expensive than you ever realized.

Speaking of expensive, let's also consider the high cost of public education and the never-ending cries for more money to correct increasingly expensive mistakes. If you already know that the average per-pupil expenditure in American public schools now tops $7,000, you may at least want to keep closer tabs when your local school budget expands, especially after Cafi Cohen tells you about a family providing an excellent education at home for less than $25 per child per year.

Have you ever taken a hard look at how often the pendulum of educational fads swings back and forth, as failure in one direction sends your tax dollars flying in another direction, a direction just as likely to be abandoned as so many before it? Even when the fad is recognized as a failure, the nature of the beast necessitates that it continue for years because so much money was invested in it in the first place. You can't throw away millions of dollars worth of textbooks and teacher training and advertising after just two years! It takes time to scrape around for the replacement. It takes many committees to study the proposed replacements and offer counterproposals. Textbook publishers must be alerted to the replacement fad, find the writers, and get the new books to print. Taxpayers must be coerced into paying for it all.

With more than 49 million children in grades K–12 of public schools, according to a National Center for Education Statistics estimate for 2000, imagine the dollars wasted with a system like this. Maybe it's time for more families to check out an alternative route. Stay home and use a textbook that your child picks out. Drop it if it doesn't work. Minimal financial damage, immediate correction. Better yet, read Mary Griffith's, Becky Rupp's, and Wendy Priesnitz's advice about how to keep the cost of homeschooling to a minimum; not one recommends purchasing textbooks—a staple of government schools' voracious dollar appetite—at all.

Hundreds of thousands of families have proven you can live on one income in a two-income society, with enough money left over to educate the children well with homeschooling. Still other families, with a reordering of priorities and deft scheduling, have found room for homeschooling *and* a job for both parents. A bonus, homeschooling lends itself to immediate correction should something be wrong. At educational bargain basement prices, and using the ideas you'll discover in this chapter, homeschooling could save your family a bundle. For just a little more fun, multiply that by 49 million children, and dream of the bundle it could save our nation.

8

How much does it cost each year to homeschool?

CINDY WADE ◆ Homeschooling need only be as expensive as you want it to be. We discovered that we didn't need all the trappings used in a public school classroom, like desks, chalkboard, art station, reading station. Instead, we stuff our house with lots and lots of good books. We prefer the classics because they're proven literary works with good vocabulary and strong moral values. All these books are free at your local library or through the interlibrary loan system.

There's really no need to buy expensive curricula and textbooks. Many homeschoolers get by on $200 to $300 a year per child for instruction and activities. We've found success with simple department store workbooks, a library card, computer programs, and mentors.

Cindy Wade

Homeschooling can happen when both parents feel compelled to work outside the home. Many parents work split shifts to accomplish this, one parent working during the day and the other at night, sharing responsibilities.

Remember, older children are quite capable of handling many of the chores necessary for maintaining a peaceful and efficient household. Homeschooled children develop a much more positive attitude toward parents and responsibility. They learn cooperation is necessary for survival.

Even single parents find that with a little creativeness and ingenuity they, too, can homeschool. Single parents don't live in a vacuum. There are family members, neighbors, and friends willing to help with lessons, supervision, and resources. Much depends on how determined a parent is to take charge of her children's education and of her own life.

To fairly gauge the cost of homeschooling there are two more aspects, frequently ignored but vital to consider:

- Homeschooling saves you the expense of a school wardrobe, school lunches, transportation, extracurricular activities, field trips, and fund-raising activities.

- Factor in the cost of making money. What do you spend on wardrobe, gas, breakfast, lunch, car payments, insurance, gifts for office acquaintances, day care, increased income taxes, and any other rituals associated with going off to work each day?

Wouldn't you rather live on less and spend more time fishing, swimming, talking, playing, laughing, and sharing with your child? You may discover, as we did, that homeschooling becomes a simpler, more enriching way of life rather than just an inexpensive educational alternative.

> **Wouldn't you rather live on less and spend more time fishing, swimming, talking, playing, laughing, and sharing with your child?**

CAFI COHEN ◆ The first problem is defining cost. Do you count the computer your family would have anyway? Or the encyclopedia set? Or the trip to Washington, D.C., you would have made whether you were homeschooling or not? The following answer assumes that we do *not* count those things, even though they are educational and you can document them as "school." I will also not consider the second income one parent might give up. After that, "How much does it cost?" depends on how you homeschool.

I have known homeschoolers who spend less than $25 per child per year. These families use community resources.

They frequent the library; attend school district book giveaways; accept other homeschoolers' discards; make their own math manipulatives; watch PBS and other instructional television programs; garner subject-matter expertise from neighbors, friends, and relatives; and buy occasional books and even science materials at garage sales. Teenagers in these families often volunteer in educational settings like veterinary clinics and museums and community drama groups. These older children also trade babysitting or housework for piano or French lessons. Educational sweat equity!

A cost of $100 to $400 per child per year is probably a more common expenditure for materials, once you understand the homeschooling market and learn to shop carefully. The average text for one year of math or language arts costs between $20 and $40, and families may buy anywhere from one to six texts for each child each year. Those who rely less on textbooks, as well as those who do, spend money on computer programs, real books, field trips, paper and pencils, and materials for special projects (building model rockets, for example). Families who stay in this price range also often use the strategies listed in the previous paragraphs.

It is possible to spend $400 to $1,000 per year or more for each child if you enroll your child in an independent study program; and some of the online programs for grades six through twelve can cost $700 to $2,000 per year. A few

---

THE LITTLE THINGS

Delight in every day's little things. Cherish them. This is the stuff from which life—and therefore, learning—is fashioned. From the little things your children will shape their hopes, dreams, and eventual reality.

The little things remain when all too soon paths diverge, forming the threads that bind family together through space and time's inevitable tug.

And in the most quiet of moments, when those threads glisten brightly in love's pure light, it's the little things that move your heart to smile and stir your soul to sing. That's what it's all about, this homeschooling.

The little things.

---

programs are less expensive, but most fall into these price ranges. Private tutoring may also run up the tab. While most families successfully homeschool through high school with self-instructional materials and inexpensive community resources, families occasionally hire tutors for high school math or science or foreign language.

One category of increased expense surprised our family. When our children attended school, they had time for two or three extracurricular activities—maybe Scouts, piano lessons, and soccer. As homeschoolers, our children—with more time—could easily take part in five to ten activities each week. Of course, these additional activities generated additional expenses—for supplies, uniforms, dues, transportation, lessons, and so on.

9

If I homeschool, can I continue to work and earn the income we need? How can a homeschooling family survive on one income in a two-income society?

BILLY AND NANCY GREER ◆ First you have to define your "needs." The American way seems to promote living beyond one's means and turns "wants" into "needs." Look at the costs of work as well as the income, and you may discover that you do not really gain much by

working. Day-care costs, clothes for work, transportation costs, and meals can quickly add up.

At one point Bill was working a sixty-hour-per-week job, Nancy was working a forty-hour-per-week job, and both spent Friday night through Sunday night at a residential home for handicapped kids (our children would go with us). Since then, we have both started to work from home and discovered that we can survive on less than half the income we had before.

REBECCA KOCHENDERFER ◆ I work fifteen to twenty hours a week *and* homeschool my children. Because my children are young (seven, four, and one), I have a babysitter come in to watch the kids while I work out of my home office. I have found several advantages to this arrangement.

Rebecca Kochenderfer

Two of the biggest advantages are safety and flexibility. I know exactly what's going on with my kids at all times and I know how the babysitter is treating them. If the kids get hurt, or if something exciting happens, I am just a closed door away. It's also nice to be able to nurse the baby directly instead of pumping all the time.

Also, the kids are involved in my work. They help me test products and tell me what they like and don't like. As they grow older, I hope they will help me with my writing, editing, and bookkeeping. I think they learn a lot just by being around me while I'm working. And, when they're not helping me, I enjoy a break away from them and they enjoy a break away from me.

I'm lucky to have help with the kids. Our babysitter wants to be a teacher, so she loves doing science and art projects with them. She also helps with the household duties, which allows me to spend more time on homeschooling projects.

It is also possible to work at home without hiring extra help. One homeschooling mom I know runs a successful catalog business. She has been quoted as saying, "My business has grown as my children have grown." She is able to spend more time on her business now since her children are older and able to homeschool themselves. Another friend of mine runs her husband's kung fu business while raising three young children. She takes her children with her to meetings, and they study or play quietly nearby.

You may not *have* to work. I quit my job in order to homeschool, and I was scared that we were going to starve.

> **When I quit work our expenses dropped dramatically. I no longer had those sneaky work-related expenses like dry cleaning, lunches out, gas, day care, and higher taxes. By the time I subtracted the cost of working, I discovered that my $25-an-hour job was really bringing home just $7 an hour.**

Everyone warned us that "it takes two incomes these days just to survive," but I have found that not to be the case.

When I quit work, our expenses dropped dramatically. I no longer had those sneaky work-related expenses like dry cleaning, lunches out, gas, day care, and higher taxes. By the time I subtracted the cost of working, I discovered that my $25-an-hour job was really bringing home just $7 an hour.

The book *Your Money or Your Life,* by Joe Dominguez and Vicki Robin, has really helped us get a grip on our finances by showing us how to spend money on the things that matter to us, and to stop spending money on things that don't matter to us. I know a number of homeschoolers who use the program in this book so that they can work less and spend more time with their kids.

Of course, even after reducing your expenses you may feel that you want or need to work. Talk to other homeschooling parents. I'll bet they will have some great ideas for you!

SANDRA DODD ◆ If a family feels that they *cannot* live without two incomes, maybe they can't afford to homeschool.

Some families split shifts, of necessity. Some single parents homeschool. When homeschooling is a priority, people manage to manage!

I've heard budgets described in terms of what it would have cost to have the children in private schools, to clothe them appropriately, and to pay athletic fees. Then there are the costs of having the job—dressing up, lunch out, and so on, for the mom. After all that is balanced, the loss of the second income doesn't seem so big after all.

Some families have decided that paying for a curriculum is a bad use of funds.

I was employed full time, pre-children. Luckily for us, my husband was just finishing the college degree he had procrastinated about when I first got pregnant. There were times in our financial history when it would have been more difficult to live on one income. Even now, if we really cared about driving new cars and having expensive furniture, we'd be unhappy with our finances, but we settle for older cars, used books, used furniture, and happy kids. Certainly, my kids are satisfied with hand-me-down and thrift store clothes, and are not bound by the fashion dictates of the kids at school.

Our entertainment and education are one and the same budget item (ha, if we had a budget, I mean). We don't have to spend money to relax after a hard day of school, since we're unschoolers. Budgeting, cooking, investments, home businesses—these are worked into homeschooling by many families and made learning experiences in addition to moneymakers.

10

Even if we can manage to live on one income, how can I keep the cost of homeschooling to a minimum?

BECKY RUPP
Money.
Always a sensitive topic.

For the financially strapped, there are all kinds of possibilities for low-budget (even no-budget) homeschooling. Many educational resources are absolutely free. The public library, for example, is a great source—not only for books and periodicals, but for educational videos, audiocassettes, story hours, craft programs, discussion groups, and lectures. Many field trips, with their wealth of learning opportunities, cost nothing: tours of local businesses, visits to craftspersons and other professionals, nature hikes, historical societies, museums. Flipping back through my homeschool journals, I find lists of freebie field trips. We visited a

Becky Rupp

JUDITH ALLEE'S FIVE FAVORITE FREEBIES

1. Recycled art materials are free and environmentally friendly. Ask for outdated wallpaper sample books (or ask when they are likely to be available), leftover scrap paper printed on one side from print shops and copy centers, scrap pieces of matte board from framing shops, discarded slate from roofers, and scrap wood from carpenters.

2. Free sample art lessons—including calligraphy, pencil drawing, and drawing with colored pencils—are available online: http://www.homeschoolarts.com.

3. Educational links compiled by Clonlara School have something to fascinate everyone. For example, links under "animals" include directions for building songbird houses, butterfly coloring books you can print for free, Peterson's online bird guide, information on raising llamas, and a site with links to zoos worldwide. Go to www.clonlara.org and click on "educational links."

4. Barter for private lessons in drawing, painting, pottery, music, dance, karate, gymnastics, flying, carpentry, or anything else your family would like to learn. Brace yourself for a few "no" answers, and try not to act too amazed when someone says "yes." My family traded photography services, such as a family portrait—a luxury that instructors were glad to receive—in exchange for an empty spot in the instructor's class or schedule. Better yet, your children can barter by washing dishes, vacuuming, cooking, or doing yard work if they are old enough. Help with chores around the house is mighty tempting to many piano teachers!

local orchard to watch the cider press in action, and in the process we learned how cider is made. A friend with a stable showed the boys how to take care of the horses, taught them how to ride horseback, and let them watch the farrier changing horseshoes. The local historical society (free) had a wonderful display of Native American artifacts, which sparked great interest in the history of arrowheads. A violinmaker in the next town let the boys visit his workshop and

5. Look around for educational materials you may already own, such as:

- *A tape recorder.* Create your own "talk shows" with relatives and friends, or to make your own books-on-tape.

- *A telephone book.* Real-life skills in learning alphabetization can start with the Yellow Pages!

- *A doorway.* Block with chairs and a sheet for an impromptu sock-puppet theatre.

- *Measuring cups, yard sticks, money, odometer, tire gauge, and games with points or play money, like Monopoly or Scrabble.* Use these to give math meaning.

- *Social studies materials.* Get maps, newspapers, news magazines, and National Geographic magazines for free—just post a note on the bulletin board at church or the grocery store stating you will give them a good home.

And a Hint for Harried Parents

A library card is free only if you return your books and videos on time. (I learned this the hard way.) The constant ebb and flow of books in a home-schoolers' home makes that a challenge. Designate a canvas bag, a box, or a shelf for library books in a visible place. You can keep a notebook there in which you write down names of books taken out and their due dates, and check them off when returned. Create a page to record books, videos, and subjects you want to look up on your next trip to the library.

explained the process of putting together a violin.

Used-book stores are generally inexpensive sources for books, magazines, and maps—though browsers should be cautious of used science books, which can quickly become outdated. Some homeschool supply companies specialize in marketing used (and thus greatly marked-down) educational resources.

If you own a computer, the Internet is a spectacular source for homeschool programs. Search and you'll find online books, poems, and stories, art galleries and museums, foreign-language dictionaries, tutorials in all possible subjects, biographies of famous people, history timelines, maps, quizzes, virtual field trips, science demonstrations, and much more. Once you've got the computer, this is all inexpensive; acquiring the computer, on the other hand, is a substantial investment, so perhaps this doesn't count as "keeping costs to a minimum."

Many homeschool resources can be made at home. Through our boys' elementary-level years, I wrote a lot of our materials, including science, history, and handwriting workbooks and beginning readers (precisely tailored to the interests of each child—how many first-grade science workbooks can you find that are all about submarines?); and we made a lot of our own games, equipment, and manipulatives. Making do can be an education in itself. Our boys probably learned more from making their own history board games (with cardboard, felt-tipped pens, and index cards) than from playing the commercial versions.

A local homeschool support group can be a wonderful resource for mutually beneficial tradeoffs of the "your skills for mine" variety. Ask and you'll find people willing, for example, to tutor your kids in French in exchange for carpentry lessons, or teach your kids quilting in exchange for creative writing classes.

One of our worst money drains in homeschooling—I continually kick myself for this—is what my husband calls "false starts," the purchase of stuff that simply didn't work for our kids. A good series of math books and manipulatives, for example, can be a terrific investment, lasting through many years and children—but if the kids don't like it, there it will sit, hated, on the bottom shelf of the bookcase, an educational and financial lost cause. A geography game, if the kids find it boring, is money down the tubes. I can't think of any single purchase that was financially devastating in and of itself ("Rats—the kids don't like the grand piano . . ."), but all the lesser goofs add up. Textbooks, for example, are pricey, and we've bought our share of blah ones.

There's no truly foolproof solution to this, kids being the unpredictable little intellects that they are, but wherever possible, it's a good idea to preview and pretest. Borrow the materials from someone who already uses them and see what the initial reaction is. Ask opinions and read reviews. But don't assume, just because a given program is popular ("Everybody uses it") that it's desirable for your family. I think of our experience with the (expensive) Saxon math texts, a series of much-praised math books available for all age levels, favored by many homeschool families. Our kids loathed them.

So what's the bottom line? It's certainly possible, with a little imagination, to homeschool very inexpensively, especially when your children are young.

Get the kids to share in designing the annual homeschool budget.

It's math enrichment and it doesn't cost a dime.

MARY GRIFFITH ◆ Homeschooling doesn't require much of anything you wouldn't already have around anyway. You don't need an expensive purchased curriculum (or even a cheap purchased curriculum!). You don't need special books or software or fancy manipulatives to "enrich your children's minds." In nearly ten years of homeschooling, the only thing I ever bought specifically because we were homeschooling was a teacher's planner book the very first year. I meant to use it to record, neatly organized by subject and date, what my children learned as they learned it. Within three days I realized I'd wasted my four dollars.

What you need to homeschool is the willingness to answer your kids' questions, to help them figure out what they want to know, and to help them find their answers. This could mean also buying books and equipment, but it doesn't have to. You can use the library, including interlibrary loan. You can haunt used bookstores, thrift shops, and yard sales. You can seek out people who know about whatever interests your children and get their advice. You can help your children figure out ways to make or grow or otherwise create what they need to learn.

After only a couple of years, you may find that you prefer the do-it-yourself route even if you don't need to watch your cash flow too carefully. There's much to be learned from searching out your own resources, figuring out how to make do with what you've already got to work with. (And keeping the everyday sorts of expenses to a minimum can allow you the occasional splurge on something you *really* want!)

WENDY PRIESNITZ ◆ Children do not require fancy curriculum packages in order to learn. They learn best by participating in the real world. After all, that's the way they learned how to walk and talk—two of the most difficult skills human beings ever learn. Mastery of these skills doesn't require textbooks, or even formal instruction for that matter. It requires a safe environment; somebody modeling the behavior; lots of opportunity for practice; plenty of encouragement; solace when something goes wrong; celebration when you're successful; and most of all, trust. Few parents ever doubt that their children will learn how to walk or talk. No formal instruction, no testing, no curriculum plans.

Think of learning as a drama that is unfolding with you and your children as active participants. Your role is to keep up with your child, ask questions at appropriate times, and help create bridges between new information and prior knowledge; it is not to contrive ways to teach skills or subject areas artificially. In this way, you'll do your children the honor of allowing them to be in charge of their own learning, with knowledge and skills developing in natural sequence through the exploration of an ever-expanding world. And you'll not have to spend money on curriculum materials!

Of course, books can be an excellent way to spark your child's interest in a subject, or provide more information about a topic he or she has discovered. Your public library can provide access to a whole world of historical fiction, newspaper articles, reference books, poetry and nonfiction, and is a valuable and well-used resource for most homeschooling families.

Some families feel more confident using a prepackaged curriculum program, at least when they begin their homeschooling adventure. But as children develop their skills as active learners, they inevitably demonstrate how much or how little instruction they require at any given time. It's up to us parents to listen.

> **Think of learning as a drama that is unfolding with you and your children as active participants.**

11

With all the talk about the possibility of vouchers for education, can I wait and then use this money for homeschooling?

MARY McCARTHY ◆ Talk is cheap. You can no more spend a possible voucher than you can spend a possible lottery jackpot.

However, should vouchers ever become a reality, it seems reasonable that the taxpayers who are supplying the money—in the form of a voucher—would want you to account for how you spent their money. They might even want to exercise control over your curriculum choices, as demonstrated in the potential problem with using taxpayer dollars to purchase religious materials. As a taxpayer I would want to see proof that my money was being well spent and that your child was being educated. I can see where vouchers would lead to standards and mandatory testing in addition to paperwork and accountability procedures.

ANN ZEISE ◆ I wouldn't keep putting up with a bad situation waiting for vouchers for homeschoolers. The Education Savings Act for Public and Private

Ann Zeise

Schools is an IRA account in which you may set aside up to $2,500 for home education in the U.S. Plan in advance—while your children are small—and talk to your tax accountant about how to take advantage of this, possibly sheltering some money for homeschool-related expenses.

The likelihood that voucher money will be given to homeschool families is pretty slim.

DAVID AND MICKI COLFAX ◆ To do so would be a little like not buying a computer because you are waiting for them to come out with a faster model: You lose the use of what's available while you wait. And while you can be sure that a faster computer will be produced, there is next to no chance that we will ever see vouchers being used for homeschooling anytime in the near future. Indeed, there is some reason to fear that efforts to put a voucher system in place could threaten the interests of homeschoolers, even to the point of making homeschooling illegal in some cases. A recent California voucher ballot measure—which was rejected by the voters—contained provisions that would have required a redefinition of homeschooling by legislators heavily indebted to the public education lobby, a move all but certain to make homeschooling, in a voucher-providing state, far more difficult than it is currently.

In short, don't wait for something good to happen on the voucher front; governments that have been thus far so obviously reluctant to provide vouchers so parents can send their children to closely regulated schools are a very long way from providing them with money to spend on independent homeschooling programs.

NANCY PLENT ◆ Don't hold your breath waiting for vouchers to happen. Charter schools somehow got a foot in the door, but there's a fierce battle over their existence wherever they spring up. Charter schools and vouchers take money from the public schools, and the schools won't sit still for that.

If any voucher plans do make it, I don't think homeschoolers will automatically be included in them. We'll

> **I can see where vouchers would lead to standards and mandatory testing in addition to paperwork and accountability procedures.**

have to fight for that if we want it. And doesn't it seem likely that state money would come with some unacceptable strings attached? Would we have to test our kids, send in reports, or use certified teachers to get the voucher money, for example?

There's so many books out there on being a "tightwad" to stay afloat financially, so many ideas about making money from your home, that I think homeschoolers would be better off saying "No, thanks" to state handouts and cope with the expense in other ways.

READING TO HELP YOU SIMPLIFY

Many good books have been written on the subject of simplifying your life. Here are a few of my favorites.

Andrews, Cecile. *The Circle of Simplicity: Return to the Good Life*. Harper Collins, 1997.

Dacyczyn, Amy. *Tightwad Gazette I, II, and III: Promoting Thrift as a Viable Alternative Lifestyle*. Villard Books, 1993, 1995, 1997.

Elgin, Duane. *Voluntary Simplicity: Toward a Way of Life That Is Outwardly Simple, Inwardly Rich*. Quill, 1993.

Halverson, Delia. *Living Simply*. Abingdon Press, 1996.

Luhrs, Janet. *The Simple Living Guide: A Sourcebook for Less Stressful, More Joyful Living*. Broadway Books, 1997.

McBride, Tracey. *Frugal Luxuries: Simple Pleasures to Enhance Your Life and Comfort Your Soul*. Bantam Books, 1997.

Mitchell, Jann. *Home Sweeter Home: Creating a Haven of Simplicity and Spirit*. Beyond Words Publishing Co., 1996.

St. James, Elaine. *Living the Simple Life: A Guide to Scaling Down and Enjoying More*. Hyperion, 1996.

———. *Simplify Your Life with Kids: 100 Ways to Make Family Life Easier and More Fun*. Andrews & McMeel, 1997.

Taylor, Robert, Susannah Seton, and David Greer. *Simple Pleasures: Soothing Suggestions and Small Comforts for Living Well Year Round*. Conari Press, 1997.

Taylor-Hough, Deborah. *A Simple Choice: A Practical Guide for Saving Your Time, Money and Sanity*. Champion, 2000.

CHAPTER THREE

Can Homeschool Fit *Your* Life Situation?

B EWARE.

If you've ever said, "I'd like to homeschool but (fill in the blank)," the answers to the questions in this chapter just may blow your justification out of the proverbial excuse pile. If, as an educator, policy maker, or legislator, you've ever said, "Homeschooling may work for some but not for (fill in the blank)," you have found experienced voices to correct misunderstandings. If, as a reporter, journalist, or researcher, you've tried to pigeonhole the lifestyles of homeschool practitioners, get ready for a real eye-opener.

Chapters 1 and 2 illustrate how legally safe and affordable homeschooling is, and chapter 3 is a tribute to its astonishing flexibility. Homeschooling can be fashioned and shaped by its users into a viable educational approach suited to individual family needs and circumstances. The contributors to this book were asked if homeschooling could benefit children who are labeled gifted, have special needs, are diagnosed with Attention Deficit Disorder (ADD) or Attention Deficit Hyperactivity Disorder (ADHD), or have experienced discipline problems in school. They candidly reveal how homeschooling can fit the lifestyle of a single parent, a rural family, a child coming out of school after years of attendance, or a child who wants to homeschool

> **Combine the insights contained in this chapter with a good dose of creativity and a pinch of determination, and you just may find you can be as flexible as homeschooling itself.**

part-time. Can homeschooling work if you're an ethnic or racial minority? If one child stays in school while another comes home? The answers are here.

As critics are all too happy to point out, not every family can homeschool. But it grows increasingly clear that many more of those who don't, can. Combine the insights contained in this chapter with a good dose of creativity and a pinch of determination, and you just may find you can be as flexible as homeschooling itself.

12

Is home a better place than school for my child, who has been labeled a "gifted child"?

NED VARE ◆ "Gifted" is a public relations term to make some parents believe the school recognizes talent in some children. It's self-esteem for parents; it does not benefit children. Gifted does not mean the same thing to a public school person as it does to a parent. To the public school, gifted means smart enough to be put into certain classes to be indoctrinated in ways different from the regular indoctrination. Do not make the mistake of believing that a gifted child is being given fast-track academic courses or advanced courses in those disciplines.

Yes. Home is a better place for almost any child to be educated—especially if the school considers the child gifted.

WILL SHAW ◆ Yes, and this was one reason we decided to try out homeschooling. After two years in public school, our oldest, Leah, then age seven, wasn't challenged or stimulated enough in her regular class. The so-called gifted program was, well, very inadequate. We feared her becoming a social outcast over time, so different was she from her classmates. She had already been "skipped" a grade, and we were stumped as to how to deal with the situation. As products of public schools and as former teachers, Margaret and I were burdened with conventional notions of what schools and education were supposed to resemble. But regular school was just not meeting our little girl's needs.

We heard about homeschooling and realized, "Hey, *this* is how we can make sure our child receives the variety and depth of instruction, knowledge, exposure, and room to maneuver that she needs and deserves." Homeschooling isn't as constrained by clocks and calendars or a one-size-fits-all curriculum.

You and your child can explore and pursue as deeply as you wish.

REBECCA RUPP ◆ "Gifted," surely, is one of the more conflict-laden words in the educational lexicon—what's gifted? We've all got gifted children, right?

Technically, giftedness is defined by standardized test scores: Children who score one or more grade levels above normal level are deemed academically talented or gifted. I don't know whether our children are "gifted" or not, since none has ever been tested. Josh, our oldest, is a talented and versatile writer (with a definite aversion to math); Ethan, the middle child, is intensely interested in and knowledgeable about the physical sciences (but can't spell); Caleb, our youngest, an extremely quick learner in general, is—according to his piano teacher—talented in music. Gifted? In the sense that some of their talents need more nurturing and support than my husband and I can give them, yes.

For children with unusual talents or highly directed interests, a homeschool

For children with unusual talents or highly directed interests, a homeschool environment is often ideal.

environment is often ideal. It gives them the freedom to set their own agenda, concentrating on the development of their own special set of abilities, spending their time as they see fit. A notably talented or ambitious child, however, sometimes needs more input than is readily available at home. Caleb, for example, who taught himself to read music and play the piano, clearly needed a teacher to help him progress; Ethan, determined at the age of thirteen to learn college-level physics, had list after list of questions that demanded some high-powered physics expertise. We found Caleb a piano teacher and Ethan a kindly e-mail pen pal in the Cornell University physics department.

Josh, on the other hand, prefers to work on his own. We've tried a couple of creative writing and literature classes at different levels—most recently an online class through the local community college—but none has been too helpful. Fun, said Josh, but he thinks he learns more by himself. He writes daily and is working through a self-assigned reading list, including works by Kafka, Solzhenitsyn, Isaac Bashevis Singer, and Wallace Stevens.

Gifted children—most children—are often skewed in their interests: obsessed with chemistry but indifferent to poetry; fascinated by art but unwilling to practice the clarinet; thrilled by astronomy but bored by Shakespeare. If anything creates tension in our homeschool program, it's this academic imbalance. Children given the freedom to pursue their own interests, do. The writers write; the scientists spend whole days in the basement where they've set up a chemistry lab. This means that not all academic subjects get equal enthusiasm, equal dedication, and equal time. My husband and I provide the fundamentals of a basic education, but the boys, inevitably, pick and choose. We lay it out; they take what they need. Each according to his own gifts.

13

Can my child, who's been diagnosed with ADHD, succeed at home?

SUSAN EVANS ◆ Children who have been labeled ADHD, ADD, dyslexic, hyperactive, or any of those other labels may benefit most of all from homeschooling!

Conventional schools can be failure traps for children who are not by nature quiet, compliant, morning people who are able to concentrate for long periods of time on disconnected, unrelated tasks and who are able to screen out lots of distracting sounds and activities. That's not a description of very many children I know.

Some young people, especially boys, are active and curious, focusing on several activities simultaneously—building with Lego blocks, watching television, listening to a conversation on the phone, humming a song. These children need, thrive on, and deserve an environment where they can move freely, change activities as their minds shift gears, and be able to eat, sleep, dance, and use the bathroom as their bodies require.

Time and growing maturity allow children to develop healthy patterns of eating, sleeping, working, and playing in their own time—consistent with their own personalities and temperaments. Productive responses to frustration, anger, and enthusiasm develop over time in a supportive atmosphere. In such an environment, an impulsive, too active, easily distracted boy, for instance, can grow to become an empathic, energetic, multitalented delightful young man. And rather than being dependent on drugs or rigid routine to be likable, he grows with his independence and self-esteem intact.

Many overly active youngsters thrive on physical challenge: digging in gardens, building structures, moving furniture, and so on. Often they need to eat, rest, and use the bathroom on timetables different from quieter, less active children, and they can easily be overstimulated.

These children have an internal demand for activity and need for instant response to stimuli that seems overwhelming, and they can find spending large amounts of unsupervised time with groups of other children unsuccessful. But they are delightful and happy with people who are more mature and can accommodate their temporary social immaturity, while providing positive behavioral role models.

Homeschooling can do a superb job of giving young people this supportive environment while they are growing up and "mellowing out." After several years of quiet, appropriate support and productivity, these kids will move of their own accord into a group of peers (age, interest, or both) as pleasant, successful friends. In the meantime, they've learned more about the world in a useful context than they would have as singled-out, different children in a class, who absorb the lesson that they're not quite acceptable as they are, and often can't figure out what they're doing wrong or what's expected of them.

As homeschoolers, they are useful, valued members of their families and their communities. They're the ones folks turn to when something needs to be fixed, hard work needs to be done, or a puzzle (physical or social) needs to be solved.

LUZ SHOSIE ◆ ADHD, in most cases, is a teaching disability. It means that your child learns in ways other than the way school chooses to teach. It is likely to disappear once your child is allowed to choose what, when, where, and with whom she wants to learn.

Luz Shosie

Read Thomas Armstrong, Susannah Scheffer, John Holt, Daniel Greenberg. Remember that children want to learn and they know how.

> Conventional schools can be failure traps for children who are not by nature quiet, compliant, morning people who are able to concentrate for long periods of time on disconnected, unrelated tasks and who are able to screen out lots of distracting sounds and activities.

CINDY WADE ◆ Many families new to homeschooling tell me they see the greatest change for the better in their children in the first two weeks after they begin to homeschool. They say their children seem more relaxed, more secure, and more loving. Many tell me their child's ADD or ADHD symptoms all but disappear.

I'm convinced that ADD and ADHD are conditions created by the schools to shirk accountability. Pick up any book on ADD or ADHD and just look at the "symptoms": fidgets, stares out the window, won't wait for a turn, speaks out of turn, talks loudly, unable to learn to read, accident prone, given to tantrums, noisy, mischievous, dawdles, loses things, daydreams, impulsive, needs constant stimulation, gets angry and frustrated, restless, low self-esteem, can't concentrate, and awkwardness at sports. That describes just about everyone on this planet! These are things that all children (and many adults) do innocently and naturally.

Nature provided children with short attention spans for a reason. It's part of their survival instincts. A child will, however, spend hours doing one thing provided that one thing holds his interest. My six-year-old can spend an entire day playing in his sandbox, if I let him, taking short breaks only for food and potty-runs. Try getting him to sit still at a desk for an hour or so. It's just not possible. But then sitting at a desk for four to six hours a day isn't natural, either.

I'm also convinced that children under the age of ten shouldn't be forced to attend any kind of institutionalized training such as preschool or public school. These children should be out catching frogs, building forts, raising chickens, going on hikes, playing in sandboxes, baking cookies, riding bikes, and playing make-believe. A child's play is his work. While he plays, he learns. Children this young are not psychologically, biologically, emotionally, or physiologically ready for structured learning. This is the reason so many of the male

youth in this country spend much of their frustrated childhoods labeled as ADD or ADHD and are legally drugged into submission and dependency.

I once got into a heated discussion with a mother of a teenage boy diagnosed as ADD. By her description this boy was a real terror; but after listening to her lengthy diatribe about her son's upbringing, I came to the conclusion that the boy's major problem was a combination of his public schooling experience and her parenting. She'd hauled that boy from psychologist to psychologist, yanked him in and out of any number of programs, homeschooled him, then put him back into school because it was too much trouble for her and she couldn't "handle" him. He was put on drugs only to be taken off and put back on again. The boy's life seemed like one endless experiment and psychotherapy session. All of this was done with the countless advice from the countless "experts" in the school system and psychiatry industry.

Early on in my discussion with this woman, I told her I didn't believe ADD or ADHD even existed. She argued it had to exist because "just look at all the books written about it." I took the liberty of reminding her that just because something is discussed and written about extensively doesn't mean it really exists. Take the Loch Ness Monster, for example. She eventually ended our conversation by walking away from me.

Children, especially boys, shouldn't be required to attend formal instruction until they are at least ten years old. They should be allowed the freedom of learning by doing. Let them build forts, climb trees, have lengthy conversations with their parents, raise animals, go fishing, and play while they are young, unlabeled, and drug-free.

But, you ask, what would society do with all these little boys running around loose? Maybe society would tolerate them better. Maybe society would love them more. Maybe the tolerance and love would be returned to us when these same boys reach adulthood and they do not abuse drugs or other people.

14

I'd like to homeschool my child who has special needs. Is this possible?

MICHELLE BARONE ◆ Yes, the benefits of homeschooling for all children extend to those with special needs, including serious or multiple disabilities. I truly believe these children do extremely well being nurtured at home. I was a special education teacher in a very small, self-contained, special education classroom for five years. This classroom had no more than eight students and one full-time

aide. Additional staff was available when I needed it. I cared deeply for these children and gave them my best, but I knew I could never spend enough time with each one individually, as they deserved. The need for classroom management increased as my students "learned" a variety of disruptive behaviors from each other. This cut down on the time I had to cover the material assigned by the powers that be.

In my heart I knew what I was teaching them could easily have been taught at home. Most of my students would have been much happier there, with their families, going on errands, participating in programs that truly fit their needs. Instead, so much time was spent on the bus to and from school, waiting for everyone to be ready, interruptions for snack, lunch, or outside time. I often wondered why they had to be in this classroom learning about cooking and self-care when they could learn the same things at home. This was all before I had children or had even heard of homeschooling.

When parents decide to homeschool their exceptional child, it takes great courage and love. But it is being done successfully. Here are a few suggestions: Get support from friends, homeschoolers with special-needs children, family members. Find professionals who support your decision to keep your child home. Pick their brains for ideas and good resources, and use whatever services your community offers. Always remember, you have the final decision on what is best for your child and your family.

Because you know your child better than anyone, you are in the best position to assess his or her educational needs. Consultation with experts, like speech or physical therapists, can be very helpful. With love and patience, you can learn to work with your child in these areas. You don't have to give your child over to others, but you can use others as resources so you can care for your child at home. A family I know with an autistic child hires a teacher to come in their home three times a week. This gives the mom a needed break and brings another caring adult into this child's life.

Working one-on-one gives you the opportunity to help your special needs child with daily living skills based on her individual needs. Your child will get much more attention in these areas with you than at a school.

Homeschooling a special needs child is a difficult task—you need to make sure your needs are also met. Time for yourself and a good support group are essential. Caring friends and relatives can also be of tremendous help with your child's care.

In my heart I knew what I was teaching them could easily have been taught at home. Most of my students would have been much happier there, with their families, going on errands, participating in programs that truly fit their needs.

WENDY PRIESNITZ ◆ Many families find that their special needs children blossom in the homeschool environment. For many children, the typical classroom style of teaching is not the most suitable learning method. Their cognitive or motor skills may be developing slower or faster than their age peers. They may learn better by listening than by reading or writing. Or they may simply not be interested in the subject matter being discussed and tune out. When these children have difficulty with their school work, the blame is often laid at their feet and they are said to be "learning disabled." This label adds to their already high level of frustration and low self-esteem, contributing to a downward spiral of poor school performance and antisocial behavior.

Many parents have told me that, to their astonishment, these so-called learning disabilities often turn out to have been more like teaching disabilities. In many cases they disappear once the parents are able to cater to their children's unique style of learning. Away from the pressure of a competitive classroom in which they couldn't keep up, and finally able to make academic progress at their own pace, their self-esteem returns and their behavior improves.

Children with real disabilities also tend to do well in the home-based learning environment. As a parent, you are able to provide just the right amount of individualized attention in a caring, supportive environment, which is often just not possible in a school setting.

15

Should I do anything special for a child who is coming out of public school after years of attendance?

CHRIS CARDIFF ◆ The key to a successful homeschooling transition starts with the parent, not the child. The best thing you can do is *relax.*

This is an extremely difficult assignment for most parents. After seeing their children struggle inside the traditional institutional school, they are frantic to "do something" to correct the situation. Recognize that "doing nothing" may be the best "something" you can do for them at first.

Allow your children the freedom to explore areas that interest them without placing them on any artificial schedules. They need time and space to decompress from the public school experience. The methodology of public schools (and many private schools) discourages their inborn curiosity and desire to learn. It may take some months away from that environment before a child's natural curiosity reawakens. Look for ways to encourage the reawakening rather than stifling it.

The most common mistake new homeschooling parents make is attempting to recreate the public school environment at home (aka the "school-at-home" syndrome). While "school-at-home" is a natural mistake (for many of us, it's the only model we're familiar with), it's an unfortunate one because it puts unnecessary pressure on both parent and child. For the parent/teacher, there is the frantic scramble to duplicate the schedules and curriculum of an institutional-based style of teaching. For the child/student, it's a return to an environment and style of learning that probably was the source of problems before—except now there's no way to escape it by going home.

One of the strengths of homeschooling is the freedom and flexibility it provides in contrast to the rigid structure required for mass schooling. It takes time for both

> **Allow your children the freedom to explore areas that interest them without placing them on any artificial schedules. They need time and space to decompress from the public school experience.**

parent and child to adjust to home-schooling's freedom and flexibility and decide how they want to take advantage of it. Neither of you should make any hasty decisions or rush to spend money on some fancy (and expensive) prepack-aged curriculum.

To help you explore and understand your homeschooling options, get in-volved with a local homeschooling sup-port group. Support groups are available in most areas. If you can't find a group (or the existing group doesn't suit you), you can always start your own or get involved with one of the online groups. These groups can be a major source of group activities for your children as well as an important source of in-formation for you as a homeschooling parent.

Every family develops its own philosophy and style of homeschooling. Spending time evaluating and discovering your child's learning style and matching it with an appropriate homeschooling philosophy is time well spent. Be patient with yourself and your child as you ex-plore the world of homeschooling to-gether. Give yourselves time to relax and enjoy learning again.

LILLIAN JONES ◆ The wonderful new lifestyle you're entering is almost like a

> **The wonderful new lifestyle you're entering is almost like a different dimension from the one that seemed normal up until now, so it might take some time to get oriented.**

different dimension from the one that seemed normal up until now, so it might take some time to get oriented. You'll want to be especially sensitive to your child during the transition. Take care to support his unique style of being and learning, and try to avoid thinking in terms of a thing called homeschooling.

Children just coming out of school will often go through a withdrawal or de-compression period, and will almost cer-tainly balk at any attempt to reproduce elements of school. The intensity is in di-rect proportion to how long they went to school, and to how difficult the experience was for them. You might think the summer break would have taken care of that, but it just doesn't seem to work that way.

It might be a bit un-nerving for you at times, but your child really does have an internal wisdom about his needs. Remem-ber that he's been in an un-natural situation for a long time, one in which he wasn't always trusted or respected as an intelligent, self-directed person. Time taken for the internal process of refinding himself and his equilibrium is every bit as legitimate as any academic study might be.

Try not to take it too seriously if you have some nervous moments—times when you worry that you might be doing the wrong thing, that your child is not a good candidate for homeschooling, or that you aren't cut out for this. It passes. As you gradually let go of the school model of being and learning, a new and richer way of life will emerge.

This is a special and sometimes delicate time for your family, a time for getting to know and trust in one another all over again. Relax and enjoy, read wonderful things to him, and let your child know that he's wonderful and loved just as he is. Listen to him, and respect his way of being. Provide things that interest him, science experiments, time outside in nature together, field trips, play time with old and new friends, and lots of time to vegetate in whatever way he's drawn to. It's easier if you don't watch for the kettle to boil: Occupy yourself with something else, and it will be easier to let him be. He's doing what he needs to do, and it's a healthy process. Moreover, your child very much wants and needs for you to remain available as his parent. It can unnecessarily stress your precious relationship if you turn into a teacher.

You, too, will need time to adjust. You'll need to reexamine lots of expectations. If you trust your child, give him space, and promote mutual respect, you will become a trusted facilitator. You will begin to witness the magic of homeschooling. It won't look anything like what you expected—and it will amaze and delight you!

16
My child has had discipline problems at school. Can homeschooling help?

PAT MONTGOMERY ◆ Problems are symptoms. They indicate that something needs to be fixed. Determine the reasons for your child's discipline problems. If they can be traced to the way he relates to the teacher and/or classmates, or to time scheduling and the other aspects of the school environment, home-based education may be the way to go. It may be necessary for you to observe your child in the school environment and make a judgment on whether or not he would benefit from being in your one-on-one setting (home).

Pat Montgomery

It is not an uncommon situation. Parents and students alike have reported a great release of pressure because of the move from institutional schools to home. Problems often disappear. Critics claim this is catering to a child's whims, as in the oft-repeated myth, "A child has to learn how to tough it out in this world."

Consider how a gardener tends new shoots in the nursery. Never would she take them from the heat and light of a deliberately planned nurturing environment before they have the strength and stamina to withstand the elements. Parents almost take this approach for granted when it comes to babies and toddlers. Yet children of any age have growth needs that must be met humanely if they are to develop into healthy human beings.

DAVID AND MICKI COLFAX ✦ The only possible answer to this kind of question—and we have been asked it many times at homeschooling conferences—is . . . *probably.*

Some so-called "discipline problems" are so trivial or school-specific that getting the child out of school will obviously help. Less obvious are instances in which the discipline problems are more serious or less directly related to school functions. Discipline problems relating to drugs or alcohol abuse, for example, need to be taken seriously, and rehabilitation may require more than simply removing the child from the school setting. And serious discipline problems that cannot be attributed to the school setting itself may be manifestations of more general problems, such as psychological or physical disorders and family dysfunction, and are unlikely to be helped by homeschooling programs that do not directly address these possibilities.

> While homeschooling cannot *guarantee* success—particularly where the damage inflicted, from whatever source, is substantial—patient and understanding parents who are prepared to take very seriously the at-home reeducation of their "discipline problem" child will substantially increase the odds that homeschooling will indeed help.

In general, we recommend that parents of any child who is not enjoying or doing well in school should at least consider removing him or her from that setting. But every case is different; and while homeschooling cannot *guarantee* success—particularly where the damage inflicted, from whatever source, is substantial—patient and understanding parents who are prepared to take very seriously the at-home reeducation of their "discipline problem" child will substantially increase the odds that homeschooling will indeed help.

SHARI HENRY ✦ This was not our situation, but I'd like to answer it based on the situations I've seen. A friend pulled her son (he was nine at the time, third grade) out of school halfway through last year. He had been loaded up on Ritalin and was known far and wide as one of the most difficult children at school. This particular school is widely thought of as the best public school in the area, and is located in a wealthy district full of successful, well-educated parents. I listened to various conversations about this boy over lunch at the swimming pool. If it weren't so sad, it would have been laughable to hear these people's reasons for why this child should have been made to tough it out in school. The fact is, many of these parents liked having children lower in the pecking order than their kids. It's all a big race to them—who wanted to be moved down the ladder simply by having a couple on the bottom rung pulled out?

I got tired of listening to their elitism disguised as concern. I asked why anyone would care if this kid was gone. He was nothing but trouble to the teachers; the other children didn't like him; and by removing him from school, his parents were saving the school district thousands of dollars.

The mother has since dropped the dosage of Ritalin incredibly and the child's behavior has improved dramatically. Sometimes this child comes over to play. Once, his mother forgot to send along his Ritalin and phoned, nearly panicked, to ask if he was okay. I asked him. He said he was fine and he stayed to play with my son another five hours. No problem. The most recent time they played, my son, TJ, and this friend walked through the woods to the school's playground. The boy showed TJ where he usually sat during recess. "Over there, in that corner by the fence." TJ said, "You mean you didn't swing and slide or play with the other kids?" "No, they were always mean to me. I just sat over there and played with the rocks."

The imagined scene grieved my son. It infuriated me. Did those teachers try hard enough to integrate this child into the lives of the others, or were they too exasperated by his difficult behavior? Did the other parents encourage their children to respond more kindly, or did they only use this child as an example of how not to behave? Was the boy ever, ever held up as an example and acknowledged for what he did well (he is headed toward national rankings in swimming), or was the school environment so determined to set him straight and the other children so trained to keep others in their place to maintain what is theirs that no one dared say a thing?

Words cannot express how privileged I feel to watch this young man emerge from his prison-like cocoon, his wings glistening with possibilities.

17

I'm a single parent. Isn't it hard for single parents to homeschool?

MICHELLE BARONE ◆ I have been homeschooling as a single parent now for three-and-a-half years. Single parenting certainly has its challenges, but the rewards are many. Homeschooling as a single parent is not much different than for couples. I have the same concerns, questions, frustrations, and joys as most families because only one parent is usually with the children all day long. The real difference—the big difference—is in not having the support of another parent, and money.

For this reason, gathering a strong support system around us is vital to my family, and is probably the most important step in being successful. I have friends who take my children when I have to work nights, a brother who puts up my bookshelves and fixes the light switch, a mother who buys my children their nice Christmas presents when I cannot, and a support network of other homeschooling friends who keep me connected and sane.

Find a rhythm that works for your family. As a single parent, you may be working either outside the home or in a home business, or maybe even both. This means your family may not operate on the standard nine-to-five schedule. This requires creativity and flexibility from everyone in the family. This struggle to support your family can be the most difficult task as a single parent. If you are responsible for earning an income, how do you do that if your children are not being taken care of all day in school? There are lots of different ways to tackle this problem. Some find a home business works well. For some, a job with flexible hours can work well. I know of single moms who have done manicuring, sewing, bookkeeping, direct sales, house cleaning, baby-sitting, typing, writing, crafts, tutoring, teaching, anything they could so they would be

home with their children most of the time. This dedication and commitment are a tribute to the unshakable belief that our children deserve to learn at home with us.

Homeschooling provides you with the time and opportunity to be with your children in a loving and healing way. If you are single as a result of a loss from divorce or death, then both you and your children need time together to heal. Time and closeness can provide you with the strength to mourn the loss of dreams, and courage to make new ones. The first few years of homeschooling on our own were hard, both financially and emotionally. I tried to keep my focus on the long run, knowing my children would not be children for long and we could do without a bigger house, better toys, or new clothes, but we could not do without each other.

18

What is the homeschooling situation among ethnic and racial minority populations?

DONNA NICHOLS-WHITE ◆ When I began homeschooling, I entered the world as a triple minority. I was African American, an at-home mother, and I homeschooled my children. Living in Washington was an additional problem; this state's population was, at the time, only 2.6 percent black.

I felt as if I was the only black woman who homeschooled. Whenever we attended a homeschooling function, our family stood out from the rest of the crowd.

Over the years I discovered my original premises were incorrect. Homeschooling is as diverse as the rest of American society. It's just finding the folks that is hard. Many parents shy away from going public with their lifestyle. The harsh reactions of some communities to home education can often hinder a family's desire to be noticed. Let's not forget that many advocates of schooling think families such as mine should think like them.

When I was a child, black people were fighting to get into supposedly better schools and therefore have access to equal opportunity. It's pretty painful to leave an institution that has always been credited for being the road to upward mobility and have enough trust to go it alone. It is also a relief when we discover how wonderful the homeschooling experience is.

Many ethnic and racial groups are noted for having a firm belief in education. The more degrees a person has, the more prestige offered. Homeschooling in many communities is not considered the road to a higher education. I remember a browbeating I received at a child development convention. I was accused of cheating my children out of a decent education and also harming others by supporting family education. Whenever I pointed out the plight of black children in schools (which was the reason this particular organization was formed), and noted how homeschooled children fared better, he berated me more. I thought it strange that a male of my race would defend the schools so adamantly while accusing me of harming my children. (I knew, from experience, that I couldn't help but offer an education that far exceeded that offered through institutionalized education.) John Holt once noted that the least served communities were the strongest advocates of institutionalized education.

> **When I was a child, black people were fighting to get into supposedly better schools and therefore have access to equal opportunity. It's pretty painful to leave an institution that has always been credited for being the road to upward mobility and have enough trust to go it alone. It is also a relief when we discover how wonderful the homeschooling experience is.**

I've been honored by having had the opportunity to meet, and be in contact with, a very diverse group of homeschoolers. We are here but we just aren't yelling about it.

19

My family has chosen to live a natural lifestyle. Are there enough educational opportunities available to homeschool in a rural area?

WENDY PRIESNITZ ◆ There are educational opportunities everywhere. Life itself is an educational opportunity, and children learn by being part of it. While rural children don't have easy access to museums, art galleries, and libraries, like their urban counterparts, they can learn by wading in streams, growing their own gardens, and interacting with nature.

For many rural families, the Internet opens up a vast array of information rivaling that found in the best libraries and science museums. In addition to Web sites that inform and entertain, Internet access provides people of all ages with opportunities to correspond and communicate with both age peers and communities of interest from around the world.

LOTS OF WAYS TO UNCOVER RURAL RESOURCES

- The Internet

- Educational television, videos, books on tape

- Interlibrary loan programs through your local library

- Homeschooling magazine subscriptions

- Oodles of catalogs

- Join or start a local support group

- Utilize online support groups

- Enjoy and learn from your natural surroundings

HELEN AND MARK HEGENER ◆ There are more than enough resources in the smallest community, even on a remote homestead, to enrich the life of a child beyond measure. Just as it is in the city, homeschooling in a rural environment is mostly a matter of finding and supporting your child's interests. Computers, the Internet, educational television, videos, books on tape, and other resources bring a world of learning to everyone's door. Even the smallest community libraries are often connected to a never-ending network of other libraries, and interlibrary loan programs can provide almost any book in print.

Subscribe to a homeschooling magazine, and send for educational resource catalogs. Many large school supply catalogs are free, and offer every learning resource imaginable. Sometimes the smaller, less polished catalogs will have just what your child is interested in, and often for much less money.

If you or your children need socialization with other homeschoolers, join or start a local homeschool support group. Or join an online support group via the Internet or a service provider—if you haven't been online yet, the resources and support available there will astound you! If you don't have a computer, check your local public library. They often have computers available for accessing the Internet at little or no cost.

But even without any of these resources, homeschooling rurally can be a rich and rewarding experience. What does any child really need besides love and encouragement and someone to share discoveries with?

For many years children raised on farms and ranches and coastal islands have learned by doing—raising animals, growing gardens, doing chores, tending crops, overseeing herds and flocks. A lot of what most children learn sitting in school seats is learned by these children first-hand: reading, writing, and math as they read instructions, keep records, compute feedings, adjust recipes, and so forth. In the same way, homeschooled children can find endless ways of learning and applying what they've learned.

Most of all, if you live in a rural area, count yourself and your children lucky. Fresh air, green grass, animal friends, and all the rest are usually well worth the loss of a few museums and well-stocked bookstores.

> **If you live in a rural area, count yourself and your children lucky. Fresh air, green grass, animal friends, and all the rest are usually well worth the loss of a few museums and well-stocked bookstores.**

20

What are the pros and cons of home-schooling for my military family?

ANN FISHER ◆ Military families savor many benefits from homeschooling. One thing we all know about military families is that they are likely to move regularly. Like other families who choose to travel to learn, military families can turn a potentially stressful event—moving—into rich learning opportunities. Whether you move across the country or around the world, each move brings with it new terrain, geography, history, local lore, crafts, art, language, and so much more, and plops them right under your nose for exploration.

You won't have to worry anymore about move-caused learning gaps—you know, the ones where everyone else learns the multiplication table or how to read while your child is passed out from jet lag. No gaps develop since the home-school program moves with the family—books, routines, schedules, plans, and all. Just pick up where you left off after you unpack and settle in.

Are your children stressed by the thought of leaving friends behind? Take friends along as pen pals or e-mail pals—and build writing skills effort-lessly! In time, your children may realize that they are not losing old friends as much as they are adding new friends.

Military families who live in the states usually have no trouble connecting with the local homeschooling community nearest to their installation. In fact, since military families must follow the homeschool regulations of the state in which they *currently* reside, connecting with a local support group is the easiest way to find out how to comply with the law. In some areas, you may also find a homeschooling support group for military families.

Military families who homeschool overseas may have more difficulty making connections with other families. Use the same strategies you would use if you lived in a small rural community in your efforts to find others who homeschool: Ask around, post a notice on a bulletin board, contact national and international home-schooling organizations for referrals.

As for following regulations while overseas, military families who home-school have sole responsibility for the education of their children. According to the Department of Defense Educa-tional Activity Policy Memorandum on Home Schooling, 3/27/00, military fam-ilies are asked only to communicate their desire to the local military community commander. (The document can be ac-cessed on line at http://www.odedodea .edu/foia/iod/pdf/1342_6a.pdf.)

From time to time, issues do arise that can affect military homeschooling families. Parents should contact a national homeschooling organization, such as National Home Education Network, for the most current information.

MARSHA RANSOM

The pros for the children:

- *Consistency of education.* They don't have to readjust to new schools, teachers, and teaching methods, but continue their own individualized program with one-on-one attention.
- *Positive social impact.* The children don't have to adapt to a new school's "rules about what's cool," be teased as the "new kid," or experience bullying, bad language, violence, or social rank based on their parent's military rank—all seen in military schools overseas.
- *Awareness.* Frequently exposed to different experiences, they tend to be far more accepting and curious about the world around them.
- *Security.* Having family unity and knowing what to expect educationally makes them less likely to fall into the cycles of depression and lack of self-esteem seen in many military kids.
- *Close sibling relationships.* Home-schooled military siblings look out for each other, and enjoy each other's company.

Pros for the whole family:

- *Flexibility and convenience.* Families can take trips to see family or visit muse-

ums and amusement parks when they aren't as busy as during school holidays.
- *Adaptability.* Lessons and times with Dad can be planned around odd schedules such as working nights, weekends, and holidays, or unexpected short-term times away.
- *Peace of mind.* Since military families are often stationed far away from family, it's reassuring to know that they can make plans to fly "back home" in case of a family emergency without having to worry about missed school-work or unexcused absences.
- *Comfort.* Being together makes things easier for the rest of the family when one parent leaves for a long-term foreign deployment. They can also integrate his duty stations into their schooling, while he can search foreign ports for souvenirs for the kids.

21

Is homeschooling an all-or-nothing situation, or can I homeschool one child while the other is enrolled in school?

LUZ SHOSIE ◆ Self-directed learning takes place wherever the learner chooses. If one child in the family wants to experience learning inside a school building, it should not interfere with the learning of other members of the family. If it does interfere, then compromises may have to be made—but that's learning too, isn't it?

SANDRA DODD ◆ Sandra's answer originally appeared in the August/September 1996 edition of Network News, now called *California Homeschool News,* published by the California Homeschool Network, PO Box 44, Vineburg, CA 95487.

Some people are solidly homeschoolers and happy to be so. Others are wholly involved in and supportive of the public schools their sons and daughters attend. Then there are those with a foot in each world.

Using my sister as a test case, I made a radical recommendation that she chose to implement, and it turned out well. Since then, I've given this advice several times and haven't been sued (yet). Nobody's even asked for a refund!

Here is the way my sister overcame her school codependency: She divorced herself emotionally and politically from the public school. I have one sister, three years younger than I am. I was a star pupil, junior honor society member, extracurricular queen, member of the band, all-state chorus. Younger sisters in the readership are already sympathizing with my B-student sister. She went out with the younger brothers of my boyfriends a couple of

> **Some people are solidly homeschoolers and happy to be so. Others are wholly involved in and supportive of the public schools their sons and daughters attend. Then there are those with a foot in each world.**

times. She couldn't get out of my shadow. She dropped out of high school not long before I became a teacher. I was invested in the system. She had rejected it.

Years passed, and we each had three children. While I opted not to send mine to school at all, my sister was a "room mother" and gifted-program advisory board member, and she chaperoned field trips. Her older boy wrote at the age of five. Mine didn't *read* until he was eight. The evidence that she was right and I was wrong was increasing, which must have been a great feeling for her. (It happens more and more as the years go by, and I don't mind it at all.)

Another thing was increasing, though. From once a month, to once a week, to every other day, my sister called and complained about something at school, and I would play devil's advocate, or give her considerations the teacher had that my sister might not have known. At first I was sympathetic. Then I was apathetic. After a while I got irritated, and one day I cut her off in advance of the tale of woe, saying, "You already know what I'm going to say. You don't *have* to send them to school."

It was springtime. She decided to spend the summer preparing them for the idea of staying home if they wanted to, but meanwhile she needed a way for their being in school not to ruin *her* life. I recommended that she just detach. She was not to enable the teachers to torment her children. She quit forcing them to do homework. She quit even considering punishing them for bad grades or rewarding them for good grades. Their grades were theirs, and not a reflection on the family, and not an indicator of learning. They were just grades, a contest, a competition like who sold the most candy bars, only my sister quit buying the candy bars, as it were. She quit helping with the homework.

The year after that her daughter, the oldest, stayed home instead of going to fourth grade. The boys went to school. When they felt ill they were allowed to stay home without having to have a fever or puke to earn the privilege. They became more honest. Sometimes they just said, "I don't want to go to school today." She would say, "You don't have to then. I wish you just would never go again." So their first reward was renewed and increased honesty. (When I called my sister to read this to her for verification, she asked me to add that if she had it to do over, she wouldn't be so honest as to announce to the principal, "School is optional at our house." She advises you to make assorted excuses, like the other parents do.)

The next year the daughter went back because she had missed her friends. The dynamics of that school year, though, were phenomenal. Neither my sister nor I had foreseen the extent to which this detachment would free the entire family, and hadn't considered the effect on the relationship between the children and their teachers. No longer were these children in school against their will, their parents having submitted them to a lock-up situation. On one hand, they had teachers who wanted them to stay in school. On the other hand, they had parents who wanted them to say home. How much more "wanted" could they feel? Each moment they were in school they were aware, and the teacher was aware, that they were there because they, the children, *wanted* to be there! These factors changed the way the kids responded to assignments, to interpersonal problems, and to threats from the teacher (which have little power without the backing of the parents).

In late winter, the daughter contracted a staph pneumonia and was in a hospital ninety miles from home for a couple of weeks. After that she didn't want to return to school (and her recovery was better served by staying home, too). One of her brothers left school at that time as well, and next year all three plan to stay home. When school starts and they don't go, how different it will be for them than it is in those families in which the children pine for school but their parents forbid them to go.

There are different reasons for homeschooling. School might not be an option at all in a family in which religious or social considerations take precedence. In families in which student-directed learning is the primary focus, children taking control of their own learning by deciding whether to pursue it at home or at school can be liberating for all involved, and educational in the extreme for their teachers.

Although the ideal might be children who have never gone to school a day in their lives, reality isn't always ideal. If your children press you to let them go to school, this detachment option might be a way for you to have your cake and eat it, too. The philosophies of choice, freedom, child-led learning, "bliss-led learning," and personal responsibility can be honored and spread to new audiences by parents treating children as humans with rights and responsibilities whether they are sixteen, twelve, or eight years old.

22

Can my child combine school attendance with homeschooling, picking and choosing what to learn where?

PAT LINES ◆ The most interesting new development in homeschooling is the emergence of public school–home school partnerships. Alaska pioneered such arrangements, assigning teachers in Juneau to work with students located all over the state, staying in touch by mail, telephone, and occasional visits in person. Although designed for students in remote areas, Alaska made this service available to all, and today a majority of its students live in the Anchorage area. North Dakota has had a distance learning program for older students for many years, and is now extending it to younger ages.

Elsewhere, these kinds of partnerships have emerged at the district level. In California, for example, a child can enroll in a public school in an independent study program, and base his or her studies in the home. In Washington and Iowa, state law requires public schools to enroll children part time if they apply. (The district can claim a portion of the basic per-pupil assistance for the enrollment.) In these states interested districts have organized education centers where families may obtain resources, find instructional support, and/or sign up for scheduled classes. Some other states or districts also allow part-time enrollment, "shared schooling," "dual enrollment," or similar part-time school attendance. Often, children may enroll in programs anywhere in the state. These fledgling programs often rely heavily on electronic learning and communications programs.

They offer a preview of education in the twenty-first century, where the electronic workplace and the electronic school bring back neighborly communities.

JUDITH WAITE ALLEE ◆ Even a few years ago, many schools had never been asked! Many, though, have now received inquiries about one program or another—perhaps a specific class, like chemistry or calculus; an "enrichment" class, like music or art; or an extracurricular activity, like theater or math club.

Those "pioneer" families who first asked may have triggered the school to set a precedent of some kind, or to judge whether part-time attendance "works" based on their experiences with just a few families. This issue is still new enough that by asking now you may be setting a precedent for other families. Therefore, it is still important to approach school officials in a respectful manner. Bear in mind that one reason officials dread being asked these gray-area questions is that they fear they may set a precedent they could later regret. (It is the path of least resistance to say "no," which can always be changed later. A "yes" is harder for them to rescind if they later regret their decision.) It's ironic that some school officials say in one breath that homeschoolers are socially deprived, and in the next breath forbid kids to participate in the parts of school that meet their needs.

Coupled with this issue is a family's decision whether a child who starts a class has to finish it. If we let our kids quit, are we teaching them to give up on something as soon as it becomes difficult? And yet, how can they make an informed choice about school when it is outside their range of experience? Will you require your children to finish the class once they start it, or can they take the class on a trial basis? Decisions, decisions.

When our daughter decided to attend high school, we took the opposite approach—if she wanted to attend, we expected her to get herself ready and complete her part without a hassle. Otherwise, she needed to homeschool, which was our preference anyway. (She attended for two years before deciding to complete high school through homeschooling.)

All that said, I'm leery about homeschoolers partaking in school. Yes, I know your tax dollars pay for it, but I believe homeschool freedoms are endangered when you utilize tax-funded school programs. Tax money comes with strings and controls. Once the camel pokes its nose in your tent door, its head and body tend to follow.

ISABEL LYMAN ◆ Yes, but let me clarify. If by "school" you mean "public," then it depends on where you call home, sweet home. In Bozeman, Montana, for instance, homeschoolers can access a minimum of two public high school classes. In Oklahoma, conversely, homeschoolers cannot participate in public school classes or sports. You will need to become familiar with the laws of your state and the quirks of your school district to figure out what opportunities are available to your child.

Personal note: When my husband and I ran a small, private school in western Massachusetts, we admitted homeschoolers to the school on a class-by-class basis and pro-rated the tuition accordingly. It worked out very nicely for all parties. Perhaps there are like-minded souls in your community. Grab the Yellow Pages and start calling.

Finally, you can enroll your child for classes in the nearby community college or state university. Nowadays it's not uncommon for high-school age homeschoolers to bypass conventional high school classes, take college-level courses, and earn credits toward a degree. Personally, I think this is a much better option than sending your child, even part-time, to a public school. Heaven knows what unsavory socialization skills he or she will pick up in that environment.

SUSAN AND LARRY KASEMAN ◆ Yes, many states provide free public education for everyone of school age. The term "shared services" is used when private school stu-

dents, including homeschoolers, take courses in public schools.

However, before participating in shared services, many families ask:

- Are there better ways to learn, perhaps an informal tutorial, an apprenticeship, or volunteer work?
- Will the benefits justify both the disruption to our family life and the time, energy, and expense involved?

Susan and
Larry Kaseman

- Will our children benefit from school social life? How will they be influenced by "the culture of school"?
- Will attending school really meet our children's needs? Are there better ways of accomplishing whatever goals led us to consider shared services in the first place?

Attending a conventional school is not necessary or even an advantage. Many homeschoolers learn math, science, foreign languages; make friends; and play sports on community teams without attending school. One homeschooling mother observed: "There is nothing public schools offer that I can't find, and probably in a better way, in the community."

Increasing numbers of grown-up homeschoolers are showing that experience in conventional schools is not necessary to get a job, do volunteer service, travel abroad, or go to college. In fact, many of these young people are doing so well because they chose homeschooling over conventional schooling.

Participating in shared services can undermine homeschooling freedoms. It puts homeschoolers under the jurisdiction of public schools, promotes the idea that conventional schools are a necessary part of learning, blurs the distinction between public schools and homeschools, and sets precedents of government control over homeschoolers that may then be applied to homeschoolers who do not even want shared services. For example, public schools may require that homeschoolers pass tests to show that they are qualified to enroll in certain classes. Critics of homeschooling will then find it easier to argue that all homeschoolers should be tested.

> **In short, homeschoolers who are considering shared services should ask themselves whether the benefits they hope to gain are worth the costs involved.**

In short, homeschoolers who are considering shared services should ask themselves whether the benefits they hope to gain are worth the costs involved.

If homeschoolers want shared services despite the downsides, it is better to make arrangements with local schools than to seek a law requiring school districts to provide shared services to homeschoolers. The following suggestions may help.

- If officials claim that they are not required to provide shared services to homeschoolers, remind them that the statutes require that free public education be provided to everyone of school age.
- If school officials claim there is no precedent or policy for shared services, explain that virtually every public school in the nation regularly enrolls private school students in special education classes on a part-time basis.
- If school officials claim that the district cannot afford to provide shared services to homeschoolers because the state does not reimburse them for the costs, remind them that in most states property taxes cover a substantial part of the school budgets.
- If school officials fear that homeschoolers' participation in shared services will disrupt their planning, explain to them that homeschoolers are a very small minority (less than 2 percent) of the school-age population. Of these, only a few homeschoolers will be interested in shared services.

23

If our circumstances change, by choice or otherwise, are there any problems when a homeschooled child returns to school?

HELEN AND MARK HEGENER ◆ The problems children face by returning to public school are the same ones they would face if they had never been homeschooled, because the problems of schooling are inherent to the system, the bureaucracy. Some children can work with them, can learn to fit into the schedules, the expectations, the unfairnesses, but other children never will, especially if they've been unschooled for any length of time.

If your child needs or wants to return to school, the best source of information will probably be your local homeschooling support group. They should be able to tell you if problems have been experienced with certain districts or individuals, what the school personnel will be looking for, how best to make the transition.

In the January/February 1998 issue of *Home Education Magazine,* in an article titled "My Daughter Has Special Powers," Martine Palmiter writes:

I don't care too much for schools. I went to one. It wasn't that awful, but still it stifled my life. I learned some good things, but looking back, I see now how much I missed.

And now, I've seen that schools have become even more stifling. Even more rigid. Skewed reward systems, commercialism, more emphasis on behavior management than on asking questions and being curious. Books and subjects so watered down and "politically correct." Not much juicy learning. Overcrowded classes with disruptive students.

Still, Martine's daughter wanted to attend school, and Martine agreed to let her go. She continues:

I sent my daughter fully expecting her to see the light and quit. Well . . . she loves school, and her teacher and her classmates. She gets up early, gets dressed, eats, eager to get on the bus. She comes home happy and exhilarated. What's not to like? I even like her teacher. She supports many of my homeschool philosophies. No homework because kids should play after school, no grades, lots of moving around in class, lots of singing and dancing, and much emphasis on children being read to by their parents "in their laps." Lots of manipulatives. Heavy emphasis on home life. I feel so lucky that Olivia is in good hands.

On the other side, I miss my family being together. I want to read to her some more. Take her to parks and to dance class. Want to see her running free in the grass and laughing. I want her to quit.

NANCY PLENT ◆ I had homeschool friends who divorced, and the mother had no choice but to return her children to school so she could work. One son adjusted pretty well. She left the other one crying at the school door every morning while she hurried off to her job, also crying. The oldest son's teacher blasted at my friend during their entire first parent-teacher meeting for "ruining him." By the middle of the school year, that same boy was above grade level. Today both children, now grown, have positive memories of their homeschooling. Yes, there were painful problems, but the same grit that made this mom try homeschooling helped her get through the rough places.

Most of the parents who change their minds and return children to school still have good things to say about the experience. Often they used the time to reconnect with their children, or enjoy a peaceful hiatus in lives that had been too hectic. Many have told me that, even if they couldn't see themselves continuing, it had given them and their children a fresh start with a positive attitude.

In either case, I think children are different persons for the experience and will cope. You will have taught them that school isn't the sacred necessity we all grew up thinking it is, and that they are really the ones in charge of their learning and their lives.

School officials generally don't offer much resistance to returning students, except in high school. High schools are often reluctant to admit a student at the level his mom-teacher places him unless he brings some kind of certificates or testing results.

JUDITH WAITE ALLEE ◆ (Adapted and excerpted from *Educational Travel on a Shoestring,* Copyright 2002, by Judith Waite Allee and Melissa L. Morgan. Used by permission of Shaw Books at WaterBrook Press, Colorado Springs, Colorado.) Typically, homeschoolers do fine academically when they return to school, and teachers often comment on how refreshing it is to have a child in class who likes to learn. Before high school age, children can usually enter school at an age-appropriate grade, although some schools require a placement test. If so, you might have the test in the spring, work on any weak areas over the summer, and retest in the fall if needed.

To avoid testing, you can request that the teacher review samples of your child's work. Schools routinely deal with trans-

> **Most of the parents who change their minds and return children to school still have good things to say about the experience. Often they used the time to reconnect with their children, or enjoy a peaceful hiatus in lives that had been too hectic.**

fer students from other states or countries. These students have varying skill levels, but normally assimilate into their own age level without any big deal. Most policies are negotiable. When parents of a six-year-old, a fluent reader, were told he would have go to kindergarten instead of first grade, they said, "Never mind, then. We'll continue to homeschool," and that prompted the school to reverse itself. Such problems rarely come up before high school age, though.

Teens are vulnerable because more is at stake concerning grades, credits, college admissions, and graduation. While the school has to enroll your teens, getting credit for homeschool studies is another story. First, check out school policies. One may give standard course credit if the student passes final exams for the class. Another may give placement tests. Some will consider your documentation (sample work or other demonstration of proficiency) and make a case-by-case decision. If you homeschooled through a satellite program or correspondence school, that program may help you to negotiate with the school.

Some schools may refuse credit for homeschool work under any circumstances. What then? You might check into private schools. Another option—and this may sound radical: Your students can go ahead and take high school classes *without* worrying about gradua-tion. Then, if they want a diploma, they can combine their existing high school credits with homeschool documentation, and graduate through a satellite school or a distance-learning program. For example, the Clonlara Home-Based Education Program works with teens to custom-design a program to finish off a high school degree and help them complete any missing credits. In some cases, they can graduate by simply documenting their experiences.

You can also negotiate to register your children for French II in high school, even if the school won't let them have credit for French I. One school tried to insist that a youngster take the "prerequisites" for French III, even though she had lived in France. Her parents fought it and prevailed.

Taking the GED test (General Equivalency Diploma) is another option (GED hotline: 800-626-9433). But a GED is not as valued as a high school diploma, right? Perhaps, but a high school diploma is not all that revered. Does it surprise you that colleges seldom require a high school diploma—that even Harvard and Yale do not? Consider having your teenager take a few college classes, in person or through distance learning. That makes a high school diploma pretty much moot. What matters is documenting readiness for college. A portfolio showing independent learning, internships, volunteer work, and travel experiences can have more impact on a college application than a high school diploma.

The diploma may be more important for teens who do *not* go to college. A traditional diploma (versus a GED) may sound better to some employers. A more common concern, though, is what to write under "schools attended" in those little boxes on employment forms. You can name your homeschool (Smith Home School, Life Academy) or write "homeschooled." Armed forces may actually prefer a homeschooler to a student with a GED, but their policies are in flux, so check if relevant.

24
Is there an ideal situation for homeschooling?

JEAN REED ◆ Are you living your idea of an ideal life in the ideal place? If not, are you making the best of your particular circumstances? Everyone has a mental image of an ideal place to live and raise a family. We would have our ideal house, in an ideal place, and enough income to do just what we want. A nice dream, and there's nothing wrong with it, except that life isn't like that for most of us. Most of us don't have everything we want. In reality, we have to make the most of what

we have. Homeschooling is a way of life and, as with the rest of our lives, we have to make the most of whatever we have.

History proves that neither location nor financial status place limitations on great thinkers or the ability to learn. Some great men and women have come from impoverished homes, and some of the sons and daughters of the very wealthy have been idiots. Learning can take place anywhere, anytime. Money can buy resources, but it can't insure learning any more than it can buy happiness.

We ship homeschooling materials all over the globe. No matter where you live you can learn. Where you live is, or should be, an irrelevant detail in respect to learning. It's taking advantage of wherever you live that is important. There are advantages and disadvantages to all places. If you lived someplace else you would learn something different. If you live in the city you will learn some things you wouldn't learn on the farm and vice versa.

We couldn't live in the city, which doesn't mean that our children went without some of the advantages of city living. Although there is nothing like being at a live concert or visiting a good museum, we found reasonable substitutes through books, magazines, on radio, CD, videotape, and television. The television, for all the junk shown, can be a very useful tool. Sometimes you see more than you would if you were there in person.

You can't have an extensive garden, orchard, or raise a lot of animals in the city, but you can grow many plants, even small trees, in pots or in a small yard. You can raise a number of small pets even in an apartment.

I think it's up to us as parents to help our children be aware of the great variety of human experience, cultures, beliefs, and places to live in this world. Books, magazines, field trips, radio, television, videos, computers, and libraries can make the world accessible to us all. These are tools we can use wherever we live.

Most of all, I think homeschooling parents want their children to be happy as children; to grow up to be strong, happy, productive adults. All we can do is provide them with love and encourage them to make the best of their own lives. This is a matter of philosophy, not location. This can be achieved wherever and however you live.

LILLIAN JONES ◆ Every homeschooling scenario offers unique advantages and disadvantages, although people often think someone else has the ideal setting. *Hard Times in Paradise,* by David and Micki Colfax, is an inspiring and thought-provoking book—the fascinating account of the personal hardships and challenges the whole family had faced and mastered while struggling to build a homestead, eventually creating a successful goat farm. That ongoing project, along with the

family's social/political activism, was the kids' education! Academic preparation, which started in early adolescence, was basically just a means to an end, a way to get into and through college, and on to the real and important things they would later want to do with their lives. Their pragmatic education in learning how to learn got the kids scholarships to Harvard, not anything they learned in a book.

I fretted a bit, when I finished that book, to think of how underprivileged my own son was. Poor kid—born into a relatively affluent family, raised in a snug house, no particularly important work to do, destined to miss the opportunity to struggle and to have to figure out the mechanics of survival. So sheltered. Soft. What would become of him? I chuckled later, as I recognized my own exaggerated perception of the grass on the other side of the fence. I'm sure the Colfaxes might have had a moment or two during their adventures when they would have traded with us in a flash, too.

There is no ideal situation for homeschooling, any more than there is an ideal situation for living in general. Once you let go of the notion that there is an almost tangible plan or pattern called "homeschooling," it's a lot easier to appreciate the opportunities life has to offer in any number of settings and lifestyles.

Those who don't fit into the prevailing lifestyle, religion, or racial group of their region might have a tougher time because of isolation. On the other hand, there are a growing variety of homeschoolers in most places. If you look hard enough, and with an open mind, you can usually find like-minded souls. It might take some creativity to find your niche.

One of the marvelous things about homeschooling is the way it forces us to let go of old familiar notions of how things should be. The whole family benefits deeply from an ongoing process of growing into new ways of thinking. Parents who have had basic educational needs handled by schools for many years often unconsciously expect homeschooling to be much the same way. They want a format. They want to know how it's all supposed to be. The good and the bad news about homeschooling, they discover, is that it's all up to them. That may feel scary at first, but it's inevitably the thing we value most.

Now that you've read Lillian's account of the Colfaxes' homeschooling situation, here are the Colfaxes' thoughts on the same question.

DAVID AND MICKI COLFAX ◆ The ideal setting for homeschooling? On a remote mountaintop in northern California— with plenty of electricity and water, great

---

All we can do is provide them with love and encourage them to make the best of their own lives. This is a matter of philosophy, not location. This can be achieved wherever and however you live.

---

soil, and a pile of money! But as our book, *Hard Times in Paradise,* shows in sometimes too painful detail, one can do a fair-to-middling job of homeschooling without *all* of those things. "Ah, but your situation was ideal for homeschooling," is a line we've heard many times from homeschoolers and non-homeschoolers alike. All that space, few distractions, the opportunity to learn new things, do real work, no television . . .

Unlike realtors, however, homeschoolers have little reason to concern themselves about "location, location, location." By now we have plenty of evidence that homeschooling both flourished and floundered in urban and rural areas, in all parts of the country, and in homes rich, poor, and somewhere in between. Indeed, every homeschooling family, to a greater or lesser degree, constructs its own image of what constitutes a "good" or "ideal" homeschooling situation, the elements of which often vary radically from family to family. Elsewhere, we have compiled a list of some of the characteristics of what we regard as successful homeschooling efforts— parental commitment to keeping the love of learning alive, a skepticism of educational fads, intellectual openness and flexibility—which, without exception, are *attitudinal* rather than *spatial* or *circumstantial.*

Unfortunately, too many parents who hear about homeschooling are made to feel that it is something they cannot do because their home or economic circumstances are so different from what they perceive to be the "ideal." Those of us who are homeschoolers perhaps need to consider the extent to which we have promulgated—however unintentionally—the idea that homeschooling is a Dick and Jane, June Cleaver sort of activity, best conducted in a middle-class, two-parent family living in a nice house with a big yard in a nice neighborhood, a family in which the children are bright and well-behaved, mom stays home, dad has a good job (or they all work together in a family business), surrounded by supportive relatives and friends who are themselves homeschoolers. The realities of homeschooling are infinitely more diverse, and we do a disservice to the movement when we fail to remember that homeschooling does, indeed, take place everywhere, and under all kinds of conditions.

25

Our family wants to take advantage of homeschooling's flexibility and travel. What are the pros and cons?

JUDITH WAITE ALLEE ◆ You can learn a lot about geology, writing, or Abraham Lincoln from a textbook. There is a big difference, though, when you explore actual caves; talk with a real, live author; or visit the modest frame house the Lincoln family lived in before Abe became President. When you travel, your living quarters may be small—a tent, RV, or motel room—but your backyard is huge!

Learning starts even before you leave—your children can research your destinations, find interesting spots en route, and help you stretch your travel dollars by finding bargains. (Giving them a commission on the savings may inspire a more wholehearted effort and provide them with spending money for your trip.)

Not being bound by school schedules, homeschoolers can travel at "off-season" rates. When a parent has a business trip, the family can go too. Some families take off for extended or even full-time travel. The von Trapp family (about whom *The Sound of Music* was created) emigrated to the U.S.A., earning their living as the Trapp Family Singers. Each time they left on concert tours, the younger children stayed behind weeping for their mother in convent boarding schools. To everyone's delight and relief, the whole family was able to travel together when Maria Trapp discovered homeschooling.

Today a whole community of homeschooling families travel, part-time or full-time, often in recreational vehicles

(RVs). *Families on the Road* (FOTR) is both a print newsletter and an online discussion list published by Shelley Zoellick, "for families who RV full-time . . . or want to!" (www.familiesontheroad .com)

So, how can these families afford to travel extensively? The choices for travel money for the average Joe (not the celebrities) generally boil down to these: living on your savings or your home equity, starting a traveling "home" business, working for a company that requires travel, or finding temporary or seasonal jobs along the way. One family handcrafts dulcimers all year, then travels to music festivals and craft shows during the summer to sell them. Linemen, construction workers, pipefitters, welders, and electricians can travel wherever work is available without leaving their families behind. So can people who travel with rodeos, circuses, and carnivals. For full-timers without a house or apartment to maintain, the costs of living on wheels can be about the same, or less, than living in traditional housing.

Over the years, my family has visited homeschoolers in fifteen states while traveling to photograph conventions and reunions. We met our host families by participating in a homeschool directory sponsored by *Growing Without Schooling* magazine (now defunct). Our hosts shared the insider's view of their hometown, the popular as well as the off-the-beaten-path places to see. We saw each city from the front porch of a new-found friend, instead of as strangers in a motel room or campground.

So far I've noted the pros of educational travel. As for the cons, well, I've never been able to come up with any. Happy trails!

SPECIAL NEEDS BIBLIOGRAPHY

(Compiled by Marsha Ransom)

Armstrong, Thomas. *In Their Own Way: Discovering and Encouraging Your Child's Multiple Intelligences.* J. P. Tarcher, 2000.

Boyles, Nancy S., M.Ed., and Darlene Contadino, M.S.W. *The Learning Differences Sourcebook.* Lowell House, 1997.

Davis, Ronald D. *The Gift of Dyslexia: Why Some of the Smartest People Can't Read and How They Can Learn.* Perigee, 1997.

Freed, Jeffrey, and Laurie Parsons. *Right-Brained Children in a Left-Brained World: Unlocking the Potential of Your ADD Child.* Fireside, 1998.

Gray, Carol. *The New Social Stories: Illustrated Edition.* Future Horizons, 2000.

Hartmann, Thom. *Attention Deficit Disorder: A Different Perception.* Underwood Books, 1997.

Hensley, Sharon, M.A. *Homeschooling Children with Special Needs.* Noble Publishing Association, 1995.

Herzog, Joyce. *Learning in Spite of Labels.* Greenleaf Press, 1994.

Kumin, Libby, Ph.D. *Communication Skills in Children with Down Syndrome: A Guide for Parents.* Woodbine House, 1994.

National Association of the Deaf. *Legal Rights: The Guide for Deaf and Hard of Hearing People.* Gallaudet University Press, 2000.

Oelwein, Patricia Logan. *Teaching Reading to Children with Down Syndrome: A Guide for Parents and Teachers.* Woodbine House, 1995.

Palladino, Lucy Jo. *The Edison Trait: Saving the Spirit of Your Nonconforming Child.* Random House, 1997.

Rendoff, Patty. *Special Needs Resource Guide: For Home Schooling and/or Supplementing Education.* Diggies Do It All Inc., 1994.

Rivero, Lisa. *Gifted Education Comes Home: A Case for Self-Directed Homeschooling.* Gifted Education Press, 2000.

Willis, Mariaemma and Victoria Kindle-Hodson. *Discover Your Child's Learning Style: Children Learn in Unique Ways—Here's the Key to Every Child's Learning Success.* Prima Publishing, 1999.

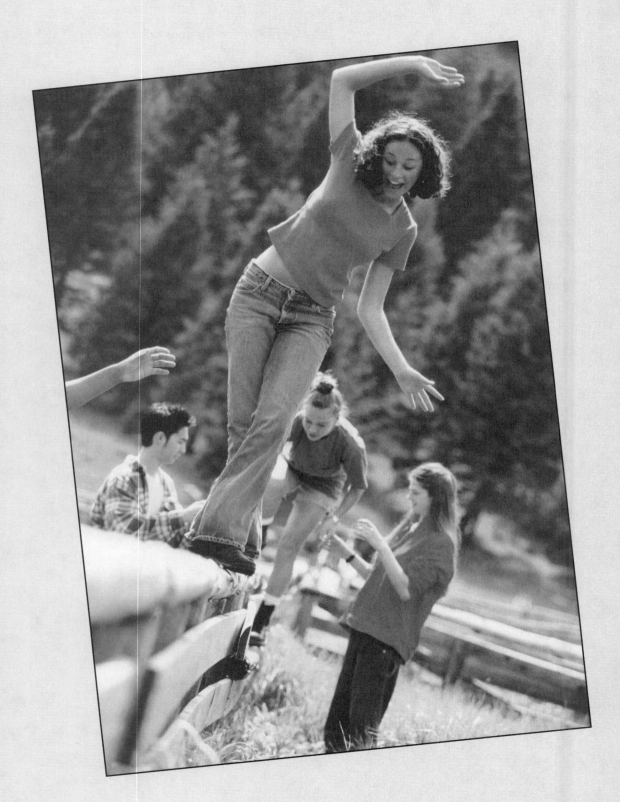

CHAPTER FOUR

Rest in Peace, Fears About Socialization

N O OTHER aspect of homeschooling has garnered more attention, commentary, and criticism over the years than the socialization of its children. I can't believe anyone really thinks we make the decision to homeschool so we can lock our children in closets, chain them to the kitchen table, or otherwise see to it that they don't interact or communicate with other human beings. Think about it for a minute: Wouldn't that make it that much more difficult to educate them? Wouldn't that make it that much more difficult to be around them for large portions of each day? Wouldn't that be downright counterproductive to a parent's natural inclination to raise well-rounded children into adulthood?

So why the big fuss over socialization? Rather than being related to any real problem homeschooled children have meeting and mingling with fellow humans, it seems to be a problem with the thinking of some adults. These folks think it's "weird" that families would have the audacity to decide for themselves with whom, where, when, and how much or how little "socialization" occurs. The converse of this, of course, is that someone outside the family decides these things for our children. Thus, in recent history, it has been decided that children's socialization occurs in the institution of school, away from the rest of the world, much as the prison institution keeps inmates away from the rest of the world. And the constancy and intensity with which this decision is defended, mostly by those with a vested interest (read paycheck!) in making sure the institution stays full, is cause for pause. This focus on school as children's socialization device is an even more recent invention than public school itself.

What can we learn from this? That (a) the educational decision makers believe the public school system's job extends beyond teaching academics; (b) these same decision makers need a strong criticism of a growing educational alternative that bypasses their control; or (c) both of the above.

The proliferation of topics addressed in schools, from drugs to sex to health to peer counseling to values training, coupled with the giant "strings attached to federal aid" programs such as Goals 2000 and School-to-Work, shows that choice "a" above is definitely true. And it is all accomplished under the seemingly benign term of socialization.

Research and personal evidence show that homeschooled children get along with others as well as, and in some cases better than, their publicly schooled counterparts. If what the educational decision makers mean by socialization is the ability to get along with others, familiarity with even a small amount of research would reveal the criticism as absurd.

> **Listen to the voices of experience, those who dared to by-pass control and decided to define, value, and actually practice "socialization" on their own terms.**

But if their definition of socialization reaches beyond the ability to get along with others, and encompasses a standardized list of behaviors, attitudes, values, and thinking they wish to implant in all children, then, indeed, homeschooling has bypassed their control and choice "b" is also correct, making "c" the right answer.

If you didn't choose answer "c," don't worry. I'm a home educator; I'm not in the habit of grading people like slabs of beef. It just means it's most important for you to read this chapter carefully. Get the other side of the story from those who don't hire public relations firms to put their own spin on this issue. Listen to the voices of experience, those who dared to bypass control and decided to define, value, and actually practice "socialization" on their own terms.

From this vantage point, it's easier to put the modern definition of school socialization into perspective. From this vantage point, you and your family can see how homeschooling offers you *real* choice now that the importance of parental choice in education grows increasingly important to our children.

26

How can my children meet other children and find friends if they don't go to school?

BILLY AND NANCY GREER ◆ This is part of the big "socialization" question that always seems to come up when discussing homeschooling. First of all, we think it is important to point out that socializing and socialization are two different things. Socializing is basically talking and playing with other kids; socialization involves learning the proper rules of behavior for a culture.

Neither of these tend to take place in a school environment (at least, not in a beneficial way). Socializing is typically punished in school. Kids are not supposed to talk and play in the classroom. During the day they have little opportunity to socialize, except perhaps briefly at lunch or recess.

The socialization they get is very artificial because the environment is very artificial. They are grouped with kids their own age. The rules for behavior in their culture say that older kids don't play with younger kids. If you like computers you're a geek, if you like sports you're a jock, if you're small you're a target for bullies.

Our five-year-old daughter and a nine-year-old homeschooled girl are best friends. This probably couldn't happen if they were in school. It's common at homeschool activities to see children of all ages working and playing together.

There are lots of activities available for homeschoolers now. Field trips, clubs, activities, and sports are readily available. In fact, you have to be careful not to overcommit yourself. There are probably more homeschoolers who are doing too many activities and meeting too many people than there are those who are isolated. Our opinion is that it is better to have a few deeper friendships than to have a lot of acquaintances you don't really know very well.

JANIE LEVINE HELLYER ◆ Because school is where most children spend the bulk of their waking hours, it's naturally the place that comes to mind when considering the opportunities children have for meeting others and developing relationships. The traditional classroom, however, can be compared to the workplace in that children do not choose those they are grouped with. While a "working relationship" may develop, there is little time to actually get to know others and nurture true relationships. No matter where a child is educated, true relationships seem to be formed outside of the classroom.

Let's first consider the young child. Is there a need for young children to be surrounded with age-mates all day? No. Before young children can interact with a social group in a positive way, they must first have established their own identity and feel secure. Too often, young children are placed in social situations before this develops, and so are not sure that it's "okay" to be themselves. This is the first step to lifelong peer pressure and control.

The home, family, and neighborhood are natural places for children to begin to explore relationships at their own pace and as they are ready.

The home is the first social unit. Young children at home learn to recognize the structure of the family, and acquire important values and skills that will assist them as they move out into the world. As children grow strong and secure in the concept of self, it is natural that they will begin exploring the world outside the walls of their home.

Most youngsters grow up in neighborhoods, play with neighbor children, and get to know them well. An important aspect of this stage of social development is that children playing in their own neighborhood are free to leave a group or activity when they are tired, uncomfortable, or when they choose not to participate for some reason. Real friends are those we choose to spend time with, not people we are forced to be around, and the experiences youngsters have in their neighborhoods allow them to freely choose the time, place, and individuals with whom they wish to spend time and develop lasting relationships.

As children grow older, no matter where they are educated, there are many positive social activities to choose from outside of the classroom. Homeschooled youngsters participate in the same positive activities as their schooled peers. These include things like Scouts, 4-H, YMCA, sports activities, church groups, and community-based youth groups.

Most communities also have special activities and organizations for homeschoolers. As our children grow into young adults, most homeschoolers are out in the community pursuing their interests. This provides opportunities to meet others who have the same interests.

Homeschoolers are not confined to friendships with those exactly the same age as they are, and so tend to be comfortable with a wide variety of ages. When strong relationships are developed with various age groups, peer pressure is less of a factor, leading many to view the social opportunities of homeschoolers as superior to those of schooled children.

When strong relationships are developed with various age groups, peer pressure is less of a factor, leading many to view the social opportunities of homeschoolers as superior to those of schooled children.

27

But what about the prom?

NANCY PLENT ◆ Strange thought, isn't it, that no childhood is complete without a formal dance at the end of it, wearing expensive, uncomfortable clothes! We've certainly bought into the school lifestyle when we ask this question. Families who have a lingering regret about their children missing the prom (a highly overrated affair to many, by the way) may have a lingering doubt about whether they're doing the right thing by homeschooling. You can't blame them; rituals are comforting and important, a way to mark certain passages in life. If we give up traditions, something feels a little incomplete.

I think it may be important for homeschooling families to develop meaningful rituals of their own. I know one mom whose traditional graduation gift to each of her children was a short European trip. It probably meant at least as much to them as a ceremony. As support groups grow, many will probably duplicate school functions like the prom. In a way that's too bad, to copy what we've left behind; with a little more time, maybe we can come up with something better.

SHARI HENRY ◆ After chaperoning a youth group trek to the local roller rink,

then subjecting myself to watching children aged nine to fourteen "slow dance" at set-aside times, then watching boys skate while girls lined up alongside the rink with their hands held out and the boys passing by to "smack" the hands of the "cute" girls and then vice versa, I became even less concerned about the prom than ever. Certainly, nine- to fourteen-year-olds could much better spend their time preoccupying themselves with a host of other activities than pre-mating games. So, about that prom, it would be my desire that my kids have plenty of friends of the opposite sex by the time they're prom age, and perhaps (but perhaps not) they would be asked to attend a dance as such. But I'm glad they won't be in school where the event takes on undue importance. It's just not, nor should it be, that big a deal.

SUSANNAH SHEFFER ◆ The simple answer is that homeschoolers can usually find a way to go to a school prom if that's what they want to do, or to create a parallel opportunity by organizing a homeschoolers' dance (or a community dance for both homeschoolers and schooled teenagers). Long before they reach prom age, homeschoolers have had many ways to meet and interact with school students, and one easy way to go

Susannah Sheffer

to a prom is to be invited by someone who attends that school.

But not all homeschoolers (or, for that matter, all school students) actually want to go to the prom. When *Growing Without Schooling* magazine asked one homeschooled teenager about missing the prom, she replied, "I didn't go to the prom because I would have had to go with someone who went to the high school, and my boyfriend goes to college. I probably could have gone if I really wanted to, but it wasn't that important, and all my friends ended up having a horrible time. It wasn't something that I felt I missed out on."

I love this comment because of the reality check it provides for adults who may romanticize the trappings of conventional teenage social life more than the teenagers themselves do. And even if the prom was truly the highlight of one's teen years, who's to say that experience is intrinsically more fun than a weekend-long gathering organized by homeschooling teenagers, for example?

The question, "But what about the prom?" may seem to be a simple question about access, but I think on a deeper level it's about parents' fears and hopes for their children. What will it be like if my children's experiences are different

> **The question, "But what about the prom?" may seem to be a simple question about access, but I think on a deeper level it's about parents' fears and hopes for their children.**

from mine? parents wonder. Homeschooling may attract parents precisely because it offers something different from schooling, but "different" is also scary. After all, what usually happens to children in school who are "different"?

A school student who doesn't want or can't gain entrance to the popular crowd, the conventional social arena, may have little choice but to be an outcast. Homeschoolers, however, can redefine the terms and can think about what kind of social life they truly want rather than only what the movies, or even their own parents, tell them they should want. It's reassuring to hear about homeschoolers who go to dances and football games and parties, who date and have groups of friends. I know plenty of homeschoolers who do all these things. But I find it equally reassuring to know homeschoolers who don't date and don't have to defend that choice, or who prefer a few close friends to a large group, or prefer adult friends to peers, or like to spend a lot of time alone, or whatever other variation suits them. I like seeing that, in the social as in the academic arena, homeschooling means that young people can find—and create—the kind of set-up that best works for them.

28

I've always considered public schools the place where children learn how to get along with each other. How do you compensate for this at home?

DEB SHELL ◆ Most people believe schools are teaching young people how to get along with each other. Unfortunately, this is probably true. Sassiness, disrespect for the personal property of others, fighting, and cheating, as well as succumbing to peer pressure at younger and younger ages (resulting in early sexual experiences, body mutilation, and drug and alcohol abuse), are behaviors now considered by many educators, social workers, and mental health professionals to be the normal developmental stuff we should expect our kids to exhibit as they mature.

I've had a very different experience raising four children at home. Just from living in our family, and as members of our community, my children learned how to get along from birth on. Their models for appropriate social behavior were other adults who valued individual differences and demonstrated effective interpersonal communication skills. Our children learned fairness by being treated fairly, respect by being respected. They learned to trust themselves because we gave them real opportunities to explore self-responsibility. They held others in

high regard because we held them in high regard. Their self-confidence increased as their real skills improved—as measured against their own development, not some arbitrarily standardized concept of achievement.

The value of not using grade levels or grades enables children to feel right about themselves, no matter where their stage of development happens to be. The effects of manipulation and coercion into activities that hold no appeal or meaning may produce behavior that, when taken out of context from its cause, may result in the child being pathologically labeled (for example, ADD, ADHD, oppositional disorder). Very often, children who are labeled in school have their symptoms disappear once they are removed from the social system that supports such coping behaviors.

My favorite book about the socialization of children, *The Continuum Concept* by Jean Liedloff, is a tribute to what many homeschoolers know to be true: Children learn how to get along while naturally living as integral members of their family and community. Like all children, ours also wanted to participate, to be included, to be contributors. A loving family is the natural place from which to learn how to get along. Schoolchildren have to learn how to get along as members of an organization that sets up within-the-ranks competition, supports the use of rewards and punishments as motivational tools, and sets up unnatural consequences for disobeying rules that may benefit the school bureaucracy rather than the educational needs of its students.

Now that my children are teenagers and beyond, I am frequently met with amazement from parents and educators of schooled peers. My children get along with each other and with their parents, as they do with all ages and races of people. Who wouldn't be proud to say their children are compassionate, considerate, responsible human beings?

CAFI COHEN ◆ First, examine your assumption that public schools are "the place where children learn how to get along with each other." Visit your local school for one entire day and simply sit and watch. Watch how the children treat each other, in and out of class. Watch how teachers treat the children and vice versa. Total the amount of one-on-one adult attention for each child.

I have done this in schools in three different states and always found three things. First, there is not much time for meaningful interaction, certainly no time for in-depth relationships. Second, the atmosphere is—more often than not—petty and mean-spirited. And last, the

social pecking order leaves many kids more isolated than they could possibly be in any home-based program.

If I were to design an environment to enhance my children's ability to function socially, I would never propose anything resembling school. I would never design a place where my children principally see those born in a one-to two-year period who also happen to live in our zip code, a place where they have little adult contact.

Instead, to enhance our children's abilities to get along with others, we focused on our community. Our children satisfied their needs for age-peer socialization through groups like 4-H and Civil Air Patrol and church choirs and softball teams. In addition, they had friends of all ages through various community activities—classes, drama groups, political campaigns, hobbyist organizations, various volunteer jobs. Our teenage homeschoolers befriended people of all ages from a much larger socioeconomic spectrum than is present in most schools.

Our children meet and make friends much as you and I do—through their interests and through current friends, neighbors, and relatives. We always knew when school dismissed because the phone started ringing. Finding social opportunities was not a problem. Our real prob-

> **If I were to design an environment to enhance my children's ability to function socially, I would never propose anything resembling school.**

lem was keeping a lid on it: "No, you cannot go out again tonight; you have been out every evening this week, and I need the car."

I never worried about compensating for school "social" experiences. We did not want what schools provided. Our family and the larger community presented more opportunities to meet a greater range of people. And homeschooling provided something attendance at most schools precludes—*time* to develop and maintain friendships with people of all ages.

CHRIS CARDIFF ✦ Actually, if you think about it, exactly the opposite is true. Many of the pathologies of youth are associated with public schools—peer pressure, age segregation, cliques, isolation, and persecution of nonconformists. Logically, how could it be otherwise? Yes, children *are* learning social behavior from other children. However, what most parents want is for children to learn social behavior from adults. The home is the natural environment for this training.

Chris Cardiff

Homeschooling does *not* mean that children interact only with their parents and siblings. This popular homeschooling myth (also known as "The Isolation Myth") suggests that homeschoolers have no academic or social interactions outside the family. Reality is far different, as homeschoolers work, play, and learn within the community in ways that resemble "real life" much more than the artificial environment of the institutional school.

Homeschooled children participate in their full share of traditional extracurricular activities: 4-H Club, Little League, Cub Scouts, Brownies, dance, karate, gymnastics, music, and more. All of these activities provide boundless opportunities to interact with other children, both homeschooled and public schooled.

Moreover, as the popularity of homeschooling soars, any activities normally found in institutional schools are being duplicated by entrepreneurial members of the homeschooling community. Spelling bees, choir, band, sports leagues, science fairs, foreign exchange students—homeschooling specific versions of these are all available somewhere, providing more opportunities for children to work, play, and learn together.

A primary source of additional academic and social opportunities for homeschooling families is local homeschooling support groups. Weekly park days provide opportunities for social interaction (for kids *and* parents!). Field trips and group learning opportunities are also typical activities sponsored by individuals within the group. Children are usually not age-segregated (although age guidelines are provided for some activities) and parental involvement is high, ensuring more positive interactions. With their flexible schedules, homeschooled children have much more opportunity to interact with a wider variety of people than children confined to institutional schools. The results of these interactions are children who capably communicate and interact with people of all ages.

29

Without siblings in the house, how does my only child learn social skills as we homeschool?

MARY McCARTHY ◆ Oh, my dear Linda, are you implying his parents don't have any social skills?

LUZ SHOSIE ◆ We learn social skills by interacting with people. We included Cassidy in our interactions as much as we could when he was a baby and as much as he wanted as he grew older. He learned to interact with all kinds of people of all different ages.

We get together with homeschoolers, neighbors, friends and relations, and coworkers, not to learn social skills, but to live a full life.

My favorite answer to the socialization question comes from Mary Beth Nelsen, the president of the Connecticut Home Educator's Association: "We did

tend to over-socialize when we first started homeschooling, but I think we have it under control now."

WENDY PRIESNITZ ◆ When we think about socialization, we need to consider quality as well as quantity. How much social interaction do children actually require? What is the quality of the socialization at school compared to what is available outside of school? Do speaking and other social skills get as much attention as listening skills?

Life for children in school is public. They have virtually no time or space to which adults can be denied access. Children who find psychological privacy by daydreaming are labeled as inattentive or disinterested. On the other hand, life for unschooled children—even ones without siblings—is a mixture of personal and shared time, which allows them to get to know themselves, at the same time as they learn to value—yet be discriminating about—the time spent with others.

My observation of thousands of home-educated children over the past twenty years suggests that another factor outweighs any kind of peer or sibling interaction in its influence on social development. Feelings of security and self-confidence are created in children who have the freedom to venture into sophisticated social situations at their own speed. This positive self-concept is nurtured by warm, loving interaction with parents who respect their children. As some of the main ingredients in a child's proper social development, these even outweigh the contribution of continued social contact in creating a child who functions well in society.

These observations are reinforced by developmental and social psychologist Dr. Urie Bronfenbrenner of Cornell University, who has spent many years studying children in various societies. He has noted that overexposure to a peer group during a child's early years can be damaging and has found that until the fifth- or sixth-grade level, children who spend more time with their peers than with their parents or older family members become peer dependent. This, he claims, leads to a loss of self-worth, optimism, respect for their parents, and trust in their peers.

At any rate, even home-schooled children with no siblings often have much more contact with a wider variety of people than they would if they were in school. They interact on a personal basis with people in the community from all walks of life, with the result that they learn about the adult world without losing any sense of the child world. Because they're not segregated in a school building all day, their lives can be full and integrated into all aspects of community life.

30

Have there been any studies about how homeschooling affects a child's ability to get along with others and make the transition into the adult world?

PAT LINES ◆ First a word about studies:

My observation of thousands of home-educated children over the past twenty years suggests that another factor outweighs any kind of peer or sibling interaction in its influence on social development. Feelings of security and self-confidence are created in children who have the freedom to venture into sophisticated social situations at their own speed.

There is no conclusive research suggesting that time with same-aged peers is preferable to time with individuals of varying ages. Limited testing of a self-selected group of home-schooled children suggests above average social and psychological development. At the very least, anyone who has observed home-schoolers will notice a high level of sharing, networking, collaboration, and cooperative learning.

People disagree on whether homeschooling helps or hinders a child's social development. Children engaged in homeschooling spend less time with same-aged children and more time with people of different ages. Most spend time with other children through support and networking groups, scouting, churches, and other associations. Many spend time with adults other than their parents, through community volunteer work, running home-based businesses, tutoring or mentoring arrangements, and in other ways.

The stereotype of the isolated family does not fit any homeschooling family that I have met to date. To the contrary, homeschooling families seem highly connected to other families and other institutions. I would suggest that you make an effort to meet experienced homeschooling families and talk to their older children. If you enjoy meeting them, and they can discuss a variety of topics knowledgeably, then that may be the best test.

> **There have been research studies done in which homeschooling children score high in self-concept, leadership skills, and community involvement—all reflectors of positive socialization.**

KATHARINE HOUK ◆ There have been research studies done in which homeschooling children score high in self-concept, leadership skills, and community involvement—all reflectors of positive socialization. These findings are borne out by my experience with my own children and hundreds of other families. "Getting along with others" means being able to move beyond one-

self to consider the position and point of view of another. It is the realization of and ability to live with the fact that something other than oneself is real. Another word for this process is "love." What better place to foster these realizations and skills than in the family? Such family learning stands children in good stead when they come in contact with those with different opinions. A strong sense of self is what enables people of any age to move beyond themselves for mutual solutions when dealing with one another.

When my own children found themselves in disagreement with each other to the point of tantrums, each learned that in order to retain a playmate, he or she would have to work things through. The family can be a safe place for this to happen, and it behooves us as parents to learn and pass on conflict-resolution skills. Because children are involved in their communities, they also learn social skills from friendships with people of all ages, church, classes, volunteering, and jobs—in other words, in the "real world." People homeschooling today are at an advantage because of their flexible schedules and the large number of opportunities available to them through homeschooling groups, learning centers, travel networks, and other places where people meet and share their knowledge and ways of life. The ability to get along well with others is valuable to homeschooled teens as they begin working or applying for college; and by the time they have reached sixteen or seventeen, most homeschoolers have a strong sense of their aptitudes and their direction in life and are not afraid to pursue their dreams.

A friend of our family once told me that what impressed her most about our children was that they could, with ease and confidence, carry on a conversation with adults. I've noticed that they also take pleasure in carrying on conversations with babies and toddlers. They've never learned that younger people and adults are stupid or somehow inferior because of age differences. This stands in sharp contrast to what I learned in school, where upper-class students always looked down upon younger ones and peers "ruled." Psychologists and counselors are dismayed that so many teens today behave as though they hate their parents.

When we began officially homeschooling many years ago, the superintendent of schools told us that our choice would ruin our daughter's life. I suppose there may be families who isolate their children and stunt their growth; but if these families exist (I don't

know any personally, though every once in a while one reads a horror story in the papers), they must be a tiny minority. My husband and I have seen many young people, including our own, become independent, self-supporting, involved members of their communities. Homeschooling can facilitate getting along with others and moving into the wider world.

31

How can I be sure my child is growing socially without trained school personnel assessing this growth?

JOHN TAYLOR GATTO ◆ How can you be sure you got a good haircut? How can you be sure that wearing a bikini to your sister's church wedding is the wrong thing to do? How can you be sure whether the soup you just ate was tasty? A huge part of professional assessment is fraud.

I don't mean to be flippant, but forced schooling can only ensure its own sovereignty by making its clientele mistrust their own judgment. And the more you do mistrust your own judgment, the worse your judgment will indeed become. Formal assessment is institutional school's mechanism to mediate this fatal process.

Think of it this way: Abundant models of success (as you personally define success) are available everywhere in profusion. Look at them for your indices. There are no templates of "social growth" a trained schoolperson is charged with conveying except these:

- Stay in the "class" to which you have been assigned.
- Respond to the bell and other reflexive commands.
- Do what you are told.
- Confine yourself to your specified place in a world of children.

Does that sound like a formula calculated to produce what any sane person would call "social growth," or is it a formula for making a hierarchical, intensely corporatized, fundamentally totalitarian future work by providing a trained proletariat for it? A hive world.

You can be sure your child is "growing socially" if he or she is curious about all kinds of people, the details of their lives, their motives; you can be sure your child is okay if he can find pleasure, satisfaction, profit in talking to all different ages, responding appropriately to the challenges and opportunities presented by those older and those younger than himself. You can be proud of your child's social growth if he relishes responsibility

and looks on work as a lovely thing instead of a mere duty; if he can be alone with himself for long periods without boredom; if he confronts his own cowardice with people unlike himself and is learning to swim easily, like some noble fish in all human environments.

But most of all, you can be "sure" by learning to trust yourself. Study those people you admire yourself with great and continuous intensity, analyze precisely what it is that makes them socially valuable people, show your child by your own example, your conversation, and your choices that you yourself are growing socially (for surely none of us is ever fully done with this challenge).

And for pity's sake, encourage your children to develop at least one social talent: play the piano, sing, fill a room with humor, listen creatively, be graceful, whatever. Look at the people you *like* to be around and you'll see that every one of them has some attribute which makes her socially valuable. Many such attributes are natural and only need a little encouragement in youth to blossom on their own; some are more sophisticated and require disciplined effort to acquire. It can't hurt to make your child self-

> **Forced schooling can only ensure its own sovereignty by making its clientele mistrust their own judgment. And the more you do mistrust your own judgment, the worse your judgment will indeed become. Formal assessment is institutional school's mechanism to mediate this fatal process.**

aware—which is not the same thing at all as being self-conscious.

But throw away your fears about what school calls "socialization." You'd have to be nuts not to see the dehumanization/depersonalization intended by that deadly umbrella word.

MICHELLE BARONE ◆ The first issue we must make clear is this: Just what *is* socialization? I define a socialized child as one who easily and cooperatively fits in with other humans, someone who has the skills to live in society. The next question then must be, Do children learn to be social beings in a confined, same-age group of other children? Studies have shown that children learn to socialize in a positive way by spending time with people who love them and have a compelling interest in helping them learn to be a part of society.

Michelle Barone

They learn this skill by being with people of all ages and by following the models of the adults around them in a healthy way. They learn by being with friends and siblings, shopkeepers, and

---

PRESCRIPTION FOR FAMILY EMPOWERMENT

Take the experts with a grain of salt. Then do what you know is right in the morning.

At their best, the "experts" spread advice based on families and children they know. At their worst, many do and say whatever will bring in the most money. Child care and public education are quite susceptible to "fads" that are based on the expert-of-the-moment's ideas, fads that come and go with the wind.

But each and every child is unique, just like every family—and its circumstances. Whether you need to address silly everyday problems or major crises, you, the parent, are the expert on your child. You are the best informed about your child at any given time in any given circumstance.

Give over your time to discovering within yourself the means to raising your children. Both you and your children will be better people when you do.

neighbors, learning what works and what doesn't. You will know your child is growing socially by simply observing, seeing her mature before your eyes. One month she will have such difficulty sharing her toys, and the next month she is loaning her things to everyone. My experience has shown that children who have been with their families as their primary teachers are truly socialized. They are a part of the world, learning what is most important to them, to their families, their community.

We have been led to believe children learn to socialize by being only with children of their own ages in a very structured setting, with punishment and shame as the motivating force for behavior. The truth is, children want desperately to belong to the world of adults, to become competent, contributing members of society. This can only happen when a child is allowed to be a part of the world, not apart from it.

A child's temperament also influences his social growth. It is important to honor your child's pace and temperament. If your child is slow to warm up to a new setting, give her the time to adjust. If you have a very social child, find enjoyable activities and people for him. Socialization is always the big question with new homeschooling families. In reality, it is usually not a problem to find friends and activities. If you live in an isolated area it may take some effort; but again, children truly learn to be happy, well-adjusted social beings by spending time with their families, with other adults, and the world at large.

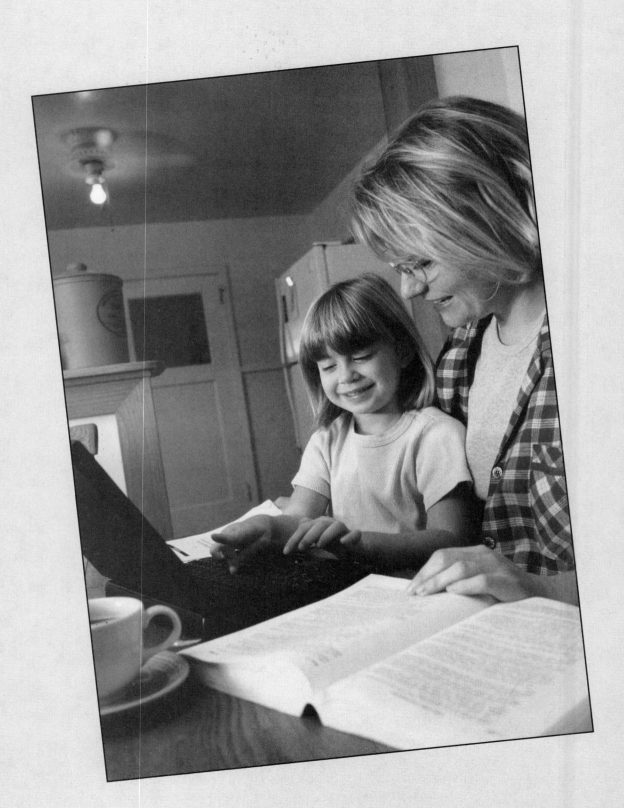

CHAPTER FIVE

"Educationese" You Can Understand

THE TOOL most frequently used to make parents think long and hard about removing their children from public schools is criticism of home-schoolers' socialization. The secret language of education runs a close second.

Fearing they won't be able to toss out the right jargon to explain their concerns, many parents don't question teachers and administrators. Those parents who do dare to speak up are often barraged by unfamiliar terms, and quickly fall prey to the "professionals'" implications that *they* know a lot more—and better—than an untrained parent.

If you are trying to stay involved with the education of a child in public school, you might want, for example, to bone up on the differences between types of assessment: authentic, alternative, group, valid, peer, portfolio, or self. Which does your child's school use?

You could study the implications of outcome-based education (OBE), and whether your child's school is in the stage of traditional OBE, transitional OBE, or transformational OBE.

Heard talk about CIMs and CAMs? Do you know what they are? Where they came from? Whether your child's school plans to drop traditional diplomas when adopting them?

Did you wonder what was wrong with "old" math when you studied "new" math in school? Do you know how "new new" math differs from both? (I'm not making this up, folks!) And, by the way, how do your child's metacognitive skills measure up?

Truth is, each of the "educationese" terms can be explained in a few, plain English sentences. Within fifteen minutes you'd have a handle on it all and be capable of discussing it with anyone. (And I strongly recommend doing so!) As easy as the jargon is to translate, though, it's totally unnecessary to the practice of home education. Educationese is the language of an institution concerned with management, efficiency, teachers' unions, and funding. This language needn't be applied to a home where the only concerns are the needs of one or a few children surrounded by supportive family.

> **Educationese is the language of an institution concerned with management, efficiency, teachers' unions, and funding.**

Ironically, many of the current educational reforms are attempting to take what works in a home setting and institutionalize it, mostly with disastrous results. It stands to reason that if you take what works in an institutional setting and put it in the home, the results will be equally calamitous. Indeed, personal reading and anecdotal evidence suggest that it's those homeschoolers who create "school at home" who suffer the highest incidence of stress and burnout and send their children back to school in frustration.

There are many ways to go about homeschooling without resorting to school at home, and an explanation of just a few of these approaches are all the "educationese" you'll need to better understand homeschooling. Unschooling, interest-initiated learning, and unit studies will help you see how many different ways there are to go about helping your child receive an education, and probably get you thinking of a dozen more ways.

For a special treat, read the fascinating essays about some of homeschooling's earliest advocates. First, Susannah Sheffer, author and editor of the popular *Growing Without Schooling* magazine, and Nancy Plent, who founded the Unschooling Network twenty years ago, share their memories of John Holt and his work. Then Dr. Raymond Moore and Dorothy Moore describe their world-famous Moore Formula, a customized low-cost, low-stress, readiness-oriented plan for achievement, behavior, and sociability through a study-work-service balance.

It's "educationese" you can understand—and enjoy.

32

The name John Holt comes up frequently in articles about homeschooling. What was his thinking about education when he began to encourage homeschooling?

SUSANNAH SHEFFER ◆ Holt had been a schoolteacher for several years when his book *How Children Fail*, published in 1964, brought him to public attention. It was an account of life in a fifth-grade classroom, and it looked closely at why the students—supposedly bright, privileged, successful—weren't learning what Holt was trying to teach. He was surprised and puzzled to find that most of the children in his classroom were bored and frightened, intent primarily on figuring out what the teacher wanted. The classroom was not the place of active learning and exploration that Holt had imagined it would be.

While teaching in school, Holt was also spending time with the young children of relatives and friends. He saw in these young children the energy, enthusiasm, and skill at learning that were almost wholly absent in fifth-grade students. What was it, he wondered, that turned such active and curious human beings into the timid and evasive strategists he met at school?

He began to suspect that the fault lay in the way children were treated in school and in the entire assumption that learning was something separate from life that children had to be made to do or shown how to do. Children are good at learning, Holt eventually asserted, and that phrase is a good short summary of his beliefs. (In his second book, *How Children Learn*, he wrote, "Everything I am saying in this book can be summed up in two words: trust children," so there's an even briefer summary.)

Holt spent many years at the forefront of the school reform movement, talking, writing, and working for more freedom, choice, and innovation in education. For a while he felt hopeful; it seemed as if many people were interested in the ideas he and others were putting forth, and change seemed forthcoming. But, by the mid-1970s, many "free schools" closed; innovative teachers were fired; audiences seemed less receptive. Holt later wrote that he came, slowly and reluctantly, to see that "very few people, inside the schools or out, were willing to support or even tolerate giving more freedom, choice, and self-direction to children."

At the same time, Holt's own thinking was being challenged and expanded by his contact with Ivan Illich, author of *Deschooling Society*. Holt began to consider that school might not be "a good idea gone wrong," but rather "a bad idea from the word go." The whole idea of compulsory learning and of a society that judges people on the basis of their schooling seemed wrong to him. Holt began to imagine what growing up without schooling would be like; at the same time, he began meeting parents who had actually taken the step of allowing their children to learn outside of school entirely. To support such families, to provide a forum in which they could communicate with one another, and to explore and develop his own ideas, Holt founded *Growing Without Schooling* magazine in 1977.

NANCY PLENT ◆ John was one of those rare people who adjusted his vision when new information came his way. His thinking about education was in Stage III when I met him. First he had tried teaching in public school and began to talk and write about how they should change.

Then he encouraged families who couldn't wait for change (which might take years, the way bureaucracies move) to get together and form their own schools (Stage II). It turned out that these schools rarely lasted very long, and he saw that.

So to parents who were discouraged with the membership wars that went on in co-op schools, John suggested the most

> **The whole idea of compulsory learning and of a society that judges people on the basis of their schooling seemed wrong to John Holt.**

direct route to get what they wanted was to take on the job themselves.

I often wonder what insights we may be missing because he's not around today to point out what Stage IV should be.

33

What does "unschooling" mean, and how is it different from homeschooling?

NANCY PLENT ◆ I was stunned when my first homeschooling friend showed me her basement schoolroom. She started lessons from her teacher's desk every day right after breakfast. Her kids had desks lined up in front of her, just like in public school. I couldn't understand it. Wasn't that what we were all trying to escape? She was what I would call a "home schooler"—somebody who duplicates school at home to a high degree. I've since realized that my reaction was because *I* was trying to escape everything that looked like school, but that by itself didn't make me an "unschooler."

Each person's definition of *unschooling* is a little different, and that's appropriate. Unschooling is about helping your child learn by doing the things that excite him, that fit his inner drives, rather than trying to motivate him to work at a generic "Goals 2000" curriculum.

Biographies of famous people are packed with examples of how well child-centered education works. Read about Thomas Edison, Noel Coward, Andrew Carnegie, Woodrow Wilson . . . and hundreds of others, all lucky enough to have parents who helped them travel their own unique unschooling road.

KATHARINE HOUK ◆ Most people understand homeschooling to mean learning outside of the institution called school, yet some families refer to what they do as unschooling. The term unschooling has been used in a couple of different ways.

Unschooling sometimes refers to homeschooling without a set curriculum, wherein what happens each day is based on the interests and curiosities of the people involved. Sometimes this process is called natural learning, the discovery method, or

Katharine Houk

experience-based learning. Many families, including my own, have enjoyed this family- and community-centered way of living and learning for many years. To some this may not look like "education" at all because it so closely resembles daily life. And daily life it is—with a focus for both adults and children on exploration, problem-solving, discov-

ering where to look for answers to the hundreds of questions that naturally arise, all intertwined with the tasks involved in keeping a household running smoothly.

Becoming unschoolers was an evolutionary process for our family. At first I was worried about "covering" the same topics that children in school were learning. I borrowed books from my local district but found that my children's daily explorations at home and in the community went far beyond what they would have learned from those books. Using our home and public libraries, going fun places and meeting interesting people, taking care of home, pets, and the garden, and attending homeschooling gatherings filled our days with discovery. My task as an unschooling parent has been to create a rich learning environment (which has included everything from dance classes to textbooks to travel), provide guidance and direction when appropriate, and nurture interests. This is not to say that a family homeschooling with a set curriculum cannot also do these things, time and energy permitting.

The term *unschooling* is also used by homeschoolers to describe the process of shedding notions that institutional education has bestowed on us, both parents and children. These notions may include the idea that learning is a chore and must be coerced with rewards and punishments, or that teaching is necessary for learning to take place, or that there is a uniform timetable for learning certain things such as reading.

Letting go of these ingrained ideas is a recovery process, best helped by developing trust in our children and ourselves, which can be nurtured by learning from experienced unschoolers whether in support groups, online, or by reading articles in publications. My children have been my best teachers in my efforts to unlearn what my schooling has taught me and it's an ongoing task. It's been my love for them that has opened my eyes to what they really need, to what captures their minds and hearts, to what has helped them grow up to be healthy, knowledgeable adults.

One scary aspect of unschooling, if you live in a state that requires reports, is translating this kind of learning into a form that school officials can understand; therefore my husband and I have put in valuable time explaining to education officials what we are doing and how it is working. Translating our children's natural learning into "educationese" can be tedious, but doing so has enabled us to

> **The term *unschooling* is also used by homeschoolers to describe the process of shedding notions that institutional education has bestowed on us, both parents and children. These notions may include the idea that learning is a chore and must be coerced with rewards and punishments, or that teaching is necessary for learning to take place, or that there is a uniform timetable for learning certain things such as reading.**

keep on with what has been working best for our family. Some unschooling families enroll with a support group such as Clonlara, which acts as a buffer/translator between them and school officials.

The flexibility of unschooling has allowed our children to develop in directions that might not have opened to them had we stuck to the school's (or some other) curriculum. They've become self-directed learners. Unschooling has worked well for our family and for many others, but there is no right way when it comes to homeschooling. You and your children are the experts on what is best for your family.

DONN REED (EDITED BY JEAN REED) ◆ There are as many ways to homeschool as there are people and families. Unschooling is one way of homeschooling, just as different religions are different ways of celebrating life and worshiping God.

Differentiating between unschooling and homeschooling requires a definition of homeschooling. I believe homeschooling occurs when parents take personal responsibility for a child's development and education outside of the traditional public school environment. That's a simplistic definition. Homeschooling is actually much more. It's a lifestyle involving and bonding the whole family. For us it means recognizing that learning takes place at any time or place; that life itself is an ongoing education not confined to a particular time, place, or age.

Homeschooling allows us to give our children more than test-taking and money-earning skills. Our global society is changing. We feel it our responsibility to give our children more than just academic skills to meet these challenges. Our children need the ability to evaluate, make responsible judgments, and resolve conflicts peacefully with open minds and creativity. We also want our children to be happy now. We feel that childhood is important in itself; it shouldn't be spent only in preparation for adulthood.

Unschooling advocate John Holt said, "Children do not need to be made to learn, told what to learn, or shown how. Given access to enough of the world, including our own lives and work in that world, they will see clearly what things are truly important to us and to others and they will make for themselves a better world than we could make for them."

> **Homeschooling is . . . a lifestyle involving and bonding the whole family. For us it means recognizing that learning takes place at any time or place; that life itself is an ongoing education not confined to a particular time, place, or age.**

Some parents feel allowing children freedom to learn "by doing" without interference constitutes unschooling; that parents shouldn't offer advice or "teach" unless asked or "invited" to share their knowledge as opposed to teaching how to do it: a statement of faith in children's innate curiosity and abilities.

We found that leaving our kids alone, letting them study when and what they wanted, worked at some times, but not always. It worked for Mowgli and Tarzan; other times we've wondered why so few of the great educators have children of their own. If I interrupt my son's woodworking to show him a way to start the saw-cut without nicking a finger, am I interfering with his ability to learn by himself? If I withhold the same information from an adult, and he becomes aware of it, he may very well resent me. Letting a child struggle with a task without offering advice that would make it easier is not showing respect; and, once he realizes you could have helped but chose not to, probably will not increase his respect for you. Perhaps it is the manner used to convey the information.

Our experiment with different learning styles continued throughout twenty-four years of homeschooling. Our conclusion: Any philosophy, carried to its "logical," consistent extreme, can become ridiculous and indefensible. We all learn in different ways at different times. Homeschooling should allow each child to learn in the manner that is best for them at that particular time. We've always liked Emerson's comment, "Consistency is the hobgoblin of little minds."

34

What is "interest-initiated" learning, and how do I learn how to do this?

LUZ SHOSIE ◆ Have you ever watched a baby learning to pull herself up to reach a toy, or a seven-year-old figuring how many weeks' allowance it takes to buy that new game, or a sixteen-year-old planning college-entry strategies? That's interest-initiated learning. Humans, and all other living beings, come into the world with the ability and the need to learn and grow into adults. They know how to do it.

Many of us who spent a lot of time in school were taught that we must be forced to learn, that learning is difficult, and that only experts know how to do it. For us, some unlearning is required. I recommend reading John Holt, carefully observing young children, and joining (or starting) an unschoolers' support group.

Our son, Cassidy, and I have made several cross-country trips and stayed with homeschooling families. Usually one of the first topics of discussion when we meet a new family is how do we do it? I would always say that we don't do lessons, that we answer questions or give help when asked. They would say, "That's the way we do it, too, but we thought we were the only ones because our support group always talks about how to teach math or how to choose a curriculum."

So I decided to start a group for those of us who are struggling to overcome our years of schooling and trust ourselves and our children to be learning all the time. We meet at each other's homes on Saturday afternoons so the children can play and the parents can reassure each other and exchange ideas. We publish a mailing list so people can get in touch. It's Schoolaholics Anonymous—when you think you can't make it through another minute without *teaching those kids a lesson,* get out your phone list and call an unschooler. We all have those days. It will pass.

> **It's Schoolaholics Anonymous—when you think you can't make it through another minute without *teaching those kids a lesson,* get out your phone list and call an unschooler. We all have those days. It will pass.**

SANDRA DODD ◆ You're asking how to learn something? You're asking someone you think would know? *That's it! You've got it!*

You could have taken a course in interest-initiated learning, maybe, and bought a $60 book and read the chapters in the order the teacher listed, at the speed the syllabus recommends, taken two tests and a final, written two papers . . . that is *not* interest-initiated learning.

That's submitting yourself to scheduled torture. That's lying down and letting someone else tell you to learn more slowly, learn more quickly, don't ask *that* question, it won't be on the test, anyway.

Sandra Dodd

If I need to be at a meeting in a neighboring town at a certain time I would plan time to get there, no side trips, no stopping, no

---

THE DEFINITON OF "TO EDUCATE"

Educate: from Latin: *ex* (out) + *ducere* (lead). You have to look long and hard to uncover this original definition in your dictionary, but you will search forever to find evidence of it in the way we typically approach our children's learning lives.

To lead out what does this definition tell us? It tells us that perhaps we are experiencing so many problems teaching our children because we are going about it backwards. We consider education as putting information into our children when true education is the act of "leading out" that which already exists inside.

This simple definition can transform your family's perspective on learning. Through it we recognize learning s natural connection to life. The artificial experience of reading and memorizing (pouring in) pales in comparison to real life learning through which your child learns by discovery (leading out). Only you as parent can allow your child the opportunity to touch true education.

Memorize this definition. Let it lead your entire family to the joy of learning.

changing my mind. If I'm going to drive for four hours without a destination, turning where fancy leads, staying as long or as short a time as seems good to the children, we will do and see things we could never have chosen in advance. A flexible willingness to experience what comes will open up the world.

If, after a lifetime of schedules, deadlines, and year-ends, you want to experiment with interest-initiated learning, I think the best way is to play. Play board games, word games, work jigsaw puzzles side by side with your children (even if they are seventeen years old). I predict two things will happen: You'll be surprised at the connections to history, geography, math, language, culture, science, and so forth that will unfold from your game *if* you can consider it an opportunity instead of "just" a game. You will have an opportunity to talk with your child on a calm and personable level. The game or puzzle creates a space in which you are facing the same direction, and you have a need and excuse to sit still, without jumping up out of anxiety or discomfort. It creates a calm area and a shared space.

Another shared learning experience can be reading aloud. With younger children, this is obvious. With middlin' children, you can read books that would be too hard for them to read on their own, a chapter or two at a stretch, or read them to sleep. They'll gain vocabu-

lary and a feel for written English beyond what they can get visually. With older children who are proficient readers, you could take turns reading, maybe in the car, or they could read to you while you sew or do dishes. You could read to them while they work on a model or draw or work puzzles or sand furniture. Reading in the car or listening to books on tape can be a great way to share literature, and car trips are good opportunities for long discussions.

Once you've seen half a dozen instances of getting to a subject area you hadn't expected to reach, or of the children asking questions you would never have thought to set up or to coax from them, you'll gain confidence. I can't tell you what your children will ask or learn because that would be a curriculum, a set of facts or activities you all could pass or fail. I'm talking about cross-country thinking. Get off the paved road and explore.

What if you don't "do history in order"? Probably you'll learn a lot more history! Just get out there and play around with words, ideas, concepts, and connections.

Another approach is to think of the things you have learned outside of school, and how you learned them. What hobbies or authors or subjects or crafts have you learned just because you developed a curiosity and burning interest? What collections do you have, what skills or special knowledge do you have that you've developed gradually or quickly without paying a teacher, without being tested or certified?

35

A friend told me she finds out what her children are interested in learning about, then turns that into a unit study. Is this an effective way for children to learn?

PAT LINES ◆ I'm not experienced in child-directed learning over time, and I know of no studies on this topic, so I must give a very general answer. I don't know how you can "teach" a child who is not interested in the subject. On the other hand, I don't know how a child can become interested in a topic unless there is some initial exposure. In a rich environment, where there is much natural exposure to many topics, I would expect this approach to work. Most children have a natural curiosity about a wide range of things, even those that are more focused on a single topic. We do expect children to learn a range of skills and subject matter, but I don't think the order in which they learn it will be that important ten years from now.

SHARI HENRY ◆ I imagine it is an effective way for many children to learn.

> **My middle child, at age seven, became fascinated with Greek mythology, thanks to a fantastic Renaissance art exhibit in town.**

We don't work that way in our house, at least not formally. My children do take off on learning tangents, but I've never felt the desire to turn it into a formal unit study. My middle child, at age seven, became fascinated with Greek mythology, thanks to a fantastic Renaissance art exhibit in town. A painting of Europa and Jupiter spurred months and months of reading myths, creating books of her favorite gods and goddesses, making paper dolls with changeable goddess clothing, playing make-believe myths with friends (where they would each transform into a famous mythological character and role play for hours), and decorating her bunk beds with leaves and grape clusters to make it look like a "Greek island." There, she'd escape for hours at end. This all led into a study of the planets and filtered into other areas of study as well. She now knows more about mythology than most college graduates, helps bail her father out of tough spots in crossword puzzles, and is on her way to what I consider a high school level study of space and the planets. I didn't do anything but help her browse shelves at the local bookstores, place a few catalog orders, and look up some pronunciations.

While I know unit studies work well for some families, they feel a bit contrived to us. And, to be honest, I'm not looking for more work!

36

What is the Moore Formula approach to home education?

DR. RAYMOND MOORE AND DOROTHY MOORE ◆ The Moore Formula provides a great deal of freedom within guidelines that target (1) readiness for formal learning, (2) the student's interests, and (3) a balance of study, work, and community service. This offers a certain security that most curricula don't provide, with little or no burnout. It also contrasts with packaged curricula that fit nicely into conventionally minded families but sharply restrict creativity and lead to burnout.

Freedom embraces the *readiness* principle for all tasks. Whatever children need or want to do—physically, mentally, or spiritually—if they are mature enough, they learn faster, with less stress. Although they are ready for simple physical jobs as soon as they can walk, such as putting away toys, they are usually not ready for formal study until at least age eight to ten or twelve. Until then, there should be much informal learning, including useful work, learning games (phonics, math, and

> **Once you have their interests, motivation seems automatic, instead of being a dilemma to both teachers and students as in conventional programs.**

so on), life experiences (bakery, market, fire station, post office), and true stories read to them on many subjects (language arts), including religion (history), nature (science), biographies (history), and travelogues (geography). The longer such learning continues, at least until age ten, the better the foundation for their superstructure of formal learning. Meanwhile, some skills naturally develop, although never through parental pressure. If you live in a state requiring school at age six or seven, label your informal learning with typical subject names as above in parentheses.

Freedom here is a principle that measures to responsibility. Kids thrive on freedom that rhymes with authority. Yet integrity and common sense say authority must be limited to ability to accept responsibility. So states require maturity and responsibility levels before it awards driver's licenses. When youngsters see this clearly and sense the meaning of authority, motivation reigns. The Formula doesn't function exactly the same in every family or with every student. There is a built-in flexibility that's limited by student mastery of learning tools. Given that prospect, we customize to the interests, aptitudes, attitudes, and abilities of each student. The big thing we have going for us here is targeting student interests instead of giving each grade the same stack of books, which tells them we think they are all alike. Once you have their interests, motivation seems automatic, instead of being a dilemma to both teachers and students as in conventional programs.

So we follow the three guidelines above, which aren't optional. For example, *study* with balanced *work* and *service* usually means as much or more work and service as study. Work usually relates to earning money, and service here is volunteering without pay. Together they shatter selfishness.

37

My research has turned up so many different homeschooling styles that my head is spinning! What are the unique aspects of each?

MARSHA RANSOM ◆ School-at-home, or traditional homeschooling, follows the typical course of study as implemented in an institutional setting, with mother as teacher, children as students. "Read the chapter, answer the questions, review and take the test." There are many pre-packaged curriculums available for purchase that follow this approach.

Unit studies, sometimes called thematic units, cover all the curricular areas while following an interest or topic. You can purchase a pre-planned unit, plan your own, or keep records of the things a child does to follow a specific interest (what I call "relaxed unit studies"). Since all material is integrated, rather than presented in unrelated bits and pieces, children make connections more readily, boosting retention.

Charlotte Mason, an early twentieth-century British educator, believed children learned best by using living books (books that bring the subject to life in an interesting way) as opposed to dry textbooks. Children homeschooled using the Charlotte Mason approach are encouraged to use their creativity and curiosity to explore their world. Lessons in the basics (reading, writing, and math) take the child's ability and developmental level into con-

Marsha Ransom

sideration, are short, and don't include busywork. Parents model good habits and good character and snatch teachable moments during the day's activities to reinforce such behaviors. Real-life experience is used to teach all other areas, so nature walks, keeping journals, touring art museums to view original works, reading good literature, and attending concerts are included.

Unschooling is sometimes called interest-oriented, real-life, or child-led learning. John Holt, who coined the term, observed that children retained much more when they were interested and self-motivated. Most unschoolers let their children's inner timetable guide them as they teach by example and modeling, rather than imposing external structure. Unschoolers also help their children learn from life as they involve them in household chores and projects, community service, and working in the family business. Some unschooled kids have also started their own business, based on an interest or hobby, later turning it into a lifelong career.

The Waldorf approach is a holistic approach that considers the changing developmental stages of the child, while using classic literature, well-written children's stories, and nonfiction books instead of textbooks, plus imaginative play and natural materials for creative arts and crafts.

The Montessori method promotes providing a natural and life-supporting environment for the child, observing the child, and constantly adapting the environment so the child may fulfill his or her greatest potential emotionally, mentally, spiritually, and physically. A basic premise of Montessori education is that children are all born with a unique potential that can be developed.

Finally, the eclectic approach allows you to treat all the approaches as a smorgasbord, picking and choosing the ele-

ments you feel will work best for you, and leaving the rest. One of the best things you can do for your children is provide a personalized program that fits their unique qualities.

JUDITH WAITE ALLEE ◆ There seems to be a homeschooling continuum. On one end are families who "unschool," learning through living and encouraging a child's interests and passions rather than following a set curriculum. On the other end are those who "school-at-home." They purchase a "fifth-grade curriculum" for their fifth grader, using textbooks and workbooks to cover all the standard subjects.

There is a stereotype that "school at home" families are involved in the Christian homeschooling movement, while "unschoolers" populate the secular homeschooling movement. From where I sit, though, I don't see many families on either end of the continuum. Most are somewhere in the middle, picking and choosing among materials and methods. Some people call this flexible approach "eclectic homeschooling," implying a judicious mix with a broth of interest-led learning, seasoned with parental prerogatives.

Unit studies tie in traditional subjects to one topic at a time. With the Konos Character Curriculum, for example, one month the focus is on patience, and learners read about Thomas Edison and how he tested hundreds of materials to find the appropriate filament for the light bulb.

Our foster son, Danny, a struggling reader, had never paid attention to the newspapers until hearing, as part of our study of civil rights, a Filipino nun speak about civil rights violations when Ferdinand Marcos was in power. Suddenly he began watching the front page, following Marcos's fall from power. Then a Peace Corps worker told us about the common foods, poverty, climate, and cultural differences in the Philippines We tried Philippine foods, doubling or halving the recipes. Under a single topic, we tied together social studies with reading, weather science, and cooking math.

You don't have to "home" school at home, or by yourself. Learning "co-ops" spring up in creative ways. For example, six families who use Konos meet every Friday with the parents alternately preparing an activity and craft. An Alabama homeschool group sponsors formal classes one day a week. An Illinois mother we know homeschools six teenagers; two are her own, one a niece, one a neighbor, and two are friends' children who were unhappy and struggling in school. The other families pay a small fraction of what a private school would cost. A learning cooperative can also be as simple as rotating children between two or three families—you take mine on Tuesdays; I'll take yours on Fridays.

Both "school at home" parents and "relaxed homeschoolers" can use Charlotte Mason's theories. Charlotte Mason, a Christian educator from the late 1800s in England, founded a school for governesses, the primary "homeschoolers" at the time. Mason promoted the narrative method of learning—meaning that a child should retell the story or passage he or she just read or listened to—and build good work habits and character. She encouraged the use of "living books" that make history and literature come alive. Her own series of six books, including *Home Education,* are still in print.

Another theory making a comeback is classical education. While logically it might fall into the "school at home" category, it's quite different from the curriculum used in today's schools. The focus is on stages of learning for different ages, called the *trivium.* Classicists teach facts and memorization during the "grammar" phase (which is why elementary schools used to be called grammar schools). The second stage, for middle schoolers, is "logic." They study relationships between various subjects and events, and develop logical thought in speaking, writing, and reading. The sthird stage, "rhetoric," focuses on high-school-level problem solving and original thought.

The latest twist is distance learning programs sponsored by public schools. I guess you could call this "public school at home," rather than homeschooling, since the school controls the curriculum. This is not really new—Alaska has had a home-based option for decades, originally for children in remote areas but open to anyone. Now some states make a conscious effort to woo students away from homeschooling and back under the public school umbrella with online classes, often offering a free computer as enticement. This approach offers a ready-made curriculum along with a public school diploma, and the schools get to keep the students on their rolls, but not in class.

One concern is that the schools will co-opt the homeschooling movement, which encourages freedom and experimentation, and put it under tight controls. That free computer and curriculum are strong lures; however, the same-old textbooks and drudgery remain, only now the student works alone in front of a computer.

I have seen happy and successful homeschooled families from every philosophy, style, curriculum, and method. While so many options are daunting to new homeschoolers and some veterans alike, remember that your decisions don't have to be "all-or-nothing." You can combine methods and materials in any way that works for your family. And you can change your mind if you see that what you are doing is not working, or if you want to try something new.

CHAPTER SIX

Okay, the Kids are Home— *Now* What?

FOR SOME folks, the *decision* to homeschool is a piece of cake compared to actually facing the first day of complete responsibility for their children's education. I know; I've been there. There can never be a definitive "how to" book for this occasion, no matter how loudly a title may shout it. Why? Because that momentous "first day"—and, for that matter, all subsequent days—are unique to each family. Let's meet just a few of the broad "groups" of new homeschoolers to help you understand how the experience that all call by the same name—homeschooling—starts from many different places.

Let's begin with the I-Always-Knew-I-Would family. They've known since their first child was born—and maybe even before—this was the only way to fly. For them, the first day of homeschooling is not the first day of school during the year their child turns five or six years old. Rather, their child simply turns five or six during the learning rhythm of day-to-day life, and they're well aware from the get-go that each day provides opportunity and experience galore for learning. There is no easily recognizable first day of homeschooling for this family.

The Oh-No-He's-Almost-School-Aged family makes the decision to homeschool when the day to sign up for kindergarten looms ever closer. Likely, friends and acquaintances with children the same age busily go about the rituals associated with starting school: taking their children to "readiness tests"; buying new clothes; checking bus schedules; making sure all vaccinations are up to date. The Oh-No-He's-Almost-School-Aged family is less likely to recognize the learning rhythm of all the days that have passed before and enter into what may be termed "substitute" rituals: a quest to find the magical list that outlines what all the other kindergartners will be learning that year (aka curriculum); a frantic materials- and book-buying spree; a series of late-night "Are we doing the right thing?" conversations; a tenth phone call making sure they've got the right day and time for the next homeschool support group meeting. For the Oh-No-He's-Almost-School-Aged family, there will be a first day of homeschooling, and it will be a "happening."

> **For some folks, the *decision* to homeschool is a piece of cake compared to actually facing the first day of complete responsibility for their children's education. I know; I've been there.**

The first day of homeschooling is different still for the I-Don't-Want-Him-in-School-Anymore family. Each of this group's families has their own reasons for this, be it religious, philosophical, academic, social, growing fear for their child's safety, or an intricate combination of some or all of the above. One or several of their children have gone to school for a year, maybe a few years. Their children are still quite young, but even in this relatively short time period, the family has grown assimilated to the school routine. The I-Don't-Want-Him-in-School-Anymore family will not only have a first day of homeschool "happening," this family is likely to make sure it starts on time and occurs in specific subject areas at specific times of the day, to boot—just like school!

And last, meet the My-(Pre)Teen-Is-Coming-Out-of-School family. They have spent a *long* time in the school routine, and their child may be bored or overwhelmed academically, ditto for socially, acting out, caving in to peer pressure, or sensing that school isn't all there is. The idea to homeschool may have been Mom's or Dad's, or it may just as easily have been suggested to them by their child.

This child may have many strong ideas about where he wants to go with homeschooling and jump right in with little or no help or guidance from parents. Another teen, used to having others set the learning schedule and agenda, could easily require—or even demand—strong guidance from a parent. In either case, the first day of homeschooling is different here than it is in the I-Don't-Want-Him-in-School-Anymore family's house, as an increasingly independent teen approaches *everything* differently than an elementary school-aged child does.

We could go on, but from even these few examples you can begin to see how many varied places there are from which a family begins to homeschool. Homeschooling is neither easier nor harder for any one of these broad groups of new homeschoolers; it's simply different. And with so many different starting points, you can begin to see how each family will soon be traveling its own homeschooling path in its own way.

This chapter addresses the practical aspect of homeschooling, and the included questions and answers were chosen to be useful no matter where you're starting from. Here you'll find out what experienced homeschoolers do all day. Equally important to notice is what they *don't* do all day! You'll find out how they feel about the use of textbooks, curriculum, and computers. They share ideas on finding the best resources, keeping records, and meeting the needs of several children of different ages at the same time. From sports activities to motivation to learn, this chapter is guaranteed to help you get off to a great start, no matter where your starting place is!

38

What do you *do* all day?

CAFI COHEN ◆ Our teenage home-schoolers do what needs to be done. That includes shoveling snow, planning and cooking dinner, practicing piano, bathing the dog, volunteering at the hospital, working math problems, attending diving practice, memorizing a speech for 4-H, and teaching a rocketry class at a Civil Air Patrol meeting.

We also do whatever strikes our fancy. On this list are biking, drawing, playing games, seeing old movies, reading for hours on end, entering writing contests, and getting together with friends of all ages.

We have no typical days, no set schedule. Our activities vary tremen-dously, in accordance with the children's changing interests. One day my son might spend five hours with a new computerized flight simulator and the remainder of the day mowing the lawn, helping his dad with car maintenance, and reading—all of which we count as "school." The next day might include science homework (from his community college class), piano practice, math problems, weight training, and a 4-H meeting.

Sometimes the children are very productive. On other days it looks like they do very little—maybe just some household chores, visiting friends, and curling up with a favorite book for the fifth time. And we drop everything for family crises, unexpected travel opportunities, and great weather (best time to hike and ski!).

I do not worry about these apparent down times. Every day need not be the educational equivalent of the Fourth of July. Often enough (two to five days each week) the children are busy with activities that many professional educators would not only approve of, but envy.

It looks messy, but it works.

LUZ SHOSIE ◆ We create for ourselves a life worth living and work worth doing and try not to do what doesn't fit into that framework. We invite our son to participate in our activities as much as he wants and is able. Sometimes we insist that he join in the work of keeping a house and family operating. Sometimes he invites us to participate in his activities or asks us to help in his work.

We try to remember that we are all learning all the time, that life is not divided into math, social studies, science. Whatever we choose to do or pay attention to will teach us and lead us to the next learning experience. We do not choose or create activities for the sake of learning; we learn by doing what interests us and what needs to be done.

SUSAN EVANS ◆ The activities in our home change week to week and season by season. There are times when big projects overtake all of our lives for a period of time: an upcoming conference, finishing requirements for a Boy Scout Eagle badge, painting the house during the last week of nice weather in the fall. Mostly, though, life is pretty low key, variable, and focused on what any, few, or all of us are interested in at the time.

For many years our family life looked much like "advanced preschool at home," even when one of my "preschoolers" topped six feet tall! Our days were built around daily chores, errands around town, cultural enrichment (trips to the library, museums, zoos, plays, concerts, movies), field trips (farms, small businesses, factories, restaurants), time to think, time to read and dream, attention to personal interests (collections, crafts, research), time for hugs, laughter and tears, long-term focused obsessions (Lego bricks, drawing, poetry, gardening).

For a while I described our approach to living and learning as being like the "gifted and talented" curriculum (while successfully skipping much of the "grade appropriate" curricula): hands-on exploration of interests; lots of messy projects; quiet, deep, long-winded conversations; scientific, spiritual, and philosophic wonderings, with no pressure for a final, definitive answer.

The main focus of our "homeschooling" time has been real life, taking care of important matters like homemaking, housekeeping, family rituals. Our most important work has been loving and supporting one another by taking the time and energy to deal with personal crises (large and small) in a direct, open, and honest manner. We've tried to attend to the real issues in life rather than artificial ones. So challenges like growing up to be ourselves, becoming responsible for ourselves and our actions, finding our true work in our lives, and creating the kind of lives that nurture our souls and challenge our spirits are in the fore.

What we've put aside are the issues and pressures that seem manufactured and rather pointless in comparison: "Are you ready for the science quiz?" "Did you write the 500-word paper that will count for half of your final grade?" "Are you wearing colors that start with the letter P today?"

After almost twenty years, I've come to see the truth in the statement that one can get straight A's in classes and yet flunk real life. What we do is real life: making a home, being actively involved in our geographical and cultural community, seeking and doing worthwhile work, seeking ways to support ourselves financially, spiritually, and emotionally.

> **After almost twenty years, I've come to see the truth in the statement that one can get straight A's in classes and yet flunk real life.**

39
How do I develop a curriculum or plan of study?

PAT MONTGOMERY ◆ The question is not "How?" but "Why?" I taught in public schools and parochial schools for fourteen years prior to starting Clonlara School in 1967. For fourteen years I never used that word, nor did my associates, teachers, or administrators. Textbook companies studied whichever curriculum a school district adopted. The textbooks were what teachers used in classrooms. Sometimes these were the only teaching devices employed.

Curricula are designed by committees of teachers and administrators or by university college professors. These compilers of curricula usually observe and test children on each grade level to find out what the average child is interested in and can learn relatively easily.

It was only when home-based education became known to school officials sometime in the early 1980s that the word "curriculum" took on significance in relation to home educators. It was as though school officials, initially threatened, strained to find something that would discourage parents from opting out of schools. How could mere parents have access to the inner workings of schools—to curriculum? It became a buzz word.

Many home-educating parents bite the bait. They accept the myth that educating is about curriculum, textbooks, tests, and lesson plans, the trappings of institutional schools. I submit that the design of a child's education ought to be about the child. What are his interests? Her needs? His capabilities? Parents are not bound by the constricts of schools, which deal with such large numbers of students that they find it easiest to teach to the average students.

Parents are in the enviable position of being able to observe their own children and to develop a curriculum based upon their real interests and abilities and needs. This has been the practice at Clonlara for its entire thirty-plus-year existence. We have no other curriculum than the individual child herself.

Everyday life in the home can be the basis around which a plan is built. The ordinary has a magical aura for very young children. Building on a sense of wonder, following trails from how a key works to where the squirrel ran off is curriculum aplenty. As children grow, the home and the wealth of activities and wonder within it open out to the neighborhood, the community, even the world. Listening to a child's questions, finding answers together, and creating more questions is living curriculum. Those things that in schools are broken down into twenty- or fifty-minute segments can be studied for as long as an interest remains.

It was only when home-based education became known to school officials sometime in the early 1980s that the word "curriculum" took on significance in relation to home educators. It was as though school officials, initially threatened, strained to find something that would discourage parents from opting out of schools.

Curriculum and a plan of study are not mystical things. They were designed to let the student know facts about the world around him. We would never dream of establishing a curriculum for a baby or toddler, yet we know that a child learns more in the first three years of life than in all the rest of it put together. Why destroy this method of education in favor of an institutional school approach designed to pour facts into a child's mind? Your child has been making connections and using her mind actively since birth. She learns in ways peculiar to her own style. Study *that*. Then design a plan to nurture and support *that*. Education ought to be the parent's goal, not schooling. Education and schooling are not synonymous terms.

JOHN TAYLOR GATTO ◆ I'm glad you asked this. Nobody can develop a curriculum for you that isn't, at the very best, *second* best and, at the very worst, a rather diabolical exercise in mind control—even if its intentions are honorable.

Consider that the term "curriculum" comes to us from the classical period of ancient Rome and refers to a race course upon which animals, chariots, and drivers all "run." You don't have to be a rocket scientist to see similarities between race courses and mazes through which rats are run for the amusement and satisfaction of academic masters. Curricula, by their very nature, assume the surrender of volition—free will—for some presumably valuable goal that will be achieved in some presumably worthwhile future.

John Taylor Gatto

These are pretty big assumptions (and there are more assumptions inherent in the idea, had we the time to think about them) considering that the most efficient schoolmen and curriculum designers of history were the north German states of Prussia, Saxony, and Hanover, where every moment of the day fell under orders and directives of one kind or another—including the directive that women must report the onset of menses each month to the local police. These social planners caused the three biggest wars in modern history so far, although everyone agreed the "education" was superb.

The problem with buying someone else's *comprehensive* curriculum for personal development (limited curricula—like those for mastering a musical instrument, are not part of my [...] is that it will be certain not to fit you[...] certain because the assumption that the[...] are only a few types of humanity, and that all are sufficiently plastic or empty to take on whatever shape is imposed upon them, is an insane utopian idea contradicted by common experience. It *is* possible to shoehorn people into a few kinds of *classes* or types and spend oceans of energy and money convincing those so confined that such a course conforms with human nature. Schools do it every day. But the mutilations necessary to achieve the appearance of regular human ordering cause a lot of problems in an open society. Run to the library and read H. G. Wells's *The Island of Dr. Moreau,* which dealt prophetically with this very social initiative one hundred years ago.

To develop a curriculum of your own, you must be determined to know yourself and what you expect of yourself. This is a wholly different thing than studying and guessing what others expect of you. As you begin to know yourself (and the roads to self-knowledge are multiple but always begin with silences, solitudes, intense reflections, and self-study done obsessively until the programmed layers begin to flake away), you will begin to see what racecourse you *want* to build for your family to run on, and begin to fashion it by arranging experiences and planning time dispositions which lead in that direction.

O'S RECOMMENDED READING LIST
URRICULUM

of Benjamin Franklin: Franklin provides an account of
rior to his role in the early U.S. government. He started
without wealth or position, but achieved greatness as a well-rounded citizen—from scientist to entrepreneur, from public servant to national leader—all the while adhering to the guidance of industry and thrift.

2. *Autobiography of John Stuart Mill:* John Stuart Mill was the subject of a massive experiment by his own father to test how much a mind could be force-fed in childhood. You can derive two genuine values from Mill's later musings about his own experience. First, how criminal an abuse it is to trivialize a young mind with thin, insubstantial garbage; but second, how it is possible (though not likely) to err on the other side of exploitation of intellect at the cost of the affections. You will learn in detail the actual curriculum used and Mill's mature thinking about what he missed, and the effect it had on his character.

3. *The Autobiography of Norbert Weiner:* Weiner, a legendary teacher at MIT, is often called the "father" of cybernetics, the creation of artificial intelligence. Mill's curriculum was adapted by Weiner's father to deliberately create a scientific genius. Again, the precise curriculum is reflected on in detail, with its glories and inherent contradictions.

Think of it this way: If the goal of your race is to have your child go to Harvard, work his way up an international corporation's ladder, and get rich, you will move the foundations of his day in such a fashion that attitudes, habits, and interests suitable for such a competition are prepared. I hope that isn't your goal, but what the hey, I'm not you.

On the other hand, if a strong, independent person filled with courage, resourcefulness, curiosity, humor, and in possession of a livelihood not dependent on fitting into a collective is your hope, then a *much* different course has to be run. (For this latter I again recommend the eminently readable *Autobiography of Benjamin Franklin.)*

4. "The Lost Tools of Learning," a 1947 essay by Dorothy Sayers (not diffi-cult to find): The famous detective story writer and social thinker (she created Lord Peter Whimsy) generally analyzes how people, of the upper classes mostly, were taught to think for themselves for hundreds of years through the classical tradition preserved in every one of America's elite private boarding schools. Whether this is your cup of tea or not (and I confess it is mine), if you think about what you are hearing from Sayers you will have no difficulty realizing that an aristocratic educa-tion—unlike the education of a technician—costs absolutely nothing to deliver and is accessible to all. Read this short piece at least six times on different days.

5. *Angela's Ashes*, by Frank McCourt: Pick up this book that's been atop the bestseller list since 1996. You will learn how a boy with weak eyes can be beaten, starved, humiliated, and hounded every single day of his young life, in the worst curriculum the twentieth century has to offer, and still—because his mother and drunken father provided him a curriculum of tough love—could grow up to be an honorable and successful teacher in America's most prestigious high school, an entertainer in his spare time, and a multimillionaire from writing about it.

Some important part of the curricu-lum of growing up will have to be sup-plied by the young person, even in babyhood. I think it's a bad idea to be doctrinaire about this—how much ex-actly is something you have to play by ear—but the guardians have to be en-thusiastic about it as well as the guarded or else it will degenerate into a bad thing for everyone. In the words of the im-mortal Chris Mercogliano at the Albany Free School, you have to make it up as you go along in this regard.

Reading and studying other people's curricula, as long as they are explicit about selection of items, methods, justifications, outcomes, and assessments over time of the life results, can be extremely useful in showing you different ways such thinking can proceed. I don't mean you copy necessarily what others do; but by observing how and what they think you can sharpen your own mind.

But remember, it's not a contest. There are many, many ways to grow up right, and many "good" lives that can be enjoyed. Too many for any person to have them all.

SUSAN EVANS ◆ Fortunately, every homeschooling family comes equipped with curriculum experts: curious children.

What are your children's interests?

What sorts of places do they like to visit: airports, parks, libraries, museums, malls, the backyard, rock shops, zoos, factories . . . ?

What sorts of questions do they ask or wonder about?

What do you and your children enjoy doing together: talking, eating, dancing, playing sports, reading, singing, swimming, arguing, shopping . . . ?

The world and everything in it are connected. You can start your exploration anywhere and keep traveling intellectually. Interests lead one to another, and you're sure to run out of time before you run out of new adventures.

If you live in a state with reporting regulations, it's not difficult to translate what you love to do into educationese.

If you live in a state with required testing, you might want to add political activism to your curriculum (it won't hurt the rest of us, either). From what I've seen, most children who are following their hearts and their passionate interests do well enough on the tests so that they needn't sacrifice real learning in order to meet arbitrary state requirements.

In every state with excessive regulations, though, there are parents who have figured out how to put their family's education ahead of bureaucratic paperwork. It's worth the time to seek out these parents in your state and learn from their experiences.

Back to curricular considerations: A good rule of thumb from the time your children are small is to think of purchasing tools rather than toys for holiday and gift giving. Beyond the obvious books and art supplies, think of other useful materials and resources: fabric, pins, hammers, nails, a sheet of plywood (what would *you* make out of your own sheet of plywood?), rope, duct tape, Lego bricks, embroidery thread in a rainbow of colors (good for jewelry, hanging pictures, twisting into dog leashes, weaving), shovels and rakes and a corner of the yard.

What are your children longing to "mess with"? Can you think of creative ways to oblige them?

Do what's fun, what's intriguing, what keeps you up at night wondering about. Don't worry about grade level or the paperwork, if you absolutely must make your life conform to a state's idea of a curriculum, you can always write it up later, in the afterglow of newfound wisdom and knowledge.

40
Can I find a ready-made curriculum to get started in homeschooling?

DR. RAYMOND MOORE AND DOROTHY MOORE ◆ Yes, although twenty-five years ago they were scarce. Many Christian publishers resented homeschools and would not sell to them. Today, mass-produced textbooks, workbooks, and videos make big money for these publishers, and perform a service for conventional schools. As a university teacher-education dean and curriculum specialist, I authored and coauthored many such books. Parents often choose them because that's the way they were taught. Many often are uneasy with programs that encourage freedom for imagination, and sometimes they are right; it can be overdone. Yet those who use mass education for homeschools are the most frequent burnouts.

If you want creativity and exciting quality with the best chance at major scholarships, customize to your children's abilities, aptitudes, and interests. Ready-made curricula seldom produce creative children, balanced in head, heart, hand, and health.

Dr. Ed Dickerson, who supervises Iowa homeschools, wrote about curricula for our *Moore Report International*. He says when upset parent-burnouts misunderstand and misuse curricula, he tells them a story about an imaginary shopping trip for a boy, age nine. They tell a clerk, "We'd like some nine-year-old boy shoes." He brings a shoebox clearly labeled "nine-year-old boy shoes." But the shoe doesn't fit! So the clerk concludes, "His foot must be deformed!"

Children's minds are even more individual than their feet. A nine-year-old in a ready-made curriculum at home or school will seldom fit right. So we have many "special education" misfits, especially boys, whose maturity is often misdiagnosed.

If you want to know how to teach with freedom, recheck our answer to Question 36, read our Moore Formula books, *The Successful Homeschool Family Handbook* and *Minding Your Own Business*, and send for a free basic information packet (BIP) from Box 1, Camas, WA 98607. These books are based on our research, which is the main reason that Moore Academy students are known for their creativity and many major scholarships.

Whatever your curriculum route, for your own well-being and for your

> **Those who use mass education for homeschools are the most frequent burnouts.**

children's sake, be sure that it is consistent with the research on readiness. It is a form of child abuse to force children to enroll for studies for which they are not equipped by age, maturity, ability, and aptitudes, especially for boys.

Some ask about correspondence schools. If they provide personal tutorial help, they are especially useful for college-age students or for odd courses for high school diploma needs. Be sure they provide the freedom and creativity of a sound work-study-service curriculum customized to students' interests, abilities, and aptitudes, and also embrace readiness. The president of a highly rated correspondence school recently visited us, saying he'd like to follow our plan. Given these conditions, he will come closer to producing vibrant, creative children at low parental stress levels than with average packaged curricula.

NED VARE ◆ Yes, but don't ever take them seriously.

41

At what age do I have to start formal lessons with my children?

LILLIAN JONES ◆ Life offers so many things that are fun to learn, interesting to learn, good to learn, or necessary to learn, but formal lessons are not generally helpful for the learning process—there's something clumsily unnatural about them.

A young child wants to learn about the world, about people, animals, places, the seasons, weather, the night sky, the sun and moon, natural processes like plant's growth—all things that come about naturally in the course of living, questioning, and observing. If you pay sensitive attention, it will be obvious when your child is ready to learn something.

Young children mostly need relaxed time to play and to imagine. They thrive on having wonderful books read to them from an early age. There's no hurry for independent reading—lots of time spent snuggling together while being read to will bring a deep love of reading, learning, and imagining. The places you can go together, the characters you can get to know, and the experiences you can share through reading aloud are indescribably wonderful. I've always felt sorry for families who missed out on this because of feeling their kids need to be reading on their own at young ages.

You'll eventually want to have some specialized books for a few subjects like math or science, but any learning can be approached in just the same way as helping a child to get a kite off the ground; you can be a partner in learning rather than a teacher. Children will also learn an amazing amount on their own, and you'll recognize this more and more throughout your homeschooling years. If you provide trips into the wider world, a good play environment, good conversation, construction toys, books, tools, craft supplies, dolls, and models, their growth and learning will flourish.

Parents' worries behind the issue of "lessons" are usually around the question of discipline, or whatever might need to be mastered for college entrance exams, and academic success toward a career. This is where you might want to seriously reexamine the nature of learning. A child can labor for years over those things from an early age, or he can wait until much later, and get through them pretty quickly. If he's had a healthy childhood, with plenty of time for growth and exploration, his enthusiasm and imagination will be ready for meeting the challenge of more formal study in later years—if he decides to choose that path.

Wonderful materials are available for facilitating self-directed learning, but you'll be surprised with the great amount of tangential learning kids' special interests will stimulate. Any number of little boys I know of, for instance, have been motivated to teach themselves to read by deciphering their video game strategy guides! Parents often worry about how they can teach something they don't know about or don't remember; but parents tend to underestimate the ability of kids to learn on their own, or better yet, alongside their parents.

When should you begin formal lessons? Ideally, you never will. You'll be too busy growing, learning, and enjoying life together.

PAT MONTGOMERY ◆ The human brain grows and develops in spurts. It lays out networks of axons and dendrites over which a network can be etched. For maximal growth, the child is compelled by her brain to do certain tasks over and over until the network can operate with no (or minimal) conscious thought. Grasping a rattle, pulling open a drawer, tossing a ball, assembling a balsam model, and so on, are all dictates of the brain in its quest for maturity.

Play and motion are the natural brain-developing activities of the young child. They ought not to be interrupted by lessons that an adult thinks might be more appropriate. (It helps to bear in mind that no adult had a hand in designing this magnificent

> **Children will also learn an amazing amount on their own, and you'll recognize this more and more throughout your homeschooling years. If you provide trips into the wider world, a good play environment, good conversation, construction toys, books, tools, craft supplies, dolls, and models, their growth and learning will flourish.**

creation, the human brain. Any one of us, however, can interfere with its growth and development if we are careless or ignorant.)

The child who has opportunities to explore in a safe environment (home) is learning all the time. By the time a child is twelve years old, she is ready for more formalized learning. By this time that child has a brain that has, in fact, grown to the point where all of the necessary networks are in full working order and are ready for outside direction and guidance. It is as though, having been free to explore—to play—the child possesses within herself a view of the world that makes sense to her.

At Clonlara, teachers and parents and students expect more of a formalized approach to learning. My own eldest child attended Clonlara School until she was twelve years old. In those days (mid-1970s) we did not serve high school-aged students. She played with dolls and in the sandbox and with checkers and chess and board games and letter puzzles and number games . . . you name it.

She entered public school for the first time in sixth grade. On the second day of school, she came home with her assigned textbooks, an impressively

> **It helps to bear in mind that no adult had a hand in designing this magnificent creation, the human brain. Any one of us, however, can interfere with its growth and development if we are careless or ignorant.**

heavy assortment of them. "Look, Mom," she glowed, "they gave me all of these, and if I complete them they'll give me more."

Her teachers expressed delight and surprise at how eager she was to work and how interested she was in what was presented in the classes. They often wished that the other students were as involved in learning as she. I submit that she would have been as burned out and turned off as the other students had her play been continually interrupted during those developing years Maria Montessori called play "the work of a child." I am always grateful there is a place like Clonlara where children are free to play and develop their minds and souls without coercion and interference from well-intentioned adults.

42

How do I schedule and organize our days?

JANIE LEVINE HELLYER ◆ Homeschool families can organize their days any way that meets the needs of their family. It's important to keep in mind that we are families, not institutions, and free to create what works best for the individuals in our home. We can start out with an idea of what it takes to keep our home running smoothly. Things like shopping, cooking, laundry, and housework must be done. Each of these activities are opportunities for working and learning together.

Homeschool families tend to be busy and active people. Something that is often overlooked is the need of the parent at home and her (or his!) needs and interests. While it is true that our children are only young once, and that as they grow and become independent there will be more time for us to pursue our own interests, it is also very important for parents to be active in things they enjoy. As we go about pursuing an interest, finding answers to problems, information and resources, our children are watching and learning how to do these things themselves. For this reason, it's important for us to make time for the interests of parents, too.

As for a "learning schedule," you know your children best. Some children get up in the morning and want to dive right into their projects immediately, while others do better later on in the day. Don't attempt to duplicate what goes on in traditional classrooms, for this defeats the real advantages of homeschooling! If your child is busy working on a science project, there is just no need (and no sense) in interrupting her at 2 P.M. so she can work on English literature. Over

time, your youngster will learn everything she needs to, and will most likely learn it "better" than had she been taught in a more traditional way.

Possibly the greatest advantage of homeschooling is that our families can find a balance in life. Members of the family can pursue their interests and learn in their own way, come to know what it takes to run a home and family, what work is, and become active participants in our communities. That balance of learning, real work, and community creates an environment in which young people thrive and grow into caring and concerned adults, capable of meeting each new challenge as it comes along in life. Finding that balance is different for every family, so take the time to create what will work best for yours.

43

Do I need to use textbooks?

JOHN TAYLOR GATTO ◆ You need to use *texts,* and the best ones available, because they are the cheapest, most reliable way your children can come to grips with the whole range of human intellect, and how different minds see the world, develop their arguments, and reach their conclusions. Notice I've said nothing about the content, the "facts," these classic texts will contain. With that you are welcome to make any use that suits you for it is much less important.

Textbooks, on the other hand, have been for at least a half-century, and probably longer, creations of publishers or ambitious academics written not for children, but to please textbook adoption committees. The standard followed is almost always what the states of California and/or Texas will tolerate because those jurisdictions bulk-buy for the entire state centrally; hence adoption by either of these assures the financial success of the book. In order to be acceptable, numerous concessions to the preferences of politically powerful groups of many persuasions must be made; hence not only is the information suspect (a Scott-Foresman "history" book in 1991 announced that the atomic bomb had been dropped on Korea), but it has *always* been politically doctored to reflect prejudices thought/known to exist in the textbook adoption committees. Hence you may read an expensive textbook allegedly written by a Pulitzer Prize–winning historian upside down and inside out, and in the section on Western contact with Japan in the 1850s, you will be unable to detect the interesting fact that Tokyo harbor was forced open by American gunboats. Similarly, in the references to Tibet, there will predictably be no hint that a "punitive expedition" under British General Younghusband forced open the sacred city of Lhasa, which had declined to accept intercourse with the West. Or that the international drug trade was created and militantly policed by the British government for at least a century and a quarter—and it fought two wars to protect its monopoly.

> **Textbooks, on the other hand, have been for at least a half-century, and probably longer, creations of publishers or ambitious academics written not for children, but to please textbook adoption committees.**

It is not only history that is inevitably politicized in textbooks, but math, science (especially science), literature—you name it. I said "inevitably" because I mean just that. Far too much is at stake in arranging the strength and contents of young minds to allow that to occur uncontrolled.

The answer is easy and inexpensive. The core of your text material should be primary materials, not secondary ones, and especially not books written by committees for committees. The only utility in reading those, not an insignificant one by any means, is to illustrate their deficiencies. By turning first to the index rather than the table of contents, then doing a graph by number of text lines devoted to each major and minor topic occupying more than a brief space in the textbook, you will—and your children will—be able to penetrate the code sufficiently to recognize what the book is actually selling. If rockets and space travel, for instance, occupy 180 column inches in a history of modern times, and the economic engine of capitalism only six, even a thirteen-year-old will have no difficulty understanding how his mind is being regarded once the discrepancy is pointed out to him.

CINDY WADE ◆ My answer is an unequivocal *no*. I have always found textbooks dry and void of any real learning value. Textbooks tend to make a subject choppy and uninteresting. My children find them dull and cumbersome. They prefer workbooks for the simple reason they can write in them without recopying the information or questions.

Additionally, modern textbooks have become so politically correct and void of any values we find them offensive. Use your money instead for CDs for the computer or buy a good set of encyclopedias.

Although I consider workbooks to be more valuable than textbooks, these, too, are subject to misuse. The younger the child, the less inclined they are to need or want workbooks. Before a child can read well enough to understand the directions, he's better off with quality educational manipulatives (a fancy word for toys). Workbooks imposed too early will only frustrate your child.

If you know your child is capable of doing workbooks but balks at the idea of sitting down with mom or dad to work on them, you can try what I did. When my daughter was six or seven years old, she was a very good reader. I knew she was capable of reading the instructions and completing the written work in these workbooks. When we tried to sit her down and "instruct" her, though, we would all be in tears before the session was over.

I learned to purchase several workbooks and leave them scattered about the house in conspicuous places. After a week or so, the workbooks didn't seem to budge; but when I picked them up and looked inside, they were completed with little or no mistakes! Without the need to "perform" or "be schooled," the pressure was off.

Today, my daughter is eleven. We still purchase workbooks but she helps select them, and they disappear into her room where she does them at her leisure still. And there are still few, if any, mistakes.

Our six-year-old son, on the other hand, doesn't yet read but loves to sit down with workbooks. He likes the interaction with the person reading the instructions more than he enjoys the actual work. In the meantime he fills his hours with manipulatives, such as Legos (with gears—he can make cars with front and back wheel suspensions), calculators, computers, and lots of picture books and children's magazines. He may never use a textbook until he takes a college course someday.

44

Where do I begin to find the resources and materials I need?

JEAN REED ◆ You're going to look at the world with new eyes, starting with yourself. You know much more than you think you do. You've learned where to find information if you don't know about something. That's one of the most important gifts you can give your child. You've been teaching or showing your children by example how you live and learn in this world since they were born. You started the minute you first smiled and talked to your baby. Family unity and good values aren't taught so much as shown by example. Some things you can't buy.

Very young children use their immediate surroundings to explore and learn. You can start the same way. Your own house is full of resources! Your best tool is yourself: your love, playfulness, laughter, and encouragement.

Older children will need books and materials that are harder to find. Successful homeschooling isn't so much a matter of how much you spend, as how creatively you use what you have. Ac-

cording to several surveys, the average spent per homeschooled child is $500. I'm sure we never spent that much. Mary Potter Kenyon's *Home Schooling from Scratch* has lots of good ideas. Use your library card (don't forget to check for library discards), yard sales, cheap workbooks, and occasionally good reading books at Wal-Mart.

It's amazing how much paper you'll use. Check your local newspaper office and print shop for rolls of newsprint and odds and ends left over from printing jobs. If you're part of a support group, make a list of books you'd like to borrow or lend, organize a book sale, or create a group resource library.

Look for homeschooling magazines and books that review other books and products, preferably by an author you know and trust. Donn did the very first of the homeschool catalogs years ago because we learned by trial and some expensive errors that all that is hyped as educational ain't necessarily so. As a reviewer and supplier for homeschoolers, I'm getting mounting pressure from big businesses and publishers to recommend their products. They know there are over a million homeschoolers. They want your money. They'll try to sell anything they can with big, glossy, impressive looking ads. Some homeschool publications will take any ad because advertising pays the bills. Don't discount all paid ads. Some of the books and products are excellent. Use your discretion. You'll make some mistakes; who doesn't?

Resources: Ask homeschoolers who share your learning philosophy what they like. I recommend (and admit prejudice) *The Home School Source Book*, because it covers learning resources from pregnancy through to adulthood, and liberal arts subject matter, including other homeschooling resources: everything is reviewed, satisfaction guaranteed. Second is *Home Education Magazine* because you'll find resources and how-to articles from many different points of view. Back issues of *Growing Without Schooling* magazine are extremely valuable. Even if you are not an unschooler, you will find valuable ideas. Becky Rupp's *Good Stuff* is also excellent. For Christian-based resources, I like Ted Wade's *Home School Manual*.

Becky Rupp ◆ Educational resources are a challenge these days simply because there are so many of them—and so many different opinions about their relative appeal, usefulness, and worth. Choosing resources for a homeschool program is always tricky. No matter how well you know your children, occasionally you make a choice that leaves them cold. A project, program, or book series that fascinated one child (a success, you've decided triumphantly) will bore another to tears. Homeschooling, in our hands, has always been a process of trial and error. The errors, for me, have always been a

bit of a mental struggle—that math text cost $40, I mutter to myself, watching the youngsters squirm miserably at the very sight of it. But sometimes a flop is a flop, and the only solution is to drop the thing and try something else. If the children aren't interested, they're not going to learn—or at least they're not going to learn very much or very well.

For resource-hunting parents, there are a wealth of educational supply companies and catalogs: most are reviewed in Rebecca Rupp's *Home Learning Source Book*.

Our prime information resources—for tackling such questions as "Where's Timbuktu?" "Who was Grandma Moses?" and "What do penguins eat?"—are our personal library, an ever-mushrooming collection (our kids have learned to build bookcases), the public library, and the Internet. The Internet, with its phenomenal store of information, conversation, and educational activities, is an invaluable resource for homeschool programs. One child or another around here is always logged on, searching for Civil War timelines, physics tutorials, software reviews, virtual museum tours, or foreign-language dictionaries. A good starting point, incidentally, for young Internet browsers, is the American Library Association web site (http://www.ala.org), which includes a list of over 700 excellent sites for children, categorized by academic subject.

Our children's education over the past years has involved a lot of varied resources: games, science kits, building sets, carpentry tools, popular books, textbooks, reference works, art and music supplies. We've invested in a microscope and three violins, a lot of laboratory glassware, assorted math textbooks and an excellent American history series, several educational video series, computer software, cross-country skis, and hockey skates.

Many of our most successful educational resources, however, have been simple and homemade. The boys' favorite math game for years was a family-designed buying-and-selling game which consisted of a pack of index cards, each with a picture of some desirable object—a robot, a pony, a rocket ship, the state of Colorado, the Great Pyramid of Giza, the Hope Diamond—and a (wholly imaginary) price. The kids started the game with a standard amount of money, and—in turn—bought, sold, traded, and made change, attempting to acquire their favorites.

You could get the Hope Diamond, as I recall, for a cool $1.75.

Their favorite geography game consisted of a National Geographic world map tacked to a bedroom wall, with accompanying pack of index cards, each with a geography question or challenge: "Find the country that Paddington Bear came from." "Where would you find kangaroos?" "Where did Charles Lindbergh land after his famous solo flight across the Atlantic Ocean?"

I suppose, looking back, if I had to name one resource that I found absolutely essential to our homeschool program, it would have to be index cards.

Or maybe not.

Some of our best learning experiences—the ones I truly cherish—used nothing at all. These were the times when we sat on the rug in front of the woodstove or sprawled on the back porch and simply talked—conversations that ranged from astronomy to Chinese philosophy to current events to cows, that covered books we'd read and places we'd like to visit, ideas and inventions, and just plain curiosity: "What's the difference between a hurricane and a tornado?" "Which do you like better, Beethoven or Bach?" "Do you think President Truman was right to drop the atom bomb?" "How do you engineer a gene?"

Our single most important resource is the one I never seem to have enough of.

Time.

45

Do I need to keep records? If so, how?

DEB SHELL ♦ Even though I didn't do it initially for the sake of complying with school or state requirements, keeping records of my daughters' work (the tangible stuff anyway), has served a good purpose. When they were young, I always treasured their little scribbles and hieroglyphic writing as well as early drawings, just as I had treasured their first spoken words and sentences. These were the tangible evidences of their current thinking; these attempts at communication and individual expression represented a process of learning about the world and themselves in it. So I've always saved stuff—at the beginning of each calendar year I would make a new folder with each girl's name on it. Whatever they produced (after it came off the designated "artist's" wall or the refrigerator) eventually went into their folder. This turned out to be a great record of each child's progress. What I am compelled to remind people, especially those who want a tangible record representing every designated area of study, is that just one drawing, or poem, or design, represents a holistic understanding and becomes a point of reference from which to appreciate future development.

Deb Shell

When end-of-the-year assessments approached, I chose the certified teacher option (we live in Vermont, where there are several measurement options available to homeschoolers). The folder of collected works provided evidence of development. Proof of progress is the purpose of any assessment method used.

Personally, the benefit of saving stuff or keeping records of their work included helping me to appreciate how our children progressed. As drawings became more detailed and representative, so letters became articulated; developing handwriting reflected individual styles, as did designs, stories, and poems. Themes became evident as areas of interest appeared. When she was five, our eldest daughter began taking photographs of projects she and her sisters created, which I see in retrospect as another way of recording the less sustaining yet equally important developmental events that occurred so frequently in our house full of active children.

When my daughters became teenagers, I created divided folders headed with departmental categories that roughly followed the expected areas of study represented on a high school transcript. For example, the learning components of an experiential activity such as raising a purebred Shih Tzu puppy to adulthood, selecting a sire, breeding, preparing for whelping, and caring for the litter, may be broken down into several areas of study: science (developmental canine physiology); math (accounting); geography (breed discovery, ancient Tibet and Chinese Empire); literature (James Herriot's *All Creatures Great and Small* series). Helping my daughters to examine the learning components entailed in a seemingly general activity not only helped them to develop transcripts that related specifically to things they really knew about, but also helped them to see how our unstructured homeschooling really did fulfill state high school requirements.

Rather than viewing record keeping as a negative requirement, we used it to our advantage. The difference is that our record keeping simply chronicled progress; it was never intended to influence the course of study or exploration by looking for deficits. We assumed that by the time our children were about graduation age, they would have covered the areas of study that adults consider important for adequate functioning. The big secret is that when left to follow their interests, children really do a fantastic job of this.

> **Helping my daughters to examine the learning components entailed in a seemingly general activity not only helped them to develop transcripts that related specifically to things they really knew about, but also helped them to see how our unstructured homeschooling really did fulfill state high school requirements.**

46
Do I need to buy a computer? More important, do I need to know how to use the computer?

REBECCA KOCHENDERFER ◆ When television first came into use, it was hailed as a great educational tool. Now the computer (and especially the Internet) is considered to be an educational must. Although I use the computer for my work and am very comfortable using the Internet, I have concerns that computers, like television, may not be all that great for my young children.

Before you buy a computer, you may want to consider the following:

- What will your child not be doing when he's using the computer? Will he sit in front of the computer instead of riding his bike? Will he draw pictures on a computer screen instead of using chalk outside in the fresh air? Will your children really be learning from their computer, or will it just become another electronic babysitter?

- Jane Healy (author of *Endangered Minds*), Thomas Armstrong (author of *Awakening Your Child's Natural Genius*), and Joseph Chilton Pearce (author of *Magical Child* and *Evolution's End*) all warn that computers are not good for young children. These authors believe that young children should learn about their world through their physical senses and that they should be interacting with people, not machines.

- Most child-development researchers believe that children are not developmentally ready for computers until they are about fifteen years old. After that age, these same people believe the computer to be a great asset to a child's education.
- The Internet can be a great tool, but it also has certain safety considerations. When your child watches television, it's easy for you to see and hear what's going on. Computers, because they are one-on-one, are much harder to monitor and you will have an easier time keeping your child safe if you know how to use the Internet, too.

So, do you *need* to buy a computer? If your children are young, you may be better off without one. But then you'd miss out on this great tool for yourself. I must admit that I have not come up with a great computer plan for our family. Television was easy. We simply moved it to the garage, where it's available if we *really* want to watch something. I can't keep the computer out of sight, however, because I use it every day for my work. And since my children see me using the computer so often they naturally want to use it, too. Until I come up with a better plan, I'm just going to keep reminding myself that the computer is a tool and should be used not so much for entertainment, but to achieve a purpose.

CHRIS CARDIFF ◆ Families were homeschooling long before today's personal computer revolution arrived. You and your family can homeschool perfectly well without one. From the 3 R's to history, science, and shop, there is no subject that requires a computer (with the possible exception of computer science). There are no educational materials available on computers that aren't also available through other media.

Having said that, I believe a computer can be a fabulous addition to your family's educational resources. Just as businesses large and small invest gazillions of dollars in computers every year because computers make jobs easier and faster to do, the same can be true in homeschooling—a computer can enhance a learning experience, make learning easier and faster with new tools, and allow access to enormous informational resources not easily available by other means.

Guiding your child through this informational maze is easier if you understand it yourself. However, one of the more joyful aspects of homeschooling is learning together with your children. And remember, this is how most families have done it. We are the generation that lived through the personal computer revolution and had to homeschool ourselves in their use because they didn't

---

ANN ZEISE'S TOP WEB PICKS

Beginners

AAA Math
http://www.aaamath.com
Explanations, games, and math practice.

Alice's Adventures in Wonderland & Other Stories
http://megabrands.com/alice
A dynamic eBook: the illustrations move and talk with a click of the mouse.

Exploratorium Science Snacks
http://www.exploratorium.edu/snacks/snackintro.html
Miniature versions of a popular museum s exhibits.

Funschool.com
http://www.funschool.com
Preschool through 6th grade arcade games, puzzles, and fun things to do.

GusTown
http://gustown.com
Fun, games, art, stories a clubhouse for kids.

Hatshepsut's Revenge
http://edweb.sdsu.edu/courses/edtec670/egypt/start.html
An adventure game that takes you back to Ancient Egypt.

NASA Kids
http://kids.msfc.nasa.gov/
Games and activities for learning about the earth, outer space, and rocketry.

Planet Tolerance
http://www.tolerance.org/pt/index.html

Read, play and explore, even add to an online mural of "One World" art.

Rubbish World
http://www.BruceCGull.com/game.htm

The people of Rubbish World are being held captive by the evil Rubbish Warlord, Hsart.

Wild 'N Wacky Inventions
http://www.nationalgeographic.com/features/96/inventions/images
  /games/main.html

Help Professor Lou Knee from the National Geographic build some wild inventions.

Advanced

American Red Cross Youth Services
http://www.redcross.org/services/youth/

Things kids and teens can do to help in an emergency.

Bartleby.com: Great Books Online
http://www.bartleby.com/strunk/

Classic literature, verse, and reference books online.

General Chemistry Online
http://antoine.frostburg.edu/chem/senese/101/index.shtml

For self-motivated teens, this is a free complete chemistry course right on the Web.

Microscopy Primer
http://micro.magnet.fsu.edu/primer/index.html

Java and Flash tutorials on using microscopes.

(continues)

Nutrition on the Web For Teens
http://library.thinkquest.org/10991/
Informative and interactive site. More fun than the name indicates.

Paradigm Online Writing Assistant
http://www.powa.org/
An interactive, menu-driven, online writer s guide and handbook.

Perry-Castañeda Library Map Collection
http://www.lib.utexas.edu/maps/index.html
Features very contemporary maps of places in the news, as well as a huge collection of detailed maps from around the world.

Professor Freedman's Math Help
http://www.mathpower.com/
Information about basic math and algebra. Specifically addresses the needs of the older student with math anxiety.

Project Citizen Student Forms
http://www.civiced.org/projcit_formenu.html
A set of seven forms to guide you through a project to solve any problem you may want to work on to improve your community.

The Rosetta Stone Online
http://www.rosettastone.com/HOME/aboutdemo.html
Free trial lessons in several foreign languages.

---

have computers back when we went to school.

Learning about computers, the different software programs, the online universe—all of this is an amazing learning opportunity for you to share with your child. Here are just a few samples of what you may encounter:

- Reading: "Living Books" not only tell a story but also allow a child to interact with elements of the story on the screen. Many programs teach reading through a phonetic approach. The Internet's Online Books project contains the complete texts of hundreds of classic books whose copyright has expired—Twain, Shakespeare, Kipling are all online for reading, searching, printing.

- 'Riting: Once you've used word processing software, it's unlikely you'll ever return to a typewriter or handwriting. Basic word processing today allows onscreen editing, spell checking, grammar checking, and control of what your text looks like. More advanced software created the phenomenon of desktop publishing.
- 'Rithmetic: "Edutainment" programs drill kids in basic math operations through games where success is based on correctly answering math questions. More sophisticated programs focus on real problem-solving skills. These programs seek to engage the children without boring them and provide analysis of their progress to the parent.
- Research: An entire shelf of encyclopedias is now contained on a CD-ROM disk that includes words, pictures, sound, and video. An Internet search can turn up a multitude of Web sites with information and references on a particular subject. Thousands of subject-specific Internet

newsgroups provide discussion forums for people around the world.
- Geography/History: More fertile fields for edutainment software. You can travel the Oregon Trail yourself with one program, or chase an international thief all over the world with another.

ANN ZEISE ◆ About eight years ago while giving a talk on online services for homeschooling, I said, "No, you can do just fine without a computer and online connection." Now I think you'd be doing yourself and your children a big disservice if you aren't "wired."

You certainly could live a more "natural" life if you did without the technical innovations in this new millennium, but why? The cost of the average home computer is now about $600. You can get a dedicated e-mail and net computer for about $100.

The connection with other homeschoolers, to validate what we're trying to do, to get ideas on educating in a different way than the school model, is through the 'Net, on your computer, in your home! I enjoy seeing my local homeschooling friends once or twice a week at organized activities, but I also enjoy meeting my homeschooling friends around the globe on the 'Net.

In theory, your computer and software could represent the majority of your curriculum expense. There are so many free and low-cost "lessons" online, all done in multimedia interactive format, that you'll find your kids giggling while they investigate an Egyptian tomb or plan a space mission. Libraries loan software. Our county office here in California allows homeschoolers (and others filing R4s) to borrow software from their curriculum library.

Can computers waste your time? Sure, but I can think of worse ways to do that. My husband wishes I'd spend less time writing, but the computer has freed me from tedious handwriting or typing and given me a readership. The only way my son will write is by keyboarding his thoughts into the computer. The computer has given us a medium to keep our minds sharp and an audience to view what we write or create. As homeschoolers often lack an audience for their writing or art, an online forum or art gallery can be great motivation to keep sharp.

A home computer can be a source of additional income for a hard-strapped homeschool family. Read the manual for just about any application, practice it, and soon you'll be an "expert" in creating documents in that medium—an expert others will be willing to pay.

Home networks can be problematic and thus provide handy scientific experimentation as everyone in the family gets involved trying to figure out if the problem is hardware- or software-related. (Those with Windows machines get a little more practice than Mac users, but they claim to like it that way.)

So, yes, let a computer or two into your life. It will bring the homeschool support community right into your den, give you a creative outlet, and maybe provide some extra income.

LORETTA HEUER ◆ Let me answer the second part of this question first by sharing a story with you. Gr'ma, my dad's mom, who lived across the street from us, refused to own a telephone. However, when she needed to call Aunt Lena, or the doctor, or the seed catalog company, she'd appear in our living room asking us to put through her call.

I learned from watching Gr'ma that if you're not comfortable and conversant with current technology, you lack the ability to connect—literally!—with the rest of the world unless you have an intermediary. Homeschooling is about empowerment; learn to use today's technology.

A second reason to buy (and buy into) technology is support. In 1990 when my son Tad was thirteen, homeschooling felt discouraging. Actually, we were just experiencing typical adolescent issues (homeschoolers are not exempt from them), but I had no other homeschooling parent of a teen nearby to lend support. Cafi Cohen, author of *And What About College,* who had a son a year or two older than Tad, became my confidante. Although she was 2,000 miles away, she was as near as my computer if I needed to talk things through via e-mail.

Homeschooling parents need connections with others who share similar issues. Whether you have a child with ADHD behavior, a late reader, a hormonal teen, a college applicant, there are homeschooling parents in cyberspace who have dealt with these issues; who will validate your concerns; and who will help you to see options, alternatives, and new ways of responding. Used this way, technology breaks down the isolation we sometimes feel.

Homeschoolers need accurate up-to-date information regarding their state laws, local regulations, college admissions policies, and so on. Often the most efficient way to acquire this information is through online resources.

Finally, computers permit kids to learn some things more easily. Homeschoolers do not need to use commercial "educational software," which is often of the "drill and kill" variety. Here are a few alternatives:

- Homeschoolers can use "real" software—Microsoft Office Products, Quicken, PhotoShop—to do real-life tasks. They don't need to use dumbed-down, simulated programs to do artificial projects.
- Homeschoolers can research and *construct* their own curricula using the Internet. They don't need someone to

"bundle" a package of Web sites about T. S. Eliot for them. They can do it themselves!
- Homeschoolers who are visual learners or non-linear thinkers will find Web-based learning especially appropriate.

While all these things can be done with computers at the local library, I have found that having major homeschool resources—including a computer—here in the house makes learning easier, more natural, more accessible. Watch for sales, then buy yourself a computer.

47

Do I have to stay at home all day with my children?

SANDRA DODD ◆ At home? Why? There are stores, museums, libraries, theaters, parks, rivers, mountains, beaches, friends' houses, historical sites, factories, construction sites, churches, caves, animal shelters, art galleries, fish hatcheries, foundries, and blacksmiths and . . .

What was the question?

KATHARINE HOUK ◆ Very few homeschooling parents, in my experience, stay at home all day every day with their children. In any town there are opportunities for children to do things on their own—story hour at the library, music and dance classes, Scouts and 4-H, field trips with other homeschoolers—and you have a life of your own, as well! In my own case, the children went with me to work at the food co-op, to lay out and print newsletters in a friend's office, to spend the day in their dad's office, to meetings in the Capitol to lobby for improved home education regulations, to visit friends . . . the list goes on and on.

To find out what's happening locally, check the bulletin boards at your public library, community center, or church, and read your local paper. Homeschooling support groups can provide a place for social contact outside the home by organizing a wide range of activities for both parents and children. One group in western New York sponsors an annual family camping trip—in winter. They have lively and chilling stories to tell upon their return!

An important gathering place in my small town has been the learning center I founded with friends six years ago. It grew out of the needs of families in our local support group, and it provides a place for classes, workshops, and activities two days a week for homeschooled children. The parents themselves and people from the community and surrounding area offer their skills, and classes have included astronomy, singing groups, art and craft projects, American Sign Language, French, math, first-aid, history, drama, career exploration, auto maintenance, and more.

The center also organizes field trips, group excursions to plays and museums, and trips to interesting businesses and workplaces. As a parent cooperative, it provides a place for parents as well as children to socialize and learn. The number of families involved has ranged over the years from four or five to about thirty, which is pretty impressive, considering that only 3,000 people live in the town itself. Twice a year, in December and May, children bring their projects, sing their songs, and perform their plays for Display Day. The bonds formed by all involved with this community space are marvelous to behold, and have grown and deepened over the years.

It may take some extra effort on your part to find the community resources available to your family, or to determine whether you have the time and energy to invest in a support group or learning center, but the possibilities are there. Home education need not be an isolating experience. I do wish to add, however, that being at home isn't such a terrible thing, and that engaging in too many outside activities can become burdensome and stressful. Sometimes slowing down and spending some time at home with our families feels just right and is the best thing to do.

LILLIAN JONES ◆ The homeschoolers I know relish those days when they can stay home together. There are always so many other things calling—classes, support group events, shopping, errands, and the lure of interesting field trips.

We also love to be out in the world, and homeschooling allows us more freedom to do that. We jokingly refer to some of our travels by name: American History 101, for instance, was a trip to historical sites along the East Coast. Our school friends think we're being outrageously irreverent, but I think we're actually learning more from these trips than we could from books. Notice I said "we." We learn together.

We were at the Museum of Natural History in town yesterday, gawking and talking as we went—learning and enjoying ourselves enormously. We were surrounded by school kids with worksheets they were dutifully filling in. They weren't enjoying the displays so much as going through prescribed motions and bouncing off of one another. I asked my son if he ever missed that aspect of school, the crowds of kids working together on projects and all. He looked at me quizzically, and then exploded into laughter at the idea.

Early in the game I learned not to make field trips into "lessons." Years ago, when visiting a museum, I kept calling my son's attention to this display or that,

reading him the display cards, and generally making a pest of myself to nudge him to "learn" something. After all, that was what we were supposed to be doing, wasn't it? Homeschooling? Suddenly, a guide with a stern, booming voice said, "Hey, *you!* You look bored! Come with me!" We followed him upstairs. There he dressed my son in an old soldier's uniform and took him behind a roped-off area, where he got to try out the soldiers' beds and poke around in their old tools, ammunition, and personal belongings. My husband and I got the guide to share fascinating historical stories we would never have heard otherwise. Our son got to follow his own imagination, and we all enjoyed a veritable feast of food for thought by following ours at the same time.

We often stop crowds in museums or historical sites by talking to guides about their area of expertise—their passion. These people are treasures of knowledge. One of our favorite finds was on the sidewalk in town near home. We saw a man coming up out of a manhole. A manhole! What an opportunity! We asked him what was down there, and he was delighted. He had marvelous things to tell us, *and* he let my son climb down to look around. Learning is everywhere, and the world quite literally is our classroom.

We do need ways of getting off to exercise or do things alone once in a while. That gets to be easier with time, but you really need to get creative about meeting your own needs, whatever they are. No situation is perfect, but home-schooling is by far the most natural and easy way for a family to live.

48

I hated (fill in a subject) in school. How can I possibly teach this subject to my child?

WILL SHAW ◆ I hated math. My worst subject. I routinely fell behind and re-ceived poor grades. I now know that, with math, before you move to chapter 4, you'd better have a good handle on chapter 3.

Regarding math or any subject, homeschooling can allow your child to learn more thoroughly and to move ahead with more security. In school the class would move on when I wasn't ready, when I didn't get it yet. I'd be lost in no time, and I never recovered. But in home education, you can spend as much time as needed to master the subject. You move ahead or stay put. Make sure your child doesn't experience what you did.

You can actually learn some things, and you can teach what you do know, and you can help your child to learn even when you don't fully understand it your-self. I'm not saying it's a breeze, but it's not at all impossible. The math texts, workbooks, videos, and other materials available to homeschoolers are fantastic, so much better than what I ever had in school.

There are sometimes other home-school parents with whom to share teaching cooperatively, each handling his or her favorites. If you want, you could look for a correspondence school that will take your math questions. Since you're not cooped up in school all day, the opportunities to apply math are greater and learning is reinforced. We called a publisher when we thought there was a mistake in a textbook. (There was.) One of my children once called a local college to see if the profes-sor would explain something. (He did.)

You don't have to be a professional, and you don't have to personally know and personally teach every aspect of every subject. If that were true, then only the teacher-trained chemist could teach chemistry, only the teacher-trained his-torian teach history. The public educa-tion industry would have us believe this is what happens but it's simply not true.

We've found that once our children have a firm foundation, they can go ahead on their own. You can help them learn to self-teach. Our two oldest, now in college, went way beyond their par-ents in math, way beyond what we ever knew or could (or can) do in what seems such a daunting subject. Our third child is doing it now, and our last one will, too

Our oldest will graduate from Virginia Tech next semester with a BS in math. Go figure.

DORIS HOHENSEE ◆ My major concern was not to destroy my children's interest in learning. Any subject can be ruined if it's forced on a child before he's ready or interested.

When I attended school, I developed many strong dislikes for certain subjects. Later, I discovered that each of these subjects was truly fascinating when approached in a different manner.

The subjects weren't the problem. Coercion was. It can kill curiosity dead in its tracks. I had to find a reason to want to learn these subjects before any genuine learning could take place. But this is hardly a recent discovery.

"Bodily exercise, when compulsory, does no harm to the body; but knowledge which is acquired under compulsion obtains no hold on the mind." Plato, circa 400 B.C.

MARY MCCARTHY ◆ By not teaching. You can talk, and preach, and scream, and beg, and plead until you are blue in the face; but if you don't let your child discover her own ways and interests, she is not going to learn.

Homeschooling isn't about teaching—it's about learning. Instill in your child the love of *learning* and you won't have to worry about the teaching.

Spending three hours doing a single page of division problems does not teach math—it teaches "I hate math." Remember?

49

Can others help me educate my child?

DONN AND JEAN REED ◆ Give me one good reason why we should restrict our kids to just one teacher. Would you limit yourself? Maybe for a year; maybe for very specialized study, but not for an extended period of time, especially if you are studying many subjects.

If you're thinking about finding others to help your child learn, you'll be amazed at the number of people with something to share. One of the really great things about having your kids learn with other people is that you'll be surprised by the contributions others will make that go beyond what you expected.

We always wanted our kids to learn more than just facts. We wanted them to find their own persona, what values were important for living in peace with themselves and others; to aim high; to reach for their dreams. Learning facts and figures is important, but doesn't necessarily make for happier people or better living. You and your spouse will impart through words and example what you believe. It's not likely that your kids will grow up to be imitations of you. Working and learning with others will give them the opportunity to view other lifestyles, values, skills, and points of view that will become grist for their minds.

We all need friends. Working and playing with others is the way we all live. There are lots of ways you can involve others with your kids. You may choose to find someone to tutor in a subject you feel you can't teach adequately or find someone who shares your child's interests to act as a friend or mentor.

Children enjoy being with other children. Take advantage of your support group. You can take turns teaching different subjects or go on field trips together. Reading and discussing a variety of books is a great way to share thoughts, explore new ideas, and learn from others. If you don't have a support group, start one, or just take field trips and do things with other families even if their kids are in school. If you live in an isolated area, you will have to work harder to find others to work with your children; but determination can accomplish a great deal.

You can help older children find a part-time job. Getting paid in cash is nice, but working in exchange for learning a skill can work just as well and lead eventually to a paycheck. One of our daughters volunteered in the local library a couple days a week, then was offered a full-time summer position. Her experience led to an excellent job when she left home. Explore hundreds of possibilities through some of the Peterson Guides (*Learning Adventures, Internships, Summer Jobs for Students, Summer Opportunities for Kids and Teenagers,* and more).

Life is an ongoing learning process not limited to age or place. Our world is full of people who know so much that we don't know! If we keep our minds open we can learn something different from each person we meet. Our children can do the same, especially if we don't narrow the definition of learning to just the standard school subjects.

SUSANNAH SHEFFER ◆ Of course. They do already, whether you're conscious of it or not. Living not just in a nuclear family but in the broader community, children surely learn from watching or helping or simply being around other people. But homeschoolers do reach out to teachers and mentors in more purposeful ways, too, forming connections that may be informal or highly organized, occasional or quite regular.

Sixteen-year-old Eva, for example, sought out a math mentor by putting up signs at a local university asking for a graduate student who could help her see math in a new light. Twelve-year-old Christian's chance to volunteer at a biologist's lab grew out of his involvement in another activity: He and his mother went to local Audubon Society meetings and happened to meet the biologist there.

And Mika's mother gave art lessons to a neighbor's children in exchange for the neighbor's helping Mika with algebra. This worked so well that Mika herself offered violin lessons to another family's son in exchange for Spanish conversation practice with the boy's mother.

Mentoring and support from adults outside the family can come through the mail, too. For several years I've served as a writing mentor to homeschoolers (roughly aged ten to eighteen, though some have been younger); they send me their work and ask for critical comments. I've formed close and rewarding connections with kids all around the country.

So, seeking out mentors, being open to opportunities, and thinking creatively about what you can offer or where you can find help—these are the kinds of things homeschoolers get good at. But I'm not that resourceful, you say? It gets easier with practice, and there are so many great examples by now that no one has to start from scratch. The main thing to realize is that parents don't need to be a homeschooler's only source of information or help. To be sure, homeschooling does quite frequently strengthen family bonds, but parents don't need to know all the answers or even be interested in everything in order to help a child learn. Parent and child don't even have to work well together in all respects. Fourteen-year-old Amanda, for example, found that she and her mother had trouble working together on math: "On some days Mom and I would work really well together, but on other days we would both accidentally irritate each other, and when you're crabby and tired it's much harder to understand a math concept." They found a family friend who was happy to help Amanda with math and, as Amanda said, her mom "was really nice about understanding that and not getting offended."

> Sixteen-year-old Eva sought out a math mentor by putting up signs at a local university asking for a graduate student who could help her see math in a new light.

The world is full of interesting people who have a lot to offer. Access to a wide range of helpful adults gives homeschoolers the opportunity to learn whatever specific skills they desire *and* to have a team of caring adults in their lives.

50

I know homeschoolers who only "work" in the morning. How can the homeschooled children possibly learn as much as the children who go to school all day?

BILLY AND NANCY GREER ◆ Most homeschoolers will tell you that their kids can accomplish more in a few hours at home than in a full day of school. What really surprised us, however, is that the board of education in most states will tell you the same thing. At one of our local support group meetings, Bill was talking to a woman who was considering homeschooling. Her son had been ill the previous year and spent most of the last semester at home. The school board assigned a pupil services worker to continue his school work at home. The school board said that six hours of this instruction at home was equivalent to full-time school attendance! (It was provided in three hour sessions two days a week.)

Bill was surprised and decided to ask members of an e-mail list about requirements in their states. The typical requirement was six to ten hours a week of in-home instruction.

Now please note that Bill was only surprised that most states would *admit* that a couple of hours a day of home instruction was equivalent to a full day in school. If you think about a typical school day, you can see how much time is wasted. There is attendance to take, time spent changing classes, time wasted in classroom management—and there is little individual attention. It's similar to going to the doctor's office. You may be there for hours even though the doctor only spends ten minutes with you!

Time is wasted in more subtle ways, too. Have you ever noticed children when they are engrossed in something new? They may spend hours on one activity before they are ready to move on to something else. A good teacher may get a classroom of kids excited about a topic, but just as they are getting warmed up—rrring! The forty-five minutes are up and it's time to change classes. Some kids may need more time to get a concept; or if they get excited about something, they may want to spend more time quickly moving ahead to other concepts. On the other hand, a child may get a concept in the first five minutes of class and the rest of the time she is bored to tears. An artificially predetermined time schedule disrupts a child's normal learning patterns.

> Most homeschoolers will tell you that their kids can accomplish more in a few hours at home than in a full day of school. What really surprised us, however, is that the board of education in most states will tell you the same thing.

SUSANNAH SHEFFER ◆ Ask a child in school how much of the six-hour day that particular child spends in active learning, exploration, or engagement. How much time is spent getting one's own questions answered or experiencing the "click" of a fuzzy concept suddenly becoming clear? If we're honest with ourselves, we don't even have to ask a child because our own memories remind us that much of the school day is spent waiting—waiting in line, waiting for the assignment to be handed out, waiting for the teacher to come help you, waiting your turn with a piece of equipment. Children in school spend more time than we'd care to admit staring out the window, either because they're not following the lesson and feel lost and confused and frightened of being called on, or because they already know what's being taught but aren't allowed to move ahead or do something else. Studies of how much time schoolchildren actually spend "on task" show that only a small portion of the school day is really spent in direct instruction. And even when a teacher is offering direct instruction, there are all sorts of reasons that it might not be reaching a particular child at a particular moment.

One indication that schools themselves recognize how little of the school day is spent "on task" is that when a school student is absent for an extended period—home with a broken leg or an illness, for example—and the school sends home a tutor to help the child keep up with the class, the tutor comes anywhere from two to seven hours a week, and that's considered enough. (See John Holt's book *Teach Your Own* for confirmation of these figures.)

Because homeschooling is so different from schooling—it's individualized and flexible in schedule, pacing, and approach—comparing how much time homeschoolers spend "doing schoolwork" with how many hours a day school students are in attendance is really comparing apples and oranges. If you hear that homeschooling families only "work" in the mornings, what you may be hearing is that the mornings are when they sit down for formal lessons, or for quiet activities like reading and writing, or simply for focused time with their parents. But this tells us nothing about what they may be doing with their afternoons and evenings: going on field trips, getting together with other homeschooling families for a vast range of academic and social activities, volunteering at an adult workplace, having a great discussion at the dinner table or at bedtime, spending time on any one of a million independent projects. Even if it doesn't look exactly like school, you can bet that a lot of learning is going on.

51

Can my child participate in sports programs if we homeschool?

ANN FISHER ◆ Sports opportunities for homeschooled students are available in several venues. When deciding which option suits your child, it helps to have a sense of what level of involvement you desire for your children.

For instance, do you want opportunities for your students to learn to play several sports, appreciate exercise, enjoy team camaraderie, and experience competition? For many students, casual exposure to sports through a support group—bowling, skating, skiing—meets that need and is organized just enough to be fun. For others, homeschooling teams, community and recreational sports, and classes at private clubs are the perfect answer.

Do you want a tougher level of competition? Homeschooled and other community clubs and teams can participate in competitive activities in many sports all the way through the national level under the auspices of The Amateur Athletic Union (AAU). AAU "is one of the largest, non-profit, volunteer, sports organizations in the United States. A multi-sport organization, the AAU is dedicated exclusively to the promotion and development of amateur sports and physical fitness programs." Most local amateur sports are connected with AAU if interclub competition is involved. To find out how to contact your regional association, contact The Amateur Athletic Union, c/o Walt Disney World Resort, PO Box 10,000, Lake Buena Vista, FL 32830-1000 or call at (407) 934-7200 or (407) 363-6170 or visit the Web site at http://www.aausports.org.

Does your gifted athlete want to play college sports, even compete for athletic scholarships? No problem! The NCAA states that it ". . . . does not have a different set of standards for homeschooled and traditionally schooled students. However, the certification process for homeschooled and traditionally schooled student-athletes is different." Eligibility information for homeschoolers is available at Membership Services Department, NCAA, PO Box 6222, Indianapolis, IN 46206-6222; (317) 917-6222; http://www.ncaa.org/cbsa /home_school.html. Parents of athletic hopefuls should read those requirements from time to time to make academic record keeping easier when the student applies for certification.

Sports participation may be available through local public school interscholastic programs in your state. Check with your local support group for this information. Be aware that school-based interscholastic sports are used by a very small percentage of all homeschooled students and are not desired by most. Access to interscholastic sports has sometimes been achieved through special interest legislation sponsored at the behest of parents of Superstar Athletes, setting a dangerous precedent for increased homeschooling regulation for all. Unfortunately, homeschooled athletes still must jump through hoops for chances at a slot on a public school team in those states, possibly creating animosity by shutting out public-schooled students.

Homeschooling sports leagues can be found in some areas. Let's hope the next wave of parents of promising home-schooled athletes throw their energy into building up homeschooling sports leagues. The numbers are there. Wouldn't you love to see homeschooled students across the country rise up in leagues of their own, competing and winning, as they do in academic competitions?

MARSHA RANSOM ◆ Assuming that you are asking about public school sports programs, this is something that needs to be determined by individual home-schoolers in their state and school district. This question is difficult to answer definitively because regulations vary so widely from state to state and are some-times enforced very differently from school district to school district within a state.

Start by asking veteran homeschool-ers in your local support groups or school district what homeschoolers' ex-perience has been working with the pub-lic schools. Some states have regulations that permit homeschooler (or non-pub-lic-school students) participation, while others have regulations that oppose par-ticipation by anyone not enrolled full time in the school. Such regulations are not always enforced or adhered to, and

pending lawsuits in several states regard-ing this issue add to the confusion. In still other states, participation on public school sports teams is regulated by a pri-vate athletic association, in which case, most participating schools will abide by their rules rather than lose their privilege to participate at their school district's class or level. *Home Education Magazine* and the National Home Education Net-work maintain bulletin boards and have informational articles on this subject that may be helpful as you research this question. Your NHEN state liaison per-son may be able to help you find contacts in your area who can help you with this question.

Many homeschoolers have found other options besides public school sports team participation that can pro-vide a competitive sports experience. Some homeschoolers have formed their own sports teams and state-wide leagues. Others get involved with community leagues or intramural sports at the public school. Participation in martial arts, tennis, downhill skiing, snowboarding, water skiing, sailing, figure skating, and swimming, among others, gives kids an opportunity to interact with others and experience competition. These same sports can also be pursued with the goal being competition with self rather than with others. By setting and meeting per-sonal goals (improving form, speed, or balance) and learning new techniques, homeschoolers can experience personal enjoyment now and may find an interest that will provide satisfaction far beyond the homeschooling years.

HELEN AND MARK HEGENER ◆ There are many options for sports programs for homeschooled children, but there are also many potential problems when they want to take advantage of public school facilities.

In the July/August 1997 issue of *Home Education Magazine,* Peggy Daly-Masternak addressed the question of school sports programs: "A handful of other homeschoolers, both here in Ohio and across the country, are pursuing their local school districts, departments of education, and legislatures, forcing statutes for the right not only to play sports, but for 'core' classes, extracurricular activities, even scholarships and diplomas. And sometimes, the results are much more than homeschoolers may have bargained for."

Peggy outlines how well-meaning proponents in several states are introducing bills that could lead to increased governmental regulation. She cautions, "Many of us are aware of the initiatives that are coming down the road to 'improve' education in our state, as well as the current requirements placed on enrolled students, both publicly and pri-

vately schooled. Proficiency tests are a big deal already in Ohio and School-To-Work is gaining momentum daily."

Peggy suggests finding alternative routes, such as community sports teams or organizations such as the Amateur Athletic Union, whose stated purpose is "Sports for All, Forever." Many homeschooling support groups organize formal and informal sports teams, ski trips, gaming tournaments, and more. Often all that's needed is someone interested enough to organize an event, and kids interested in playing the sport.

In the July/August 1989 issue of *Home Education Magazine,* Earl Gary Stevens described his group's Homeschool Family Baseball: "This is fun baseball. This is fooling around, three-mistakes-per-minute baseball. Catch the ball, miss the ball, nobody cares. There are no sign-up sheets, no try-outs. Come when you can, leave when you must. There are no practices, no extremely important games, no obligation to be on time."

Several years later, Earl describes how their game was started: "At the beginning I was feeling my way along and having to make many decisions. One parent thought the game should be more challenging for bigger kids. Another parent wanted it to be less challenging for little kids. Another felt it was too disorganized, while still another believed that any adult direction at all was too coercive. I listened to everybody and kept to my vision."

Sometimes a vision is all that's needed. A vision, and a few kids who want to play ball.

52

How do I meet the educational needs of several children of different ages at the same time?

DEB SHELL ◆ I never bought the idea that meeting the educational needs of my children meant teaching them what I (or someone else) thought they should be learning. Although I felt personally responsible for meeting the educational needs of my variously aged children, I assumed my children would inquire about and explore their interests as their needs arose, and that my role was to provide opportunities for discovery. The fact that we had four children spaced about two-and-a-half years apart never conflicted with our ability to meet their specific needs. Just as one child might have been learning to crawl backward down the stairs, another might have been learning how to unbutton and button her overall straps. My job was to foresee potential accidents and

> Sometimes a vision is all that's needed. A vision, and a few kids who want to play ball.

otherwise to stay out of their way while they were busy mastering new skills. Later on, while one might have been learning the written language of fractions or long division, another was hard at work putting together her first poetry book; my role was to guide according to the questions asked and follow the pace presented to me.

While my husband and I worked hard at facilitating opportunities for each of our children to develop their particular interests, neither of us felt compelled to specifically teach anything other than what we were asked. Our girls, like most children I know, did a very good job of asking.

So I relieved myself of the responsibility that compels most teachers; I didn't have to find the "right" curriculum, the "best" learning aids, nor did I have to be vigilant about discovering each child's so-called deficits or specific moments of readiness. When my children were ready to learn to read, they asked appropriate questions. We answered them. As adults, it's clear that the responsibility to learn rests within each of us. I don't believe children learn any differently or from any other sense of motivation. Observing young children learning reveals the pure motivational drive that compels all education.

We really do self-educate, even when we ask others to teach us.

So for me, the key to educating several children was listening to each child's requests for knowledge and providing opportunities for them to learn what they desired. We rarely had conflicts about me spending more time with one than another. Time spent with one inevitably spilled over to whoever else was also interested. Interests were contagious, too. For example, when one child read about children living in Japan and designed paper dolls fashioned in Japanese dress, she also invited her sisters to play "Japan" with her. Thus she taught them about what she'd found out. Reading books aloud also crossed many ages—the younger ones may not have gotten the same thing out of the story as the older ones, but they got something because they stayed and listened. When read again a few years later, new insights were brought to light. Because I didn't have preset goals in mind, each child was free to explore at her own discretion and sense of appropriate need. This really eliminated any responsibility on my part in terms of having to guess what each child supposedly needed. I was able to spend time with each child when she requested it, without excluding anyone else from the experience. Much like a one-room schoolhouse, a large family can reinforce each member's personal responsibility for guiding her own learning. Knowledge also moves up and down—what a younger child may become interested in and learn about may not have occurred to an older child. Respecting each person's individual sensibilities helps foster alliances between children, which thereby increases opportunities for learning and makes being part of a large family truly beneficial.

BECKY RUPP ◆ We have three sons, all of whom have always been homeschooled. Though we've had our share of problems, the joint homeschooling of children of different ages has not been one of them. For most projects—say, a study of the Civil War, an investigation of astronomy, or a pottery-making activity—the boys all learned together, each participating to the best of his abilities. They didn't necessarily do exactly the same things—the older children, for example, might read books about American Indian pottery and try making coiled pots, while the youngest made mud pies—but all shared the experience. In many cases, joint learning had an added plus: the boys helped and learned from each other. ("Look, Caleb, you roll the clay out like this and make a little snake . . .")

For basic subjects, like reading and arithmetic, the boys used different materials and got individual attention. Ethan, our middle son, who had a rocky time learning to read, had a special phonics program all his own; each boy progressed at different rates in math; and each preferred different kinds of math books and workbooks. Which means that our boys, through their elementary-level years, got a mix of (mostly) joint and (some) private homeschooling. It seemed to work fine.

Juggling the demands of children at different skill and age levels wasn't difficult; juggling the demands of children with wildly different interests was trickier. ("Let's do physics experiments this morning!" "No, ancient history!") Sometimes there simply weren't enough hours in the day to discuss English literature with Josh, work on chemistry problems and experiments with Ethan, ferry Caleb to his piano lesson, read Josh's latest creative writing project, help Ethan set up the telescope, and write an interactive workbook for Caleb ("I want one of my own") all about ancient Greece. Then, as the boys grew older still, demands on our time lessened as they became increasingly independent learners. "They don't need us anymore," I say ruefully to my husband, watching Josh buried in *The Black Arrow,* Ethan absorbed in building a robotic arm, and Caleb, on the computer, lost in the geographic adventures of Carmen Sandiego.

"That's the point," my husband says.

> **"They don't need us anymore," I say ruefully to my husband. "That's the point," my husband says.**

53
How do I ensure my children are motivated to learn at home?

SANDRA DODD ◆ It's pretty hard to ensure anything, but motivated to learn? People are born with the desire to learn. If your kids have never been to school, you won't have many problems (unless you try to play school, in which case you can create the same problems school creates). If your children *have* been to school, and there have learned what they should avoid (math, writing, and so on), now you have a job to do. You need to help make those things interesting, relevant, fun, tricky, amusing. One way to do that is to find them where you didn't think they were. Find writing at the movies. Find math at the swimming pool. Mix life up. Scramble ideas. Sprinkle your days with granulated information. Whatever you do, don't "do school" just like you think school is doing it. After all, if that works, why would you keep your children home?

School teaches that there is a minimal set of information that will guarantee a child success. That is simply untrue and unfair. There is no end to information, and rather than try to guarantee your child enough of the right information, you will do better to present him with the freedom and means to find it joyously and to want more.

We've found the best way to make information interesting is to show an interest ourselves. If I were to say, "Oh, I hate Egypt, but *you* go read that book about Egypt, and you make a model of a mummy, and just keep me out of it," what I'd really be saying is, "Egypt is stupid. You have to do something because you are a kid. Learning about Egypt is a kid-thing and when you're grown you can forget the whole thing." Interest and enthusiasm are infectious. Cynicism and derision are harmful. A positive attitude and a sharing of interest are motivational.

> **Mix life up. Scramble ideas. Sprinkle your days with granulated information. Whatever you do, don't "do school" just like you think school is doing it. After all, if that works, why would you keep your children home?**

When we first bought pattern blocks, my husband and I played with them ourselves and wouldn't let the kids mess up our patterns. We talked about the degrees of the angles and the kids overheard it, but we weren't talking to them. They were saying, "Let me try!" and we'd give them just a small portion of the blocks. They were dying to get the whole set, and we told them they would be next. Ever since that first night, they see those blocks as something so fascinating that adults love them, and very often I still put them out when adults will be over and we play with them on the table while we're talking.

WENDY PRIESNITZ ◆ Children learn as surely as they grow. Watch a toddler, motivated by her boundless curiosity to explore her surroundings, and you'll understand that children are hungry to learn.

It's only when their urgent questions have been brushed aside too many times, when their innate learning agenda has been sacrificed to the more aggressive plans of a well-intentioned adult, that they become passive learners who have to be artificially motivated to internalize facts.

It may be difficult to envision young children getting enthusiastic about arithmetic or history, because we have few role models to demonstrate this internal motivation. So, with their permission, I like to use my unschooled daughters, who are now twenty-four and twenty-five years of age, as an example.

Heidi and Melanie learned math, language arts, history, geography, and science because it was part of their everyday lives. Having never been told to sit and listen to an adult teacher, they just naturally explored their world. They constantly looked for meanings and for patterns in what they were experiencing;

sometimes they asked questions, sometimes they introduced discussions about what they were learning, sometimes their father and I did. They learned by living, in other words.

Our family ran a home-based magazine and book publishing business. So when Heidi was eight years old, she started to publish a newsletter for other home-based learners. This was a real business, with real, paying customers. The experience involved bookkeeping, writing, editing, graphic design. Interaction with her subscribers led to explorations into geography, history, and foreign languages. She ran this business until she decided to enter our local public high school five years later. The knowledge and skills she'd picked up along the way were far beyond what her peers who'd been to school had managed to retain—and she'd never had a formal lesson in her life, never been tested, and never read a textbook.

CHAPTER SEVEN

It's Effective! Assessing Your Child's Growth

MANY PARENTS begin the homeschool journey full of doubt in their ability to assess their children's educational development (there are "experts" who do this, mind you!). They find it reassuring to believe that there is some sort of "yardstick" to measure progress. Yet with only four questions, this chapter on assessment is the shortest of the book. Why is what seems to be a very important aspect of school given such short shrift?

Because it's not really necessary. Experience has shown homeschooling parents that a school's need to constantly test children is a direct result of the way it goes about teaching children, not a necessary component of the learning experience itself. When you gather a large number of children together, and present to all the same information in the same way, a test to see how much was absorbed by each is the only measure available.

But if you change the way you go about teaching children—and, better still, if you proceed from the idea that the child is learning as opposed to being taught—a different, improved option of assessment automatically becomes available. This may come as a shock, but all the necessary indicators of progress come naturally—from the children themselves. Combine this with a parent who spends a lot of time with the children, understands the way they learn best, knows their strengths and weaknesses as well as she knows her own, and is attentive enough to the children to remain aware of the indicators they share, then the tests we associate with the measure of academic progress become unnecessary, time-consuming burdens.

> **Experience has shown homeschooling parents that a school's need to constantly test children is a direct result of the way it goes about teaching children, not a necessary component of the learning experience itself.**

Let's look at unnecessary measures from another angle. Many regulations exist to constantly test products from a factory. Let's use a grape jelly factory, for instance. Lots of hands touch various aspects of the product as it passes through the assembly line, and not one of the people working for a paycheck is responsible for a jar from start to finish. Due to the methods of production, these tests are necessary to ensure the desired final product, time after time after time after time.

Now, one day Grandma decides to make some grape jelly in her kitchen. Grandma is not mass-producing; hers are the only hands touching the product (she knows she should wash them first!), and she alone handles the process from start to finish. Grandma's not making jelly for a paycheck. She's making it because she knows her grandchildren enjoy it. Grandma can be trusted to make sure the final product comes out right: She has an inherent, loving interest in making sure the jelly doesn't make her grandchildren sick when they eat it! Wouldn't it be a waste of time and money—not to mention downright silly—to expect Grandma to use the same regulations and tests as the factory does?

This is why homeschoolers fight so hard against regulations that would require the implementation of testing where it doesn't exist, or any increased testing where it is already required. These tests serve no purpose and hold no value to the homeschooling way of life and learning. They're just as silly for homeschooled children as factory tests are for Grandma's jelly.

So we've addressed assessment, but in a very small space, for several reasons. New homeschoolers tend to want some means of measuring success; the few methods included will serve you well. Those who want to increase test requirements for homeschoolers need to understand there are other, family-centered methods to ensure our children are learning; the methods outlined will help you realize any other way is simply a waste of taxpayers' hard-earned money.

Most important, we've used a very small space because no more is required. After all, we all know there's no jelly on earth that tastes as good as Grandma's.

54
Do I have to give my child tests?

SUSAN EVANS ◆ What we're really asking is, "How do I know if my children are learning?"

There are many stereotypes about learning—testing, resistance, and the need to provide external motivation—that feed into worries and misgivings in this area.

But look at children who've not yet attended school. One- and two-year-olds who endlessly ask, "Whazzat?" are building their vocabulary skills. Three-year-olds who talk through all of their waking (and some of their sleeping) hours are editing and revising their oral narratives. Five-year-olds join Socrates and Plato in trying to figure out the order of things and forces in the universe: "But how can Santa deliver *all* those presents in one night? And what about houses that don't have chimneys?"

So it is with eight-year-olds writing to pen pals: "How do you spell 'Connecticut?'" "What does 'G' look like in cursive?" And with ten-year-olds reading *The Hobbit:* "What are runes? Are they still

around? Can you drive me to the library *now* to get a rune book?"

When we pay close attention to the paths of our children's interests, I think we'll very often discover that their understanding and insights about particular pieces of knowledge are much deeper and wider ranging than what any tests could capture.

Susan Evans

Over time, it's become apparent to me that, for a self-directed learner, tests not only waste time and break the flow of inquiry, they miss the whole point of seeking out and internalizing information and knowledge.

> Over time, it's become apparent to me that, for a self-directed learner, tests not only waste time and break the flow of inquiry, they miss the whole point of seeking out and internalizing information and knowledge.

Looking back over my schooling and the patterns of testing I experienced, it was as though we had a chunk of information given to us on Mondays through Thursdays in class. On Fridays we were tested to see if we got the point. Then we were finished and started anew the next Monday. (Studies show that we forgot huge portions of the information as soon as we finished taking the test—*even if* we got a good grade on the test!)

When I look at my children's understanding of the world, and when I tackle new ideas and experiences myself, I see a very different process: New information is considered from several perspectives, filed away in relationship to existing understandings, and is brought out periodically and reconsidered. Learning about Leonardo da Vinci, for example, can be an inquiry into early theories of flight, or intense studying of the art of drawing, or an ethical debate in the use of cadavers. It would be silly—and useless—to say one knows all there is to know about the man upon completion of a 500-word essay on the meaning of the Mona Lisa's smile, or a matching section on titles of his paintings. A month-long inquiry may only be laying the groundwork for larger consideration of some bit of information about the Renaissance five years or fifty years down the road. Again, any test would be useless, misleading, and a waste of time.

So when do we worry and when do we not when it comes to getting past the insulting stereotype of children resisting learning?

I always figure that if the television is off most of the time (or out of the house completely); if the children are engrossed in projects of their own choosing several times a day, or across several days; and if my calling for help with chores elicits a response of "Just a minute, I'm at a good part!" or "I need to finish this before the glue dries!" or "Fine, I'll never figure this out anyway!" then their minds are perking along, they're figuring out lots of new

things, and if I listen carefully, maybe they'll let me in on the secret of how airplanes fly, how to write beautiful poetry, or cut perfect mats for framing, or to design and make lovely glass beads. I just hope they don't try to test me before I'm ready.

55

How do homeschooled children compare academically with traditionally schooled children?

PAT LINES ◆ People disagree on whether homeschooling can help a child academically. There is no research involving controls that indicates whether the same children could do better or worse in homeschooling, or in a public or private classroom. A multitude of data does exist, and analyses of test scores are available, based on data from states that require testing or from homeschooling associations. Both sources may provide information on a select group, as not all families cooperate with state testing requirements and private efforts rely on volunteers. Keeping these caveats in mind, virtually all the available data show that the tested homeschooling children are above average. The pattern for children for whom data are available resembles those of children in private schools.

SUSANNAH SHEFFER ◆ I could answer this question by telling you how well homeschoolers generally score on standardized tests and about the research studies that compare homeschoolers' test scores with scores of other students. But I don't think these facts get at what's most interesting or most important about homeschoolers or their academic experience. What distinguishes homeschoolers, in my mind, is not just their often impressive skill and accomplishment, but their attitude toward their work, their reasons for doing what they do.

A homeschooler who's now a junior at an Ivy League university told about working on a paper for class. He turned in the paper on time, but afterward he went to the professor and said that he was still interested in the subject and would like to keep working on the paper. I don't know what grade he received, but let's suppose for a minute that it was an A, and let's suppose (because it's quite likely) that another student in the class also got an A but wrote the paper simply to fulfill an assignment, not as something that he'd willingly continue on his own time without a further grade forthcoming. By conventional measures, these two students seem the same, but to my mind, the difference between them is significant.

But there's a question that is even more relevant than how homeschoolers

> **Homeschooling, for me, is less about making sure that the children do as well as their schooled peers (or become superior to them) than it is about making it possible for each homeschooler to flourish.**

compare to schooled students. How is a child who was once in school now faring as a homeschooler? In other words, how does she compare to her former self? I always think of the fifteen-year-old who told me, just after she had become a homeschooler, that she didn't like to learn through reading. She'd always felt bad about her reading, was embarrassed to be one of the class' slowest readers, and seldom read unless she had to. After she had been out of school for a few months, she mentioned to me that she'd spent the day in the library and that she was reading *Anna Karenina*. "Wait a minute!" I exclaimed. "How did this happen?"

Things had changed; her view of herself and her capabilities had changed. Later, writing about this process, she said, "I guess because I was just doing it for me and no one else was making it horrible for me, I began to get interested in the books themselves, in the stories, instead of thinking so much about myself and how I was doing."

Again, this strikes me as a difference that makes a difference. It tells us so much about people's capacity for change and about how varying the circumstances and assumptions can allow for new possibilities. Homeschooling, for me, is less about making sure that the children do as well as their schooled peers (or become superior to them) than it is about making it possible for each homeschooler to flourish.

56

How can I do my *own* assessment of my child's academic standing in relation to her peers?

MARY MCCARTHY ◆ Why would you want to? What difference does it make if the kid next door built a full-scale working replica of the space shuttle in the backyard using just the recyclables? Your child is an individual. Celebrate the individual. *No* one is good at everything, *no* one is going to be perfect in every subject, so why would you want to compare your child to someone else's? Diversity is the blessing of humanity; individually, we lack certain skills, but put together we make a whole. If your child is learning—and enjoying it—that's success.

SUSAN AND LARRY KASEMAN ◆ Your interest in your child's academic standing is understandable. Fortunately, we homeschoolers have many opportunities to observe our children's development. We watch them exploring the world and, when necessary, translate what they do into conventional academic language. (Sorting rocks is science. Building with blocks is geometry and spatial relations. Recognizing one's name is reading.) We can see the processes our children go through and support their early efforts just as we recognized and responded to their first words. We gradually come to understand that learning about baseball or horses develops basic academic skills.

When we get concerned about academics (yes, even confident, experienced homeschoolers sometimes worry):

- We can talk with other homeschoolers, especially those with older children. They'll know what we mean when we say, "Did you wonder if your children would ever learn to multiply?"
- We can review what our children have already learned. What can they do today that they couldn't do a few months ago? Write a note? Discuss current political issues?
- We can look at the big picture. As homeschoolers, we know our children better than we would if they were attending a conventional school. We see their increasing understanding of the world; their growing ability to interact with others; their increasing self-reliance as they learn to ride a bike, drive a car, travel abroad; and their increasing maturity as they take responsibility for increasingly complex projects.
- We can realize that to become mature, responsible adults, children don't need

to follow the path prescribed by conventional schools. Children learn best by following their own timetable, at different rates in different subjects. As homeschoolers, we have the flexibility to encourage this. Many grownup homeschoolers who are doing well didn't learn to read until they were eight, ten, or older. Many who write well and are comfortable with math would earlier have been considered "below grade level." Had they been pressured to learn these things earlier, they might have concluded that they could not learn them.

A great gift we can give our children is the ability and courage to be true to themselves, to set their own standards, to identify problems and not be overwhelmed by them, to consider a wide range of alternative responses and then act. This will serve them well whether the problem is a car that won't start, a health crisis, or simply the causes of the Civil War.

- Perhaps the best preparation is the ability to learn new things. (Consider people now using computers who did not study them in school.) We can ask: Do our children recognize when they don't know something? Are they confident enough to admit that they don't know it? Do our children know how to find information they need using resources such as their common sense, the library, the Internet, and assistance from other people?
- Finally, it's great that you want to avoid standardized tests. They interfere with learning and are inaccurate, unfair, and biased against minorities, women, and anyone who does not have the same experiences and values as the developer of the test. Taking a test often undermines self-esteem. Test scores show only how well a given person performed on a given test on a given day, not how much one knows. But test results tend to be self-fulfilling prophecies. Why would we want to put our children through difficult experiences that produce unreliable results that may be harmful to them?

57

How can I tell if my children are learning what's important?

NED VARE ◆ Decide for yourself what's important for them to know. Be specific. Not geography, but where is New York? Not math, but how much money do I need to buy a baseball?

Second, decide whether it's really important for them to know it *now*. Have a good reason.

SANDRA DODD ◆ How can you tell if children at school are learning what's important? How can a teacher at school tell if children are learning what's important?

First of all, what's important? Assuming that's a simple question for you to answer, maybe the next question is, How do you know your children are learning that, the important thing? You can tell because their behavior will change, their questions will change, their actions will change. They will display the knowledge in everyday ways. If it's math, they will be able to calculate, measure, estimate, whatever. If it's reading, they'll be able to read. If it's writing, using maps, understanding mechanics . . . they will use what they've learned.

What if you think everything is important? Everything is connected, and learning is important. Consider the idea that it's not important where people start, and that people never quit learning until they finally do quit, after which *lots* of things are no longer quite as important. If a child is learning, and active, and inquisitive, and if the parents are open,

---

THE SIDE EFFECTS OF STANDARDIZED TESTING

Contributed by Ann Fisher

Standardized tests, in addition to being narrowly focused and frequently misused comparative measurements of academic progress, are powerful teachers in their own right. Are these the kinds of lessons you want your children to learn?

- Someone else knows what I should know better than my parents or I do.

- Learning is an absolute that can be measured.

- My interests are not important enough to be measured.

- The subject areas being evaluated on the test are the only things that are important to know.

- Thinking is not valued; getting the 'right' answer is the only goal.

- The answer (to any question) is readily available and indisputable, and it's one of these four or five answers here. There's no need to look deeper or dwell on the question.

- My worth can be summarized by a single mark on a paper.

and helpful, and encouraging, they are learning important things.

WENDY PRIESNITZ ◆ "What's important" is a highly subjective phrase! It depends on one's world view, definition of education, ambitions (or lack of) for a child's career, and much more.

Your family should decide on a set of learning objectives for your children, aside from any legal requirements of the jurisdiction in which you live. If you want your children to learn exactly what their schooled peers are learning, you can obtain an outline of the curriculum that's followed in your local school.

Wendy Priesnitz

My own personal goal for my children's education was for them to retain their curiosity and love of learning, and to develop their research, learning, and communication skills. The skills and

---

- The purpose of learning is to get a high score. High test scores are the only purpose of testing.

- If I score very well, I am better than other people who do not score as well.

- Poor test scores mean that I am a failure. If I score poorly, there is nothing I can do to change it. Why try?

- I haven't learned to read yet. I am not smart.

- Since I am tested once a year so I can homeschool, my parents and I have to spend the rest of the year preparing for the test.

- The test was too hard. I am not smart.

- The test was easy. I don't have to learn any more.

- The test was easy [hard]. Public [home] [private] school kids are dumber [smarter] than I am.

- The questions on the test are what is important. What I have been studying is not important.

- I have to get a higher score next year to show that I am learning.

facts they picked up along the way were largely a function of their own interests, rounded out here and there with what my husband and I perceived to be missing pieces of their own personal knowledge puzzle. But the actual body of knowledge is ever growing and changing (for instance, Saturn has more rings now than it did when I went to elementary school!) at an increasingly enhanced pace. So I felt they'd be better served by developing a questioning nature and sound literacy skills than memorizing the dates of the battles of the World Wars!

No matter what you feel your children should be learning, don't worry about being able to tell if that learning is occurring. Because you're intimately involved with each youngster on a day-to-day basis, you'll be in the happy position of observing each burst of growth and sharing each new insight.

You might get concerned from time to time that your child's development seems to have stalled. At those times, it's important to remember that learning does not proceed in an orderly fashion. It's a chaotic, fits and starts, trial-and-error sort of experience. Brains need time to process new knowledge. Your learner will move from frenetic bursts of activity through slower periods of seeming hibernation, only to surprise you one day with a pronouncement that makes you marvel at what was going on in her brain while you thought she was vegging out!

Some homeschooling families test their children on a regular basis—and some laws require that home-educated children be tested regularly. But a good number of families object to testing as a way of measuring learning.

One of the main objections to testing is that it tries to judge the growth of knowledge by measuring the performance on one test at one moment in time, rather than as a process of growth that occurs over a period of time. It's a quick and easy measuring stick that is a poor substitute for the observation which you have the opportunity to undertake.

Test scores may be unreliable for a variety of reasons. To be at all useful, a test must reflect learning; standardized tests and those administered to home-educated children by school boards cannot, by definition, be directly relevant to the individual's learning process.

An alternative used by many families as a way of assessing their children's learning growth and needs is the portfolio. A language arts portfolio, for instance, could include compositions, reports, letters, stories, favorite poems, taped recordings of oral reports or readings, book reviews, lists of favorite books, photographs of plays being presented to family members, and even artwork. The format can be whatever is suitable for the material being collected . . . from a file folder for language arts to a large cardboard box for science projects.

CHAPTER EIGHT

You Mean I Don't Need to Know Algebra?! The Teen Years

QUICK—DO you remember irrational numbers? How to factor a trinomial? Did you use the quadratic formula today?

When my oldest child was ready for algebra, he wanted my help. The terms above rang a bell but, unfortunately, it was a very distant bell. Like many other parents, it had been two decades since I'd tackled the math puzzles known as algebra, and there'd been no reason to visit them again since leaving high school. But something was different this time—my son and I had the answer book!

It's amazing what having the answers can do for your self-confidence. You don't do the problem once only to be told you did it wrong. You go back to the drawing board. You know you can figure this out and transfer what you learn to other problems. Your child gets an idea at the same time as you do and you compare notes. You play with the problem. Did I say play? You bet I did.

Armed with the answers, a "one day at a time" approach, and the notion that one could actually have fun viewing algebra as number puzzles—strolling quickly through sections we understood and slowing to a crawl when we felt we needed a little more practice—my son and I made it to the end of the algebra book.

I often wonder how many parents who are seriously considering homeschooling stop dead in their tracks when, in their mental imaginings, they reach the years they remember as high school and consider the subject matter beyond their scope. As Cafi Cohen and Luz Shosie explain in this chapter, homeschooling a teen is different, but far from impossible. Sandra Dodd and Rebecca Rupp help you see how your teens can learn the "tough" subjects even if you don't understand them.

> **Like many other parents, it had been two decades since I'd tackled the math puzzles known as algebra, and there'd been no reason to visit them again since leaving high school.**

And our homeschoolers answer still more questions about teens who learn at home and in the community. You may be worrying about diplomas, college, scholarships, and jobs. Or you may like to know how so many homeschooled teens find apprenticeships as they enjoy freedom from school schedules. The Kasemans and Susan Evans will give you and your children plenty of ideas and starting points.

I got to "play" with algebra one more time with my daughter. But just as I was looking forward to a third and last time, my youngest declared he was quite capable of doing it himself, thank you very much. You mean I don't need to know algebra? I *love* homeschooling in the teen years!

58

Is homeschooling a teenager different than homeschooling an elementary school–aged child?

CAFI COHEN ◆ Teenage homeschooling presented a new set of challenges. Our children wanted to try all sorts of things with which we were only vaguely familiar. Our son wanted a private pilot's license. Our daughter needed outlets for all kinds of creative endeavors: writing, speaking, performing, drawing, even cooking. In addition, both kids decided to tackle subjects in which we lacked expertise, most notably foreign language.

As parents of homeschooled teenagers, we began to worry about college admissions tests like the SAT and ACT. Our kids were also eager to begin researching colleges. One had a clear-cut goal, and our questions centered around the best way to help him attain it. The other could not begin to decide on a goal; and, of course, we worried about that.

In short, the kids seemed to need more expertise than we could personally provide. And we, their parents, worried more about the future than when they were younger. Were we doing The Right Thing?

Fortunately, as we discovered, teenagers can do more for themselves than younger children. Contrary to what many educationists would have you believe, teenagers *can* learn trigonometry and biology by themselves for the SAT. They *can* read college catalogs on their own. They *can* teach themselves computer skills with little outside help. They can even find resources on their own—like community drama groups and free flying lessons. When challenges arose, more and more often as the kids got older they would find a solution before we even realized there was a problem. Sometimes we brainstormed together to generate solutions.

What was the biggest difference we noticed in homeschooling our teenagers? Our role evolved from networker to facilitator. Our earlier research and our talking to experienced home educators had served two purposes: (1) We found resources, and (2) we provided a networking role model. Eventually, our kids adopted our techniques and became good networkers themselves. As they assumed more responsibility for their education, we, their parents, found we had an altered job description. We had moved from planning, motivating, and teaching to discussing, providing wheels, and writing occasional checks.

LUZ SHOSIE ◆ Our philosophy and style of learning are not different—we have always let Cassidy know that he is in charge of his own learning and we are in charge of ours. Our job has been to keep him safe and help him gain access to whatever he needs or wants to learn about. We did not ever tell him he should learn to do math, learn to read, or say please and thank you. This was not easy for a couple of former schoolteachers, let me tell you!

What is delightfully different now is seeing the proof that children can be trusted to learn and grow. The first few years of homeschooling, we pretty much had to take it on faith that what John Holt, Daniel Greenberg, and others said was true—children are born learning and they want to grow up to be responsible, effective adults. Now Cassidy is eighteen and knows enough reading, writing, and arithmetic to hold two jobs and get high scores on GED and SAT tests. And he's one of the most polite people of any age I know.

> **What is delightfully different now is seeing the proof that children can be trusted to learn and grow.**

59

How will my child learn the "tough" subjects, like algebra and chemistry, if I don't understand them?

SANDRA DODD ◆ You don't need to be your children's only teacher. Maybe learning alongside your children would be best for both of you, if you want to go that route. You can help them learn by learning *with* them. If you find yourself being surpassed, rejoice! Your child can teach you, or can go on to learn without you. There are other people in the world to help, and there are books, computer games and courses, flash cards at university bookstores, courses at local colleges or trade schools, correspondence courses and videos.

If a parent expects to be everything to a child, it limits the child's world. If I teach my children everything I know about history, they won't know as much as if I get out of the way and let them have all the books, people, photos, museums, maps, and sites in the whole wide world. I prefer to expose the children to as much as possible and let them make connections between things (with my help sometimes, but never at my insistence).

When a child has an actual need or desire to learn something, he or she can learn it. And it won't take an hour a day for nine months, either.

REBECCA RUPP ◆ Everybody, sooner or later, hits a tough subject or two. Randy, my husband, and I are both scientists, and we took algebra and chemistry in stride. Our sticking points in the course of our children's education were music, Latin, and Japanese. We coped by finding music teachers, a friendly language tutor, and a set of self-explanatory programmed texts.

In my experience, however, the "tough" subjects don't necessarily arrive in tidy blocks (LATIN) with tidy solutions (TUTOR), but surface every ten minutes throughout every homeschooling day. No matter how knowledgeable and well-educated parents are, children—with their absolutely endless curiosity—are impossible to keep up with. "How does a television work?" "What's inside a battery?" "I just read a book that says cows have four stomachs. Why? Do they all work the same? Are they all the same size?"

"I don't know," you say, dropping your dish towel, hoe, or fountain pen. "Let's go look it up."

In that sense, the tough subjects have always been my favorites. It's that experience of looking it up—of mutual discovery, of learning together—that makes homeschooling so special. A good education, to my mind, is not simply information acquisition; it's an active process of exploration, of learning how to learn.

When it comes to learning, kids are astonishingly well equipped to teach themselves. Looking back over our home-schooling years, I realize how much our children know that neither of us ever taught them: computer skills, philosophy, classical music, origami, and rock-etry—to say nothing of the aforementioned Latin and Japanese. All our children have immense subsets of knowledge that we, their parents, don't share; and in many cases their "tough subjects" haven't been the same as ours.

That, in fact, may be the answer to the whole thorny question.

Kids don't know there are any tough subjects.

Don't tell them.

> **The tough subjects have always been my favorites. It's that experience of looking it up— of mutual discovery, of learning together— that makes home-schooling so special.**

60

Will my child get a high school diploma?

Luz Shosie ◆ If he or she feels the need to have it, yes. There are many ways to go about it. One way you may not have thought about is to hire a calligrapher to make one (or learn calligraphy and make it yourself).

Cafi Cohen ◆ There are several ways that your child can get a high school diploma.

- Grant your own! Easiest, cheapest option here. The family, acting as a small private school, grants a diploma. Just check with your local print shop or stationary store and ask for a blank diploma form. Several large mail-order home-schooling catalogs also stock. Alternatively, you can design and print one on your computer. Fill out the form when your child has satisfied your requirements for high school graduation, sign it as the principal, date it. Voila! Your child has a diploma.

Will this work? Is this official? Interestingly, "official" has no official meaning— other than the school is saying, "We issued this document." You,

Cafi Cohen

as a small private school, can do the same thing. Put a seal on it and call it official if you want. It will work. Whenever your child is asked if he has a high school diploma, he should check the "yes" box.

- Hundreds of local umbrella schools (private schools that help homeschoolers homeschool) and dozens of national independent study institutions (for example, Clonlara, American School) award high school diplomas to homeschoolers. Some of these programs are accredited, some not. What that means is that some have sought and received the approval of an accrediting agency like the North Central Association of Schools and Colleges. When shopping for an independent study school, do not be overly concerned about accreditation. After all, most colleges—being much more interested in transcripts and portfolios and test scores—do not require diplomas or transcripts from accredited institutions. Look first for a program that fits your child and your family.
- In a few states, your child can earn a state-approved high school diploma by satisfying certain requirements (for example, Pennsylvania) or by completing a public school independent study program (for example, California). This is still not an option in most places. Contact your statewide homeschooling organizations for more information.
- Finally, in all states, homeschoolers may take a GED, Tests for General Educational Development, or a state-approved equivalent (California High School Proficiency Examination in California, for example). Age eligibility for the test and passing scores are established by individual states. Passing the test is equivalent to a high school diploma. The GED is considered substandard by some, most notably the military, which restricts the number of GED holders they will enlist. Nevertheless, many homeschooled students have successfully used the GED for college admissions; and, despite the restrictions, some homeschooled teenagers have enlisted in the military with a GED. Your local libraries and community colleges should be able to direct you to a source for GED testing.

61

Will my child ever be able to get into college if we homeschool, or receive financial aid or scholarships for college?

LORETTA HEUER ◆ Of course your homeschooled adolescent can go to college! In fact, homeschoolers often pick up college credits while their schooled peers sit in high school classrooms.

College courses can be taken at your local community college, during "precollege" summer programs held at many universities, or through distance learning programs. These credits acquired during adolescence will show colleges and universities not only that your child has the potential to do college level work, but that he or she has done some already!

When my sons Tad and Jed were applying to colleges, we considered ourselves both buyers and sellers. First, since a college degree is a major financial investment, we investigated each potential school thoroughly. We read several guidebooks, talked to alumni, read the course catalog (not just the viewbook), and visited each school. This helped my sons determine whether the school was a good match for what they wanted.

Second, each of my sons realized that he needed to "sell" himself to the school of his choice. By understanding what a school wanted in its students, both Tad and Jed were able to tailor their applications to show the school that they were a good match for it.

Finally, I'd advise you to find an advocate. This would usually be someone in the admissions department who can both guide you through the application process and support your candidacy when the admissions committee meets.

With regard to finances, homeschoolers fill out the same financial aid forms as traditionally educated students in order to qualify for need-based aid. Colleges also award merit-based scholarships, but these are usually based on quantifiable measures such as high school grades, rank in class, or GPA (grade point average). This meant that, although my sons were unschooled for high school we still needed to come up with a grading system. After we did this, we also asked the college to consider grades awarded in courses taken for college credit. End result? Both boys were offered merit scholarships based on this combination of homeschool and college grades.

Remember, too, that homeschoolers with flexible schedules have time to develop expertise in niche scholarship areas such as agriculture, film, community service, etc. My son Jed was awarded our town's Youth Baseball Scholarship—not as a player, but as the League's outstanding umpire!

SUSANNAH SHEFFER ◆ A homeschooler who is now at Williams College told *Growing Without Schooling* magazine, "None of the colleges that I was interested in had any difficulty with my homeschooling background and none required me to have a high school diploma or take the GED." Homeschoolers have been admitted to Ivy League schools, small liberal arts colleges, state universities, conservatories, and community colleges, and are engaged in all sorts of work, so homeschooling is clearly not a liability. Stanford University, for example, has this to say in the letter it routinely sends to homeschooled applicants who inquire: "[Homeschooled] students are no longer unusual for us, and several are usually admitted and enroll at Stanford each year . . . We are scrupulously fair in evaluating these applicants, and they are not at any disadvantage in the admissions process."

Colleges are primarily interested in what students have been doing and learning during their high school years, and homeschoolers convey this through transcripts they create or through a portfolio of work. Another option is to enroll with a homeschool program that provides a diploma after students have completed high school credits. The main thing to remember is that many colleges are more interested in seeing the best evidence you can provide of your readiness to do college work than they are in having that evidence fit a particular format. Homeschoolers generally try to convey two things in their applications: (1) Although we've done things in a nontraditional way, this student is indeed prepared for an intense and fairly traditional academic experience; and (2) Because we've done things differently, this student stands out in some particular ways and has had a chance to develop in some particular ways. Homeschoolers also fulfill the other parts of the admissions process—writing essays, describing their activities and achievements, getting recommendations (which they typically get from adult mentors or employers), and taking the SAT or ACT if the college requires it. Colleges have so far been impressed with the self-motivation homeschoolers demonstrate and the interesting activities that lead to scholarship opportunities, as was the case with a student whose many volunteer and service activities throughout her homeschooling years led to her receiving the Community Service Achievement Award, a scholarship that her college gives to a few incoming students each year.

> **As the homeschooling population grows older, we're able to see increasing evidence not only that these students can get into college, but that they can have an unusual and refreshing take on the experience once they're there.**

As the homeschooling population grows older, we're able to see increasing evidence not only that these students can get *into* college, but that they can have an unusual and refreshing take on the experience once they're there. One lifelong homeschooler, for example, said she was the only one of her friends who chose the courses she wanted to take, as opposed to writing down what her advisor told her to take. Interesting self-motivated students aren't just good admissions candidates, they're also valuable members of a college community.

WILL SHAW ◆ Ours have. Home education was no handicap whatsoever as our two oldest kids applied for admission to college and for financial aid.

Most college admissions applications ask the same basic questions, and some are kind of funny, such as class ranking. Unless you are enrolled in a correspondence school that keeps records and prepares transcripts for you, you'll have to make your own transcript, a fun project.

It helps to keep basic records so you can remember just when it was that you did that special one-semester course in whatever. As they hold weight for all college applicants, your homeschooled child will need to take the same admissions tests ("college boards") as other children (PSATs, SATs, and so on). You don't have to be a student in a conventional school to take these, and there are ready sources for them.

Many community colleges don't require college boards, or they administer their own tests to applicants.

Admission to college can seem fairly competitive, especially if you are intent on going to a particular college or if your child is not exactly an Albert Einstein. But I don't know of any public or private college or university that refuses admission to homeschoolers. Still, some prejudice may exist here and there. As a representative of homeschool interests,

a couple of years ago I participated in a panel discussion at a convention of college admissions officers. The subject was what to do about homeschoolers.

Will Shaw

One admissions officer from a stuck-up university sniffed, "They always put down that they're top in their high school graduating class." Well, the application forms ask for it, so we honestly answer!

You're on at least a level playing field regarding SAT scores and the like. And your child should have advantages on some of the other qualifications that colleges like to see, such as participation in extracurricular activities and community services. Home education offers so much greater schedule flexibility and opportunities for these. So unless you have been an especially unimaginative and unambitious homeschool parent, your child should have a fine application for admission.

Paying for college is a concern for all parents, not just homeschoolers. Homeschoolers have access to financial aid, as others do. Most financial aid is need-based, with minimal connection to academic record. Of course, once your child is in college, he could be disqualified from more aid if he does poorly in his studies. There are many kinds of schol-

---

WEB SITES TO HELP IN PREPARATION FOR COLLEGE

The following sites were selected and reviewed by the staff of Excite for the Personal Technology section of the Sunday *Seattle Times*, February 1, 1998:

Financial Aid Information—http://www.finaid.org

Sallie Mae: Helping Make Education Possible—http://www.salliemae.com/home/index_e.html

KapLoan: Student Loan Information Program—http://www.kaploan.com

Texas Guaranteed Student Loan Corporation—http://www.tgslc.org

College Edge—http://www.CollegeEdge.com

Scholarship Search—http://www.collegeboard.org/fundfinder/bin/fundfind01.pl

Kaplan's Amazing College Simulator—http://www.kaplan.com/precoll/simcoll

Your Best College Buys Now—http://www.pathfinder.com/money/colleges98

GoCollege—http://www.gocollege.com

College Board Online—http://www.collegeboard.org

Mapping Your Future—http://www.mapping-your-future.org

WebWare for the SAT Skill Lessons—http://www.testprep.com/satmenu.html

Main Quad—http://www.mainquad.com

---

arships, loans, and grants, and the college admissions offices appear to assist their applicants equally and well. Homeschoolers can and do compete for those various merit-based and need-based moneys. There are books full of scholarship opportunities. At the time of college application, and even well before then, homeschoolers can fairly compete for financial aid.

62

What happens when my child graduates, doesn't have a diploma, and wants to get a job?

KATHARINE HOUK ◆ In working with many homeschooling families, I've found that their teens are almost never asked to produce a high school diploma in order to get a job. In the event an application asks, "Do you have a high school diploma?" a young person could honestly answer that yes, she or he has successfully completed high school–level work. Some families have a name for their homeschooling endeavor (Smith Family Academy or Pine Ridge Homeschool), and in some states it may be legal for the parent "principal" to award a diploma. Homeschoolers also have the option of registering with independent study programs that do give diplomas upon graduation, such as Clonlara in Michigan or Cambridge Academy in Florida.

A third diploma option is the GED. Our daughter took the GED test to obtain her general equivalency diploma when a college became stubborn about awarding her credit for courses she had taken (most colleges are not this fussy about diplomas). The test was not difficult, and there are published guides to help people prepare for it. In some states a child must be a certain age before being allowed to take the GED, but it may be possible to obtain an age waiver. Still the chances are, contrary to popular belief, your child won't need to produce a high school diploma.

In reality, most homeschoolers have held down part-time jobs—paid and/or volunteer—all through their high school years, which are a contribution to the community and enhance their learning. Such endeavors are valuable not only in developing work experience, commitment to the community, and skills in getting along with others; they also look great on job applications, and the relationships developed with employers and supervisors often provide marvelous references and good leads to other jobs. A young person's intelligence and skills, willingness and ability to learn, strong work ethic, and respectful attitude toward others are the things that are valued more than a diploma by prospective employers.

JEAN REED ◆ A diploma from a high school or college is just a piece of paper. Colleges and employers all know that having that "paper" doesn't necessarily mean the owner knows anything. That's why we keep reading about how the educational system is failing. More than ever before, it's how skilled you are and how you present yourself that counts.

All four of our children are grown and have been independent for a number of years. I've asked them all if they ever had trouble getting into college or getting a job because they were homeschooled. I got back a unanimous "no." Three out of four of them have attended college for a while. They had no admissions problems. One did have to take admissions testing, but scored well enough so they didn't ask any questions about Brook Farm School. She now teaches software design at one of Boston's top colleges.

When filling out job applications that asked specifically where they went to high school, they wrote in the name of our school. No one has ever questioned this enough to contact us. During interviews, the children have found their homeschooling advantageous. Not that many people entering the job market are homeschooled, and there is a lot of curiosity. Cathy says it's an advantage because you definitely stand out from the crowd. She says sometimes the interview has turned out to be more about homeschooling than her skills and she has had to work to keep the interviewer on track.

Why shouldn't your child have a diploma when he graduates from your school? You've done all the work of being a "school," educating your child. Why not make your own diploma? We did. You can buy them from most office

supply stores. Can't find one? I can make one for you.

We created our own graduation ceremony, used the community hall, and invited neighbors and friends. We had music, speeches from our other children, a baccalaureate address by the minister, and Donn created a class history, class prophecy, and yearbook. Cathy wrote and read her Last Will and Testament. We presented awards to our other children and gave the graduate a diploma. The local newspaper came and took pictures and wrote a very nice article.

I've watched our children move around the country and work at different jobs. None of them has had a problem because she or he lacked a public school diploma. Sometimes they didn't get the job they wanted because there were others more qualified. Sometimes they wanted the job so badly, and had so much confidence in themselves, that they bluffed their way into the job and just learned what was needed before anyone found out. Homeschooling has been to their advantage in many ways. They have a great deal of confidence in themselves. When they have wanted to change the direction of their lives they know where to look for new information

> **When filling out job applications that asked specifically where they went to high school, they wrote in the name of our school. No one has ever questioned this enough to contact us.**

and learn what they need to know; sometimes by returning to formal education and sometimes learning on their own.

Diplomas are pretty pieces of paper, and occasionally useful. P. J. O'Rourke says, "Politicians are interested in people. Not that this is always a virtue. Fleas are interested in dogs."

63

Should my child go to community college while still high school–aged?

CAFI COHEN ◆ One of our homeschoolers took community college classes, the other did not. Certainly, for either child, I had no worries about the material being too challenging. When our oldest requested enrollment in the classes, he was first asked to take math and language arts placement tests. At the math testing, the proctor told the thirty-plus people taking the test that they could opt for either a general math (arithmetic) or basic algebra test. When he asked how many people wanted the basic algebra test, my son was the only one to raise his hand.

After our son had taken a couple of community college courses, we estimated that the level of challenge, at least for the introductory classes, was roughly the same as that at the local high school. When you look at it this way, it almost seems silly not to accumulate some college credit when the kids are teenagers. Indeed, it would have been fairly easy to earn an associate's degree by age seventeen by taking two or three classes year-round beginning at age fourteen or fifteen.

Certainly, there are benefits to taking even a few courses. Your teenager can study subjects like foreign language and laboratory science that might be too difficult to tackle independently. He will accumulate college credit in a relatively inexpensive way, even if you have to pay for it (in some cases, you will not have to pay for it, as you will be able to take advantage of agreements that the colleges have with local high schools).

The eventual transcript that the college generates will serve as independent, outside verification that your homeschooler can handle formal academics at the college level. Our son's admission to the Air Force Academy and other selective schools, plus full-ride scholarship offers, probably would not have happened without this demonstrated ability to handle college-level work—especially since he did not have sky-high SAT scores. This is not to imply that you need junior college classes to qualify for admission to good colleges, only that taking such courses may be a relatively painless way to convince an uncertain admissions officer at a selective school that your child deserves a second look.

On the other hand, if your teenager displays no interest in taking classes, or if he or she has no reason to pursue formal academics, I cannot see any benefit to taking college courses as a teenager. I have known many homeschoolers—working at everything from cartooning to emergency medicine to writing—who were better off spending their time on those activities. These teens had excellent community support and mentors for these activities; college courses would have slowed them down.

Another caution: Not everything your homeschooler takes at a given community college will be accepted for credit at a four-year college or university. If this concerns you, do check on transferability with the four-year colleges where your son or daughter will be applying.

> When the girls became focused on areas of study that suggested outside-the-home learning, our community college became an option from which they could pick and choose specific classes.

DEB SHELL ◆ Our teens have found the local community college to be an excellent resource. Since our family approached homeschool from the unschooling perspective, when the girls became focused on areas of study that suggested outside-the-home learning, our community college became an option from which they could pick and choose specific classes.

These classes may not have been the entire way (or necessarily the best way) that an area of inquiry was explored—but oftentimes community college classes served either as a jumping-off point for more serious study, or, simply as a way of getting a taste of something that intrigued them. While they were satisfying the need to further explore interests, they were also doing double duty by earning high school transcript credit (in terms of Carnegie Units, that is, the number of credits used to calculate high school graduation requirements, one semester of community college work is equal to an entire year of high school) as well as college credit, which we've found to be fully transferable to the four-year colleges our girls applied to. Also a bonus to our family, Vermont financial aid will pay for graduated student's classes.

Most of the time people we mention this to assume community college is also good preparation for "real" college. While our experience with community college classes has been positive, with such qualities as excellent teacher-student ratios, well-prepared syllabi, interesting formats, and up-to-date resources being the norm, these classes also rival the quality offered in many large four-year schools, where tenured staff and overcrowding may bring quality down.

To date, our eldest daughter has taken four community college classes and discovered that they were also good preparation for *not* going to college! She discovered that limitations placed on her by the very nature of structured classroom study were not helpful or appropriate to her way of learning about something. She earned high grades, so having been unschooled wasn't a factor in terms of her having to learn how to study or whatever else the fear is regarding people who haven't been coerced into following a curriculum. She could and did easily apply herself to accomplish this—yet the real issue remained: For her, was this the best way to explore an area of interest and to develop skills? Instead of spending a great deal of time and money just going the college route, community college offered her a chance to realize why college wasn't the way she wanted to further her education.

64

How can my child find an apprenticeship opportunity?

The Kasemans felt much more comfortable giving their answer directly to teens and those searching for apprenticeships rather than to the parents.

SUSAN AND LARRY KASEMAN ◆ One way to begin is by thinking about your interests and what you like to do. A book like Richard Nelson Bolles's *What Color Is Your Parachute?* may help you identify areas you might want to explore.

You may decide you're interested in a formal, recognized apprenticeship run through the state department of labor or its equivalent in an area like plumbing. You can request information and apply, explaining how your homeschooling experiences qualify you for the apprenticeship. Or you may be interested in an informal apprenticeship in an area where apprenticeships are less common, rare, or even unheard of. In that case the following suggestions may help.

Think about what you are willing to do in exchange for the learning experience. Are you willing to wash test tubes in order to see what goes on in a working science lab? Build sets and manage props to get firsthand theater experience? Do data entry and other general office work to see how a legislator's office functions? Potential providers of apprenticeships are more likely to be receptive if you begin by explaining how they would benefit from having you as an apprentice.

Explore resources and opportunities available in your local community. Talk with people you know about their work, what they know about the community, and whether they know anyone who works in the areas you're interested in.

Run an ad in your local paper, asking for help or volunteering your services. Don't hesitate to ask anyone who is doing something you would like to participate in. Many people who have not thought about working with an apprentice become interested in the possibility when someone proposes the idea.

To find an apprenticeship outside your local community, a book like *Internships,* published each year by Peterson's Guides, may be helpful. This book lists thousands of apprenticeships and internships available throughout the country. The book may give the impression that it is primarily for people who have completed at least two years of college, but homeschoolers who have not attended college have used it successfully. Some homeschoolers have found that it worked well to do an internship or apprenticeship that was readily available even though it was not in their area of primary interest, either so they could spend time in a different part of the country or could gain experience in a different area of work.

A contract that you write and both parties sign helps assure that both of you agree about ideas and expectations for the apprenticeship. It also helps ensure that you will not be stuck only doing routine work that no one else wants to do. When you have completed the apprenticeship, ask the person with whom you have been working for a written letter of recommendation, addressed "To Whom It May Concern," that you can include in your credentials and use when you are applying for future apprenticeships or employment.

SUSAN EVANS ◆ An apprenticeship is an age-old process to help children have the opportunity to learn the skills they will need as adults to make tangible contributions to their communities. It is an efficient, practical way to develop the means to feed, clothe, and house themselves and their families.

Families who have spent the younger childhood years with hands-on, learner-led education find that older children and teens move rather undramatically into situations we've labeled "apprenticeships." That is, they spend concentrated amounts of time with one or several adults learning about a specific body of knowledge.

For instance, a young person who loves animals and has spent several years caring for pets and making posters for 4-H fairs (or simply for hanging on a wall at home) would quite logically volunteer to help out at a vet's office or the local Humane Society. Within a short time, this capable teen would probably be invited to assist during simple (or not-so-simple) surgeries or be left in charge of the care and feeding of the animals over a holiday weekend.

I know one young man who took stained glass and lapidary (forming and polishing rocks and stones) classes as a lark. When his manual dexterity and visual skill at assessing workmanship was noticed by some senior members of the lapidary club, he was invited to work one-on-one with a skilled faceter and gold caster. He worked on new techniques and entered some local competitions, winning several blue ribbons. When his enthusiasm waned, he went on to some other interests. But he maintained several close friendships, valuable life lessons, and some exceptional skills, which will be available to him in the future if he decides to get involved in lapidary work again.

Several companies in our local geographical area offer more formal apprenticeship programs in pipe fitting, tool and die making, and other skilled trades. Most of these programs coordinate efforts with local community colleges to also confer associate's degrees upon successful completion of the training. All this while making a decent wage during forty-hour work weeks.

What interests does your child have that are shared by other people in your family or local community? Are there clubs or businesses in your surrounding area where your child could visit (alone or with you) to learn more about the skills or processes which intrigue him or her?

A field trip can provide an opportunity to ask lots of questions before approaching a possible mentor. Doing a short research project can be a perfect excuse to shadow someone for an afternoon, a month, or a year.

Apprenticeships can be formal arrangements, tied in with college credit programs, or they can be casual, informal relationships that a young person wanders into and out of as his passions lead him on the way to productive adulthood.

Like so many aspects of homeschooling, the spark of interest, the process of finding out about the world, is much more important than a finished product, a certificate, or becoming a master craftsman. In many cases, the human bonds may be many times more valuable than the original sought-after skills or knowledge.

GOOD READS FOR AND ABOUT HOMESCHOOLING TEENS

Contributed by Loretta Heuer

Doing Things Differently

- Colfax, David and Micki. *Homeschooling for Excellence*. Warner Books, Inc., 1988. ISBN: 0446389862

  Unschooling in rural California: how the Colfax kids developed a joy for learning, then met the demands of the college admissions process—and won!

- Graham, Robin Lee and Derek Gill. *Dove* (HarperCollins), 1991. ISBN: 0060920475

  Go to high school or sail solo around the world?

- Hailey, Kendall. *The Day I Became an Autodidact*. Dell Publishing, 1989. ISBN: 0440550130 (out of print)

  How Kendall decided against college attendance and designed a scholarly life for herself as an autodidact (a person who learns on her own).

- Llewellyn, Grace. *The Teenage Liberation Handbook: How to Quit School and Get a Real Life and Education*. Lowry House, 1998. ISBN: 0962959170

  So good that we have three copies in the house: mine and one for each of my two sons! Check out the chapter, "College Without High School."

- Llewellyn, Grace, ed. *Real Lives: Eleven Teenagers Who Don't Go To School*. Lowry House, 1993. ISBN: 0962959138

  What can be achieved when adolescents see no limits on their potential.

College and Career

- Barkley, Nella. *How To Help Your Child Land the Right Job (Without Being a Pain in the Neck)*. Workman Publishing, 1993. ISBN: 1563051524

  How parents and adolescents can work together to explore issues of identity and work.

- Boldt, Lawrence G. *Zen and the Art of Making a Living: A Practical Guide to Creative Career Design*. Penguin, 1999. ISBN: 0140195998

  Tons of worksheets and activities to help adolescents explore their values, talents, skills, and career options.

- Cohen, Cafi (Linda Dobson, ed.). *Homeschoolers' College Admissions Handbook: Preparing Your 12- to 18-Year-Old for a Smooth Transition*. Prima Publishing, 2000. ISBN: 0761527540

  Answers your questions about record keeping, the admissions process, financial aid, and much, much more.

- Cohen, Cafi (Pat Farenga, ed.). *And What About College? How Homeschooling Can Lead to Admission to the Best Colleges & Universities*. Holt Associates, 2000. ISBN: 0913677116

  A classic for unschoolers and school-at-homers alike.

- Estell, Doug, et al. *Reading Lists for College Bound Students*. ARCO, 2000. ISBN: 0764561014

  An excellent resource for designing a literary journey through adolescence.

- Heuer, Loretta. *The Homeschooler's Guide to Portfolios and Transcripts*. ARCO, 2000. ISBN: 0028637380

  How do you create portfolios to showcase unschooling for college admission or employment? Or design concise transcripts to show schools and employers the information they expect to see? This book shows how. A wealth of record-keeping forms are included.

- Kohl, Herbert. *The Question Is College: On Finding and Doing Work You Love*. Heinemann, 1998. ISBN: 0867094346

  Which college? Why college at all? Kohl helps families discuss these questions and provides a template to help students explore their options.

CHAPTER NINE

Kids Say the Darnedest Things— About Homeschooling

W HEN YOU hear good things about homeschooling, it's always from the parents, complained a letter written to Dear Abby late in 1997. I have to agree with the letter writer, but I wonder if she ever thought about why this is so.

While a few homeschooling parents were themselves homeschooled (contributor Helen Hegener among them), most of us attended public school, and many spent time teaching in them. This makes it quite easy to see the difference between the two approaches to education. Mostly, our best clues come from our children. There's that gleam in their eyes as they realize they have painlessly learned how to read. There are those questions that know no end and grow ever more challenging. There's that way they jump out of bed in the morning knowing exactly what they want to do, and set about doing it, free from worry about tests, the school bus bully, or being bored. As parents, we know they are approaching learning from a different place than we did, a place we can only wish we had had the chance to experience.

Seeing the difference, it's easy to get excited about what we do. We'd like other parents to know they have an option—a true choice—and that homeschooling isn't as difficult as they probably think it is. We live with proof positive of a very basic difference between the two approaches every day, and it's wonderful to share it.

On the other hand, many of our children are not making educational comparisons. Their gleaming eyes, never-ending questions, and morning enthusiasm are, in their experience, as much an expected part of the day as the sunrise. *Homeschooling is the way they live.* They're no more compelled to shout about homeschooling than they are about eating breakfast in the morning.

> **Many of our children are not making educational comparisons. Their gleaming eyes, never-ending questions, and morning enthusiasm are, in their experience, as much an expected part of the day as the sunrise. *Homeschooling is the way they live.***

That is, unless asked. In response to her reader's comment, Dear Abby put out a call for homeschooled children to share their own feelings about homeschooling, and they did so with articulate letters that spoke about homeschooling in very general terms. So I wondered. If they were asked, would homeschooled children answer far more specific questions for *The Homeschooling Book of Answers*?

The answer was a resounding *yes!* and their contributions are a valuable addition to this book. We are fortunate enough to glimpse homeschooling "from the other side of the fence." As the soon-to-be writers volunteered, I found out a little about their background—age, number of years homeschooling, interests and hobbies, current activities—so that answers would reflect each unique experience. As their answers came in, I was struck by several elements:

- No one asked for a "different" question.
- The essays required very little or, in most cases, no editing.
- The writing is straightforward, open, and powerfully honest.
- Most thanked me for the opportunity to share their thoughts and feelings.

Our glimpse comes from a wide age range, from the eight- and eleven-year-old Dodd brothers to preteens TJ Jones and Annaquista Pykosz; from young teens Theresa Hyland and Adam Dobson to mid-teens Megan Kaseman and Lindsey Johnson; from "finished-with-high-school" teens Michael Hohensee, Sara Shell, and Adam Grimm to Mae Shell, the "old lady" of the group in her early twenties. Don't miss their biographies; they're very interesting people.

I'm happy Dear Abby printed a few of the letters she received. But I'm happier still that our writers will take us beyond the cursory treatment of homeschooling so often found in the short, generic mass-media portrayals, and share more meaningful thoughts on what they're discovering through homeschooling as the way they live.

Author's Note: This chapter has been left as in the first edition . . . you don't mess with success.

65

On a day when you are doing things you like to do, what is it that you're doing and why do you like it?

KIRBY DODD, 11 ◆ I like going to my friends' houses because they're fun to play with. *[Mom's note: we know several homeschooling families, and visits don't have to wait for weekends or vacations.]*

Kirby and Marty Dodd

Board games and Nintendo are fun, because it's fun thinking fast.

I like watching videos, and movies at theaters. I like the entertainment and the stories. I enjoy voices, accents, special effects, costumes, music, and things like that in the movies.

MARTY DODD, 8 ◆ I like to play with Legos. "Why?" Now that's a harder question. Because it's fun. No, no, no. Not because it's fun. Because I like to. No, because I have them. I build with Legos. And if I don't like the thing I built, I put it back to how it used to be. While I'm playing with Legos I make the Lego men talk. I make the guys pick up the things and go. I make them pick up the pieces and put them into place. I like Aquazones.

I also like to play with Darda cars. I play with them because you can build any track you want.

I like to listen to tapes of Weird Al while I build things.

66

Who are the most important people in your life? Why? What do you consider the most important things you do? Why?

ANNAQUISTA PYKOSZ, 11 ◆ The most important people in my life are my mother, father, and my younger brother. Also, my great-grandmother, whom I call "Babcia" (that's grandmother in Polish). I think my mother and father are the most important people because they are the people who brought me into this world. Zeb, my brother, is important just because he is my little brother and I love him. Babcia is important to me in a way that is hard to describe. Babcia is just very special to me. When I go to visit her, she makes me feel welcome and important.

> **I think spending time with my family is one of the most important things I do.**

I think spending time with my family is one of the most important things I do. I also think that helping my mom at the flea markets we go to is important because I enjoy that kind of work. Reading and using the computer are important parts of my life also. Reading and using the computer are very enjoyable and relaxing for me.

Spending time with my family is very important. You can never spend too much time with your family because you never know how long you'll have them. So always spend plenty of time with your family.

67

What are some of the favorite books you've read over the years, and why are they your favorites?

TJ Jones, 12 ◆ Some of my most favorite books were written by Roald Dahl. I especially liked *The BFG, James and the Giant Peach,* and *Danny the Champion of the World.* Roald Dahl is a great storyteller. You can't really predict where he is going to go with a story. His books are completely unique.

As I've gotten older, I've enjoyed biographies and historical novels. I especially enjoy Landmark books. They have books such as *America's First World War, Remember the Alamo,* and *The Winter at Valley Forge.* I liked how the books told about the actual events while also weaving interesting stories about people throughout the pages. For instance, in *America's First World War,* the author told about how if you were in school at the time of the war, you'd have had to knit socks for soldiers.

Other historical books I've really enjoyed are The Childhood of Famous Americans series. For one thing, they're very easy and fun to read. They go into the child's life and tell what it was like to live back in the days the particular individual lived. My favorite ones so far were Daniel Boone and Davy Crockett. When I read those books, I liked to imagine myself in the story. I keep begging my mom for a shotgun based on the fact that boys like Davy Crockett and Daniel Boone got their first guns at my age. So far no luck, though!

Two books that my Dad and I both have liked around my age are *Johnny Tremain* by Esther Forbes (an all-time classic) and *The American Boys Handy Book.* My grandfather gave a copy of the *Handy Book* to my father on March 13, 1968. My dad signed it over to me on November 19, 1995. I've spent hours reading through it. It has great ideas and instructions for easy-to-make items, equipment, and generally interesting things. For example, I've made slingshots, blowguns, bird buoys, and traps. It also tells how to make camping equipment and other things for outdoor life, survival, and fun.

> **My grandfather gave a copy of the *Handy Book* to my father on March 13, 1968. My dad signed it over to me on November 19, 1995. I've spent hours reading through it.**

68

You've been homeschooling for three years after attending a parochial school. What are the major differences in these two learning experiences? Could you share a couple of your favorite activities since you started homeschooling?

THERESA HYLAND, 13 ◆ After homeschooling for three years, it's easy to see the differences between the two learning experiences.

"Classes" are much smaller when you homeschool and you can learn at your own pace. If you want (or need) to spend more time on certain subjects, you can. There's no time limit. Taking field trips, visiting museums, and talking to experts are ways to learn more, and you can do these things more often in homeschooling than in parochial school. Additionally, learning doesn't have an official "start" or "end" date. You can keep going no matter when it is. You have plenty of "free time," which you can use to expand your interests. And you can interact with people of a much wider age range than you can at school.

> **I was excited to meet homeschoolers from Japan. They brought some traditional Japanese toys with them so we got to see how Japanese children play. The visit also spurred a wish to learn Japanese and origami, the traditional art of paper folding.**

Parochial schooling restricts the amount of time you spend on a subject. The classes are much larger. You don't take as many field trips. You also don't get to socialize as much.

Two of my favorite activities since I started homeschooling are the field trips and meeting other homeschoolers. Two of my favorite field trips were to the 1812 Homestead and Gettysburg. At the 1812 Homestead I saw what a typical day in

Theresa Hyland

1812 might have been like. At Gettysburg I saw the hallowed ground of the battlefields, which gives you a good idea of what those soldiers went through at the turning point of the Civil War.

Homeschooling gave me the opportunity to meet people from different countries. In one case they even spoke a foreign language. I might not have had that chance in parochial school. I was excited to meet homeschoolers from Japan. They brought some traditional Japanese toys with them so we got to see how Japanese children play. The visit also spurred a wish to learn Japanese and origami, the traditional art of paper folding.

I have enjoyed my homeschooling experience thoroughly, and I will continue to homeschool for as long as I can.

69

What do you see different about your life compared to the lives of friends who attend school that can be directly attributed to the homeschooling lifestyle?

ADAM DOBSON, 14 ◆ First and foremost, all the free time is an excellent advantage. Getting done hours before those who go to school gives me an opportunity to spend time doing things that really interest me. For instance, I've had a lot more time to practice my electric bass, practice basketball, surf the Net, and so on. I've had a lot of time to learn about computers, then teach it to my parents!

Some of the greatest minds of all time were homeschooled. Thomas Edison, Ben Franklin, Pearl S. Buck, C. S. Lewis, Charles Dickens, John Quincy Adams, William Henry Harrison, Abe Lincoln, James Madison, Franklin Delano Roosevelt, George Washington, and Woodrow Wilson were all homeschooled, just to name a few!

> I also use some of my time in an apprenticeship at a local rock and gem shop. The owners, Kean and Kasey Riley, have taught me a lot, not only about rocks and minerals but about how a business works.

I also use some of my time in an apprenticeship at a local rock and gem shop. The owners, Kean and Kasey Riley, have taught me a lot, not only about rocks and minerals but about how a business works. (The Twin Crystal Rock Shop on Broadway in Saranac Lake, New York—now that's advertising!) Both of my older siblings' former apprenticeships have led to jobs for them.

Adam Dobson

Also it's been great to choose my own curriculum. I can take a more advanced math course instead of wasting time learning things I already know. I'm not the greatest with history, so we might spend a little more time reading, watching videos, and talking about it.

There is definitely a big advantage in homeschooling.

70

Could you share with us the evolution of your work in Shakespearean theater?

MEGAN KASEMAN, 16 ◆ When I was seven, I saw "The Winter's Tale." That evening changed my life.

The play was performed by the Young Shakespeare Players (YSP), actors ages seven to eighteen who perform full-length Shakespeare plays. During the play, I became convinced I wanted to share the magic and perform myself. The next summer I badgered my parents to get information about YSP, and I joined.

Since the directors, Richard and Anne DiPrima, don't believe in auditions or presuming to decide who will make a "good" actor, everyone is welcomed heartily. I remember with enormous fondness the experienced actors who encouraged me in my first play. They are a big part of why I stuck with it; they helped me know I could do it. Now I love supporting younger actors. It is a perfect cycle with special relationships on all sides and an example of the benefits of mixed age groups.

During nine summers with YSP, I've learned that what seems impossible (such as young people performing full-length Shakespeare plays after only seven weeks of rehearsal) is actually possible to do very well if there are people who love and believe in what they're doing and work hard at it.

From the beginning, Richard and Anne and the experienced actors shared their deep love of Shakespeare's language, making it totally unintimidating and allowing me to see for myself that it is fun and beautiful and, once you realize you can understand it, very, very cool. For example, Romeo responds to a joke from Mercutio by saying: "O single-soled jest, solely singular for the singleness."

Megan Kaseman

At first this sounds like a meaningless tongue twister. That's understandable; we don't speak Elizabethan English; we need a little explanation. "O single-soled jest" refers to the fact that a shoe with a single sole (instead of a stronger double sole) is weak, just as Mercutio's joke is weak. "Solely" means only, "singular" noticeable, and "singleness" silliness or stupidity. So we have: A joke as weak as a poorly made shoe, only noticeable because it is so stupid. Pretty cool!

Most Shakespeare is easier to understand. (If you convince yourself you can't understand Shakespeare, it's a lot harder. But if you say, "Shakespeare was a person, too; what he wrote made sense to him. I can make it make sense to me," it will be easier.) In "The Winter's Tale" Leontes greets his guests: "Welcome hither / As is the spring to the earth." The meaning is clear: You are as welcome here as spring is after winter. Living in Wisconsin, I appreciate how welcome spring is.

> **When I was seven, I saw "The Winter's Tale." That evening changed my life.**

A suggestion for parents who want to find activities kids will love: Share things you love with your kids, but don't pressure them to do things. They'll know if something's important for them. When that happens, listen to them. One interest branches into many.

Kids: Trust your instincts. If something sounds interesting, *do* it. Try different things. You never know when an evening will change your life.

71

You're just finishing a third semester at Tisch School of the Arts at New York University. How are you feeling about the future? What are your immediate plans? What are your hopes for your next ten years?

SARA SHELL, 18 ◆ I am a dance major, which means this semester I took ballet and modern dance, improvisation, acting, dance history, and music history. I handed in my term papers for the latter two courses last week, and this week I will take my exams. It is with mixed emotions that I complete my final assignments, because this may be my last semester

Sara Shell

at Tisch. I have learned a lot here and made some wonderful friends, but there are things I want to study which I am unable to here, namely environmental science, and for that reason I have applied as a transfer student to Smith College. If I am accepted, I will probably go there. It is very difficult to be in this limbo of uncertainty, having to say good-bye to my friends and teachers without knowing if I will see them again in January, but I find my comfort in the knowledge that whether I stay here or transfer, I will learn valuable things and have great experiences.

When I graduate, whether it is from NYU or Smith, I want to live in New York and try to dance professionally. If I am not successful here, I will try other cities, possibly in Europe. I also hope to have children eventually, and when the time comes for that I want to move to the country. Someday I want to get my master's degree in environmental science or ecology and have a second career in that field. All of these goals are important to me, but I don't expect them to happen exactly as I plan them. I know that people change—two years ago I never would have thought I'd leave a great dance school for a school with a less professional level of dancing and more academics. At that time, dancing was so strongly the center of my life that nothing else could come close to comparing.

One thing which I have always planned on having is a family. I wanted this even before I started dancing, and when I did, I knew that a dancer's career is short, leaving plenty of time later for children.

Her immediate plans: I took three courses at my local community college when I was fifteen. I was interested in expanding my educational process by learning in a group setting, and taking a U.S. history course with my older sister, Mae, seemed a good way to go about this. I also had a second agenda I was less eager to admit, which was that I wanted to prove to myself and the world that I measured up and was capable of college-level work. I learned a lot of history in that course, as well as how to write a formal essay and take an exam. The next semester I took psychology and environmental science, and had equally rewarding experiences. Most of the other students were at least ten years my senior, and I found their opinions fascinating and their company enjoyable.

My community college experience was really invaluable when it came to applying to four-year colleges. I am sure that having a few grades (grading was never a part of my homeschooling) and letters of recommendation from teachers were important factors in my acceptances from New York University, Hampshire College, and University of Massachusetts Amherst. Once at college, it was a help to know what to expect and what was expected from me in college-level work. The classroom skills that were easy to learn when I was taking one or two courses and living at home would have been much more difficult when I was not only taking a full course-load, but getting adjusted to a whole new life in an unfamiliar environment. College is very different from homeschooling, and community college is a great way to ease the transition. For these reasons I recommend it most highly to any homeschooler planning to attend college full time.

Beyond all the practical concerns, however, I think community college is wonderful purely for its own sake. I learned a huge amount and treasure my memories of it. Speaking from my second year at NYU, considered a very good school, I know that the quality of teaching at the community college is high, in my experience achieving standards many NYU professors I know have difficulty reaching. Perhaps even more significant is the quality of students. The people in my community college courses were mostly thirty-plus, and had kids and jobs and mortgages. They were coming back to school to

> **College is very different from homeschooling, and community college is a great way to ease the transition. For these reasons I recommend it most highly to any homeschooler planning to attend college full time.**

improve themselves and their positions in life, bringing determination, enthusiasm, and a richness of opinion that only life experience can give. They were out to get the most from each course, and because I shared that goal, I discovered I had more in common with them than I do with the NYU students who share my age and more privileged background but skim through their courses without interest or dedication.

Her hopes for the future: The woman I consider my mentor is Jae Diego, my modern dance teacher from the ages of thirteen to sixteen, and my friend. I met her at the age of twelve when my ballet class learned a piece of her choreography. I loved the dance and was eager to have the opportunity to take her class the next year. What she had to teach me was a dance technique that excited my body and mind even more than my beloved ballet, and her class quickly became the highlight of my week. I also found in Jae someone I greatly admired—she was the best dancer I had ever seen, as well as funny and smart and liked by everyone. A compliment from her meant more than five from another teacher. The next year I took her class three times a week and relished every second of it. We also found an arrangement that gave me a wonderful chance to get to know her better, as well as save my parents time. She would drive me to her house after class, where my dad would meet us to take me home, saving him half an hour of driving.

At that time, I saw Jae as perfect, and I wanted to be just like her, a goal that led to unhealthy consequences. The summer before I turned fifteen I came to realize that Jae wasn't perfect, and that I could learn just as much from her with this understanding, but follow my own path and not hurt myself by making her mistakes. At that point in my life I was making a lot of discoveries about who I was and wanted to be, and also making big choices about my future as a dancer. Jae was there every step of the way, sometimes to give advice, but more often to help me discuss and understand myself and my choices so I could come to my own decisions. I decided to audition for dance programs at colleges, and the support and knowledge she gave me were a tremendous help.

I was accepted at Hampshire College and University of Massachusetts, neither my first choice. At the same time Jae and her husband decided to move to Portland. I didn't like the idea of spending another year at home without a modern dance teacher, but after attending a summer orientation at UMass, I realized it was my best option. I stayed home, taking the classes that were available and applying to colleges again. I talked to Jae on the phone periodically, and although I missed her classes it was still a help. I was accepted at the Boston

Conservatory and New York University, both top dance schools.

I still call Jae, especially when I need advice. She has been a big help to me, and I know she's always there. I didn't decide she should be my mentor—it just happened as an extension of the student-teacher relationship, and has been an important and valuable connection in my life.

72

Now that you're settled in at Rensselaer Polytechnic Institute, what are your thoughts on home-schooling as an educational choice?

ADAM GRIMM, 20 ◆ Homeschoolers make up a colorful and diverse nation-wide community. They have chosen homeschooling for almost as many reasons as there are homeschoolers, from those who want to include religious instruction not available in local schools to those whose children's educational needs just are not met in the school system for whatever reason.

Homeschooling allows parents to collaborate with their children, if they wish, on learning. They can decide together what learning pace is appropriate without having to worry about forty other students. This is equally helpful for slow learners and those who are quick to grasp concepts. Self-paced learning is

one of the things that homeschooling advocates love to point out as something the schools are ever attempting to move towards while homeschoolers have been doing it for years.

Homeschooling is another case of getting out what you put in. Parents who are able and willing to put in the necessary time and energy will be able to find the resources needed by their children. Those who are not may not find the homeschooling experience as advantageous.

So homeschooling is viable, but is it beneficial? Does homeschooling produce well-educated and well-adjusted citizens? This is a heated debate that has been going on for quite some time between homeschooling proponents and those who advocate for public school.

Adam Grimm

Those who argue against homeschooling say that children not educated in group environments do not get enough experience at dealing with large groups of people. They also say that a parent who doesn't have a teaching degree could never educate a child as well as a trained professional.

Homeschooling advocates say that these are mostly red herrings. Most homeschooled students spend a large amount of time out in public and with groups of friends. They play sports, belong to clubs, participate in scouting, and do many of the same things as, and sometimes with, their traditionally schooled peers. Socialization, then, is not an issue. Besides, as one well-adjusted former homeschooled student said, "How does learning all the four-letter words help me learn to work in large groups?"

The education issue has been largely shown as a red herring also. By one standard, in fact, homeschoolers seem better educated than their public school counterparts. On standardized tests normed to the public schools, a majority of homeschoolers generally score in the top thirty percentile points. By other standards, too, homeschoolers seem to be well educated. Many colleges are actively recruiting homeschoolers because, among other reasons, they tend to be more self-motivated and have an easier time adjusting to the looser college environment.

One of the reasons that the reasonable education debate has persisted for as long as it has is that many homeschoolers have ideas about what is meant by "well educated" that are different from the schools. In general, the public schools use easily quantifiable standards for education. Test scores are popular. Being able to achieve a certain score at a certain age says whether or not a child is well educated. Many homeschool parents, however, use different standards to judge their children. They prefer to measure their children's total education. For many children it is more natural to read at eight instead of six. By school standards a child like that would not be considered sufficiently educated. However that same child might, at six, know more about American history than most high schoolers and be learning multiplication. Most people would consider that child pretty well educated even though s/he doesn't know how to read.

This is not to say that all homeschoolers are well adjusted geniuses, although some are. There are cases where parents shelter their children to an unhealthy extreme or fail to provide the necessary resources for their children's education. These cases, though, are the exception not the rule. Much the same thing sometimes happens in schools, too, with large class sizes and underfunded budgets taking a toll on school activities.

So homeschooling can be a good thing. It may not be the right thing for everybody but then neither is public school. Whatever the educational philosophy there is one important goal:

> **One of the reasons that the reasonable education debate has persisted for as long as it has is that many homeschoolers have ideas about what is meant by "well educated" that are different from the schools.**

Make sure the education of the child comes first. Everything else should be secondary to that.

73

Looking back, what do you think are the most important things you've learned growing up with homeschooling?

MAE SHELL, 20 ◆ This is a difficult question to answer, in part because I have learned so many things growing up with homeschooling, and also because the most valuable things I have learned are so broad it feels almost impossible to put them into words. So, here goes.

The first thing that comes to mind is the importance of my family life. And I

Mae Shell

mean this in every sense you can imagine, not simply loving but being friends with my family, enjoying their company, supporting them and knowing they support me no matter what happens. I feel very lucky to have wonderful parents who love me unconditionally, who support and respect my lifestyle choices. More than being "just parents," they are my friends, mentors, teachers, and counselors. I also cherish the friendship of my three younger sisters, and older half-brother and sister. As other friend-

ships come and go (something that is inevitable in life), I know that I will always have these rich, wonderful relationships with my siblings.

Because my three younger sisters and I were homeschooled, we spent a lot more time together than we would have if we had attended public school, and by doing so were able to form true friendships with each other. Looking back on my childhood and adolescence, and remembering all the special times I have spent with my family, I realize that it is impossible to really describe what "family life" is. For me, being part of a family was, and continues to be, much more than just living together in the same house; there are fights, apologies, differences of opinion, quiet times spent watching a movie or playing a board game, animated discussions in the car and at the dinner table, listening to one another read out loud . . . I value being a part of this intricate living quilt above everything else.

The second thing that comes to mind is the ability to believe in myself. Some would call this "good self-esteem," but to me it is so much more than that. It means having enough faith in one's instincts to choose seldom traveled paths because they "feel right"; to make objective, yet exciting choices, based on past successes; to honestly critique one's own work; to know that one is right even when everyone else disagrees; to know one's own limits yet create masterpieces within those boundaries. I feel that I have a sensible belief in my abilities, in my strengths and talents. This faith was instilled in me by my parents, who always believed in me even when I didn't believe in myself; who never criticized the bad but praised the good; who have always, and continue to, let me know they will always be there for me, no matter how far away from the nest I fly.

> **I feel that I have a sensible belief in my abilities, in my strengths and talents. This faith was instilled in me by my parents, who always believed in me even when I didn't believe in myself.**

74

What would you suggest to a teen new to homeschooling about how to make the best of educational freedom?

LINDSEY JOHNSON, 16 ◆ Make the best . . . well, the best is different for different people, so it's not easy to tell how one should make the best of her educational freedom. It depends on her own goals and ambitions and dreams. It depends on the person. The whole point of having autodidactic freedom is to be able to direct her own path, to drum out her own direction. I shall try, though, to give some suggestions for unlearning what school has taught, and for freeing oneself from the oppressive ideas of this institution most are so often dependent on.

I have never been to school. I have arrived at these conclusions by talking to friends who go or have gone to school, by reading many books on the subject, and by being in school-like situations such as driver's education that showed me what school is like. It showed me that school is not a place I'd enjoy, nor is it, in my opinion, a very good place. While there was only one "subject," it showed me that, if I went to school, I wouldn't be able to spend my life doing what is probably the best part of life—living it.

Knowing what I know now, I wouldn't dare give up my educational freedom to an institution. First, I would suggest to another teen to take a break from anything academic so as to unlearn what school has taught about learning. In school, the idea is presented that learning is a chore and a race to the finish. It is not. It is a wonderful aspect of life and a great journey. In school, she has also been told to learn what everyone else is learning. What is learned should be the choice of the

Lindsey Johnson

learner. She should try to allow herself to be inquisitive about anything that betides her curiosity and wonder. I think that all too often people are dependent on others to decide what should be learned instead of finding out what the individual heart desires to learn. That is something we must unlearn . . . something school has instilled in us from the time it was created. She should dismiss the idea that she cannot direct her own education . . . when this is done, it will be found that she is the only one who can direct her education authentically and rightly.

She should unlearn the notion that learning must happen at specific times; it should instead be realized that learning is as breathing: It happens all the time.

She needs to stop thinking in terms of "subjects" and realize that everything is dovetailed together. Everything is connected into a unified whole. She should try and rediscover this interconnected unity that she was previously turned away from. She has been taught, while being given irrelative information, that knowledge is very limited because schools separate it into "subjects" with a precise line. This is not true; everything is connected.

She should try to allow herself to question everything. In school, she is taught to focus on the answers instead of the questions, but answers are dead ends. Once one has the answer, that's it, there's nothing left to say. She should allow herself to ask questions—as immense as the Milky Way.

Most of all, don't be afraid to be real. If real means studying only cars or stars, whatever real means, be real. Be yourself. Know yourself. Find the good in yourself . . . because only when you find the good in yourself can you truly find the good in the world.

Most of all, don't be afraid to be real. If real means studying only cars or stars, whatever real means, be real. Be yourself. Know yourself.

MICHAEL HOHENSEE, 18 ◆ The best thing a teenager can do with his newfound freedom is to do whatever it is that he thinks is best. The point of being free to choose how and what you are going to learn is to set and achieve goals that are worthwhile to you. *You* have to discover what you think is worth doing. All anyone else can tell you is what *they* think you ought to do.

But don't worry, you don't have to decide what you want to do for the rest of your life just yet. All you need to do is find a subject that you think is interesting. If you're like me, you like science, engineering, and computers, but can't decide which of these fields you like best. Just find a general area of study which you'd like to pursue. Do you like literature? History? Mathematics? Bird breeding?

Once you've found an area you'd like to focus upon, you need to determine the best way to pursue it. Are you going to raise birds? You might want to find some professional bird breeders to "apprentice" yourself to, to gain experience raising birds. When I set out to breed our cockatiels, the local bird aviary was only too happy to help me choose equipment and give me tips about the care and feeding of baby birds. You'd be surprised at how much you can learn by simply doing.

> **The point of being free to choose how and what you are going to learn is to set and achieve goals that are worthwhile to you.**

If you want to go into a professional field, you'll probably need to go to college. Not only do colleges provide diplomas with which to impress prospective employers, but (if you select your college wisely) they also provide you with access to people who are interested in the same subjects as you are. A further advantage of setting your sights on college is that it helps keep your options open. You can always change your mind and set a new goal.

Since most colleges require some evidence of preparation before they will accept you, you'll have to either remain in high school, take a battery of tests, and/or take some college courses to demonstrate mastery of high school material. I recommend the latter, for I found the local high schools to be a waste of time—too much regimentation and lack of interest in learning. They were more like factories than places of learning. You are much more likely to find teachers interested in *teaching* students in college than you are in high school. Generally speaking, one semester of college is equivalent to one year of high school.

Not only is the quality of education greatly improved at college, but sampling different colleges allows you to determine what kind of college you really want to attend. I've gone to schools of different sizes and have found that I prefer smaller schools to larger ones. If you happen to live nearby the college of your choice, you may be able to attend classes and get to know the faculty. This not only may increase your chances of getting accepted, but also helps you learn whether the school is right for you. In any case, college courses look better than high school courses on your college application.

Above all else, remember that you, and only you, can decide how you're going to learn something. This has always been the case, even when you had no choice about where you were going to study. Only you can decide whether or not to learn anything. Others can only give you advice and opportunities to learn. It is, and always has been, however, your responsibility alone. Keep in mind that you not only have the freedom to succeed in unorthodox ways, but also to fail. Doing things your own way works better, but still requires work!

FOR MY SON

When my oldest was considering whether or not to drop into high school at fourteen years of age, we spent many hours discussing pros and cons. At one point I sat down and wrote out for him the benefits of remaining with homeschooling as I saw them applied to his future. Here, maybe for you to share, too, are the top twenty.

1. You won't be motivated by the "crowd."

2. You'll question opinions presented as facts.

3. You'll enjoy learning throughout life.

4. You'll grow into the person you are, not become someone somebody or something else wants you to be.

5. You'll stand up for that which you know is right.

6. You'll listen to and try to understand "the other guy."

7. You'll welcome differences in people, cultures, and circumstances.

8. You'll be comfortable with people both older and younger than yourself.

9. You'll find that time spent in quiet and solitude is time well spent.

10. You'll know that thinking is but one of several faculties at your command.

11. You'll make decisions based on your thoughts and feelings, not those of others.

12. You'll know how to find out anything you may need to know.

13. You'll be confident that choices you make and actions you take are the best for you.

14. You'll understand that doing something for others is more rewarding than doing something for yourself.

15. You'll discover that many things are not black and white/right and wrong.

16. You'll know about the world in which you are growing up, and in which you'll spend your adult life.

17. You'll realize that life is precious and is the true school you were intended to attend.

18. You'll know nobody but you can decide how and when it is best to learn something.

19. You'll be able to find the best in others because you will have found it in yourself.

20. You'll learn how to make choices that serve you and truth well.

My son stayed home, at least until he was sixteen and tested the community college waters. It's five years later now, and he's already seen enough challenges to put this list to a good test. Watching him deal with the many aspects of his independent life—friends, family, work, and community activities—is proving the list quite accurate.

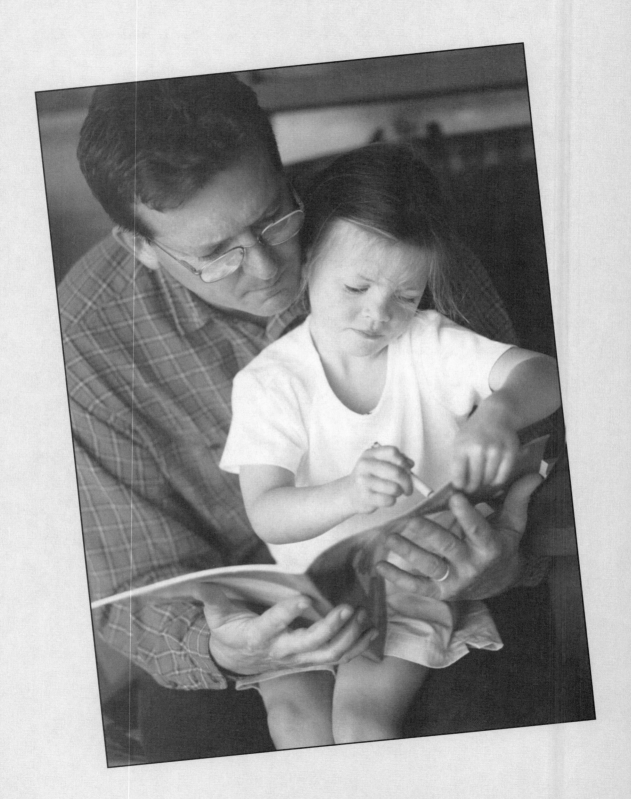

CHAPTER TEN

The Home in Homeschool

"HOMESCHOOLING" IS such a misnomer that I often wish the word had never been invented. It implies a mere link of home and school when, in reality, it is much, much more. But because this is the name now popularized in the mainstream, and it's the name most people associate with what we do, I'm afraid we're stuck with it for a long time to come.

Because of this name, and because this lifestyle frequently begins with an educational decision, all too often the "home" in homeschool disappears. Conversations, news reports, and local school authorities focus on the "school" in homeschool. But as even this misnomer implies, both home and learning are equally important parts of the whole. They cannot be separated. Since you've read much of this book at this point, I'm sure you're beginning to realize this.

So now it's time to give the "home" in homeschool its due, because there will always be those days when it's just as challenging to figure out how you're going to get the laundry done as it is to figure out those algebra problems! Home is much more than housekeeping, though, so we'll also find out what to do about relatives who don't like a decision to homeschool. And where fathers fit into home education.

Now it's time to give the "home" in homeschool its due, because there will always be those days when it's just as challenging to figure out how you're going to get the laundry done as it is to figure out those algebra problems!

We also don't want to be left out of the increasing national fervor about family values. Lawyers, legislators, ministers, governors, and school administrators spend an awful lot of time talking about missing family values. Here we'd like to share what just may be the very best idea on the planet to find them again. It's simple, really. When you put the "home" in homeschool, it grows easier to find the "home" in everything else we do with our children. And home is where the heart—and the values—are.

75

How do I take care of housekeeping when the children are home all day?

BILLY AND NANCY GREER ◆ Well, we have to admit that housekeeping is one of our lower priorities. Since we also have a home business, and lots of other activities, having an immaculate house isn't one of our most important concerns.

Billy and Nancy Greer

The level of housekeeping you do is up to you. It is important to us that our children participate in the upkeep of the house, so they help with certain cleaning tasks. This can be a challenge at times, but it is

something that they will have to face when living on their own.

JANIE LEVINE HELLYER ◆ The parent at home is often busy from daybreak to sunset, and the thought of having our children home all day and doing all we need to do can seem overwhelming. Instead of thinking of homeschooling as "one more job" to do during the day, begin to consider creating an environment where everyone can pitch in and help. This way everyone has more time to pursue interests and no one individual is left feeling like the family housekeeper.

When we begin introducing our children to housekeeping, it sometimes takes more time than it would to do it ourselves. Take enough time so that your child doesn't feel rushed, laugh a little, and have some fun. Believe it or not, this is the stuff that fond memories are made of. Even the youngest child can help sort laundry, match socks, and dust. School-aged children often enjoy running the washing machine, hanging out clothes in the sun to dry, and vacuuming the floors. When we have a positive attitude about housekeeping, children naturally want to participate. They feel like they are making important contributions to our homes and families—and they are!

One of my sons thought that cleaning the bathroom was so much fun, no one else could do that job for years. I finally figured out why one day when I passed by the downstairs bathroom while he was cleaning. There he was drawing a huge picture on the tub surround with a soapy cleanser. No other job in the house offered him the opportunity to draw life-sized pictures, so bathroom detail was actually a treat for him.

Think about why we do housework. Most of us do it because it makes our homes pleasant places for our families to be. Don't think of housework as a negative, something unpleasant that has to be done. Instead, put on some music and include the kids. Doing our work at home can be a wonderful opportunity to spend time doing things with our children, enjoying their company, introducing them to some real life skills, and having some real fun in the process. Who knows, you might actually find that you have more time to pursue your own interests than you did before.

There he was drawing a huge picture on the tub surround with a soapy cleanser. No other job in the house offered him the opportunity to draw life-sized pictures, so bathroom detail was actually a treat for him.

DONNA NICHOLS-WHITE ◆ Ha ha ha ha ha ha!

Okay. Now that I've finished laughing, I'll offer some helpful suggestions. These I've gleaned from the expertise of those whose homes are a lot cleaner than mine.

First of all, since you aren't the only one who uses your home and creates the messes, you shouldn't be the only one cleaning it up. You have a cleaning crew built-in. One of the best ways to develop cooperation and life skills in your children is to always include them in homemaking activities. This includes toddlers. As soon as they show an interest in the toilet bowl brush, hand them one and show them how to clean with it.

What about cooking? What toddler can resist pulling up a chair to the stove while mom or dad cooks? Let them work right alongside you as soon as they are willing. I've let my children cut vegetables with real knives as early as the age of two or whenever they showed an interest in food preparation. My relatives and friends have screamed over the sight of a three-year-old chopping carrots, and have even gone as far as to chastise the children for using these utensils. (And wouldn't you know it? The kids only hurt themselves when these folks scream.) I firmly believe that if allowed to use a tool properly, a child will work responsibly.

Some families devote one full day per week to overhauling the house. My personal favorite is decluttering. I love going through closets, the garage, bedrooms, and cabinets and weeding out anything we haven't used within the past eighteen months. I ship most of these items off to charity. (If you like garage sales, here's your opportunity!)

Realize you are not like the neighbors, friends, and relatives whose children attend school all day. You don't have six-plus child-free hours each day. Breakfast, lunch, dinner, and snacks are served in your home every day.

If push comes to shove, tell yourself that cleaning fanatics are control freaks! (Now I'm going to have to apologize to all of my friends who have spotless homes.)

When I get the mid-winter blues, I find it's because the house looks bad. That's when I'll assign the family on a major work detail such as window cleaning or wall washing. A couple of days of intense housework exhausts me to the

point where I can rest and enjoy the new look. It also convinces me that the rest of the house doesn't look so bad after all.

Don't expect to have a home that looks child-free. We're homeschooling parents. Our children are home with us for good reasons. One important reason is to enjoy their childhoods. Set your standards and have them work alongside you to create a home your family enjoys.

76

How do I handle relatives, friends, or neighbors who don't think homeschooling is a good idea?

MARY GRIFFITH ◆ The best way to handle skeptics is to let them see for themselves what your kids are like, how they spend their time, what interests them, what sort of people they are becoming. Unfortunately, this usually takes years to be effective.

In the meantime it helps to know what about homeschooling your skeptics particularly object to so you can address those issues directly. What's tricky about dealing with relatives and friends—people you have continuing relationships with, as opposed to the store clerk who remarks casually that homeschooling seems kind of odd to her—is that their expressed objec-

Mary Griffith

tions may not be what really bothers them about homeschooling. Your best friend may not be so much upset about your children's socialization as she is that you're doing something entirely different from the norm, and she may feel an implied criticism in the very fact of your homeschooling. Your neighbor may simply fear that your children will eventually trample her prize azaleas. Your mom may still think of you as that gawky kid who kept forgetting to turn in her milk money and had a hard time with algebra, and fear that you'll never be able to keep up with your children and their needs.

Your best friend may not be so much upset about your children's socialization as she is that you're doing something entirely different from the norm, and she may feel an implied criticism in the very fact of your homeschooling.

Whatever the situation, what you need above all is confidence in what you are doing. *You* have to know that you are doing what you believe is the best thing for your children. If you can develop that confidence and faith in your own judgment and in your children, you'll be able to keep those niggling questions and comments in perspective. They'll become the breaches of etiquette, the intrusions into your privacy, the hypothetical commentary they really are.

Which brings us right back to that little matter of time. We all need time to develop that confidence in our homeschooling lifestyle, to learn how our children learn and how we can best help them. Most of us seem to manage this within a year or two. (If we don't, we perhaps need to figure out what secret doubts about homeschooling we're still harboring within ourselves.)

Meanwhile just keep answering those skeptics' questions as best you can, and know that—eventually—time will tell.

SUSAN EVANS ♦ Nonsupportive family members and friends can be one of the most frustrating aspects to homeschooling. I've found it helpful to sort out those whose opinions matter, from those whose don't.

It can lessen your internal conflict to assume that most people are acting out of love for your children and concern for their future. So perhaps they'll simply need more information in order to see the wisdom of your actions and will then move from being critics to being your strongest supporters.

In the end, though, consider where your obligations lie. Are you obliged to keep the neighbors and relatives stress-free, or to raise your children the best way you know?

If the situation is hostile, surround yourself with support: people you admire who respect and support your decision,

THE TEMPORAL NATURE OF MESSES

When our oldest son first moved out of the house, we wound up rearranging everyone's sleeping quarters to create space for a much-needed office. On the appointed day, the bed and dresser were moving out (look at all those crayons back there!), the desk was coming in from the garage (yuk!), the tangle of computer wires was becoming frustrating, and the piles of papers and files rescued from their various storage spaces were growing higher in the middle of the office floor when the phone rang. It was an invitation to present a couple of workshops at a large homeschooling conference.

"We'd like you to present your homeschool advocacy workshop. And could you do one on 'scheduling and organizing your day'?" I could hardly answer I was laughing so hard. If the caller had been able to see our home at that moment (I will never have a video telephone!), he never would have asked!

I was, of course, able to do the workshop. The chaos that was home at that moment was only temporary.

Our time to share homeschooling with our children is temporary, too, and all too soon the Play-Doh messes, scattered Legos, and daily works of art for the refrigerator disappear. Currently, in my home, these have been replaced by paint messes, huge jigsaw puzzles, and scattered science experiments. But I know well that these, too, will fade away in what seems the blink of an eye.

To some it may look like a messy house. To those who know the secret, though, it's the hallmark of a home filled with love, life, and learning.

books that speak to your heart and sustain your faith in your decision to homeschool, periodicals that bring a new round of helpful ideas on a regular basis. Mostly, look to your children. Their growth and progress, even through rocky times, will buoy your spirits and remind you that you've made a good choice.

If all else fails, give yourself permission to tune out negative people, even if they're close friends or relatives. You alone are responsible for decisions on what is best for your family. No doubt you will be reexamining and reevaluating your decision to homeschool on a regular basis. You don't have an obligation to other people to constantly second-guess yourself.

77

If our religion is a main reason for choosing to homeschool, how can I find others who share my religious values?

DR. RAYMOND MOORE AND DOROTHY MOORE ◆ We sympathize with your desire to associate with those of like faith. Why don't you ask of local churches, synagogues, or other places of worship? Home education is now widely accepted, so don't be shy. We can give you names of state groups if you send a self-addressed, stamped envelope to Box 1, Camas, WA 98607.

For your children's sake, be sure their associates model good character and behavior. The associates' examples may be more important than their religion. Church members often don't live by their principles.

But we have a question for you! What do you think of Christ's teaching and example about reaching out to others not of your faith or race? In his associations, he didn't first ask about their faith. Take, for example, Cornelius the centurion, Zaccheus the publican, Mary Magdalene, and the Samaritan woman.

We think of the Tetzlaffs in the early 1980s. Their son, Josh, did not mesh well with the Iowa schools. He was too advanced. "About this time," writes his mother, Barb, "I saw Dr. Moore on the *Phil Donahue Show* and knew that homeschool had to be our solution. I kept my husband, Wayne, up into the wee hours of the night convincing him of this new idea."

Dr. Raymond Moore and Dorothy Moore

When she encountered a belligerent school superintendent, she called for our help. Before the days of good laws, if the issue hadn't reached court-case status, our phone call seemed always to make court unnecessary. When new homeschoolers felt very alone, we supplied information on other homeschoolers in their area and suggested they get together, inviting all homeschoolers or others who were interested. This resulted in a room full of families who formed the "O! KIDS" support group.

In those days nobody said anything about religion, even though many were Christians. They were so glad to find a common ground in homeschooling they banded together *equally* to work for

their concern. Al-
~~ffs~~ were not Chris-
~~that~~ they saw and
~~C~~hristians. This was
~~~~an leaders began to
~~those~~ not of their faith and divided state groups that won good laws in
the early years of the movement. The
Tetzlaffs express gratitude that they
weren't caught by this exclusion.

Why do Christians exclude when
Christ did otherwise? The Christian
leader who started exclusion needed a
constituency, and this was his method.
He misinterpreted two Bible texts: 1
Corinthians 5:9–11 and 2 Corinthians
6:14 KJV. Here, St. Paul
was warning about associat-
ing with "brothers," meaning Christians who are
greedy, adulterous, and so
on. If St. Paul were warning
to stay away from worldly
people, he would have to
leave this world. Home-
school groups are not "un-
equal" in preserving the
movement.

Homeschool support meetings aren't
church services, nor do they need to be
unilaterally dominated by a single belief.
Even the U.S. Senate allows prayer. If we
practice the Golden Rule, families can
learn with the counsel of experienced
home educators from whom they are

now excluded, and in unity the movement could lead the world.

78

How can homeschooling contribute to encouraging our family values with our children?

CINDY WADE ◆ Homeschooling provides a family with some very important
benefits. One of these is *freedom,* the
freedom to choose with whom your
children will learn, what your children
will learn, where your children will learn,
and when your children will learn. Freedom to create a custom
curriculum for your chil-
dren or the freedom to use
no curriculum at all. Freedom to make mistakes and
the freedom to learn from
those mistakes.

Another benefit is
time. Time to rise up in the
morning all rested, enjoy a
leisurely breakfast in the
company of your children
while talking to them about *their* goals,
their hopes, and *their* daydreams. Time to
get to know your children. Every day is
Saturday when you homeschool.

With time on your side you also get
your children at their best—in the morning, when they are clean, rested, fed, and

> **If we practice the Golden Rule, families can learn with the counsel of experienced home educators from whom they are now excluded, and in unity the movement could lead the world.**

raring to go. With schooling, children are sent away from home and certified strangers have them when they're at their best. Parents get them back at the end of the day when they're tired, dirty, and hungry. With schooling, there's the added stress of peer pressure, doing homework, after-school activities, and often no supervision at all until parents arrive home from work. Not a healthy situation for anyone. Encouraging and supporting homeschooling could mean a significant decrease in the amount of child neglect in this country.

Still another benefit is *healthy socialization*. Education doesn't take place in a vacuum, but schooling does. Homeschoolers are out in the real world living real lives. You can instill *your* values and set examples for your children. Homeschooled children live and socialize in a more natural setting by being with parents, siblings, grandparents, relatives, neighbors, and other acquaintances. They learn to live within their communities as they shop at local stores, go to the library, help with a home business or in their parent's shop, campaign for a candidate, open a savings account, perform in community or professional plays, or volunteer at local events. The list goes on and on.

Homeschooling also gives you *choice*. You decide the curriculum and budget. You set the rules and the pace. You can't get that kind of parental involvement and, therefore, values, by letting government school raise your child.

It's difficult to fathom that some educators and politicians seriously believe parents will damage their children by homeschooling them. Do they honestly think your intention is to purposely harm your children by providing them with an alternative to government-run public schools? I have yet to meet a homeschooling parent whose intent was to shelter, corrupt, or damage her child by choosing to homeschool.

Homeschoolers are like wise gardeners. They know better than to plant a tomato seed directly in the garden in the month of May. You raise tomatoes by starting the seed inside a warm and safe environment. You grow it until it can stand alone outside—and even then you must still protect it from certain elements from time to time.

Finally, there is *love*. No one loves your child more than you do. You know what's best for your child. Parents have instincts. If your instincts tell you something is or isn't right for your children then you have every natural and God-given right in the world to act upon those instincts.

You know your children best and you have the right to raise them in your own way with your values. The state and federal governments have no business or right to tell you otherwise.

MICHELLE BARONE ◆ The term "family values" has lately become a weapon in political debates, swinging from left-wing liberal rhetoric over into fundamentalist right-wing intolerance. But everyone was raised in a family, and every family has certain values, principles, and beliefs formed from observation, experience, modeling, and maturity.

Family values simply mean what we, as parents, want our children to cherish, principles such as honesty, integrity, hard work, generosity, faithfulness.

Though some will deny it, we all have values. Schools, in particular, struggle to promote value-free education, but this is always going to be a losing game. Teachers and other adults who work with children are, by their very presence, modeling values; and most of these are good ones, although perhaps not the same as a family's. This can be a good thing, exposing children to different ideas. But large numbers of same-age peers also influence a child's growing sense of values. Ruthless competition, bullying, blind consumerism, distorted body concepts, cruel teasing of younger or weaker children, and racism may not be the pro-social values we would like our children to absorb. With a loving and concerned adult to guide them, children are able to put these influences into a perspective that will guide them throughout their lives.

In order to ensure our children develop values our family sees as important, it is essential our children spend time with us, lots of time. The more time we spend with our children, the more positive influence we will have on them.

When the clerk in the grocery store forgets to charge you for the magazine you are holding, do you return and pay for it? Do you clean up your dog's mess from the neighbor's lawn without hesitation? Do you discuss propositions and candidates with others, and then vote? When you homeschool, and have your children with you, they are watching.

THE QUALITIES OF HOMESCHOOLING THAT ENCOURAGE FAMILY VALUES

Freedom   Choice

Time   Love

Healthy socialization

They are learning your family values, in context, not adrift or in the abstract.

79
What is the father's role in home education?

CHRIS CARDIFF ◆ There is no set, predefined, optimal role for fathers in home education. The father's role can vary broadly from family to family, ranging from the traditional breadwinner to the stay-at-home dad who is the primary teacher. Flexibility and freedom are hallmarks of homeschooling. Families taking advantage of them will all make different choices, including the different roles individual family members will play at different times and in different circumstances.

Even the most conventional roles of student and teacher get reversed in homeschooling. For example, my girls know much more about music than I do. When my middle daughter started learning piano at the age of six, she would follow up her lessons in the afternoon by sitting me down in the evening and teaching me what she learned. We both loved our roles as student and teacher. She would be boiling over with excitement about "teaching daddy," and I enjoyed learning and sharing her infectious enthusiasm.

Despite this flexibility, there is still the need to earn a living. In a majority of homeschooling families, the father takes on the traditional role of breadwinner while the mother is the primary teacher, coach, facilitator, educator, chauffeur, organizer, helper, coordinator, and drill instructor.

Assuming the desire to participate, getting the father involved in this situation is largely one of time management. In a single-income household with the father away from the family forty to sixty hours a week, there isn't as much time available for the father to participate in homeschooling.

In our family, which fits this model, we've discovered a few things that work for us. First and foremost is my responsibility to provide emotional support to the primary teacher. This support may come in the form of affirming the family's decision to homeschool when criticized by friends and relatives—facing these as a united front makes a big difference in these situations.

Sometimes the support is just verbal encouragement—an "attagirl" at the end of the day. At other times, it's playing the role of teacher's aide and helping to sort through the occasional homeschooling chaos by taking care of some mundane homeschooling chores (like chauffeur duty).

On a more practical level, we take advantage of the flexibility of homeschooling to let our girls sleep in a little later than kids going to traditional schools.

This allows them to stay up later at night when I'm home from work. To take advantage of this we schedule some homeschooling activities during the evenings and weekends when I'm available. For example, I coach a Math Olympiad team for homeschoolers on Wednesday evenings and get a significant turnout of participating fathers. The same is true of our Geography/Culture group, which meets on weekends.

At the end of the day, homeschooling allows families to choose the educational options and arrangements that work best for them as a family. There is no magic formula that works for everyone and one of the joys of homeschooling is working together as a family to find what works for you.

MARK HEGENER ◆ It's simple: All you have to do is display unwavering faith, trust, hope, love, and courage. These are the things that help bind families together, the important things that make families work. Getting to this point has taken me over twenty years plus lots and lots of patience, love, and understanding from my own family.

Along the way it would have been easier, and probably more financially profitable, to become isolated from my family, to lose track of my place and let the family drift apart. Perhaps not physi-

cally drift apart, but to drift emotionally, to lose the daily experience of simply living together and the perspective it has developed within each of us.

HELEN HEGENER ◆ Because Mark and I have homeschooled our five children while building a business that allows us both to work from home, we've been able to build a family closeness and unity that might be unusual in today's fractured and compartmentalized world. And yet our five children are incredibly independent individuals, as comfortable away from the family as within it. This seems like the primary role of any parent, father or mother: to provide his or her children with a sense of safety and security from which to confidently explore the world.

I know my own parents placed this concern for their children foremost in their lives. It gave me a sense that I could be responsible for what happened in my life with the security that no matter what I did, no matter how badly I blew it, my parents would still be there for me, and would still love me unconditionally. They gave me the courage and the freedom to challenge assumptions, to ask questions fearlessly, to search for new answers. My greatest reward as a parent is watching their grandchildren continue the search.

CHAPTER ELEVEN

Personally Speaking

THE PHONE rings. It's a complete stranger asking if you have a few minutes to speak with her about homeschooling. Experience has taught you to turn off the oven and sit down. This is going to take more than a few minutes.

Mostly, you listen. You listen to a variation of a story you've heard umpteen times before. She tells you about herself, her children, her children's school experiences, and anything else she can think of now that someone who understands is listening—finally. Bottom line? The stranger is searching for a different way—a better way—for her children to go about the process of receiving an education. And within a very short time, she is not a stranger anymore.

She's not a stranger anymore because she has opened up to you and, in answering her many questions, you, too, have shared a large piece of your life and lifestyle with her. She may come to your local support group's meetings where homeschoolers gather and, in a refreshing, honest, and open way, others will also listen to her story and share their own.

In a very real sense, this whole book could be called "Personally Speaking": It's filled with the same honest and open sharing that has helped countless new homeschoolers get off to a good start in meetings and get-togethers throughout the country. But the title's been saved for this chapter, the one containing the most personal half-dozen questions asked and answered. They're questions you may often have thought about but were afraid to ask.

New homeschoolers are often filled with self-doubt; you question whether you've got "the right stuff" for homeschooling, and wonder where those who pursue this path find the courage to go about it. Will your children be forever tied to your apron strings if you homeschool, or can they really learn how to think for themselves? The answers, I think, will please you.

If you really want to get a gathering of homeschoolers buzzing, just bring up the subject of television, our consumer culture's two-edged sword. The answers to the "boob tube" question here are just as lively as at any meeting as homeschoolers share their feelings about whether you really should *kill* your television.

Don't worry if you've been living this lifestyle for a while; you haven't been left out of this heart-to-heart. Have you ever wondered if you're the only one in the world who stresses out about some aspect of homeschooling? Are there ways around (or through or under or over) your stress? Oh, and speaking of stress, we're even going to question whether it's possible to share news of homeschooling without coming across as a "homeschool snob."

Even if you've been afraid to ask these questions, thankfully, our contributors were not afraid to answer.

80

How do I know if I'm cut out for homeschooling?

SUSAN EVANS ◆ Are you a parent?

Do you enjoy your children most of the time? Some of the time?

Are you curious about all those interesting nooks and crannies in the world that you didn't get to explore when you were in school?

Do you find manufactured stresses and crises (school projects, tests, teacher conferences) annoying? Would you rather not have a parade of strangers telling you who your children are and what you should be making them do?

Do you plan to have a good, solid, close relationship with your children when they're grown? Do you want to lay the solid groundwork for that now?

Are your children some of your closest friends? Would you like them to be?

If you answered, "Yes!" to any of these questions, you have what it takes!

REBECCA KOCHENDERFER ◆ Families homeschool in a variety of ways. Some families set up school-at-home. They study the same subjects as the public school, take tests, and issue grades. Other homeschoolers unschool their children. With this approach, children are free to set their own goals and evaluate their own progress.

Parents choose homeschooling for a variety of reasons. Some homeschool for religious reasons. These parents want to combine their children's academic education with their religious education. They want to pass along their family's morals and values. Some parents homeschool for educational reasons. These parents believe that their children will be able to receive a better, more thoughtful education at home rather than at school. Some parents homeschool because they do not want their children to spend their formative years in age-segregated institutions, learning what someone else thinks is important. Still others homeschool because they live overseas or because they live too far from school.

What are *your* reasons for homeschooling? The question of whether or not you are cut out for homeschooling depends a lot on your reasons for choosing homeschooling in the first place. If

it's a good fit for you and your family, homeschooling will probably work out well for you. If you are forcing yourself to homeschool against your better instincts, it may not turn out as well for you. I would advise you to explore all of the educational alternatives available. Just because homeschooling is right for me and mine doesn't mean that it is right for everyone. Find out what's available, think about what you want, and go with what feels right.

81

Where does one find the courage to pursue an education so different as homeschooling?

NED VARE ◆ The false idea is that going to school gives us an education. It takes common sense, not courage, to realize that. Trust your own, and your children's, intelligence.

Continuity of our culture and society *depends* on the passing along of its collective world view. That is not something to be ashamed of or to deny our children. It is as necessary and inevitable as night following day.

The danger that is being caused by the public schools today, at the insistence of the few in charge of the federal department of education, is that the continuity of culture and society is being broken, on purpose, in order to promote a global government and society. Schools are being changed from their traditional educational purposes and turned into job training centers where children are trained and adjusted for attitudes, opinions, and adaptability to become workers—human resources—for the "global economy" comprised of the businesses that have the ear of political leaders. It is a fraud. As Eda LeShan said to her mother, "Let me be how I grow."

MARY GRIFFITH ◆ Sending my children to school and watching them learn to tolerate mediocrity and boredom would take courage. Sending my kids to school and letting them believe history is what's contained in textbooks would take courage. Letting my children eat up hours each day waiting for the next event, waiting for the "later" to delve into the things that really interest them would take courage. Teaching my children that I think the most important thing in their lives is to achieve higher test scores than their peers would take courage. Teaching my children they shouldn't trust in their own values and judgment would take courage.

Homeschooling doesn't take courage. Choosing homeschooling is easy.

> **The false idea is that going to school gives us an education. It takes common sense, not courage, to realize that. Trust your own, and your children's, intelligence.**

82

Parents must get stressed out over homeschooling sometimes. How do I cope?

LILLIAN JONES ◆ It's a rare beginning homeschooling parent who doesn't go through some stress. There can be a real disequilibrium over leaving the known for the unknown, staggering under the heavy weight of the responsibility for your child's future.

Reading books like this one by seasoned homeschoolers is a great help in coping with that particular stress. Also, make sure you're getting this kind of support from beyond just your local support group. People often become involved in activities with their support groups in a busy way that doesn't include discussing their anxieties about homeschooling. Homeschoolers do tend to love to talk about homeschooling, though, so asking questions can get some great discussions going. You'll find that others are sometimes needing the same kind of support.

A steady source of support can also be newsletters and magazines, as well as online homeschooling forums if you have access to a computer. *Home Educa-*

tion Magazine is a wonderful support to have arriving in your mailbox on a regular

Lillian Jones

basis. Also, search the Internet for online support groups. These resources can sometimes feel like a warm hug on a cold and bitter day.

The best homeschool experiences come with no attempt to re-create school at home, and re-creating school at home is the single most stressful force against successful homeschooling. This message is hard to grasp sometimes, but it is a vital one. Pay heed.

The best (yet too often overlooked) way for getting through any homeschooling stress is to focus on enjoying your children. If you're not putting school-like stresses on your children, you will see beautifully whole and healthy individuals emerging before your eyes. There will be magical moments when the beauty of the whole situation is so crystalline that you wonder how you ever could have doubted.

Nevertheless, you might occasionally doubt everything you ever believed; times when you suddenly and inexplicably feel you've made a terrible mistake by thinking you could leave the system.

> **Anxiety passes, and . . . reappears less and less as you see your children growing strong and enthusiastic for life.**

That anxiety passes, and it reappears less and less as you see your children growing strong and enthusiastic for life. Make sure you're finding ways of nurturing yourself, too; get exercise and pursue your own interests. Your children don't need you to hover as much as you might think.

Don't worry. When you trust your children, you eventually all settle into a place of comfortable self-assurance.

NANCY PLENT ◆ Most of us are the authors of our own stress. We want everything to be perfect and go according to schedule, everyone in the family to be happy all the time, we want . . . well, life just doesn't run that smoothly. We need to identify stress as a useful signal that it's time to change something.

When my son was small, I preserved my sanity by getting up at 5:00 A.M., taking a predawn bike ride, puttering in the garden, and listening to the birds greet the morning. I'm not a morning person, so the first ten minutes were horrible! But the rest of it—the exercise, the solo cup of tea on the back porch afterwards—was good for the soul. The rest of the day I could cope with anything. Other parents have told me they avoided burnout by occasionally tossing out their careful plans for the day and doing something spontaneous that the children suggested. It's too easy to fall into thinking that you have to "do school" for six hours a day, five days a week, even though homeschool doesn't take *nearly* that long!

You know the saying: "If momma ain't happy, ain't nobody happy." Momma has to be realistic about what she wants her homeschool to be. Make a cup of tea, go for a walk, decide what's really important, and ruthlessly cut out the rest.

83

How will my children develop their own world view if I'm teacher as well as parent?

MARY McCARTHY ◆ Interesting question. I'm not sure we want our children to develop a view too far from our own. Isn't it a parent's responsibility to instill basic values in our children before the world influences them?

Our world view is from a previous generation, theirs has to reflect their generation in their time. I'm afraid we live in a media-drenched world. We catch the headlines on TV—the whole world, live, via satellite—before sitting down to read the paper at breakfast. After a few quick lessons, including such worldly subjects as history and geogra-

phy, our children can hop on the Internet and communicate with the entire world. I always figure I could never have purchased the education my son obtained on his own from the Internet. Where else can a kid ask a college student a question and get a reasonable answer? Where else can he find out what's going on in Tokyo? Or know off the top of his head what time it is in Paris? I think as parents we give our children their foundations—then they adapt their views from everything else to create a world view uniquely their own. Besides, whose child ever grows up to be just like his parents? There's a scary thought.

DAVID AND MICKI COLFAX ◆ Is the implication here that without contact with an outside-of-the-family teacher the children will not develop an independent "world view?" If so, it raises the more fundamental question of whether or not it is desirable for children to develop world views that are different from those of their parents. We all know liberal parents who have raised conservative children and conservatives who have raised young liberals. But in most cases the schools have had very little to do with it. Indeed, there is considerable evidence that schools, right on through college, have remarkably little impact on the values that inform the "world views" of young people. Schools may dumb down, teach passivity and conformity, and encourage peer-dependence, but only rarely do they significantly transform the basic value structure or set of assumptions that the child brings from home and family.

Perhaps this question is better understood as an expression of concern that some homeschooling parents, unlike those who put their children in schools, are able to indoctrinate their children with what some would characterize as narrow and stultifying world views; indeed, that they could be creating intellectual and ideological clones of themselves. According to these critics, bereft of the influence of teachers and the culture of the school, these children have few opportunities to be exposed to values and perspectives that prevail in the society at large—to develop ideas and understandings that extend beyond those which exist within the confines of the family. The school thus viewed does both more and less than educate; "Give us your children and we will *socialize* them" becomes the rallying cry of its advocates.

And while homeschooling parents can be overbearing, overly protective, and yes, even narrow-minded and rigid on occasion, the very *openness and prac-*

> **When we speak of how homeschooling allows more time and opportunities for thinking, reading, working on self-directed projects, and interacting with people of different ages and stations in life, we are talking about the very activities and conditions that nurture the development of independent "world views."**

tice of homeschooling provide children with opportunities to learn and to expand their horizons that are denied their peers who have to cope with the rigidities, inequities, and absurdities of conventional school life. Homeschooling is precisely what the schools claim to be but most emphatically are not: an approach to learning that fosters both intellectual liberation and genuine socialization. When we speak of how homeschooling allows more time and opportunities for thinking, reading, working on self-directed projects, and interacting with people of different ages and stations in life, we are talking about the very activities and conditions that nurture the development of independent "world views." How do we know this?

Talk to the children.

Does TV have a place in the homeschooler's home?

MARY MCCARTHY ◆ Sure, why not? I think it's great that you can turn on the

TV and see the world. It opens so many doors, inspires so many interesting topics, and shows you the rest of the world. There are all those diverse viewpoints and lifestyles. Then there are videos, where you can learn about something by just sitting down with a bag of popcorn. Television really expands the possibilities for learning.

SHARI HENRY ◆ Well, it sure does in ours! The children each choose thirty minutes of TV programming an afternoon. The girls usually pick PBS shows such as "Arthur" and "The Magic Schoolbus"; TJ likes ESPN. Also, we watch lots of great stuff on C-SPAN, Discovery Channel, Animal Network, and History Channel. Television enriches learning, spurs new ideas, and entertains. In moderation, it can be quite useful, though I wouldn't want my children to trade too much of their time exploring in the woods, reading great literature, or baking cookies for staring at the television. More than any single issue, television seems to require that ever-elusive balancing act.

Shari Henry

BILLY AND NANCY GREER ◆ Whew! This is a very difficult question to answer. We'd have to defer to the personal preference of parents when making this decision. We personally take the middle ground. While we do not ban television, we do believe that too much television is negative. From our own experience, we think it is an "addictive" medium and time better spent on "real" living is wasted. Our children mostly watch public television (shows such as "Bill Nye" or "Wishbone") or videos. By avoiding commercial television, our children are not exposed to advertising that we'd prefer they not watch.

Some people feel that restricting TV viewing creates a desire for forbidden fruit. We have not seen this with our children. For us, television is such a powerful medium that monitoring its use is akin to preventing them from running in front of a car and getting hit.

Others just toss out the TV, but we have seen benefits to our children watching science and nature programs on public television. They now have such vast reservoirs of animal facts that quite often I've had to go to them for information! Most educational tools have drawbacks and much of what is on television is of little worth, but the

> For us, television is such a powerful medium that monitoring its use is akin to preventing them from running in front of a car and getting hit.

same is true of many educational software packages. I find it humorous that many people will limit TV because they don't want their children to be couch potatoes, but they think it is fine for them to spend all day on the computer where they become mouse potatoes.

85

After homeschooling for several years, I've noticed a difference in my children. I want to share this difference with people; but, frankly, it's hard to explain to other parents without risk of them feeling as if I'm criticizing *their* choice to have their children remain in public school. How do homeschoolers who want to share their discoveries overcome this very natural and understandable tendency?

CHRIS CARDIFF ◆ It is an unfortunate fact of life that some people feel threatened by other people's choices. You will be unable to overcome some people's defensiveness no matter what you do. For others, however, the right approach will make a huge difference.

It's important to keep in mind that typically the choice to homeschool is more than just an educational choice—it's a lifestyle choice. In that sense it can be as controversial and soul-wrenching as the "mommy wars" between the stay-at-home moms and the go-to-work moms. There is huge potential for implied guilt, with both sides arguing they are doing what's best for their children.

To avoid igniting such a volatile confrontation, I favor a soft-sell approach to homeschooling. There is no reason to shove homeschooling down someone's throat—if you do, they are likely to just spit it back out at you. A better approach is to let them come to you with their questions.

More often than not, your children will be the best (and only) "advertisements" for homeschooling that you will ever need. Adults in particular will notice their social skills and comment on them. This usually provides the opening you need to introduce them to homeschooling and a brief discussion of the corollary benefits (other than academic) your family derives from homeschooling.

One key point to make early on is to acknowledge that homeschooling is not for everyone. This lowers defensive barriers by validating their current educational choices.

In many cases, parents may not even be aware they had an educational option like homeschooling available to them. This will be an eye-opening, consciousness-raising, mind-expanding, revelatory experience for them—the realization that there *are* educational choices for their family. This can lead to a wide-ranging discussion on the myriad ways to homeschool.

Take advantage of the positive opportunities you have to share the benefits of homeschooling. A gentle, affirming approach will negate any implied criticism of alternative choices and allow others the freedom to really listen to what you have to say.

> **In many cases, parents may not even be aware they had an educational option like homeschooling available to them.**
>
> **This will be an eye-opening, consciousness-raising, mind-expanding, revelatory experience for them—the realization that there *are* educational choices for their family.**

86

What about *me*? Will I be able to attend to my own needs and goals, and to my relationship with my spouse?

ISABEL LYMAN ◆ Will you have a life? Sure. But for a season, this is your life— all homeschooling, all the time. And guess what? It can be a wonderful life if you have the right mindset and aren't afraid to be creative. My family and I have entertained Nelson Mandela's grandson in our backyard for a Halloween party, as well as had Pat Buchanan over to the house for lunch. Homeschooling, frankly, has given me the excuse to think outside the box and take the initiative to bring the world into our home.

This educational adventure is going to consume a good chunk of your leisure time for many years. You will have to stare down discouraging days, face endless housework (since your home will be lived in as opposed to being treated like a Motel 6 pit stop), and maybe put big dreams on a back burner. It's probably not the best time in your life to run for the U.S. Senate or compete in the Ironman Triathlon. On the other hand, you could campaign for the school board and run in 10Ks.

Downsize your vision, and keep your life simple. But, by all means, make time for bubble baths, dinner dates with your spouse, and espressos with a fellow homeschooling parent. Your children will get older and become more independent, and you will, once again, have the energy that's required for working a full-time job, getting your doctorate, or doing whatever. Fact is, when you get to that stage, you might even miss the good ol' homeschooling days, like I often do.

If possible, try to homeschool as a partnership. I'm not a member of the

National Organization of Women, but neither am I crazy about the model of Dad earning the bread while Mom does all the teaching. Maybe both Mom and Dad can work part time and share the household and homeschooling duties. Maybe the parents can run a home-based business together. Maybe one of you is savvy enough to invest bucks in real estate and stocks and draw from that money for, say, a year, and dedicate that time to the family. (Read *Rich Dad, Poor Dad* by Robert T. Kiyosaki for financial ideas.) Puh-leeze don't give in to the materialistic, entertainment culture that makes you feel like your kiddies are deprived if the family doesn't live in a fancy house in the suburbs with expensive toys. You are giving your children the greatest gift of all—your undivided attention.

MARSHA RANSOM ◆ Yes, and it's extremely important that you plan your time so you may do so. Whether you are coping well or not, children pick up on your feelings and the dynamics of relationships in the home. As more than one person has said, "If Mama's not happy, nobody's happy!"

Make sure you take time for yourself. Some homeschoolers get up before their children and have a cup of coffee or tea, read, answer their e-mail, meditate, or listen to music. Counting on this time every day helps them cope when things get hectic. Others enjoy kicking back once the day is over and the kids are settled for the night. What you choose will likely depend on whether you're an early bird or a night owl!

It's vital to make time for you and your spouse to spend together, apart from the everyday activities. Some homeschooling parents have a weekly "date"; others spend a little time together in their room each day with no interruptions allowed, perhaps when the breadwinner arrives from work. Some defer pleasure and take a couple of retreats a year, with grandparents keeping the kids. You are the best judge of how much time you and your spouse need. Include yourselves at the top of your list; your relationship is just as important as planning your children's curricula or choosing what books to use.

Some homeschoolers find fulfillment in running a business from home, doing community service, or pursuing their own hobbies, such as scrapbooking, writing, or quilting. Others enjoy touching bases with other homeschoolers via e-mail lists, and exchanging stories and tips. Although I have to talk myself almost daily into keeping up with my exercise regime, I've found that I feel better when I walk and work out every day. I reap the benefits of more energy, a positive feeling about doing something good for myself, and less depression. To keep from being bored while exercising, I listen to books on tape. To minimize interruptions during "my time," I have my kids either work through a list of chores and projects, have quiet time in their room reading, or watch a video for a treat. Making healthy meals is also a priority; and planning, preparing, and cleaning up from these meals becomes a part of our family's homeschooling curriculum.

Making time to enjoy some of your favorite activities and taking care of yourself will keep you happier and prevent burnout.

ANN FISHER ◆ This is such an important question! Yes, of course you will, though you may need to plan more than your mother did. Your question points to the fact that a successful homeschooling lifestyle means that the needs of *all* family members are important. You absolutely *must* find ways to take care of your needs, goals, and personal relationship with your spouse for your homeschooling lifestyle to succeed. Here are a few tips that may help:

• Find a role model or three. Most of us weren't raised in a homeschooling family, so where can we learn what works best? Look for a book, a friend, a support group, an online e-mail list—any resource that will show you ways other people manage to create a successful homeschool lifestyle.

• Don't rush to abandon goals, but do think about rebalancing your priorities from time to time. Once homeschooling has moved solidly into your life as a cherished goal, previous goals may occupy the back burner. Although homeschooling does take time, it takes less than you might think, so don't give up goals unnecessarily.

• Schedule time for yourself regularly—daily is best for some. For example, I got up early in the morning to work on projects, then caught up on sleep at naptime or gave myself an early bedtime. Weekly, monthly, even yearly time for yourself can refresh your soul. Try a Dad's Night Out or Mom's Weekend Retreat for personal renewal. Take turns with your spouse or trade kids with a friend for a day or evening.

• Schedule "couple time" faithfully. (You probably got this advice when your children were born, only now it is more important than ever!) Without careful planning, those days and weeks when you and your spouse hardly see each other can slip into months and years—not a good family strategy! Try different arrangements to see what works for your family: a weekly date night? time together each morning or evening? a week or weekend for the kids at Grandma's? Trade Friday night babysitting with a neighbor. Time spent keeping your relationship strong is as important to your children as any other lesson you can teach them.

• Participate in your career or other personal goals part time, if possible. Working one or two days a week can keep you involved in activities you love without causing overload.

• Some careers and activities overlap well with homeschooling, enabling you to better use your time. For instance, if your hobby is sewing or crafts, set up your work area near where your children play or do their work.

• Sequence your goals to coincide with your children's level of development. No one plans to run a marathon the year the new baby arrives. Similarly, a goal of *House Beautiful* is more attainable after the paint, juice, and mud years are history. Writing your novel may need to be put on hold until your children are immersed in reading and writing and projects of their own, but you may have time to create short stories and poems in the meantime.

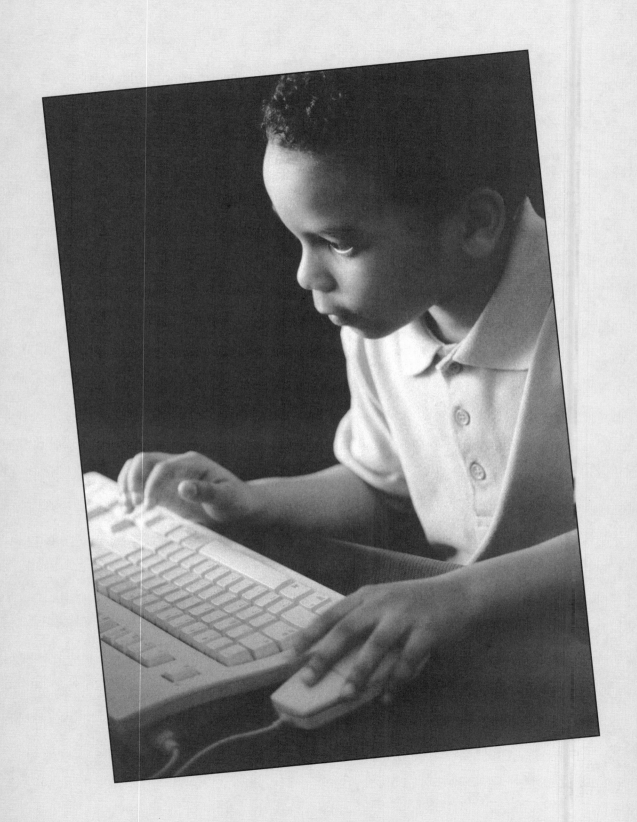

CHAPTER TWELVE

Twenty-First Century Homeschooling

I T H A S only been four years since the first edition was printed, yet that brief period ushered in many new challenges and opportunities. Homeschooling is an educational alternative still evolving, suffering occasional growing pains while boldly moving forward into the new world of educational experimentation and customization. Gone are the days a new homeschooler is considered a weirdo, as homeschooling has gone mainstream—in part because major magazines and newspapers have said so. For example, in August 2001, *Time* magazine asked, on its cover, "Is Home Schooling Good for America?"

As we enter the new millennium, the number of families turning to homeschooling continues to increase, and that includes a growing number of families with children who have special needs. Here you'll find out why.

As record numbers of homeschooled children are hitting college age, you might wonder whether homeschooling has helped or hindered their entry into higher education. This question, too, will be answered.

The twenty-first century finds the Internet and homeschooling growing up side by side. Sometimes this is a blessing, sometimes a curse. Computer-based distance learning programs, for example, seem to multiply daily and provide additional educational alternatives. Are these programs right for your child? And how can we keep from experiencing "homeschooling information overload"?

The list of twenty-first century homeschooling legal issues is topped by the push for educational accountability (as deemed necessary by the faltering state of public schooling), as well as the similarly inspired focus on truancy. Additionally, charter schools, one of the growing number of educational alternatives endorsed by the existing system, have discovered home educators as a market for their wares. It's important that you understand what these issues mean—or don't mean—to your homeschooling family.

Reporters often ask for predictions about the future of homeschooling, but I've yet to find the crystal ball that allows me to answer with any measure of certainty. If history is any indication, we can expect that whatever happens will be as interesting as it is challenging, will have a significant impact on society in general, and will be a result of the continuing phenomenal growth of family-centered education.

87

So, just how many homeschoolers were there when the new millennium began?

ISABEL LYMAN ◆ Sigh. That question gets asked almost as often as the "what about socialization" one.

No exact figures presently exist, but general agreement is that homeschoolers comprise at least one percent of the school-age population—around one million students. When I wrote *The Homeschooling Revolution*, I came up with between 893,217 and 990,817 for the 1998–1999 school year. I arrived at those numbers by contacting education agencies in each state and asking how many homeschoolers were in their state.

About thirty very helpful bureaucrats responded.

Some states, such as Mississippi and California, don't track homeschoolers, so I had to ask home education advocates to offer a guess-estimate of those populations, and that's how I arrived at the other numbers. Keep in mind that a portion of homeschoolers don't want to be counted for either religious or political convictions, and aren't involved in any homeschooling networks, so they aren't reporting their whereabouts to the authorities. The "mystery of how many students are taught at home" would stump even Agatha Christie—a homeschooler herself, by the way.

ANN ZEISE ◆ Linda, I really tried to get some numbers. A handful of states that required registration had numbers. The confusion came over whether they were counting "homeschools" or "homeschooled students." You see, some count "private-schooled students" but not "homeschooled students," so homeschoolers get lumped in with all the students in large private schools. The state "guessed" that all private schools with five or fewer students are probably homeschools. What about large families that homeschool? I guess they aren't counted as homeschoolers!

Some homeschool families are totally "under the radar," believing that they need not follow state registering laws. Can't count those children easily!

Many homeschool associations are willing to share the number of members they have. You might suppose that their members are all homeschool parents, but you'd be wrong; some members are "interested parties" and not parents. Do both parents join or just one? My guess is that association membership is at best an indication of the growth in interest in homeschooling, but certainly does not yield an accurate count.

A large religious organization likes to report its membership figures and then interpolates that number into a statistical "guess" at the number of homeschoolers. The range is huge: 1.2 to 2 million in the United States. The association's members are "joiners" and fairly easy for researchers to find and study.

Are they "typical"? They are probably not a good statistical sample.

Then there's the debate about which families are "really" homeschooling. Are students in publicly supported independent study programs (ISPs) and charters "official" homeschoolers just because they educate at home? What about those in distance learning programs of private schools? What about kids with private tutors? While we could lump just about all family-oriented educational alternatives under homeschooling, that blurs the definition of homeschooling into an unrecognizable mess. If we include them all, though, we get a good idea of how many people have abandoned the public and private school systems.

So, sorry, Linda, I can't give you any accurate count of homeschoolers.

88

Politicians seem pretty serious in their push for accountability, particularly across-the-board, mandatory, standardized testing. How will this affect my child if she is homeschooling?

JUDITH WAITE ALLEE ◆ While I think it's too late for politicians and teachers' unions to bring about an out-and-out ban on homeschooling (homeschooling works, and the general public knows it), let us not get complacent about our freedom to homeschool. Legislators and the educational bureaucracy can shackle us with their regulations and interpretations. They can hinder the experimentation, the ability to customize for each child's needs, and the freedom that makes homeschooling work so well. When Ohio went from being

Judith Waite Allee

one of the worst states to being one of the best for homeschoolers, there was no change in the law. Only the way Ohio's law is regulated and interpreted changed. Those could potentially change back to a more restrictive mode. In this regard, our fate may be tied to that of private schools, and we need to partner with them to lobby against more restrictive policies.

However, whether you fight such policies or not, you may still have to live with them. While you may be required to subject your children to tests, you can avoid stressing them at home. I read a suggestion in *Growing Without Schooling Magazine* that, if you are affected by testing, one response is to acknowledge to your children that, yes, we have to do this silly testing thing, but that is not what real learning is about. So let's get that stuff out of the way and get back to unschooling (or whatever method you use). In other words, you do not have to

turn the test into some kind of heavy, authoritative monster, or let it weigh heavily on your children. You can do what you have to do, but acknowledge that you don't agree with it.

Our family was "underground" in the mid-80s because we didn't apply for permission to homeschool. We kept out of sight during the day, and my heart went pitter-pat every time the phone rang or someone knocked at the door. If we had to go to court, my game plan was to impress the judge with the great strides my foster son had made. In brief, I tried to do way too much way too quickly. He did make great strides from my point of view, but not necessarily in ways that would have shown up on testing. It was a good year in some ways but unnecessarily stressful. Personally, I would consider moving to another state if again faced with a similar situation.

Let us not get complacent about our freedom to homeschool.

Sometimes families submit to testing because the school treats it as a requirement, may even believe it is a requirement, when in fact it is not. To get the inside scoop, read your state's laws and regulations for yourself, and network with local and state homeschool groups.

LORETTA HEUER ◆ First, *timing is everything*. For the past decade taxpayers have been justifiably concerned about the state of public schools and low student achievement. The irony is that while government has been operating in a high accountability mode, contemporary educators are favoring alternative assessments similar to those that homeschoolers use on a routine basis.

Second, *This, too, shall pass.* There has been a recent upsurge of parental and teacher backlash directed at the amount of time devoted to testing (in some districts over thirty days per school year!) and at high-stakes testing that determines promotion, graduation, and college admission.

It is crucial to remember, however, that it is the *public* schools that are being held accountable for their poor results. Homeschoolers need to remind school administrators and legislators of this whenever an official proposes greater supervision of homeschoolers. Be ready to ask the key question: *What, exactly, is the problem that this regulation is intended to solve?* Usually, there *is* no real problem, just speculation about problems that might occur . . . someday. It is imperative that homeschoolers confront this kind of thinking and nip "catastrophizing" in the bud.

I guarantee that as a homeschooler you're *far* more experienced using alternative assessments than most classroom teachers! However, even if you use alternative evaluations on a daily basis, it helps to speak the language of assessment when proposing alternatives to standardized tests. Terms such as *performance assessment, embedded assessment, formative assessment, tasks, rubrics,* and *benchmarks* should be familiar to homeschoolers. Because of this, I included a "Glossary of Assessment Terms" and a chapter on "Assessment Basics" in *The Homeschooler's Guide to Portfolios and Transcripts.*

One last comment: Your school administrators should be comfortable with a repertoire of assessments, not just standardized tests. Assess *their* assessment literacy—and hold *them* to high standards!

> **Your school administrators should be comfortable with a repertoire of assessments, not just standardized tests. Assess *their* assessment literacy—and hold *them* to high standards!**

89

What are "homeschool charter schools"?

ANN FISHER ◆ Aren't you suspicious, as I am, of a term that includes the word "school" twice? This term befuddles me. Too bad, too, because these programs have a lot to offer to some folks. Why not call them something like parent-partnered charter schools instead? From such a label, you could tell that families co-create educational opportunities for their children with school authorities.

But to answer your question, what are parent-partnered [homeschool] charter schools? In the first place, they are charter schools, subject to the laws of your state. Publicly funded, charter schools enjoy more educational freedom than do conventional public schools, such as freedom to select their own curriculum. State laws usually require charter schools to comply with certain requirements, such as days of compulsory attendance and standardized testing, in order to qualify for funding. In some cases, parent-partnered programs are not technically charter schools, but alternative schools.

Whether funded as charters, alternatives, or something else, the public school programs may have the following in common. Some aspects of homeschooling—such as parent involvement in classes, parent influence on curriculum, parent tutoring at home, small group instruction—are coupled with some aspects of public schooling, primarily schoolteachers and instruction, materials, use of schoolbooks, and access to school facilities. The combination can create a successful educational program for families who do not want to shoulder the entire homeschooling burden themselves.

These programs are an apparent win-win situation in some areas. Families save money on materials and have access to school-type educational pro-

grams for their children, while still providing one-on-one instruction for their children.

And the schools! Savvy school administrators love these programs because they draw the tax dollars for each child enrolled—at a comparable rate to that of full-time students, but with considerably less stress and strain on the budget, the school, and teachers, due to all the parental involvement and learning that takes place at home.

But is it homeschooling? You decide. Homeschooling, by its very definition, implies that parents do it all and pay for it all. That means each and every homeschooling parent is the teacher, the janitor, the principal, the bus driver, the school superintendent, the budgeting committee, the truant officer, the legal department, the school board, the PTA, the lobbyist, and yes, the beleaguered "taxpayer" who buys every book and crayon.

Homeschooling parents take full responsibility for every educational decision and expense. Whether parents share responsibilities with other families, sign students up for a class, or contract with a correspondence school for support is not the issue. The issue is this: Who is in charge?

Parents who take full charge of their children's education strengthen their family immeasurably. Children have a notably different learning experience than when responsibility is handed off to school employees. The buck stops with Mom and Dad, and the route to Mom and Dad is short and sweet. Can you say the same about parent-partnered [homeschool] charter schools?

ANN ZEISE ◆ When the charter school movement took off in California, the thought was that these schools would be "brick and mortar" alternative schools catering to specific community needs not met in the regular public schools. Pretty soon some saw that forming a charter school for homeschoolers was a good way to earn a great living, with low overhead, and "help" homeschoolers at the same time. Recently, the government of California decided to crack down on the "too profitable" charter schools for homeschoolers.

I looked into joining a charter school as an advisor (or whatever they were calling the "teachers" who were going to "help" the homeschool families). I found out that I'd mostly be forcing my friends to report plans and activities to the state government, something they didn't have to do when freely homeschooling. The lure was $100 a month per child for ten months of the year. As a charter school "teacher," I'd make that for my own children as well as for each of my assigned students. Sounded like an easy way to make a living from home. So why didn't I leap at the chance? My gut reaction was that something seemed fishy. I knew

these people weren't setting up this charter school out of the goodness of their hearts. There had to be more to it.

I watched our support group of over a hundred members dwindle as homeschooled moms found enough support through their charter school groups. Why turn to amateurs when you had "expert" homeschoolers to turn to? So what if your support group friends gave you their used learning materials? The charter would buy you new stuff! The charter would help you keep organized and make sure your kids were learning "the right stuff," while your support group friends pretty much approved of whatever you did, or tried to convince you into homeschooling their way.

I listened as my friends worried about getting their homeschool materials through the approved charter school vendors' catalogs. Apparently, the $100 couldn't be spent just anywhere. The charters had made lucrative deals with specific vendors to have their products on the "approved" list. The orders had to go through "advisors," some of whom, I guess, were swamped with too much paperwork. By the time the materials got to the families, they'd moved on to other interests or had advanced beyond that material, having learned by other means. Oh, and when the charter folded, the families were given a few weeks to return all the curriculum materials, so were suddenly left high and dry, without the materials they had ordered. (You didn't think you'd get to keep the stuff you bought with state money, did you?)

Why add a layer of bureaucracy to your life? Figure out a way to make a few hundred bucks from the comfort of your home if you need funds for homeschooling. Many a mom used to provide support groups with for-fee lessons that most likely covered their own homeschool expenses. You can find ways to get both support and a little funding without turning to state-sponsored charters.

90

Can we take advantage of distance learning for homeschooling?

LORETTA HEUER ◆ What image does the term "distance learning" conjure up for you? A student sitting at a computer taking a course for high school or college credit?

This is the most basic type of distance learning, a correspondence course where students complete assignments on a word processor and then submit the work (such as essays, practice exercises, problem sets, and examinations) via e-mail attachments. A more contemporary variation of this model would be one in which the text or course material is provided in CD-ROM format.

However, distance learning can be far more than that. Usually students work with online course material, accessing information from the Internet to complete assignments. In this case the teacher will have created a course Web site that contains an outline, readings from texts and related Web sites, and accompanying assignments. These assignments are then submitted through the school's "intranet," a system of internal communication accessed by a student password. My son Jed, when a "senior," enrolled in an online course entitled "World Wars Through Literature and Film." He read three novels—*All Quiet on the Western Front*, *Dr. Zhivago*, and *The Third Man*—then watched the corresponding films and completed written assignments. While this sounds very similar to the traditional correspondence course mentioned above, it had an added dimension. Jed needed to do independent Internet research when finding Web sites that dealt with the politics and history of the three eras. This research was then shared with his "classmates" on a course bulletin board that had password access. Although not a component of Jed's particular course, other online courses may "meet" in a chat room at a certain time each week for "class discussion." Some even have video and audio links. This is called "synchronous" online learning. One Web site that discusses these dynamic features can be found at: http://www.learningcircuits.com/2001 /may2001/hofmann.html

In addition to credit-oriented courses, there are other informal distance learning scenarios. An online writers' group, for example, may be just what you need to critique the novel you're writing. A quilters' network may offer a course to help beginners through their initial projects. This type of online learning doesn't provide course credits, but it does offer camaraderie and an extra nudge of accountability, especially for long-term projects where a weekly check-in with group members can keep you motivated and on track.

Whatever model you choose, distance learning is well suited to homeschoolers who want to take a traditionally structured course or two, but still do not want to give up their flexibly scheduled lifestyle. Just make sure you are clear about content, delivery system, course expectations, price and refund policies, how your records are kept, and the procedures for forwarding your information to schools or colleges in the future.

Sites that offer links to discussions about the philosophy of distance learning as well as links to online learning resources include these two:

http://elearners.com/
http://e-learning.start4all.com/

MARSHA RANSOM ◆ Definitely! Many homeschoolers already do take advantage of distance learning programs, and you can, too! What do you think of when you say distance learning? Many homeschool support schools and correspondence schools provide assignments that students complete and then send in for grading. Some homeschool support schools also have online classes that offer everything from a complete curriculum to selected classes or electives. A number of colleges provide high school credits via correspondence or online. More and more support schools and distance learning providers are popping up on the World Wide Web, providing distance learning opportunities by the class or by the complete grade level from kindergarten through high school graduation.

Remember that most distance learning providers will have clear-cut guidelines for you to follow, including policies about record keeping and time frames for returning assignments, grading, and so on. Be sure you understand the provider's policies, including their refund policies, in case you are not satisfied once you have started.

> **Whatever model you choose, distance learning is well suited to homeschoolers.**

Some programs require an assessment test to help place your child at the appropriate level. If your child doesn't do well with testing, this could be a problem from the start. Remember that if your child has been having difficulties doing verbal-linguistic and mathematical/logical work (such as completing worksheets, reading selections and answering questions, or doing pages of math) in an institutional school, switching to a distance learning provider may not be the answer to his or her problems. It's a good idea to know your child's strengths and weaknesses, his or her learning style and interests, before you make such a decision. If your child is one who marches to a different drummer in the learning arena, you will want to search for a provider offering a flexible program that takes learning differences into consideration. Both the Moore Foundation and Clonlara Home-Based Education Program help homeschoolers plan a flexible program based on activities, projects, and real-life learning; this better suits some children's learning styles and abilities.

As with all choices homeschoolers make, finding the right fit—the one that optimizes learning for the child—is key to choosing a distance learning provider.

ANN ZEISE ◆ Have you noticed that during the "shakeout" of online businesses, the distance learning programs (DLPs) are still going strong, and new ones are springing up all the time?

Several pages on my site are devoted to a different aspect of distance learning. There are correspondence schools that will send you materials and assignments, all supervised by a remote teacher. Other DLPs will just send materials based on grade level. At "cyberschools" your child meets regularly in "chat" to discuss subjects with a teacher he has never actually met. Some DLPs cater to religious groups; others to students with learning disabilities. While many are accredited and will provide your son or daughter with a transcript and diploma upon completion of the program, others are more casual—offering interest-based courses for those who don't care about credits. You may want to select just one course rather than a whole grade-full of courses.

If the DLP is in a state other than the one in which you reside, state education code may require you to register as a homeschool in your own state. If the DLP is in your own state, you then legally become a student body member of their private school. You need not register as a homeschool family. A few states make it so hard to homeschool independently that DLPs are the easiest option.

When a family asks me about the possibility of homeschooling in a foreign country, I suggest they register with a major DLP catering to expatriates.

These DLPs have long experience in helping families of missionaries, military personnel, diplomats, and corporate employees who must work in remote locations. The families are then legally under the "umbrella" of a private school until they figure out the legality of homeschooling independently in their new country. As these DLPs have had experience with distance learners in a wide variety of places, they can help a family understand how to use their program in their host country.

DLPs aren't for everyone. Parents will still have to oversee much of the learning, as it will take a child some time to get into the routine of doing work assigned by an instructor who isn't right there. DLPs can also be costly. You often need a good deal of technology these days to successfully interact with a cyber-oriented program. A top personal computer, fast online access, and equipment such as a fax, scanner, and even digital camera may be required. Often the cyberschools like to tinker with new technology such as "white boards" that don't always work as expected. Some high-tech features, for example, only work with Windows machines and not with Macintoshes.

Occasionally, these DLPs just vanish into thin air—even ones that have been around a long time. I hear from people who can't get a transcript from programs into which their children put years of

work. Make sure you don't invest in a fly-by-night DLP. Find a Web message board where people discuss the reliability of various programs and ask about their experiences with any DLP you are considering.

DLPs offer students a plethora of wonderful educational opportunities. Students can often access some of the finest online teachers in the world this way. The potential for all sorts of customizable education is ever increasing through these innovative programs. Homeschoolers who wish to learn through a distance learning program should make their concerns and goals known to administrators of such programs. Let them know we don't care whether their program meets Goals 2000 standards. We want better than that!

JUDITH WAITE ALLEE ◆ Oh, my, yes! Although most of us think of the Internet these days, correspondence courses are a time-honored form of distance learning (DL). Whether you "correspond" by mail or electronically, you can take classes for all grade levels.

Calvert School, which has offered children's correspondence classes since the early 1900s, shared this bit of their history: "Calvert curricula reached the farthest outposts of civilization, delivered to the hands of eager parents by dogsled, camel caravan, even parachuted from airplanes . . . The young daughter of an American missionary in Africa wrote to apologize that she was behind in her Calvert home-school studies, because 'the lions roaring all night keep us awake.'"

The American School, another longtime correspondence program, offers sixty-five DL courses ranging from algebra and civics for college-bound students, Practical English and Essential Math for a general high school diploma, and vocational classes such as Blueprint Reading for the building trades.

DL also provides an opportunity to earn college credit, regardless of age, as long as the student is capable of the work. College-level work counts twice—once as a high school credit (if you are concerned about that), and again as advanced college credit. Once you can show you are already successful at college-level work, a high school diploma is pretty much moot.

Distance learning (DL) also offers highly specialized topics you may not be able to find elsewhere, such as repairing dolls or writing children's books. Jennie Chancey, who was homeschooled in the early 1980s, became passionately interested in historic costume design. She now teaches an online class through the Costume Classroom (http://www.costumeclassroom.com) to students world-

wide, including many homeschoolers. She teaches students how to create historically accurate patterns and designs, and how to start a vintage clothing store. The Internet is a perfect way to find expertise in esoteric topics, no matter where you live.

It would be easy to fill an entire curriculum with DL classes. However, would I have wanted my daughter to stick with DL? No way. In general, I think DL "classes" have many of the same drawbacks that other forms of school have, such as an artificial focus on "testable" facts and less-than-exciting textbooks. Another concern with online DL is the amount of time students spend on computers.

Clonlara School's Compuhigh offers high school classes online. The students have an enthusiastic online community with a secure, monitored chat room, and some of them have formed lifelong friendships around the world. They passionately interact about literature and history and other subjects. Clonlara, however, discourages students from graduating with DL credits alone, and students must be age thirteen to eighteen to enroll in Compuhigh. Why? Because Clonlara believes online classes can be a valuable part, but not the whole, of a young person's education. Also, ac-

> **DL "classes" have many of the same drawbacks that other forms of school have, such as an artificial focus on "testable" facts and less-than-exciting textbooks.**

cording to some developmental experts, computer use not only swallows up time the younger children need to spend on physical activity, but can be harmful to their development.

Are some families happy with an all-DL curriculum? Yes. Maybe it's partly a question of semantics, though. Whereas they consider taking karate lessons and participating in their church band to be "extracurricular," maybe I would consider them just plain "curricular." The upshot: DL offers low-cost choices today that were not available even a few years ago.

> **Children with special learning needs are terribly vulnerable when their placement situation does not mesh well with their unique challenges and gifts.**

91

Why are so many parents of children with special learning needs turning to homeschooling?

ANN FISHER ◆ You've noticed that too! There are so many reasons for this educational choice. A common reason is that "one size fits all" schooling—especially special education programs—inadvertently sends families in search of an alternative. Children with special learning needs are terribly vulnerable when their placement situation, even when supposedly individualized, does not mesh well with their unique challenges

and gifts. Even a seemingly small mismatch can have horrifying results.

For instance, one boy with both autism and possible mental limitations was placed in a public school classroom for mentally limited students. It was such a disaster! That misplacement took years for his parents to correct through homeschooling, and the young man still thrives while learning at home. So escaping a bad situation—providing sanctuary—is a strong motive to homeschool.

More important, though, is what families are moving *toward*. Homeschooling children with special learning needs seems natural if you reflect on how learning takes place.

Through an individualized program, parents can tailor materials precisely to fit the child's needs. They can move through concepts at a rate that matches the child's learning pace. Parents know the child and his abilities very well and waste no time, matching instruction to ability accurately and

Ann Fisher

effectively. The consistency of family life and a regular routine minimizes disruption, further optimizing the time the child spends learning.

Why are these advantages of homeschooling so urgently important? Remember that, despite their special needs, these are everyday kids who just happen to have an additional burden to carry. They need playtime, rest, fun, chores, social experiences with friends, entertainment, exercise, and good food—just like everyone else. Their goals and dreams need time to develop.

Parents may find that special needs programs in schools necessarily include many extraneous experiences—exhausting bus rides, crowded classrooms, a changing parade of teachers, difficult social environments. Each nicks away at time available for focused learning tasks. Parents notice, too, that time spent navigating the system is time *not* spent learning and living a full life.

The child's time, parents discover, is most profitably spent learning and growing up in the familiar home environment.

JUDITH WAITE ALLEE ◆ Let me tell you a story. When my foster son, Danny, was eleven, he was in a special education class for kids with learning disabilities (LD). (Did you know that LD stood for Little Dummy at school?) There was nothing—not one thing—at school that Danny felt good at other than, perhaps, manipulating his teachers and keeping things in a turmoil. I spent more time in the principal's office in one year as Danny's mother than I did during my entire school career as a child. I looked into a private school that specialized in LD, but it was over an hour away and the tuition cost was more than our annual income. We felt that our time to help our son was running out, and we were desperate to find an alternative.

Then I found an exciting program that sounded perfect for Danny. This program featured a curriculum individually designed for each child. The children could learn about math by doing cooking or carpentry, volunteering at the food co-op, and participating in other hands-on experiences. Instead of a "reader," each child could pick out a magazine about something that especially interested him or her and receive a subscription for it. Social studies included volunteering at a shelter for battered women and talking with Civil War re-enactors in costume. Even the field trips were designed around activities the children were excited about—such as a night visit to an astronomy professor at a nearby college. The kids could get school credit for working on 4H projects or for taking gymnastics. In every subject, the children would be working right at their own level—not hopelessly struggling nor being bored to tears by repetition of what they already knew.

How could we possibly afford it? The costs were kept low because the parents volunteered to provide transportation, help create learning materials, and participate in activities with the children. Parents were expected to read to their children daily, and were involved in exciting field trips to real businesses, factories, and courtrooms.

This sounded too good to be true. I was skeptical, fearful, and overwhelmed by the commitment. Yet it was all true—and this exciting program is what we call homeschooling.

Homeschooling offers (or can offer) the dream curriculum a special-ed teacher would love to provide, but cannot, due to logistics and cost. Just as "special ed" offers IEPs (Individualized Education Plans), homeschooling provides every child with a customized plan. No child needs to qualify as a "Little Dummy" to have this "special" program. Every child can be successful.

MARSHA RANSOM ◆ Parents of children with special learning needs are finding homeschooling the answer to the problems they have encountered over and over in institutional school settings. Some children need extra help because they have specific learning disabilities. Others get left behind because their learning style is not addressed. Children identified as gifted often have their needs minimally met by placement in a pull-out program for an hour a day or a couple of hours a week, making these children feel "different" and as if they are

missing what happens in their regular classroom while they're gone. While law states that all children are entitled to an education appropriate for their needs, children with physical and mental handicaps of all kinds need continual intervention and advocacy when they are enrolled in a public school program; such effort can be costly and exhausting for parents.

Homeschooled children with special learning needs are flourishing with the one-on-one attention, unique learning programs designed specifically for them, and positive reinforcement of progress experienced in homeschools. Measuring personal progress is quite different from trying to measure up to someone else's, or to an arbitrary "norm." Families of children with disabilities—such as autism, auditory hypersensitivity, Down syndrome, and sensory integration dysfunction—may develop their own IEP (Individualized Education Program), which may include activities such as horseback riding or learning sign language. Parents of gifted children can arrange for their kids to work at their own level twenty-four hours a day, seven days a week. Homeschoolers in general find that they can complete their work more efficiently without the distractions of keeping a large group of children on task, and the parents of children with special learning needs are no exception. Children whose learning styles simply don't fit the typical institutional setting often blossom when learning activities are planned based on their interests, personalities, and learning styles.

Some parents utilize support schools that provide flexible, adaptable programs; IEP planning; and other services for children with special needs. A variety of online resources and newsletters are also available for homeschooling families with special needs. Many parents of children with special learning needs have found that, after even a short period of homeschooling, their children are more interested in learning, develop better feelings of self-worth, are closer to other family members, and feel more capable.

> **Many parents of children with special learning needs have found that, after even a short period of homeschooling, their children are more interested in learning, develop better feelings of self-worth, are closer to other family members, and feel more capable.**

Independence, Missouri, enacted a daytime curfew, the Home School Legal Defense Association (HSLDA) reported that the ordinance "made it unlawful for any minor subject to compulsory school attendance to be in any public place between 8:30 A.M. and 1:30 P.M. Monday through Friday . . ." An exception was made in the ordinance for children who are in the company of their parents.

I think it's wise to keep the following in mind:

1. It is in your family's best interest if you contact your local elected officials to find out whether your community—or a community you might be visiting—has such ordinances.

2. Accompany your children on outings or delegate another adult to be present at all times. Unchaperoned kids plus nosy neighbors equals a disaster waiting to happen. This is, alas, a sad reality about the times. Unfortunately, the curfews being enacted and the truancy laws being enforced are a result of public school parents and school administrators not having the backbone to keep an eye on the children in their care.

3. Make sure you and your children don't give the authorities reason to apply these ordinances to you. Be considerate

---

92

With the proliferation of daytime curfews and growing attention to truancy, will my children and I be bothered as we use the world as our classroom?

ISABEL LYMAN ◆ That depends. If you are escorting your children around your community, you should not face any serious problems. When the city council of of public property (don't litter, for example), show respect to those in charge of law enforcement, and put a good (smiley) face on homeschooling.

4. Teenagers should be aware of the above precautions and be taught to accept responsibility for their safety and behavior. Encourage them to communicate with you frequently (get them a cell phone if necessary), and exhort them to make productive use of their away-from-home time. Don't be shy about contacting a lawyer if public officials unfairly bother you. Children have civil rights, too, and zealous adults should be called on the carpet if those rights are violated.

5. If your town or city decides to pursue enacting a daytime curfew, by all means use your First Amendment right to make a stink because these curfews stink.

93

Help! I'm a victim of "homeschooling information overload"! Is there any way to get this under control?

ANN FISHER ◆ The best strategy, if you can do it, is simply to walk away. That overwhelmed feeling of "information overload" is a glaring neon sign telling you to take advice from your ultimate expert: yourself. The wellspring for homeschooling success is within you and your unique family. Only you, with your spouse, can choose the approach that is right for your family.

So how do you take advice from yourself? If your brain is swimming with bits of scattered data, you have too much information overloading your system, so take yourself off the planet for a breather. Knit, garden, paint, shoot hoops, read fiction, go to the beach—do whatever you do to give yourself time to process information. Then, when you've refreshed yourself, take your own ideas about how you homeschool, no matter how tentative and "iffy" your ideas feel, and do it! Don't wait. Start with what you know now and let the rest develop as you go. You really need stay only one or two steps ahead of your family.

Having said that, we both know there is still a glut of information coming at you every day. Really now, how *can* you process it all? While you may enjoy devouring favorite books and journals from cover to cover, as I do, there are more efficient ways to glean key facts and needed support.

Try letting other people do some of the reading and research for you. Three pivotal subscriptions can make your life easier. Subscribe to at least three (one each of local, state, national) of the most inclusive and broad-based homeschooling newsletters, journals, or e-mail lists. These will keep you apprised of key political and legal issues that affect homeschooling on local, state, and national scenes, and will shower you with useful tips, activities, and support to boot.

Another way to share the reading load is through a homeschooling book club. Use journals and newsletters that publish reviews to help your group select books to read.

For material you want to read for yourself, try serendipitous reading to sort out which books and materials you want to read cover to cover and which need a place on a reference shelf. You will be surprised at how quickly you reap the juiciest bits in the process. It is fun and easy.

I often put unread material in handy places in case I find a spare minute: in the car, in my purse, in my bedroom or bathroom, on the kitchen counter. Then, when waiting for coffee to brew or swimming lessons to end, pick up a book or magazine, skim through the table of contents or the index, and read whatever appeals to you. Or simply flip through pages until something catches your eye. Read as little or as much as your interest demands and see where that tidbit takes you. Use sticky notes to tag sections that you want to reread.

Finally, remember that you can't know it all anyway. Have you noticed the symptoms children show when they feel overloaded with new information? Their whining or complaining soon becomes a neon sign, telling us to make some changes. They need a change of pace just

as you and I do, so why not take a break together?

Ann Zeise ◆ Used to be there wasn't enough information, and now there's too much! I like to steer new homeschoolers toward Ed Dickerson's spiral-bound notebook, "Destinations." It has a jaunty nautical theme, pointing out that a family's homeschool journey is like a unique sailing voyage. You need goals, plans, and a good compass.

Those without goals will find themselves blown about by the strongest winds (educational opinions) that come their way. Setting goals takes some effort and time. Ed takes you through goal-planning sessions you can do alone and with the whole family. Having a handful of agreed-upon goals for the year posted on your fridge can help you determine whether or not some new information fits in where you are headed. (It is well and good to know about Spain, but if you have decided to go to Bora Bora, then Spain will have to wait!)

Even the most diehard unschoolers can incorporate some plans into their lives. Child-led learning does not mean child-dominated learning (you'd wind up with a spoiled brat!). Children should be encouraged to be part of the planning process, their goals and interests taken into account, just like you take into account your goals and interests when you plan a family vacation. Getting used to this freedom to set educational goals as a family and planning ahead may take a bit, but it will definitely save you time and money to do so. There's too much out there!

Your compass is your internal will to stay on course, to keep trying to reach your goal in spite of unfavorable winds. You may need to "tack" or stop on an island refuge to visit a bit, but your compass will guide you to where you want to end up.

When Ed led us in a goal-setting session, no one listed things like "spelling" or "handwriting" in their goals lists. What people wanted their children to learn read more like the Boy Scout laws, you know, "to be honest, trustworthy, courteous, friendly" and so on. What is important to your family? What can you do to ensure your children have those values in their heads by the time they are out of your control at about age eighteen?

It is okay to have goals that other families do not. It is okay to emphasize what schools do not. One family may highly value music, another sports; yet another family values business sense, computer literacy, or environmental concern. The world needs a few less "well-rounded" people and a lot more people who are devoted to making the world a better place through their passions and skills. I like to quote Steve Wozniak, in-

ventor of the Apple Computer: "Do what you love to do, and learn to do it very, very well, and some day someone will pay you very well to do it for them."

94

I'm noticing a lot of communication and media coverage about record numbers of homeschoolers reaching college attendance age. Has this resulted in any changes in how homeschooled applicants are received?

ISABEL LYMAN ◆ Yes. As homeschoolers come of age, they are demonstrating that they have the brains and drive to achieve in college, and admissions officers are noticing. Consider that the National Merit Scholarship Corporation selected 137 homeschooled finalists in 1999 and 150 in 2000. Homeschoolers are participating in online Advanced Placement courses available to all. In 2000, homeschooled students scored higher on the ACT (a college-entrance exam that measures achievement in English, mathematics, reading, and science) than traditionally schooled peers. The *Washington Times* noted that while "the average ACT assessment score was 21 nationally, home-educated students scored an average of 22.8 . . ."

If that information doesn't make you burst with pride, consider that *The*

Chronicle of Higher Education reported a boom in homeschooled students winning admission to selective colleges. For example, in 1995, Houghton College in upstate New York had 11 homeschoolers in its freshmen class of 340. Dr. Brian Ray's 1997 book, *Strengths of Their Own— Home Schoolers Across America*, surveyed the post-graduation endeavors of 232 high school homeschoolers. Writes Ray, "Immediately after high school graduation from home education, 25.4% went to a four-year college on a full-time basis, 12.1% went part-time, and 8.2% went to community college."

The talent from the home-grown team is mighty impressive. Some of my favorite all-stars include Danny Nolan, who graduated from the U.S. Naval Academy; Barnaby Marsh, who spent his maiden semester of school and college at Harvard University; and Alexandra Swann, who earned a master's degree in history from California State University at age sixteen. (See *Homeschoolers' Success Stories* for in-depth reports on many other homeschooled "grads.") And our critics have the nerve to worry about socialization! That's so . . . 1980!

LORETTA HEUER ◆ Students who use pre-packaged curricula, receive grades, or participate in an umbrella school program pose less of a dilemma to college admissions staff. But what about homeschoolers such as my sons, who designed their own hybrid programs of unschooling and classwork? Or those who have totally unschooled?

Colleges are actively struggling to figure out how to evaluate these traditional homeschoolers who are, by definition, non-traditional students. The good news is that some schools are seeking input from homeschoolers themselves. One place this is happening is on a listserv that links teenaged homeschoolers, their parents, and college admissions officials. Families can ask questions, such as how to deal with the standard two-year foreign language requirement, or whether having a GED helps or hinders a homeschooler's chance of admission.

To join the conversation, contact listserv@list.pace.edu and ask to be placed on their HSC-L list (transition of homeschooled students into post-secondary education).

By engaging in dialogue with homeschoolers, admissions officials are able not only to share information about their school's policies but also to get feedback about what the world of teenage homeschooling is really like. Hopefully, this will inform future policy-making. However, a problem can occur if a college develops a standard policy for *all* homeschoolers, confusing competency for college work with the route the student took to arrive at this level of competency.

In a situation like this I'd suggest two things: First, attempt to negotiate. Assume that the school is more open-minded and flexible than the printed policy implies. The term "non-traditional student" holds a clue. Ask how the college assesses non-traditional students such as students from abroad, GED recipients, forty-somethings returning to school, recent immigrants who gradu-ated with less than four years in an American high school.

Then, if you're still met with resistance, you may want to reconsider the school. Ask yourself whether you'd be comfortable in a school that doesn't seem to value diversity of educational experience.

CHAPTER THIRTEEN

Lifeboats:
Final Inspiration

I NEVER SET out to become a homeschool advocate, though that is what I'm often called. As I watched three young hearts and minds blossom in an educational experience antithetical to my own, it was impossible to keep the discovery—the joy, the love, the obvious "naturalness" of the process of learning—to myself. Fourteen years ago it was pretty hard to find more than a handful of people to speak with directly about such a revelation, so I began writing about it. I helped start a support group, and wrote some more. That writing led to invitations to speak, and thus an advocate was born.

While my advocacy began as a desire to share the "good news," it continues today for a different reason. Homeschooling has given me reason and opportunity to ponder, discuss, dissect, and question both what I've been taught and what I've assumed. When educational teachings and assumptions didn't hold up to this scrutiny, there were reason and opportunity to look at other teachings and assumptions related to children and family, the building blocks of a healthy society.

To put it plainly, what I uncovered is appalling. I look around and see my family and I are afloat in a sea of suffering where families and children are concerned. For every one of the increasing number of children reported to end his life, or wind up in jail, or become addicted to drugs, or suffer violence at the hand of another, there is a family, a family whose members' lives are forever changed in a wave of human connection, and the ripples are far-reaching. For each of these children who allow anger and resentment to turn his or her life into a series of conflicts (and isn't that what youth violence really is?), a mother fears, a brother hopes, an uncle mourns, a friendship dies.

In the midst of this sea of despair, I feel compelled to offer homeschooling as a lifeboat. Yet I can only offer the boat. Each family must work together to fill it with their own breath of life and love, hope and commitment. Only *they* can rescue themselves.

I know there will be many whose politics, personal or governmental, won't allow them even to consider an approach to education that contradicts the *one* method chosen for the masses and practiced in the monopoly public school system. Others may desperately want a lifeboat, but they spend so much time and energy simply staying afloat in the sea of suffering it seems impossible to find more time and energy to inflate the boat.

If you don't have much practice thinking alternatively or cooperatively, common-sense solutions may sometimes slip by you. But consider this: If just a few of those safely on their lifeboats gladly keep others afloat as they blow up their boats, soon all would be rescued. The community of the drowning would save itself.

Every contributor to this book has offered that help so selflessly, so joyfully, their kindness will live in my heart forever. They offered up their time, their devotion, their combined 500-plus years of experience in an unprecedented effort to keep members of our society afloat long enough to gather their life and love, hope and commitment. One family at a time. Doing it for themselves.

If there is another lifeboat in addition to home education that can so profoundly enrich parents' and children's lives together, I have yet to find it. And I have looked hard. Homeschooling has been so uplifting it's only appropriate to leave you readers on a note of inspiration, and to offer you your very own, personal lifeboat.

95

All I ever read about in the newspaper is exceptional homeschooled kids doing exceptional things. Are there any normal homeschoolers?

SUSANNAH SHEFFER ◆ They're all normal—and they're all amazing. Does that sound like I'm dodging the question? All homeschoolers do seem normal to me: They're regular kids, with ups and downs and immaturities and bad days, just like everyone else's kids. And all homeschoolers do seem amazing to me: They've each got something special that homeschooling, more often than not, allows to flourish.

It's worth remembering that newspapers cover what they consider newsworthy—in other words, what seems out of the ordinary. The first homeschoolers to be accepted by Ivy League universities got intensive media coverage. Now that homeschoolers are routinely accepted to selective colleges, it's less common for any individual acceptance to make the news. It's also true that with so many skeptics questioning whether homeschooling works, people within the homeschooling community will sometimes want to hold up examples of obvious success in order to counter criticisms. People are understandably proud when a young person not only does something great, but attributes her success to her homeschooling background.

Nonetheless, a newspaper is unlikely to write about the fact that eight-year-old Jane sat with her dolls all day long in a wonderful luxury of fantasy play; or that twelve-year-old Jonathan woke up eagerly, with many things he wanted to do that day, whereas last year his mother could hardly coax him out of bed to get to school on time. Yet these sorts of things may be what the families themselves are thrilled to observe. Years ago a homeschooling mother wrote to *Growing Without Schooling* magazine, "It's okay to be ordinary, living your days out well and happily without newsworthy accomplishments, just every day going forward, living and learning." That's a sentiment many homeschoolers would heartily endorse. At the same time, with so many skeptics out there—not just about homeschooling, but about children in general—news of good things young people do challenges negative stereotypes and benefits us all. The key, it seems to me, is to make a point of talking about what went into the accomplishment or what was behind it: what steps were involved, what kind of support and help were necessary, how challenges were faced and handled along the way. In thinking about education, what we want to understand is what's possible for human beings and then what helps make it possible. That way, we can learn from others' success and try to offer similar opportunities to all children.

JEAN REED ◆ Normal! What's normal? Who is normal? Are you normal?

Exceptional people will make the headlines. Exceptional kids will make bigger headlines. Homeschooled children are essentially no different than children in public schools. Like people everywhere, we all have our strengths and weaknesses. If there are any differences it's because homeschooling can allow all children, gifted or not, to grow more freely and pursue an interest to the point of excellence.

Our four children may resent me for calling them "average, normal kids," but that's what they are. They are not geniuses, yet they have done some exceptional things because they had the freedom to investigate and follow their special interests. Average children can do exceptional things when interested and encouraged. Susan, who never considered herself to be a great, or even good, writer, won a provincial writing contest. Cathy spent hours studying dinosaurs in third grade and acquired an exceptional knowledge of the subject. Derek got hooked on sharks in about fourth grade

and read everything we could find for him. He read through everything in the provincial library and we had to go to the Library of Canada and enlist the aid of friends and relatives to find resources to help satisfy his insatiable curiosity. He began reading on high school and college levels because he really cared about what he was learning. Karen finished her entire high school studies in two years, tackling every subject in *High School Subjects Self-Taught,* including some advanced courses we tried to dissuade her from doing. We couldn't see that she would need them. We were wrong, of course. She's used what she learned and been glad she did it all.

Our kids were just like kids all around the world. They argued, fought, played, failed at some things, and have done some outstandingly great things.

Not every one goes to Harvard, or wants to. Not everyone can write a symphony at age eleven, win a national spelling bee, or be outstanding in some field. Most adults don't make headlines. It's the exceptions who do. If we don't have exceptional kids, that's all right. The point of homeschooling is not to compete for headlines, but to give our children as much freedom and enjoyment as possible in their learning and to

> **The point of homeschooling is not to compete for headlines, but to give our children as much freedom and enjoyment as possible in their learning and to help them prepare themselves for their own future.**

help them prepare themselves for their own future.

96

How can I find out where and when homeschooling conferences and curriculum fairs will be in my neighborhood?

NANCY PLENT ◆ Here are the four top ways to locate those invisible homeschoolers in your neighborhood:

- Find a book about homeschooling in the library (like this one!), and call a group listed in appendix A.
- Talk to your librarian. She probably knows local families because she's helped them find materials.
- Ask for names at roller rinks, park programs, any fun or educational place. Local homeschool groups probably go there.
- Call your local newspaper and ask for the last reporter who wrote about homeschooling. He or she will have family names in his file.

Notice I didn't suggest you call the local school. They often tell you they don't *have* homeschoolers in their district. Or can't give out the names.

If you follow up every connection you can think of and network until your eyes glaze over a bit, you'll be rewarded by finding an amazing network of homeschoolers who can fill you in on local and statewide events.

SANDRA DODD ◆ Join local and state organizations to receive local information. Subscribe to national magazines to get information on regional conferences.

SUSAN EVANS ◆ Conferences may be among the best sources of support, information, and refueling for homeschooling families. Finding one in your neighborhood isn't difficult, but it depends on what you consider your neighborhood . . .

> Conferences may be among the best sources of support, information, and refueling for homeschooling families. Finding one in your neighborhood isn't difficult, but it depends on what you consider your neighborhood . . .

Find out about local conferences through local and statewide networks. It doesn't hurt to be in touch with two or three networks if your state has them. (If it doesn't, you might want to start some!) Conferences will be listed in newsletters, or announcements may be sent out in special mailings to publicize the events. Try going to gatherings sponsored by networks you don't usually participate in. The difference in perspective can be eye-opening. The one-on-one dialogs between diverse homeschooling families are extremely valuable in strengthening the homeschooling community.

If you subscribe to any of the fine national homeschooling periodicals like *Home Education Magazine* you'll find announcements of upcoming conferences, seminars, book fairs, and curriculum fairs. If you have access to the Internet, either through a computer in your home or at your local library, you can find listings of future conferences in your state and across the country.

There are publications that list conferences, vendors, and speakers on an annual or semiannual basis. Look for marketing guides like Jane Williams's *Home School Market Guide* or Ted Wade's *Home School Manual.* Perhaps your library or local support group can purchase a copy of these titles as reference books available to all interested homeschoolers.

If none of these avenues result in you finding a conference, chances are your neighborhood would benefit from having you (and a few stout-hearted friends) arrange to sponsor a conference or one-day seminar. Don't faint! That's how most big homeschool conferences started once upon a time. The plans don't need to be elaborate—a meeting space for the day, a couple of interesting people who have some experience homeschooling and a willingness to share what they've learned. Attendees can enjoy brown-bag lunches or a potluck. Such a day can be wonderfully renewing, without burning out volunteers or destroying any family budgets.

97

How do I find a homeschooling support group in my neighborhood? How do I start a support group?

LILLIAN JONES ✦ You can get a list of state organizations and local support groups from both *Home Education Magazine* and the National Home Education Network (www.nhen.org). If you don't find a listing for a local support group, you can usually get lists from the state organizations. Don't be discouraged if all you find at first are groups that don't fit your needs. There really are a variety of homeschoolers out there.

If you have online access, you can post messages in homeschooling forums of electronic bulletin boards like AOL or Prodigy, and on the Internet. Computers with online access, by the way, are becoming increasingly available in libraries and cyber-cafes.

Sometimes local groups are a little challenging to find. If you have no luck locating one through the magazines or state groups, you can explore the territory where homeschoolers take their children during the hours when other children are in school—playgrounds, museums, libraries, educational supply stores, book stores, parks, and amusement attractions. Keep your eyes open for people who might look like they're homeschooling, and go ahead and approach them. They usually love to meet new people. Ask librarians about homeschoolers, especially children's librarians, and leave your name and number, or a card, with them.

Scan bulletin boards at places you think homeschoolers are likely to frequent. Don't forget natural food stores, because homeschooling is one of those "natural" things. If you don't find a notice, put one up yourself, and say you're looking for other homeschoolers. The local La Leche League will undoubtedly have members who homeschool—it's a natural outgrowth from another natural practice, nursing babies. Look around at kids' classes like gymnastics or dance. Ask at skating rinks if there are homeschooling groups that have regular get-togethers there.

Check the free parent/family newspapers that are so common these days. Often ads or event notices are placed by homeschooling groups. If you don't find one, call the newspaper and ask if they know of any. Also try calling the regular town newspapers. They're often familiar with groups from doing research for articles. They might even have an education editor who keeps track of groups or individuals.

Find out what opportunities the state groups have for getting together with other homeschoolers. Some sponsor large annual conferences and hold wonderful family campouts. Getting to know homeschoolers from all over the state is great fun for the whole family.

KATHARINE HOUK ◆ I live in a rural area. When our family first took our daughter out of school, there were no support groups for homeschoolers. In fact, we were the only homeschoolers in our district. Nevertheless, I rounded up three or four families who were interested in the homeschooling idea even though their children were not yet school age, and Homeschoolers' Exchange was born. After eight years this group evolved into the Alternative Learning Center, a thriving parent-cooperative resource program for homeschooling families that has been providing workshops, activities, field trips, and classes for children for the past six years.

If you do some research and find that there is no group in your area, or the available group doesn't meet your needs, you, too, may wish to start a group. It can be as simple as getting together with one or two others who are interested in the idea; or, if you don't know anyone, you could advertise in your state homeschooling newsletter or a local newspaper. With those who respond, you can consider what you need from a group—your reasons for getting together, what you hope to learn, what activities would be involved in this learning, and what resources you have to share with one another.

Who do you wish to reach and include in this group?

- All interested people
- Homeschooling families only
- Adults
- Families with children within a certain age range
- Only the families from your church group, or co-op, and so on

What size group do you envision?

- Something small and informal
- A large and diverse group
- Something in between

What would be the purpose of the group?

- Activities, socialization, and learning experiences for the children
- Support and homeschooling ideas for parents
- Help and guidance with regard to the state laws or regulations
- Spread the good news about homeschooling through a newsletter, media contacts, or other methods
- Improvement of state laws and regulations
- Provide guest speakers or workshops on topics related to education

- Make available books, tapes, lab equipment, sports equipment, and other resources through an exchange or lending library

As your group grows, there will be other things to consider: Does the group need a name? Will there be members and dues, and if so, will you open a bank account? How can the group reach out to the community? How can you get input from the children about what *they* hope for from the group? How often should the group meet, and where? Should meetings include adults and children? If conflict arises in the group, how will it be handled? Should you start a lending library or book exchange? What about a newsletter, calendar of events, or Web site? Who will take on which responsibilities, and how can they be rotated? Should you become politically involved in improving the climate or laws concerning homeschooling in your state? What are the advantages of drafting bylaws and becoming incorporated?

There is no one best way in homeschooling, so a good group provides a way to explore diverse needs and helps parents build confidence by finding out what works best for them. Many of the above questions will be answered as those in your group communicate and grow, and all involved will benefit from the camaraderie and support that results.

JANIE LEVINE HELLYER ◆ The creation of a new support group or network is something many of us face at one time or another. If you know other families with the same needs as your own, get together and discuss what type of group would best serve you. Are you looking for an informal group in which families can get together, a parent network, or a group that focuses on children or teens? Whether you are working with others or on your own, the first task is to define what it is that would best serve your family.

Janie Levine Hellyer

Personally, I prefer informal groups where families can get together. Kids can play and visit, while parents can discuss issues in a relaxed and informal setting. Some people prefer a parent network—an opportunity to sit down with other parents away from the distractions children might create. Still others feel that the most important aspect of a homeschool support group is to provide positive social activities and experiences for children. It's important to define what you want and need and realize that you can't start out doing everything. Setting priorities allows us to focus on what is most important, then if we choose, add other dimensions.

Talk to others who have organized support groups in your state. Often these people will be very helpful. Your state support group will most likely have lists of local groups, and can refer families to you. Also, they might have names of people in your area who have contacted them in the past, helping you connect with others interested in creating a group.

Once this is done, you can set about getting the word out to others. A good place to start is with your local public library. Most librarians are more than happy to set out fliers, and you might find that your librarian knows of families who might be interested in your new group. Local newspapers often have a section devoted to community activities, and accept press releases from local community groups. If your local television station or cable company has a community calendar, you might also send them the information. Fliers can also be placed at sites other homeschoolers might frequent: museums, bookstores, and specialty shops. Often local school districts are also happy to give a flier to homeschooling families contacting them.

Probably the most important thing to keep in mind when organizing a support group is this: Do not try to do everything yourself. Work with others, learn to delegate responsibilities, and make it a group effort. Too often, a support group organizer or leader has so much responsibility that it interferes with family responsibilities, leading to burnout. Don't be afraid to ask others to help! Often, people are standing back just waiting to be asked.

98

Is there anything today's legislators can do to ensure this educational approach remains a choice for families in the future?

CHRIS CARDIFF ◆ You bet! But the answer may surprise you . . .

Unfortunately, many people have been trained to turn to government to solve their problems for them. "There oughta be a law" is a familiar refrain that is now ingrained in people. Special interest groups across society turn to legislators at all levels of government to pass laws and ordinances that favor them. One of the worst things that could happen to the homeschooling movement is for it to become just another special interest group petitioning legislators for benefits, privileges, exemptions, and regulations.

The only way to ensure the continued viability of homeschooling as an educational option is the gradual restoration of *total educational freedom for all families.* We don't need legislators passing new laws giving us permission to homeschool and telling us how and when we can do so. What we need to do is remove education from the political process and return it to families where it belongs. Today's

legislators can restore educational freedom to us not by passing new laws, but by *repealing* old laws concerning:

- Compulsory attendance
- Mandatory curricula
- Mandatory testing
- Education and credentialing requirements for teachers
- Compulsory funding

While each state has its own set of laws and regulations for education in general and homeschooling in particular, they all impose the core compulsions listed above in one form or another. Underlying these compulsions is the fundamental principle that government is responsible for what children know and learn. Embodied as laws, the further implication is that government is fully within its rights to use the full force and power at its disposal to achieve this goal.

The linchpin of government control of education is compulsory funding. Spending over $350 billion a year for kindergarten to twelfth grade, our educational system is the second largest income transfer and entitlement program in the world. This enormous amount of money attracts powerful special interest groups who need to force children into the system to help justify the continued flow of money. Breaking this financial link would eliminate much of the political resistance to repealing the rest of the state's educational framework.

The $350 billion in compulsory funding must be returned to families so they can spend it on the educational options appropriate for their family. This, more than anything else, will ensure educational freedom for all families. Educational providers will be forced to compete to provide educational services to families rather than organize politically and force families to pay them through compulsory taxation. Rather than being at the mercy of the latest educational fad, education consumers—families—will be free to choose from a smorgasbord of educational options.

The freedom to homeschool is only a special instance of a general problem. You can't ensure your freedom to homeschool unless you solve the broader issue of total educational freedom. As long as education is embedded in the political process, families will be subject to the political winds of the majority (or a special interest minority) and the educational whims of an unconstrained bureaucracy.

The Kasemans answered this question from their perspective as political writers intent on preserving and protecting our freedom to homeschool in this nation. Their answer, therefore, focuses on what we as homeschoolers can do.

SUSAN AND LARRY KASEMAN ◆ It is unlikely that homeschooling will be outlawed in the foreseeable future. However, pressure to increase government regulation of homeschooling and to require that homeschools become more like public schools will undoubtedly continue. Many school officials (some of whom are well-intentioned) and some members of the general public have the mistaken idea that homeschoolers would benefit from guidance from experienced professional educators. Despite all the evidence that homeschooling works, some public officials are not yet convinced that homeschooling parents can be trusted. In addition, new state and federal standards in education and greater emphasis on state and national testing are increasing government control of education and making public schools more standardized. Homeschooling parents will increasingly be expected to meet these standards, and perhaps even administer state-mandated tests. These and other developments would reduce homeschoolers' opportunities to decide how they will homeschool.

Therefore, if we homeschoolers are going to maintain the right and freedom to homeschool without unnecessary and increasingly restrictive government regulation, we need to act. We are in the best position to do this, because we have the strongest motivation and we understand the importance of homeschooling. If we don't work to maintain our freedom, no one else will do it for us. Among the things we can do are the following:

- As we are planning our homeschooling, we can budget some money, time, and energy to spend working to maintain our freedoms in some of the ways listed below.
- We can read and interpret homeschooling laws ourselves and refuse to do more than the minimum required by law. (See Question 2.)
- We can understand the basic foundations of our homeschooling rights and freedoms, including the difference between compulsory attendance and compulsory education. (See Question 5.)
- We can work with other homeschoolers through inclusive grassroots homeschooling organizations when they exist or start them ourselves, if necessary. (See our book *Taking Charge Through Homeschooling: Personal and Political Empowerment,* pages 149–164.)
- We can work to increase public support, or at least acceptance, by sharing our homeschooling experiences with friends, relatives, and acquaintances; getting positive homeschooling reports into the media; countering negative press; and so on.
- We can counter individuals and organizations that threaten to decrease our homeschooling freedoms through carelessness, lack of understanding, or willingness to sacrifice homeschooling freedoms for the benefit of some other agenda.
- Most important, we can enjoy living and learning with our children, activities that will be much more difficult to do if our homeschooling freedoms are reduced.

ISABEL LYMAN ◆ Like the motto of Texas, the message homeschoolers need to continue to broadcast to their legislators is "Don't mess with us!" Time and time again, homeschoolers have proven they know how to exercise their political clout. In 1994, for example, homeschooling parents overwhelmed Capitol Hill switchboards for several days in their efforts to get Congress to drop a drive that would have forced parents to get teaching certificates before they could homeschool. Of this intense lobbying effort, the *Congressional Quarterly* noted that House members were besieged by homeschoolers with "calls, letters, and faxes for over a week . . ." Result? The House voted with home educators, 424 to 1, on that issue. Yahoo!

Isabel Lyman

There have also been a smattering of politicians and wannabe politicians who are homeschooling parents. Gex Williams of Kentucky, a homeschooling father, came close to becoming the congressman for the fourth district in 1998; State Rep. Kevin Calvey of Del City, Oklahoma, has two children who are homeschooled; and former State Rep. Bob Forrey of Nampa, Idaho, has grandchildren and great-children who are all homeschooled. Homeschoolers serve in state legislatures, on city councils, and on school boards. Not only do we need to support such brave souls, we need to teach our children the importance of lobbying elected officials, so future generations will continue to enjoy these hard-won rights.

99

Who are the homeschool experts?

WILL SHAW ◆ This depends on the aspect of homeschooling and what you mean by expert. People who have homeschooled for a while can say what they have done and what appears to have worked, and maybe why—for them. But being experienced doesn't make you an expert. Some individuals have tried hard to learn what's happening, what's available, who's doing what, what's new. Some may possess more knowledge on a given subject. They can give their perspective, which can have value.

But homeschoolers need to rely on themselves. They should gather information from many sources and use their own judgment on methods, resources, and issues. There are a wealth of books about home education. Look at various books, and read new ones as they're published. Associate with local homeschool groups or networks, and join a statewide homeschool organization (or at least subscribe to its newsletter). You should also read national homeschool magazines. Stay informed so you can wisely think for yourself about your educational choices, your rights and responsibilities. If you never go to curriculum fairs or conventions, don't get state organization newsletters, and so on, you will be clueless when a fantastic homeschool resource appears or if the homeschool laws in your state are about to be fundamentally changed.

Some *think* they are informed, but aren't. They may belong to a local homeschool organization that is connected with a certain state organization that is associated with a certain national organization that is connected with a certain national homeschool magazine, and they all hear and read the same homeschool viewpoints and spokespersons. So some homeschoolers really only get one perspective and don't realize it.

Make the connections, get the newsletters and magazines, but be sure they represent a true variety of sources and resources.

MICHELLE BARONE ◆ Our culture really likes experts. It is comforting to be told what to do and how to do it. That way, when things go wrong, we can abdicate responsibility and point a finger somewhere else. Homeschooling is an entire movement based on the principle of accepting responsibility for our children's education, and still we seem unable to shake the notion that someone else knows more about our children and their needs than we do. Those of us who have been homeschooling for a few years may have many wonderful ideas and suggestions to share. We may have read lots of books, gone to conferences, field trips, and lectures. Talking to us can be helpful when you are new to homeschooling and uncertain of your path.

Remember when you were pregnant the first time and it seemed as though every woman you met could not stop herself from telling you her story—in all the gory detail? But you went to classes, read all you could, talked to doctors, midwives, experienced moms. When the day came and you gave birth, it was in your own unique way. The same is true of homeschooling: You will do it your way, the unique way that fits your family.

There are many wonderful, bright, interesting, motivating people who are writing and lecturing about homeschooling. Here you are, reading a book full of "experts." But I would venture to guess all these experienced homeschoolers would be the first to encourage you to take your own path, let in all the in-

---

NO MATTER THEIR AGE, EACH DAY PROVIDE YOUR CHILDREN WITH A MINIMUM OF AT LEAST ONE

- Kiss
- Hug
- Compliment
- Chance to share
- Opportunity to teach something
- Reason for learning something new

---

formation that works for your family, let the rest go. Truly, you are the homeschooling expert for your children.

100

What lasting impact of homeschooling is evident in your grown children?

LORETTA HEUER ◆ Ahhhhhhh, what a lovely question!

Both my sons have internalized their own standards of excellence. Homeschooling allowed Tad and Jed to engage in self-evaluation, to determine *their own* criteria for success, which usually exceeded the culturally imposed limits of what a young person "could" do or "should" do.

Each of my sons also has a strong work ethic. Jed, for example, designed his schedule at art school to allow for a day "off" from class. However, this break was not recreational. He might spend the day at St. Patrick's Cathedral, drawing an interiorscape, or at the Metropolitan Museum of Art, studying Rembrandt's drawings.

This may sound facetious, but homeschooling turned Tad and Jed into delightful conversationalists! Because of their wide experiential background, they can discuss just about anything with just about anyone. The tensions in Northern Ireland? Walt Whitman's Civil War poems? Shoreline erosion and flood insurance? They can handle it. In addition, each has an area of specialization—Jed in art, Tad in politics—that allows them to have something interesting to say.

Loretta Heuer

Both boys—young men!—are creative, independent thinkers. Without homeschooling, Tad probably would have accepted the prevailing political philosophy of our town's social studies teachers. Instead, with access to political information from both the left and right, he was encouraged to make his own philosophical decisions. Jed, had he gone to school, would have engaged untold hours of penmanship exercises. How would this have compromised his left-handed/right-brained "wiring"? Is his current creativity related to homeschooling's uninterrupted hours of drawing time?

And what about the real world? Are homeschoolers sheltered? Well, one son resides in London, the other in New York City. They are safe, street-smart

> I would venture to guess all these experienced homeschoolers would be the first to encourage you to take your own path, let in all the information that works for your family, let the rest go.

young men, each delighted to be living in a dynamic, cosmopolitan metropolis.

Finally, homeschooling has created bonds that transcend age and location. It has made and kept us a family. Nowadays, when Tad or Jed returns for a visit, I feel that I am meeting a cherished friend. They are wonderful company, both to each other as siblings and to us as their parents. If either has a problem, he is able to share his concerns. When things are going well, they call to share good news.

Happy kids. Competent, caring young adults. Isn't that what homeschooling is all about?

ANN FISHER ✦ Ah, the ultimate accountability question: Do homeschooled kids make it as adults?

Erin and Alice are certainly not cookie-cutter people; my daughters' uniqueness shines through in who they are and what they do. While both have very different personalities and interests, they do share significant traits that I attribute primarily to the homeschooling lifestyle.

While I have often been astonished by their ability to solve problems, I suspected my opinion was tainted by a mother's rose-colored prejudice. No more! I am convinced that their abilities are quite real. Time after time, their ability to think on their feet, learn quickly, and problem-solve has prompted comments by employers, co-workers, and others. Neither has a slacker bone in her body. (Because of all that unschooled freedom?) Creativity, willingness to do a good job, and self-management seem to be embodied in all they do. Time after time, employers have gone out of their way to open doors for them.

Of course, my kids have gaps in their knowledge and skill base. Who doesn't? What I didn't anticipate was how realistic and accurate my daughters would be in determining who they are, what they know, and where they might improve. Unencumbered by excessive or misleading grading and testing during the early years, they have only their own self-evaluation skills to rely on as they find their way in the world. As Alice told me, "Self-evaluation leads to self-motivation to improve upon the point being evaluated." Both have become crackerjack critical thinkers.

As many families do, ours suffered difficult times. During those times, the family connection—strengthened by a homeschooling tradition—was a lifeline that kept us grounded. When I asked my daughters how they experienced those tough periods, both assured me, "I know I have a family that loves and supports me, no matter what." The attachment still grows.

Both daughters have always been mature for their age. I credit homeschooling in that they matured at their own rate instead of at a school-mandated pace. However, that "pre-mature maturity" has created some interesting learning challenges. The delayed maturation of many of their age-mates has appalled them for years. Their dismayed observations continue to this day, triggering many useful insights into human behavior. Alice and Erin have learned to choose friends carefully.

One more thing: My most secret fear was that my children would feel like outsiders, living forever on the fringes of society because my choice to homeschool them was far from mainstream. Ha ha! I was wrong, wrong, wrong, and should have relaxed! When I shared that gnawing anxiety with them, both took me in hand, each saying in her own way, "Knock it off, Mom! Be glad, not sad. Homeschooling is the best thing you could have done for me, and I am sooooooo glad you kept us out of school as much as you did. *I had a happy childhood!*"

101

What have homeschooling parents learned from this experience?

MARY GRIFFITH ◆ I've learned that my children are just as curious as I am, that they want to know how their world works, and that they're capable of learning far more than I am capable of teaching them. I've learned that my children are essential members of this family, that they often find solutions I've missed for problems we've faced. I've learned (and keep learning, over and over again!) that my children are the best judges of how and when and what they need to learn. I've learned that my children, like me, learn most from doing real, useful work rather than from make-believe projects. I've learned that learning is the best part of life, that learning is something I will do until the day I die. And I've learned that my children already know all this. They won't need to be thirty-five years old before they finally figure it out.

HELEN AND MARK HEGENER ◆ We've learned to trust our children and ourselves. Trust is not easy to come by, and it's made even harder by schooling, which teaches us not to trust ourselves or our own instincts and feelings, but to rely on expertise and authority instead. Schooling utilizes a top-down chain of command, a hierarchical student-teacher relationship, but homeschooling doesn't need to replicate this hurtful pattern. Homeschooling encourages the development of a loving relationship based on caring and trust between parent and child, and this is the best possible environment for real learning to take place. Real learning—such as how to talk to other people about minor and major things, how to determine what needs doing and the best way in which to get it done, how to find one's rightful place in a confusing and complex world, how to truly live a life filled with goodness and worthiness and love.

While this learning is happening to our children, similar learning is happening to us as parents. We begin to question long-held assumptions about children and learning and our own place in the puzzle. We begin to see that what we were told about certain things like education and earning a living and what's worth doing with our lives is not necessarily true, and we find ourselves searching for answers to questions we thought we already knew the answers to.

As parents for over twenty years now, we've learned that we don't have all the answers. Sometimes our children have better answers than we do, especially as they've grown older. We've taught them to think carefully, and to consider several angles and approaches to a situation when necessary, but we're not as good at it as they are now. We've learned that being open to new ideas, new ways of looking at things, is a valuable approach in life, but old habits and old ways of doing things can be difficult to let go. Our children are helping us learn to let go and embrace new ways of seeing, hearing, feeling.

As parents for over twenty years now, we've learned that we don't have all the answers. Sometimes our children have better answers than we do, especially as they've grown older. We've taught them to think carefully, and to consider several angles and approaches to a situation when necessary, but we're not as good at it as they are now.

We've often quoted an old saying, whose author we've long forgotten, that goes something like this: "We can teach our children to have courage, faith, and endurance; they can teach us to laugh, to sing, and to love." In the final analysis, these lessons are probably the most important ones.

BECKY RUPP ◆ Each homeschooling family doubtless has its own list of unexpected revelations. What Randy and I have learned from our homeschooling experiences could fill a book. Homeschooling has been much more than we ever expected. In a way, it's like those little sponge capsules about the size of a vitamin pill—the kind you drop in water and suddenly it swells to the size of a pancake and turns into an octopus.

We've learned, from hands-on experience, that a true education is something that each person does for him or herself. It's not what we teach that makes an education; it's what they learn. This may not sound like much: these days it's accepted homeschool dogma. Observing it in practice, however, in our very own living room, was something else again. I hadn't realized that "pursuing their own interests in their own way" was going to be so emphatically individual. Each of our sons assimilated something different from his homeschool experience and used it to build a unique education—and the outcomes, in each case, are not necessarily the educations we would have chosen for them. Instead, these are the educations they chose for themselves.

When we decided to homeschool our boys, starting some eleven years ago when our oldest was just reaching kindergarten age, we had a number of goals in mind. We wanted to raise children who could think for themselves, undeterred by peer pressure. We wanted the boys to develop as individuals, with the confidence to march to the beats of their own—perhaps very different— drummers. We wanted the boys to have time and freedom to pursue their own interests and set their own goals.

There's an old saying: "Be careful what you wish for, because you just might get it." Homeschooling gave us just what we wished for: It turned out three unconventional and independent thinkers. This means that our sons don't always think like we do and it means that we don't always agree with each other. It's not quite what we expected. But we wouldn't trade it for anything.

LINDA DOBSON ◆ I wish I'd had the opportunity to learn what I've realized through homeschooling much earlier in life. That's probably why I look at homeschooled children, including my own, with awe and respect and optimism. I emerged from high school confused and unsure, told to jump into a new world when I didn't know if or where it had a place for me. These children generally finish homeschooling comfortable and confident, moving gracefully through growing independence into a world where their place is well established through years and exposure.

What was the vital difference between my experience and theirs? The answer is as clear as the stars on an Adirondack winter night. You see, the homeschooled children were never forced away from the world in the first place. And this has made all the difference.

Homeschooled children have experienced educational freedom in as many forms as the term freedom implies. Educational freedom means children's minds, hearts, and hands are delivered from restriction, schedule, and agenda externally imposed. Thus freed, the children have room—lots of space and time—to discover self. This discovery is a necessary foundation, an essential first step before any learning can possibly become meaningful and significant.

This step leads to the ability of self-determination. It's the self-determination of which Thomas Jefferson spoke so eloquently when he imagined an educated populace charged with electing forthright government representatives, the same self-determination implied in the phrase "life, liberty, and the pursuit of happiness." Yet self-knowledge and self-determination are made impossible by the very nature of any educational "system," most notably one that locks children away from the world.

This, I believe, is the most important of a long list of homeschooling lessons I've learned. When an educational system is set up to discourage self-determination from the start, and when I must financially support this discouragement of self-determination under threat of losing my home, then connections to life, liberty, and pursuit of happiness have been severed. A system like this must be a vehicle for something else. The evidence, too plentiful to include in this short piece, points to a "systematic" replacement of self-determination with dependence. The system serves up a curriculum—no, a lifestyle—that readies children for dependence on government for, just to name a few, increased police protection, health care, child care, jobs, housing, and food; in short, survival.

Did you notice the common thread running through all three of the other answers to this question?

Mary Griffith wrote: "[My children] often find solutions I've missed for problems we've faced."

The Hegeners wrote: "Sometimes our children have better answers than we do."

Becky Rupp wrote: "Our sons don't always think like we do."

This is anecdotal evidence of homeschooling children's self-determination—from three out of three families. These children are not being educated for dependence on government or anything or anyone else. If you prefer scientific evidence, I know of only one formal study of adult homeschoolers, which was undertaken by J. Gary Knowles and reported in 1991. None of the adults who were homeschooled as children that Mr. Knowles surveyed were unemployed (a large percentage had their own businesses), and none were on *any* form of welfare assistance.

The lesson is elementary: An education that starts with self-determination will finish with self-determination. Homeschooling parents and children alike are pressing the concept of educational freedom against its boundaries—and beyond—and reclaiming our ancestors' promises.

The value of educational freedom is a lesson too important to keep to ourselves. Throughout this book we have freely shared it with you. If you appreciate your home, you may be forced to keep supporting the system with your money, but you don't have to support the system by feeding it your children. You *can* choose to allow them to remain in the world.

And this will make all the difference.

Resources: Terribly Incomplete, But More Than Enough to Get You Started

I N MANY WAYS the search for resources was a lot easier for beginning homeschoolers fifteen to twenty years ago: What you wanted was either available from a limited number of suppliers or you went about creating it yourself! In one sitting I could quickly put together a resource list that covered most of the territory. But with homeschooling's growing popularity and acceptance, putting together a *complete* resource list has become a monumental task, and the quantity of suppliers fills many books devoted specifically to that task.

This list is not an attempt to duplicate those heroic efforts; it's just a way to get you off and running to collect the information and materials you may feel you need to get started—a little of this and a little of that. As you read books, subscribe to periodicals, and start sending away for information, ever more resources will come to your attention. Look at it like a treasure hunt: You'll dig in a lot of places in order to uncover those few gems that fit your unique needs.

Throughout this book experienced homeschoolers have echoed a similar refrain. Despite our learned thinking to the contrary, you don't need to spend a lot of money and buy a lot of "stuff" to provide a quality education for your children. Like most of the contributors to this book, I remember all too well spending money on materials I initially felt were essential, only to watch them sit on shelves collecting dust and wishing I had back just *half* of the money spent to do it over again.

At the same time, I encourage everyone to check out every resource that looks even remotely interesting to your children. Materials are as diverse as the people you've met in this book who use (or don't use) them. You never know when a book, a story, a documentary, a game, a movie, or a little-known occupation will ignite an imagination and set a child off on a life-influencing exploration.

One caveat: *Take it easy!* There's a lot of great "stuff" out there, but you don't need it all and you certainly don't need it all at once. Homeschooling doesn't have to be a "budget buster." In fact, when education is seamlessly integrated into living life, the ordinary becomes educational. "Educational" toys, books, games, videos, audiotapes and more are gifts happily welcomed by youngsters as birthday and Christmas presents. While it felt a bit "tacky," I would always compile a list of all those neat things I saw in catalogs throughout the year, then provide Grandma and Grandpa, aunts and uncles, with the list and catalog ordering information when holidays rolled around. Ordering information was necessary because many of these great resources just aren't available on local store shelves; and since many of the suppliers are home educators with home businesses, I want to support their efforts.

After reading this book, you also realize that homeschooling frees our minds from the compartmentalization of subject matter, so many of the available resources defy strict categorization. A good child's magazine may focus on history, for example, yet provide your son with knowledge of geography, science, and throw in a few great art projects for good measure. For the sake of making the following list as easy to use as possible, it has been broken down into categories, so just remember the lines between those categories are thin and flexible. Be sure to look around as you may find that I listed a resource where you might not have.

Since this is an incomplete list, please keep in mind that just because a resource *isn't* included, that doesn't mean it's not a good one. Any lack of inclusion simply means *we're out of room, folks!*

I leave you with many best wishes for an enjoyable, enlightening romp through learning at home with your children. Happy learning . . . always.

SUPPORT GROUPS

Homeschool support groups come in all shapes and sizes. They may focus on serving homeschoolers around the nation, or simply around the neighborhood. Most, regardless of scope, work on shoestring budgets, so including a stamped, self-addressed envelope when you are requesting receipt of printed information is always greatly appreciated, as is your use of e-mail or Web sites.

National Homeschool Groups and Allies

Most of the following organizations focus on special areas of homeschooling. Others address home education in the broader areas of alternative education, legal issues, and parental involvement in education.

The Adventist Home Educator
PO Box 836
Camino, CA 95709
530-647-2110
E-mail: tjshewmake@juno.com
Web site: www.adventisthomeed.org

Alliance for Parental Involvement in Education
PO Box 59
East Chatham, NY 12060-0059
518-392-6900
E-mail: allpiekjh@aol.com
Web site: http://www.croton.com/allpie

Alternative Education Resource Organization
417 Roslyn Road
Roslyn Heights, NY 11577
800-769-4171
Fax: 516-625-3257
Web site:www.edrev.org

American Homeschool Association
PO Box 1083
Tonasket, WA 98855-1083
509-486-1351
E-mail: AHA@americanhomeschoolassociation
.org

Web site: www.americanhomeschoolassociation
.org

The Association of Canadian Home-Based Education
Fax: 815-366-5342
E-mail: homeschool-ca-admin@flora.org
Web site: http://www.flora.org/homeschool-ca
/achbe

Canadian Alliance of Homeschoolers
272 Highway 5, RR 1
St. George, Ontario N0E 1N0
Canada
Wendy Priesnitz: 519-448-4001

Discovery Bay Homeschooling Resources of Hong Kong
http://www.geocities.com/discoverybayhk/

Education Otherwise (United Kingdom)
Web site: http://www.education-otherwise.org

Family Place (Malaysia)
03-5636-7562
E-mail: info@familyplace.com.my
Web site: www.familyplace.com.my

Family Unschoolers Network
1688 Belhaven Woods Court
Pasadena, MD 21122-3727
Voice Mail/Fax: 410-360-7330
E-mail: FUN-@unschooling.org
Web site: www.unschooling.org

Foundation for Educational Renewal
PO Box 328
Brandon, VT 05733
800-639-4122

Future of Freedom Foundation
11350 Random Hills Road, Suite 800
Fairfax, VA 22030
703-934-6101
E-mail: info@fff.org
Web site: http://www.fff.org

Holistic Education Press
Box 328
Brandon, VT 05733
1-800-639-4122
E-mail: info@great-ideas.org
Web site: http://www.great-ideas.org

Homeschoolers for Peace
PO Box 74
Midpines, CA 95345
209-742-6802

Moore Foundation
PO Box 1
Camas, WA 98607
360-835-5500
Fax: 360-835-5392
E-mail: moorefnd@pacifier.com
Web site: www.moorefoundation.com

National Center for Fair and Open Testing
342 Broadway
Cambridge, MA 02139
617-864-4810
E-mail: info@fairtest.org
Web site: www.fairtest.org

National Coalition of Alternative Community
    Schools
1266 Rosewood, Unit 1
Ann Arbor, MI 48604
734-668-9171
E-mail: ncacs1@earthlink.net
http://ncacs.org

National Coalition of Homeschoolers
    (South Africa)
PO Box 14
Dundee, 3000
South Africa
E-mail: durham@liadun.dundee.lia.net

Native American Home School Association
PO Box 979

Fries, VA 24330
Web site: http://expage.com/page/nahomeschool

Network of Black Homeschoolers
9709 Virginia Centerway Place
Glen Allen, VA 23060
804-515-1980
E-mail: gwnbhl@aol.com

Students Against Testing
Web site: www.NoMoreTests.com

Odysseus Group
Web site: www.johntaylorgatto.com

Otherwise Japan
E-mail: owj@comax.net

Pacific Justice Institute
PO Box 4366
Citrus Heights, CA 95611
916-857-6900
Fax: 916-857-6902
braddacus@pacificjustice.org
Web site: www.pacificjustice.org

General Homeschooling Information on the Internet

A to Z Homeschool: http://www.gomilpitas
    .com/homeschooling
Best Homeschooling: http://www.besthome
    schooling.org
Eclectic Homeschoolers Online: http://eho.org
Home Education Magazine: www.home-ed
    -magazine.com
Homeschool.com: www.homeschool.com
Homeschool Zone: www.homeschoolzone.com
Kaleidoscapes: www.kaleidoscapes.com
National Home Education Network:
    www.nhen.org
Teach at Home: www.teach-at-home.com
Unschooling.com: http://www.unschooling.com

Religion-Specific Support Groups

This list provides opportunity for contact (primarily electronically) with just some of the support groups that combine the religion they hold in common with discussions on homeschooling.

African American Homeschoolers of
    Christian Faith
Simon of Cyrene Association
PO Box 26357
Rochester, NY 14626

African Methodist Episcopal Church
http://www.yahoogroups.com/subcribe
    /AMEC-homeschool

Buddhist
http://www.yahoogroups.com/subscribe
    /Buddhist-homeschool

Catholic Homeschool News
http://www.yahoogroups.com/subscribe
    /CHSnews

Christ-Centered Unschoolers
http://www.yahoogroups.com/subscribe/ccu-list

Evangelical Lutheran Church of America
http://www.yahoogroups.com/subscribe
    /ELCAhomeschoolers

Episcopalian
http://www.yahoogroups.com/subscribe
    /Episcopalian-homeschool

Freewill Baptist
http://www.yahoogroups.com/subscribe
    /FreewillBaptist-homeschool

Hindu
http://www.yahoogroups.com/group
    /hindu-homeschoolers

Jehovah's Witness
http://www.yahoogroups.com/subscribe
    /Jehovahs_Witness-homeschool

Jewish Home Educators Network
http://snj.com/jhen

Latter-day Saints
http://www.yahoogroups.com/subscribe
    /bountiful_fhe

Muslim
E-mail to: majordomo@muslimsonline.com
In body: subscribe madrasah-net <your e-mail
    address>

Mennonite
http://www.yahoogroups.com/subscribe
    /Mennonite-homeschool

Messianic
http://www.yahoogroups.com/subcribe
    /MessianicHomeschool

Missionary Baptist
http://www.yahoogroups.com/subscribe
    /MissionaryBaptist-homeschool

Pagan
E-mail to: PHSlistparent@yahoo.com

Pentecostal
http://www.yahoogroups.com/subscribe
    /Pentecostal-homeschool

Presbyterian
http://www.yahoogroups.com/subscribe/Presbyterian-homeschoolers

Quaker
E-mail to: quakerhomeschool@topica.com

Seventh Day Adventist
http://www.tagnet.org/ahe

Southern Baptist
http://www.yahoogroups.com/subscribe
    /SouthernBaptistHomeschool

Traditional Roman Catholic
http://www.littlesparrow.org/homeschool.htm

Unitarian Universalists and Humanists
Send e-mail to: listproc@uua.org
In body: subscribe HUUH-L <your name>

United Church of Christ
http://www.yahoogroups.com/subscribe
    /UCC-homeschool

Special Interest E-mail Lists Sampler

Combining homeschooling and work
Blank e-mail to: WORKandHOMESCHOOL
    -sub@yahoogroups.com

Combining eBay pin money and
    homeschooling
http://groups.yahoo.com/group/homeschool
    _and_ebay

Homeschool Editors (of homeschooling
    publications big and small)
http://groups.yahoo.com/group/Homeschool
    -Editors

Homeschool Upper Grades
http://groups.yahoo.com/group/homeschool
    -upper-grades

Homeschooling U. S. military in Japan
http://members.xoom.com/MHESG

Homeschooling moms with disabilities
Blank e-mail to: hswm-subscribe@yahoogroups
    .com

Organize to homeschool (part of Messies
    Anonymous)
http://groups.yahoo.com/group/Organize-to
    -Homeschool

Overweight homeschooling moms
http://communities.msn.com/Overweight
    HomeschoolMoms

The Unschooler
Blank e-mail to: Theunschooler-subscribe
    @topica.com

State and Local Support Groups

Local, regional, and state support groups may be among the most important contributors to homeschooling's success. Sources of information, inspiration, activities, and lasting friendships, these backbones of the homeschooling movement are overwhelmingly started and maintained by volunteers doing what they love, and sharing what they do.

Because of the voluntary nature of these groups, contact information is ever-changing. As careful as I've been to provide the most accurate way to get in touch with a support group near you, chances are very good that *somewhere,* on the day after I put the information on paper, someone "retired" or moved or served her term and handed over the reins to another volunteer.

The good news is that a former volunteer can lead you quickly to the person you need. If this fails, you can always use any of the terrific ideas the writers in this book provided about how to contact a local support group. And remember, if all else fails, you can always start your own.

Good luck, and happy meetings!*

Canada
London Educational Alternatives Program
    (Ontario)
E-mail: womble@zap.wwdc.com

*Most of this collection is courtesy of the efforts of *Home Education Magazine.* Please remember that addresses, phone numbers, and e-mail addresses change frequently.

Montreal Metropolitan Support Group for
     Home-based Education
E-mail: zil@intlaurentides.qc.ca

Ontario Federation of Teaching Parents
77 Washington Street Paris, Ontario N3L 2A6
E-mail: oftp@kingston.net

Yukon Home Educators Society
PO Box 4993
Whitehorse, Yukon Y1A 4S2
867-667-6659

Alabama
Alabama Homeschooling Organization
Web site: http://www.alabamahomeschooling .org

Central AL Resources for Home Educators
E-mail: Mi4Angels@aol.com
Web site: http://www.geocities.com/Athens
     /Agora/7633/cafsg.html

Catholic Home Educators of Mobile
E-mail: mobilecath@xoommail.com
Web site: http://members.nbci.com/mobilecath/

Elmore County Homeschool Organization
E-mail: echo@onlineus.com
Web site: http://www.onlineecho.com/

Home Educators of Alabama Round Table
PO Box 1091
Huntsville, AL 35807
205-933-2571
Web site: www.educationalfreedom.com/heart

Homeschool Advocates
5962 Chalet Dr. N.
Mobile, AL 36608

North Alabama Home Educators
E-mail: NAHE@NorthAlabamaHomeEducators
     .freeservers.com
Web site: http://northalabamahomeeducators
     .freeservers.com

Alaska
AK Homeschool Network
E-mail: AHN@akhomeschool.net
Web site: http://www.akhomeschool.net

AK Homeschoolers Association
PO Box 230973
Anchorage, AK 99504-3527

Alaska Homeschoolers Mailing List
E-mail: Akhomeschoolers@yahoogroups.com

Anchorage Home Spun Educators
PO Box 798
Girdwood, AK 99587
E-mail: HomeSpuned@aol.com
Web site: http://members.aol.com/homespuned
     /webpage.html

Homeschoolers Unlimited
PO Box 56836
North Pole, AK 99705-1836
E-mail: Info@homeschoolersunlimited.org,
Web: http://www.HomeschoolersUnlimited.org

Sitka Home Education Association
506 Verstovia Street
Sitka, AK 99835
E-mail: dross@galenaalaska.org

Arizona
Apache Junction Unschooler
PO Box 2880
Apache Junction, AZ 85217
E-mail: ajunschl@aol.com
Web site: http://members.aol.com/ajunschl

AZ Families for Home Education
PO Box 2035
Chandler, AZ 85244
800-929-3927
Web site: http://www.expage.com/page
     /homeschoolersunlimited

SPICE
10414 W Mulberry Drive
Avondale, AZ 85323
Susan Taniguchi: 602-877-3642
E-mail: pompey@juno.com

TELAO Home Educators
4700 North Tonalea Trail
Tucson, AZ 85749
520-749-4757

Arkansas
Arkansas Home Educators Association
PO Box 4025
North Little Rock, AR 72190
501-758-9099

Coalition of AR Parents
PO Box 192455
Little Rock, AR 72219

Home Educators of AR Voicing Excellence Now
8 Glenbrook Place
Sherwood, AR 72120

Live & Learn
E-mail: HSOK1@aol.com
Web site: http://www.geocities.com/Athens
/Aegean /8673

California
All Ways Learning of San Jose
Web site: http://people.netscape.com/ccardiff
/awl.html

Antelope Valley Homeschoolers
805-947-3674

Bay Area Homelearners
Web site: http://home.earthlink.net/~hawk141/

Bayshore Homeschoolers
PO Box 13038
Long Beach, CA 90803
562-434-3940

E-mail: BayShSch@aol.com
Web site: http://www.bayshoreeducational.com
/homeschoolers.html

CA Homeschool Network
PO Box 55485 Hayward, CA 94545
800-327-5339
E-mail: mail@cahomeschool.net
Web site: http://www. californiahomeschool.net

Central CA Homeschoolers
7600 Marchant Avenue
Atascadero, CA 93422
805-462-0726

East Bay Family Educators
1090 Mariposa Avenue
Berkeley, CA 94707
510-524-1224

Excellence in Education (Monrovia)
818-357-4443

Family Centered Education of Los Angeles
818-766-8914
E-mail: Writer42@aol.com

Family Village Support Group
510-528-6510
E-mail: robinreed4@aol.com

High Desert Homeschoolers
760-956-1588

Home Learner
PO Box 90638
Industry, CA 91715
562-693-4232
E-mail: comfynest@aol.com

Homeschool Association of CA
PO Box 868
Davis, CA 95617
888-472-4440
E-mail: info@hsc.org
Web site: www.hsc.org

Humboldt Homeschoolers
477 Crosby Road
Ferndale, CA 95536
707-786-4157
E-mail: hchs@webtv.net

Independent Homeschoolers
310-788-9788

LA Homeschoolers Westside
E-mail: Copykatz@aol.com

Lompoc Valley Home Educators
3343 Via Dona
Lompoc, CA 93436
E-mail: ctykeson@hotmail.com

Los Angeles Homeschoolers
PO Box 1166
Malibu, CA 90265
310-456-5447

Marin Homeschoolers
905 Tiburon Boulevard
Tiburon, CA 94920
415-435-0768

Monterey Bay Christian Home Schoolers
1558 Flores Street
Seaside, CA 93955
408-394-9504
Web site: http://www.redshift.com/~mizmooz

North Bay HomeScholars
PO Box 621
Vineburg, CA 95487
Cyndie Moi: 707-939-9525
E-mail: CynMoi@metro.net

Queen of Angels Homeschooling Support Group
5 Sierra Drive
Salinas, CA 93901
831-757-3288
E-mail: champr@netzero.net

Riverside Area Home Learners
3356 Freeport Dr.

Corona, CA 92881
909-272-6132
E-mail: Las@mikeshores.com

San Diego Home Educators
619-560-8866

San Francisco Homeschoolers
3639 Webster Street
San Francisco, CA 94123
415-673-8092

Santa Clara Valley Homeschooling Group
E-mail: Raywasing@aol.com

Sierra Christian School Association
PO Box 2023
Portersville, CA 93257
E-mail: mishel@lightspeed.net

Sonoma County Home Schoolers
    Association
7009 Baker Lane
Sebastopol, CA 95472
707-573-4750

South Bay F.R.E.E. Scholars
408-773-9201
E-mail: tlscwall@kepnet.com

South Street Centre
PO Box 227
Boulder Creek, CA 95006
831-338-2540
E-mail: southst@cruzio.com

South Valley Homeschoolers Association
7500 Chestnut Street
Gilroy, CA 95020
408-847-2017 (after 1 P.M.)

SPICE (Sacramento Valley)
PO Box 282
Wilton, CA 95693
916-687-7053
E-mail: spice-sacramento@juno.com

Tri-Valley Explorers
925-462-8264
E-mail: Cris@techie.com
Web site: http://members.nbci.com/homeschool

Venture Home Schoolers Resource
231 Market Place #328
San Ramon, CA 94583
E-mail: ventureschool@hotmail.com

West San Fernando Valley Playgroup
20555 Dumont Street
Woodland Hills, CA 91364
818-888-2480

West Valley Homeschoolers
Web site: http://wvhomeschoolers.tripod.com
    /WVH

Whittier Homeschoolers
7432 Duchess Drive
Whittier, CA 90606

Yolo County Homeschoolers
530-759-1106

Yosemite Area Homeschoolers
PO Box 74
Midpines, CA 95345
209-742-6802

Colorado

CO Home Educator's Association
3043 S Laredo Circle
Aurora, CO 80013
303-441-9938
E-mail: pinewood@dash.com

CO Home Schooling Network
1247 Harrison Street
Denver, CO 80206
303-369-9541

Colorado Springs Homeschool Support Group
PO Box 26117

Colorado Springs, CO 80936
800-532-7011
E-mail: board@hschool.com
Web site: http://www.hschool.com

Concerned Parents of Colorado
PO Box 547
Florissant, CO 80816
719-748-8360
E-mail: Treonelain@aol.com
Web site: http://members.aol.com/treonelain/

Denver Northwest Homeschool Community
http://www.denverhomeschools.org

The Homeschool Support Network
719-596-1162

Independent Network of Creative
    Homeschoolers
5984 S Netherland Circle
Aurora, CO 80015
303-766-7882

The Ken Caryl Homeschooling Network
Littleton, CO
303-948-3308
E-mail: unschoolmom2@yahoo.com

Longmont Homeschool Co-op
PO Box 6674
Longmont, CA 80501
E-mail: Homeschoolcoop@yahoo.com
Web site: http://www.geocities.com
    /homeschoolcoop

Mesa Verde Homeschoolers
PO Box 134
Mancos, CO 81328
970-892-7802

Pueblo Home School Association
14 E Cellini Dr.
Pueblo West, CO 81007
719-547-4054

Secular Homeschool Support Group
719-749-9126
E-mail: shssg@mindspring.com

West River Unschoolers
779 Jasmine Ct.
Grand Junction, CO 81506
970-241-4137
E-mail: wracademy@aol.com
Web site: http://www.geocities.com/wracademy

Connecticut

CT Home Educators Association
80 Coppermine Road
Oxford, CT 06478
203-732-0102

CT Homeschool Network
47 Daniel St.
East Hampton, CT 06424
860-267-6358
E-mail: cthmschlntwk@aol.com
Web site: http://www.mardicon.com
    /cthomeschoolnetwork.htm

CT's CURE (CT's Citizens to Uphold the
    Right to Educate)
PO Box 597
Sherman, CT 06784
203-355-4724
E-mail: CtsCure@yahoo.com

The Education Association of Christian
    Homeschoolers
25 Field Stone Run
Farmington, CT 06032
800-205-8744

Unschoolers Unlimited
22 Wildrose Avenue
Guilford, CT 06437
203-458-7402
Web site: http://www.borntoexplore.org
    /unschool

Delaware

Brandywine Valley Home Education Resource
    Organization
Web site: http:///www.geocities.com/bvhero/
E-mail: bvheroes@hotmail.com

DE Home Education Association
500 N. Dual Hwy. PMB 415
Seaford, DE 19913
E-mail: jcpoeii@juno.com

North Wilmington Homeschool Group
302-984-2931
E-mail: nwhomeschooler@juno.com

Support for Home Educators and Resources
    in Dover
Web site: http://www.geocities.com/tdand31k/

Tri-State Home School Network
PO Box 7193
Newark, DE 19714
302-234-0516

Unschoolers and Others
E-mail: Unschoolersandothers@juno.com

Florida

The Family Learning Exchange
2020 Turpentine Road
Mims, FL 32754
407-268-8833

Florida Home Educators
PO Box 677523
Orlando, FL 32867
407-568-1191
E-mail: FlaHomeEd@aol.com

FPEA
PO Box 50685
Jacksonville Beach, FL 32240
877-275-3732

Florida Inclusive Home Education Network
http://fihen.org/fihen

Home Educators Assistance League
904-682-2422

H.O.M.E.
E-mail: mesjlls@n-jcenter.com
Web site: http://www.angelfire.com/fl2/home4
    ourchildren

Home Education Resources and Information
904-565-9121
E-mail: herijax@juno.com
Web site: http://www.heri.net

Home Educators Assistance League
3343 Shoal Creek Cove
Crestview, FL 32539
904-682-2422

Home Educators Family Network of Venice
941-492-5905

Home Educators Lending Parents Support
5941 NW 14 Court
Sunrise, FL 33313
954-791-9733
E-mail: Info@HelpsOnline.org
Web site: http://www.HelpsOnline.org

Homeschool Alternatives
7030 - 32nd Ave N
St Petersburg, FL 33710
E-mail: uumom@ivillage.com
Web site: http://www.geocities.com/homeschoolalt

The Homeschool Network
Web site: http://www.homestead.com
    /homeschoolnetwork/intro.html

Lake County Homeschool Groups
E-mail: scalish@earthlink.net
Web site: http://www.lchsn.org

Marion County Home Educators
E-mail: magnolia@dm.net
Web site: http://www.homestead.com/mche

Parkland Home Educators
407-381-3081
E-mail: samiot@cfl.rr.com

SOAR
Holly Palermo: 407-997-9874

South County Home Schoolers
561-638-2602
E-mail: info@southcountyhomeschoolers.org
Web site: http://www.southcounty
    homeschoolers.org

South Florida Homeschool Association
PO Box 840554
Pembroke Pines, FL 33084
954-435-9867
E-mail: AmyKCA@aol.com
Web site: http://www.southflorida
    homeschoolassociation.com

Teaching Our Own
155 Flamingo Drive
Boynton Beach, FL 33435
561-493-3679
E-mail: teachingourown@juno.com
Web site: http://h-e-a-t.org

Georgia
Atlanta Alternative Education Network
1586 Rainier Falls Drive
Atlanta, GA 30329
404-636-6348
E-mail: mickaels@mindspring.com
Web site: http://www.mindspring.com/~lei/aaen

Alternative Learning Group
770-554-8994
E-mail: TammyBristow@aol.com

Athens Area Homeschoolers
1855 Jot-Em-Down Rd
Danielsville, GA 30633
706-789-2159

Augusta Area Home Education Network
PO Box 15963
Augusta, GA 30919
E-mail: ReedAcademy@home.com
Web site: http://augustahen.mybravenet.com

Catholic Home Alliance of North Georgia
    Educators
Marietta, GA
E-mail: change@catholichomeschool.org
Web site: http://www.catholichomeschool.org
    /change

Creative Home Educators
404-978-1262, ext.3369
E-mail: Nessa@creativehomeeducators.com
Web site: http://www.creativehomeeducators
    .com

Douglas County Home Educators
3855 Jims Court
Douglasville, GA 30135
770-949-3297

Family Educators for Christ
PO Box 16619
Savannah, GA 31416
912-354-5204
E-mail: fefc.sayh@juno.com

Free to Learn at Home
4439 Lake Forest Drive
Oakwood, GA 30566
770-536-8077

Georgia Home Education Association
245 Buckeye Lane
Fayetteville, GA 30214

Georgians for Freedom in Education
103 Sarazen Circle
Sharpsburg, GA 30277
770-463-1563

Home Education Information Resources
PO Box 2111
Roswell, GA 30077
E-mail: info@heir.org
Web site: www.heir.org

Intelligent Education, Inc.
3811 Stonewall Terrace
Atlanta, GA 30369
770-518-4880
Web site: www.intelligenteducation.com

Lifetime Learners of Georgia
861 Franklin Rd., Bldg. 2, Apt. 14
Marietta, GA 30067
770-419-8680
E-mail: mrslarak@yahoo.com
Web site: http://llg.freeyellow.com

LIGHT
PO Box 9473
Columbus, GA 31908
E-mail: terrillyn1@yahoo.com
Web site: http://www.lightsupport.homestead
    .com

Robins Air Force Base Homeschool Network
PO Box 563
Lizella, GA 31052
E-mail: TyphoonT45@aol.com

Rockdale Evangelical Association of Christian
    Homeschoolers
Conyers, GA
E-mail: kpstover@bellsouth.net

Hawaii
Christian Homeschoolers of Hawaii
91-824 Oama Street
Ewa Beach, HI 96706
808-689-6398

Hawaii Homeschool Association
PO Box 893513
Mililani, HI 96789
808-944-3339
E-mail: HawaiiHomeschoolers@hotmail.com
Web site: http://www.hawaiihomeschool
    association.org

Homeschool Adventures
Web site: http://mauisfreepress.com/supplements
    /homeschool/index.html

Kauai Home Educators Association
808-245-7867
E-mail: swimmerjean98@yahoo.com

Idaho

Family Unschoolers Network
1809 North 7th Street
Boise, ID 83702
208-345-2703
E-mail: ndjensen@qwest.net

Palouse Home Learning Alternatives
802 White Avenue
Moscow, ID 83843
208-882-1593

Southeast Idaho Homeschool Association
E-mail: joyfuljoyc@aol.com

Southern Idaho's Great Homeschool Trackers
E-mail: nsight@onewest.net

Illinois

Grassroots Homeschoolers
E-mail: GrassrootsHS@yahoo.com
Web site: http://GrassrootsHS.tripod.com

Homeschooling Families of Illinois
630-548-4349

HOUSE
2508 E 22nd Place
Sauk Village, IL 60411

708-758-7374
E-mail: illinois_house@hotmail.com
Web site: http://www.geocities.com/Athens
    /Acropolis/7804

Jewish Homeschool Association of Greater
    Chicago
773-764-5137
E-mail: BHP@BnosHenya.org
Web site: http://bnoshenya.org

Northwest Chicago HOUSE
773-637-9085
E-mail: Hallshorj@aol.com
Web site: www.drawcomics.com/nwhouse
    /index.htm

Raising Kane Home Educators
E-mail: wonblurose@ameritech.net

Rockford Area HOUSE
815-395-0843
E-mail: Heylu52@aol.com

Indiana

Families Learning Together
1714 E 51st Street
Indianapolis, IN 46205
317-255-9298
E-mail: whemul@earthlink.net

Homefront
812-347-2931

IN Association of Home Educators
1000 North Madison #S2
Greenwood, IN 46142
317-638-9633

L.E.A.R.N.
9577 E State Road 45
Unionville, IN 47468
812-336-8028

Life Education and Resource Network
9998 West State Road 43

Bloomington, IN 47404
E-mail: nancyw@bluemarble.net
Web site: http://www.bloomington.in.us/~learn

Wabash Valley Homeschool Association
914 Barton Ave.
Terre Haute, IN 47803
E-mail: WVHA@aol.com

Iowa

IA Home Educators' Association
818 N. Utah Ave.
Davenport, IA 52804
319-323-3735

Iowans Caring About Homeschooling Internet
Support
515-466-3311
E-mail: Muste5@aol.com

Iowans Dedicated to Educational Alternatives
3296 Linn-Buchanan Rd.
Coggon, IA 52218
319-224-3675
E-mail: hsinfo@juno.com
Web site: http://home.plutonium.net/~pdiltz
/idea/

Network of IA Christian Home Educators
Web site: http://www.the-NICHE.org

Kansas Circle of Homeschoolers and Unschoolers in Central Kansas
RR 1, Box 28A
Rush Center, KS 67575
913-372-4457

Heartland Area Homeschoolers' Association
823 West Street
Emporia, KS 66801
316-343-3696

Konza Homeschoolers Association
7675 Jenkins Rd.
St. George, KS 66535

785-494-2884
E-mail: hackney@kansas.net

Lawrence Area Unaffiliated Group of
Homeschoolers
913-597-5579

Teaching Parents Association
PO Box 3968
Wichita, KS 67201
316-945-0810

Kentucky

Bluegrass Home Educators
600 Shake Rag Road
Waynesburg, KY 40489
606-365-8568
E-mail: bhe@ky-on-line.com
Web site: http://ky-on-line.com/bhe

Home Educators Resource Center
502-261-9858

KY Home Education Association
PO Box 81
Winchester, KY 40392-0081

Louisiana

Homeschoolers Learning from Mother Earth
14189 Ridge Road
Prairieville, LA 70769

Homeschoolers Organizing for Progressive
Education
5229 Hwy. 3276
Stonewall, LA 71078

Louisiana Home Education Network
Web site: www.la-home-education.com

Northshore Home Educators
Web site: http://members.xoom.com
/nshomeedu/nhe.html

Westbank Homeschool Organization, Inc.
E-mail: whoedu@bellsouth.net
Web site: www.angelfire.com/home/whoedu

Wild Azalea Unschoolers
6055 General Meyer Avenue
New Orleans, LA 70131
504-392-5647
E-mail: wildazaleas@hotmail.com

Maine
Central Maine Self-Learners
36 Country Acres
Monmouth, ME 04259
207-933-5055
E-mail: Cmslhomeschool@aol.com
Web site: http://members.aol.com
     /Cmslhomeschool/home.html

Homeschoolers of Maine
337 Hatchet Mountain Rd.
Hope, ME 04847
207-763-4251
Web site: www.homeschool-maine.org

ME Home Education Association
800-520-0577

Southern ME Home Education Support
     Network
42 Hammond Rd.
Parsonfield, ME 04047
207-883-9621

Maryland
Educating Our Own
686 Geneva Drive
Westminster, MD 21157
410-857-0168 or 410-848-3390

Glen Burnie Homeschool Support Group
6514 Dolphin Ct.
Glen Burnie, MD 21061
E-mail: HS6Whetzel@aol.com

MD Home Education Association
9085 Flamepool Way
Columbia, MD 21045
410-730-0073
Web site: www.MHEA.com

Montgomery Home Learning Network
301-916-1132
E-mail: ElissaJC@concentric.net

North County Home Educators (Anne Arundel)
1688 Bellhaven Woods Court
Pasadena, MD 21122
410-437-5109
E-mail: NCHE@IQCweb.com

Northern Montgomery County Home
     Schoolers
301-916-6315

Prince George's Home Learning Network
E-mail: ccjw@mindspring.com

Unschooling Family Connection
301-916-1132
E-mail: ElissaJC@concentric.net

Massachusetts
Cape Ann Homeschoolers
978-281-6927

The Family Resource Center
PO Box 308
Salem, MA 01970
978-741-7449
E-mail: FamilyRC001@aol.com
Web site: www.FamilyRC.com

The HOME Club
617-876-7273

Homeschooling Together
24 Avon Place
Arlington, MA 02174
E-mail: ses@world.std.com

Web site: http://people.ne.mediaone.net
/jrsladkey/hst

Jewish Homeschoolers of MA
E-mail: FernReiss@aol.com

MA Home Learning Association
PO Box 1558
Marstons Mills, MA 02648
508-249-9056
E-mail: Lisawood@aol.com
Web site: www.mhla.org

Merrimack Valley Homelearners Group
13 Ashdale Road
N Billerica, MA 01862
Alysa Dudley: 978-663-2755
E-mail: alysad@mediaone.net

Newburyport Area Homeschool Network
978-388-6448
E-mail: HappyFiddlers3@aol.com

North Suburban Home Learners
978-744-4796
E-mail: KathrynJB@aol.com

Shadows on the Shore—Cape Cod
Homeschooling Network
508-430-7122
Web site: www.bearabletimes.org/shadows
shore.html

Michigan
Ann Arbor Area Unschooling Support Network
Web site: http://community.mlive.com/cc
/unschooling

Belleville Area Homeschool Association
734-699-0787

Celebrating Home Under Rome—Catholic
Homeschoolers
517-349-6389
E-mail: RWittLans@aol.com

Christian Home Educators of the Blue
Water Area
E-mail: chebwamail@yahoo.com
Web site: http://www.members.tripod.com
/chebwa

Christian Home Educators of Michigan
248-380-3611

Families Learning and Schooling at Home
21671B Drive North
Marshall, MI 49068
616-781-1069

HELP Michigan
906-475-5508
E-mail: up4hmsklrs@aol.com

Hillsdale Area Homeschoolers
5151 Barker Road
Jonesville, MI 49250
517-287-5565
E-mail: klinefam@dmci.net

Older Homeschoolers' Group
9120 Dwight Drive
Detroit, MI 48214
313-331-8406

Restoring Education and Cherishing Home
248-377-1513
E-mail: abmorris@home.com
Web site: http://reachhomeschool.homestead
.com/index.html

Minnesota
Creative Twin Cities Homeschoolers
Web site: http://www.creativehomeschoolers
.com

Home Educators and Youth
218-984-3503
Web site: http://homeeducatorsandyouth
.homestead .com/HEY.html

MN Association of Roman Catholic Home
   Educators
7211 Sherwood Echo
Woodbury, MN 55125
612-730-8101

MN Homeschoolers Alliance
PO Box 23072
Richfield, MN 55423
612-491-2828 or 888-346-7622
E-mail: mha@homeschoolers.org
Web site: http://www.homeschoolers.org

Mississippi
Christian Home Educators of Hattiesburg
601-544-5195
E-mail: jsbmcb@c-gate.net
Web site: http://www.geocities.com/cheh_ms

Coast Military Home Educators
601-388-4522

Home Educators of Central MS
102 Hollow Hill Dr.
Florence, MS 39073

Oxford Homeschool Network
E-mail: shuhart@watervalley.net

MS Home Educators Association
RR 9, Box 350
Laurel, MS 39440
Web site: www.mhea.net

Missouri
LEARN
PO Box 10105
Kansas City, MO 64171
913-383-7888
E-mail: Kwilson898@aol.com,
      Krissmoose@aol.com
Web site: www.kclearn.org

Ozark Lore Society
HC 73, Box 160
Drury, MO 65638
417-679-3391
E-mail: deb@wiseheart.com

St. Louis Homeschool Network
4147 East Pine
St. Louis, MO 63108
314-534-1171
E-mail: regtill@swbell.net

St. Louis Secular Homeschoolers Co-op
314-781-5640
E-mail: unschool@swbell.net

Sugarcreek Homeschool Support and Play
   Group
314-963-7307
E-mail: sugarcreek_2000@yahoo.com

Montana
Bozeman Homeschool Network
406-586-1025

Mid-Mountain Home Education Network
c/o 3300 CB Loop
Helena, MT 59602

MT Coalition of Home Educators
PO Box 43
Gallatin Gateway, MT 59730
Web site: http://www.mtche.org

North Choteau Country Home
RR 1, Box 732
Big Sandy, MT 59520
406-378-3257

Whitehall Area Home Educators
83 1st Road
Whitehall, MT 59759
406-287-2250

Nebraska

LEARN
7741 E Avon Lane
Lincoln, NE 68505
402-488-7741

Nevada

Home Schools United—Vegas Valley
702-870-9566
E-mail: homeschooluvv@yahoo.com
Web site: http://homeschool8.tripod.com

Homeschool Melting Pot
702-320-4840
E-mail: homeschoolmeltingpot@onebox.com
Web site: http://www.angelfire.com/nv
    /homeschoolmeltingpot/

Northern NV Home Schools, Inc.
PO Box 21323
Reno, NV 89515
702-852-6647
E-mail: NNHS@aol.com

New Hampshire

Derry Area Homeschoolers
603-898-0828

Homeschooling Friends
204 Brackett Road
New Durham, NH 03855
603-664-9673
E-mail: newcomers@homeschoolingfriends.org
Web site: http://homeschoolingfriends.org

NH Alliance for Home Education
17 Preserve Drive
Nashua, NH 03060
603-880-8629

NH Homeschooling Coalition
PO Box 2224
Concord, NH 03302

New Jersey

Educational Excellence—School at Home
E-mail: HomeschoolSummit@aol.com

Homeschoolers of Central New Jersey
609-333-1119
E-mail: kfridkis@kldigital.com

Homeschool Playgroup
908-454-4574

Homeschoolers of South New Jersey
1239 Whitaker Avenue
Millville, NJ 08332
609-327-1224
E-mail: Tutor@Pulsar.net
Web site: http://www.pulsar.net/~tutor

Unschooler's Network
2 Smith Street
Farmingdale, NJ 07727
732-938-2473

Unschooling Families Support Group of
    Central NJ
150 Falwell Station Road
Jobstown, NJ 08041
609-723-1524

New Mexico

Enchanted Families
505-837-9495
E-mail: twavebks@swcp.com

Home Educators of Dona Ana
2022 Rubina Ct.
Las Cruces, NM 88005
505-525-2358

Home Educators of Santa Fe
505-466-4462

Homeschooling PACT
PO Box 961

Portales, NM 88130
505-359-1618

NM Family Educators
PO Box 92276
Albuquerque, NM 87199
505-275-7053

New Mexico Homeschooling
2905 Tahiti Ct., NE
Albuquerque, NM 87112
505-299-2476
E-mail: SandraDodd@aol.com
Web site: http://expage.com/NewMexico
    Homeschooling

NM Loop
E-mail: Kraf3@aol.com

New Mexico Tumbleweeds
5909 Buena Vista NW
Albuquerque, NM 87114
505-899-6916
E-mail: monimiura@yahoo.com

New York
Buffalo Area Homeschooling Association
8750 Tanawanda Creek Rd.
Clarence Center, NY 14032
716-741-4755

Columbia County Homeschooling Mothers'
    Group
29 Kinderhook Street
Chatham, NY 12037
518-392-4277

Families for Home Education
3219 Coulter Road
Cazenovia, NY 13035
315-655-2574

Fingerlakes Unschoolers Network
201 Elm Street
Ithaca, NY 14850
607-273-6257
E-mail: Laundress@aol.com

Home Education Network of Central
    New York
Web site: www.geocities.com/hencny

Homeschool Network of the Southern Tier
1560 Red School Rd.
Corning, NY 14830
607-722-8269

Kids' Place of Choice (Freeport, LI, NY) South
    Nassau Home Educators' Resource Room
516-868-5766
E-mail: Devww@aol.com

Lake-to-Lake Homeschoolers
1399 Maryland Rd.
Phelps, NY 14532
315-548-4026
E-mail: mail@lake2lake.org
Web site: http://www.lake2lake.org

New York City Home Educators Alliance
8 East 2nd Street
New York, NY 10003
212-505-9894
Web site: www.nychea.com

Oneida Lake Area Home Educators
PO Box 24
Sylvan Beach, NY 13157
315-762-5166

Oneonta Area Sharing in Homeschooling
PO Box 48
Gilbertsville, NY 13776
607-783-2271
E-mail: dabajian@citlink.net

Rochester Area Homeschoolers Association
275 Yarmouth Road
Rochester, NY 14610
Voice mail: 716-234-0298

Tri-County Homeschoolers
PO Box 190
Ossining, NY 10562
914-941-5607
E-mail: chofer@croton.com
Web site: http://www.croton.com/home-ed

Tri-Lake Community Home Educators
7 White Birch Lane
Saranac Lake, NY 12983
518-891-9021
E-mail: hoytfarm@juno.com

Ulster County Home Ed Resource Person
914-255-1870
E-mail: Y.Aspengren@WorldNet.ATT.NET

Woodstock Home Educators Network
12 Cantine's Island
Saugerties, NY 12477
845-247-0319
E-mail: msklaroff@ulster.net

North Carolina
Caldwell County Home Educators
1427 Bushville Dr.
Lenoir, NC 28645
E-mail: ryearwood@twave.net

Cary Homeschoolers
114 West Camden Forest Dr.
Cary, NC 27511
919-851-5157
Web site: www.caryhomeschoolers.com

Families Learning Together
1670 NC Highway 33 W
Chocowinity, NC 27817

E-mail: cn2464@coastalnet.com
Web site: http://fltnc.cjb.net

Franklin County Home Educators
888 Carlyle Rd.
Zebulon, NC 27597
919-404-0898

Lunch Bunch Learners
PO Box 5715
Greensboro, NC 27435
336-375-3861
E-mail: hopperme@earthlink.net

Many Paths of Stanly and Union County
737 E. Oakwood Ave.
Albermarle, NC 28001
704-986-4797
E-mail: ManyPaths@onebox.com

North Carolinians for Home Education
419 N Boylan Avenue
Raleigh, NC 27603
919-834-6243
E-mail: nche@nche.com
Web site: www.nche.com

Robeson County Homeschool Support Group
910-671-8553
E-mail: mommyt@interstar.net

North Dakota
ND Home School Association
PO Box 7400
Bismarck, ND 58507
701-223-4080
E-mail: ndhs@wdata.com

Ohio
Association of Ohio Homeschoolers
3636 Paris Boulevard
Westerville, OH 43081

Creative Learning In My Backyard
E-mail: wew99@sssnet.com

Families Independently Schooling at Home
Ashland County: 419-945-2319
Richland County: 419-747-7286
Wayne County: 330-262-4489

Families Unschooling in the Neighborhood
4132 Spring Flower Court
Gahanna, OH 43230
614-794-2171
E-mail: roy@qn.net

Families Unschooling in the Neighborhood—
    Mid Ohio
5668 Township Road 105
Mount Gilead, OH 43338
419-947-6351
E-mail: laurie@redbird.net

Growing Together
1676 Trendril Court
Columbus, OH 43229

HEART
7979 Greenwich Road
Lodi, OH 44254
330-948-2941
E-mail: ncarter@neo.rr.com

HELP—Central OH
4132 Spring Flower Court
Gahanna, OH 43230
614-470-2219
E-mail: help.columbus@pobox.com
Web site: http://www.help.columbus
    @pobox.com/~help.columbus

HELP—Northern OH
10915 Pyle—S Amherst Road
Oberlin, OH 44074
216-774-2720

HELP—NW OH
PO Box 98

Perrysburg, OH 43552-0098
419-478-9729 or 419-476-1088

Home Education Resource Organization
170 W Main Street
Norwalk, OH 44857
419-663-1064

Home Educators Advocacy League
26140 Yearsley Road
Raymond, OH 43067
513-358-2450

Homeschool Network of Greater Cincinnati
3470 Greenfield Court
Maineville, OH 45039
513-683-1279

Newark Area Home Learners
614-787-2947
E-mail: hsfamily@alltel.net

Inclusive North Columbus Home Education
    Support
614-878-8419
E-mail: oneill@netset.com

Learning in Family Environments
PO Box 2512
Columbus, OH 43216
614-241-6957
E-mail: Lifehmsl@aol.com

OH Home Educators Network
PO Box 38132
Olmsted Falls, OH 44138
E-mail: ohen@grafixbynix.com
Web site: http://grafixbynix.com/ohen

Our Uniquely Challenged Homeschoolers
30213 Robert St.
Wickliffe, OH 44092
440-944-4782 (mailbox 44)
E-mail: RCHOSEN@juno.com
Web site: http://www.community.cleveland.com
    /cc/ouch

Parents and Children Together
8944 Weiss Road
Union City, OH 45390
937-692-5680, 937-968-4942

Oklahoma

Fellowship of Shawnee Home Educators
RR 1, Box 23681
Tecumseh, OK 74873
405-598-8517

Green Country Home Education Resource
    Organization
183 Fox Run Circle
Jenks, OK 74037

Home Educators Resource Organization
302 N. Coolidge
Enid, OK 73703
580-446-5679
E-mail: HERO@OklahomaHomeschooling
    .org
Web site: http://OklahomaHomeschooling.org
    /oklahoma.htm

Oklahoma Home Educators Network
PO Box 1420
Blanchard, OK 73010
E-mail: OK-HE@att.net
Web site: http://home.att.net/~ok-he

Oregon

Greater Portland Homeschoolers
PO Box 82265
Portland, OR 97282
Voice mail: 503-241-5350
E-mail: gphnews@hotmail.com
Web site: http://www.expage.com/page
    /gphomeschoolers

Online Inclusive Support Group for Oregon
    Homeschoolers
E-mail: orsig-owner@yahoogroups.com

OR Christian Home Education Association
    Network
17985 Falls City Rd.
Dallas, OR 97338
502-288-1285
E-mail: oceanet@oceanet.org
Web site: www.oceannetwork.org

OR Home Education Network
PO Box 218
Beaverton OR 97075
503-321-5166
E-mail: ohen@teleport.com
Web site: www.teleport.com/~ohen
Web site: www.ohenconference.org

OR Pagan Homeschool Association
PO Box 129
Madras, OR 97741
541-546-6108
E-mail: crew@goddessmoon.org
Web site: http://www.goddessmoon.org

Pennsylvania

Blue Mountain Homeschoolers
636 Almond Road
Walnutport, PA 18088

Bucks County Homeschoolers
125 Mountain Oaks Rd.
Yardley, PA 19067
215-428-3865
E-mail: pporter321@aol.com

Catholic Homeschoolers of Scranton
1317 St. Ann Street
Scranton, PA 18504
717-344-8866

Center City Homeschoolers
2203 Spruce Street
Philadelphia, PA 19103
215-732-7723

Central Philadelphia Homeschoolers
215-482-7933
E-mail: vallone@dellnet.com
Web site: http://cphomeschoolers.tripod.com

Christian Homeschoolers of Mercer County
705 S. Center St.
Grove City, PA 16127
724-458-0837
E-mail: basicallydon@juno.com

Homeschoolers Association of Warren County
RR 1, Box 87B1
Youngsville, PA 16371
814-489-3366
E-mail: Cyndi@Penn.com

Hosanna Homeschoolers
1615 Termon Ave.
Pittsburgh, PA 15212
412-732-0900
Web site: http://members.xoom.com
    /homeskooled /homeschooler.htm

McKeesport Area Homeschoolers
404 Owens Avenue
Liberty Borough, PA 15130
412-672-7056
E-mail: pageclan@msn.com
Web site: http://www.ontv.com/school-cgi
    /schoolHook

MD/PA Home Educators (Mason-Dixon area)
PO Box 67
Shrewsbury, PA 17361
717-993-3603

Northeast PA Homeschoolers
PO Box 884
East Stroudsburg, PA 18301
717-476-9321

PA Home Education Network
285 Allegheny Street
Meadville, PA 16335

412-561-5288
Web site: www.phen.org

PA Home Education News
PO Box 305
Summerhill, PA 15958
814-495-5651
E-mail: Karenleven@aol.com
Web site: www.phen.org

People Always Learning Something
105 Marie Drive
Pittsburgh, PA 15237
412-367-6240

Rolling Green Home Education Resource
    Room
2725 Aquetong Road
New Hope, PA 18938
215-862-2968

Southwestern PA Home Education Network
429 Union Avenue
Pittsburgh, PA 15205
412-922-8344
E-mail: Pasage@juno.com
Web site: www.phen.org

Valley Unschoolers Network
565 Forgedale Rd.
Barto, PA 19504
610-845-8941

York Home School Association, Inc.
717-292-5379
E-mail: YHSA@juno.com
Web site: http://www.geocities.com/Heartland
    /Prairie/2819

Rhode Island
Parent Educators of Rhode Island
PO Box 782
Glendale, RI 02826

RI Guild of Home Teachers
PO Box 11
Hope, RI 02831
401-821-7700
Web site: http://members.tripod.com/righthome

S.O.S. for Home Schoolers
55 West Log Bridge Rd.
Coventry, RI 02816
401-392-3386
E-mail: HollysHomeschool@aol.com

South County Homeschoolers
500 Carolina Back Road
Charleston, RI 02813

South Carolina

Carolina Superschooler
103 Dill Circle
Landrum, SC 29356

Christian Home Educators of Laurens County
200 Carolyn Dr.
Clinton, SC 29325
864-833-4502
E-mail: sowingseeds@go.com

Inclusive Network of Columbia Homeschoolers
E-mail: INCH@teacher.com
Web site: www.inch-homeschool.com

Lancaster Area Homeschool Support Group
1528 Carmel Rd.
Lancaster, SC 29720

Network of Inclusive Coastal Home Educators
E-mail: photo6keiki@sc.rr.com
Web site: http://photo6keiki.tripod.com/NICHE

Palmetto State School's Out Support
Web site: http://communities.msn.com/PS*SOS

South Carolina Homeschool Support Group
242 Weathers Farm Rd.
Bowman, SC 29018
803-563-9322

South Carolina Homeschoolers Discussion List
E-mail: dbroughton@infoave.net

South Carolina Homeschool Network
Web site: http://www.schomeschool.com

Together in Education and Support
E-mail: selaacademy@netzero.net

T.O.R.C.H. Morning Star
1136 Lining La.
Charleston, SC 29407
843-766-4651

Tri-County Educational Association of
　　Community Homeschoolers
PO Box 651
Summerville, SC 29484
E-mail: teachhomeschool@yahoo.com
Web site: http://www.geocities.com
　　/teachhomeschool

South Dakota

SD Home School Association
PO Box 882
Sioux Falls, SD 57101
605-338-9689

Tennessee

State of Franklin Homeschoolers
494 Mill Creek Road
Kingsport, TN 37664
423-349-6125
E-mail: kramerbg@mounet.com

TN's Homeschool Information Site
E-mail: Kay@TnHomeEd.com
Web site: http://TnHomeEd.com

TN Homeschooling Families
214 Park Lane
Oliver Springs, TN 37840
423-435-9644

Unschoolers of Memphis
901-757-9859

Texas

Austin Area Homeschoolers
510 Park Boulevard
Austin, TX 78751
Web site: http://www.austin360.com/community
/groups/homeschoolers/index.html

Central TX Homeschoolers (Temple)
E-mail: morron@vum.com

Heart of TX Home Schoolers
1710 Vincent
Brownwood, TX 76801
915-643-1182
E-mail: charlotte@gte.net

Highland Lake Area Homeschoolers
RR 1, Box 239
Burnet, TX 78611
512-756-2982
E-mail: tolliver@tstar.net

Homeschoolers EXCEL
E-mail: ListGrrl@onlineworks.com
Web site: www.yahoogroups.com/group
/hsers-excel-public

Houston Unschoolers Group
9625 Exeter Road
Houston, TX 77093
713-695-4888
E-mail: MHFurgason@hotmail.com
Web site: http://www.geocities.com/Athens
/Delphi/1794/hug.html

Metrocrest Home School Support Group
PO Box 59627
Dallas, TX 75229
214-358-5723
E-mail: Homeschl@gte.net
Web site: www.mhssg.org

Minority Homeschoolers of TX
Blank e-mail to: MHOT-subscribe
@yahoogroups.com
Web site: http://www.mhot.org

North TX Home Educators' Network
E-mail: infor@nthen.org
Web site: www.nthen.org

North TX Self Educators
150 Forest Lane
Double Oak/Lewisville, TX 75067
817-430-4835

Southeast Area Home Education Network
E-mail: sahen@cog7.org

Parents Encouraging a Christian Education
E-mail: homeschoolmom@teacher.com
Web site: http://peacetalk.bizland.com/index
.html

South Fort Worth Christian Home Educators
PO Box 16573
Fort Worth, TX 76133
817-249-1975
E-mail: robbjh@flash.net

South Texas Self-Learners
1005 Delta Drive
Corpus Christi, TX 78412
512-992-7549

SW Dallas Home School Association
PO Box 1104
Cedar Hill, TX 75106
E-mail: StoryLadee@aol.com
Web site: www.swdhsa.org

Sugar Creek Christian Home Educators
281-499-6958
E-mail: info@SCCHE.org
Web site: www.SCCHE.org

SW Homeschooling Network
PO Box 960004
El Paso, TX 79996

Tarrant Home Educators Association
PMB-109 S. Hulen Drive, Suite 360
Fort Worth, TX 76132
817-421-1761
Web site: http://www.theaonline.org

TX Advocates for Freedom in Education
E-mail: sjf@jsoft.com
Web site: www.jsoft.com/archive/taffie
　/index.html

Wharton County Christian Homeschool
　Organization
409-543-1999
E-mail: car@wcnet.net

Woodlands Innovative Scholastic Environments
130 N Rushwing Circle
The Woodlands, TX 77381
713-364-8074

Utah

Beyond Books Homeschool Co-Op
Web site: http://www.creativewebpagemagik
　.com/beyondbooksm.html

Charlotte Mason Study Group of the
　Salt Lake Area
PO Box 900983
Sandy, UT 84090
E-mail: PennyGar@aol.com
Web site: http://members.aol.com/PennyGar/

Latter-day Saint Home Educators' Association
2770 S 1000 W
Perry, UT 84302
801-723-5355
Web site: www.ldshea.org

Salt Lake Home Educators
801-501-0344
E-mail: shark@xmission.com
Web site: http://www.xmission.com/~nprw
　/SLHE.html

Southern Utah Home Educators Network
Web site: http://sgarea.homestead.com

Utah Home Education Association
PO Box 1492
Riverton, UT 84065
888-887-UHEA
Web site: http://www.utah-uhea.org

Utah-hs E-mail Support Group
E-mail: Utah-hs-owner@yahoogroups.com
Web site: http://www.yahoogroups.com/group
　/Utah-hs

Vermont

Christian Home Educators of VT
214 N Prospect #105
Burlington, VT 05401
802-658-4561
E-mail: GESA97@aol.com

Right at Home
RR 2, Box 145
E Wallingford, VT 05742
Cindy Wade: 802-259-2394
E-mail: cwade@vermontel.com

United Homeschoolers
264 Tortolano Rd.
South Royalton, VT 05068
802-763-2837
E-mail: dltimian@together.net

VT Association of Home Educators
RR 1, Box 847
Bethel, VT 05032
802-234-6804
E-mail: liberty@together.net
Web site: www.vermonthomeschool.org

VT Homeschoolers' Association
RR 2, Box 4440
Bristol, VT 05443
802-453-5460

Virginia

Blue Ridge Area Network for Congenial
    Homeschoolers
255 Ipswich Pl.
Charlottesville, VA 22901
804-974-7149
E-mail: amy@pcsp.com

Children's Circle
RR 1, Box 132A
Mouth of Wilson, VA 24363
703-579-4252

Community of Independent Learners
PO Box 16029
Alexandria, VA 22302

Fauquier Unschoolers Living Classroom
PO Box 51
Goldvein, VA 22720
Rene Pleasant: 540-752-2478

LEARN (Northern VA Homeschoolers)
1111 Waynewood Boulevard
Alexandria, VA 22308

Learning in a Family Environment
125G Clubhouse Dr. #2
Leesburg, VA 20175
E-mail: abbey@anent.com

Many Paths for Excellence
E-mail: jdfriestad@erols.com
Web site: www.manypaths.f2s.com

Richmond Educational Alternatives for
    Children at Home
PO Box 36174
Richmond, VA 23235-8003
804-795-7624
E-mail: carmel@compuserve.com
Web site: http://www.geocities.com
    /Heartland/Plains/7440

Tidewater Educators Association for Christian
    Homeschooling, Inc.
Hampton Roads, VA
E-mail: teach@springmail.com
Web site: www.teachhomeschool.com/index.htm

VA Home Education Association
PO Box 5131
Charlottesville, VA 22905
E-mail: info@vhea.org
Web site: www.vhea.org

Washington

Family Learning Organization
PO Box 7247
Spokane, WA 99207
509-467-2552
E-mail: homeschool@familylearning.org
Web site: www.familylearning.org

Fun Family Homeschool Group
421 NE 12th St.
North Bend, WA 98045
E-mail: fisler@msn.com

Granite Falls Homeschoolers
3526 Robe Menzel Rd.
Granite Falls, WA 98252
360-691-7429
E-mail: M8land@aol.com
Web site: http://groups.yahoo.com/group
    /GraniteFallsHomeschoolers

Home Educators Cooperative of the
    Mid-Columbia
41005 E. Hacienda
Benton City, WA 99320
509-967-3301

Homeschoolers Support Association
PO Box 413
Maple Valley, WA 98038

Ignatius Scholars
Spokane, WA
509-487-3154

Island Home Educators
509-463-9060
425-746-5047

Kittitas Valley Homeschool Association
PO Box 1492
Ellensburg, WA 98926
509-925-4033

Life Education Activity Resource Network
PO Box 8783
Lacey, WA 98509
E-mail: LEARNatHomeFam@aol.com
Web site: www.homeschoolerslearn.org

Military Homeschool FAMILIES of Kitsap
    County
Web site: http://community.silverlink.net
    /pheconnection/index1.htm

Network of Vancouver Area Homeschoolers
162 Krogstad Road
Washougal, WA 98671
360-837-3760
E-mail: 71230.66@compuserve.com

North Central, WA Homeschool Co-op
PO Box 147
Curlew, WA 99118

Olympia Christian Homeschool Group
PO Box 8823
Lacey, WA 98509
E-mail: OlyHSGroup@yahoo.com
Web site: http://www.geocities.com/Athens
    /Olympus/3331

Peninsula Homeschool Exchange
419 Benton St.
Port Townsend, WA 98368

360-385-3830
E-mail: dcarroll@cablespeed.com

St. Thomas More Home Education
3853 76th Avenue SE
Mercer Island, WA 98040
206-232-2680

Spokane County Homeschoolers Association
PO Box 184
Mica, WA 99023
509-891-1370
E-mail: SoSpokaneCoHs@hotmail.com

Teaching Parents Association
PO Box 1934
Woodinville, WA 98072
206-505-1561, ext. 1274
E-mail: info@washtpa.org
Web site: www.washtpa.org

Valley Home Educators
1413 Easthills Terrace
E Wenatchee, WA 98802
509-884-1237

WA Home Education Network
E-mail: gardnfev.em@gte.net
Web site: http://www.homestead.com
        /WaHomeEdNet/WHENmain.html

WA Homeschool Organization
6632 S. 191st Pl. #E100
Kent, WA 98032
425-251-0439
E-mail: WHOoff99@foxinternet.net
Web site: www.washhomeschool.org

Washington, D.C.
Bolling Area Home Educators
E-mail: ritsfam@juno.com

BWHE (Network between Baltimore and
Washington inclusive homeschoolers)
Web site: http://groups.yahoo.com/group
/BWHE

West Virginia
Kanawha-Putnam Home Educators
PO Box 7541
Cross Lanes, WV 25356
304-766-9877
Web site: www.kphe.org

Morgan County Homeschoolers
1417 Fairfax St.
Berkeley Springs, WV 25411
304-258-5414

WV Home Educators Association
PO Box 3707
Charleston, WV 25337
800-736-9843
Web site: www.wvheahome.homestead.com

Wisconsin
Dodge County Home Educators
755 East Center St.
Juneau, WI 53039
920-386-0387
Web site: http://www.geocities.com
/dodgecountyhomeeducators/index.html

HOME
5745 Bittersweet Place
Madison, WI 53705
608-238-3302
E-mail: amckee73@hotmail.com

Home Scholars of Sheboygan County
920-528-7057
E-mail: darcymz@execpc.com

Milwaukee Area Home Learners
W260 N7751 Jay Lane

Sussex, WI 53089
414-246-3604

Ozaukee Explorers
4410 Bittersweet Lane
Cedarburg, WI 53210
414-377-7734
E-mail: PIPPENN@aol.com

Spooner Area Home School Group
PO Box 343
Spooner, WI 54801
E-mail: sp_hm_sch_group@hotmail.com

WI Parents Association
PO Box 2502
Madison, WI 53701-2502
Web site: http://www.homescholing-WPA.org

Wyoming
Casper Area Christian Home Educators
307-638-8179
E-mail: Lovs6kids@aol.com

Homeschoolers of Wyoming
PO Box 926
Evansville, WY 82636
307-745-3536

Laramie Home Education Network
429 Hwy. 230 #20
Laramie, WY 82010

T.E.A.C.H.
PO Box 3150 Evans Mobile Home Ct. #1
Jackson, WY 83001

Unschoolers of Wyoming/Laramie Home
Education Network
429 Hwy. 230, #20
Laramie, WY 82010

Wyoming Catholic Homeschoolers
Web site: http://www.yahoogroups.com/group
/wychs

Resources, Resources, and More Resources

The title of this section says it all!

Books: Just a Bit More to Read About the Homeschooling Lifestyle, Including Books Mentioned Within . . .

The number of books devoted to homeschooling has exploded in the last decade as more and more parents seek useful information. While most of the titles below deal specifically with homeschooling, the others are included because they are recommended by this book's contributors for the information they provide to aid in the homeschooling lifestyle.

Armstrong, Thomas. *Awakening Your Child's Natural Genius: Enhancing Curiosity, Creativity, and Learning Ability.* J. P. Tarcher, 1991.

———. *In Their Own Way.* J. P. Tarcher, 1988.

Bolles, Richard Nelson. *The 2001 What Color Is Your Parachute: A Practical Manual for Job-Hunters and Career Changers.* Ten Speed Press, 2000.

Cohen, Cafi. *Homeschoolers' College Admission Handbook: Preparing 12- to 18-Year-Olds for Success in the College of Their Choice*, Prima Publishing, 2000.

——— *Homeschooling the Teen Years: Your Complete Guide to Successfully Homeschooling the 13- to 18-Year-Old*, Prima Publishing, 2000.

Colfax, David and Micki. *Hard Times in Paradise: An American Family's Struggle to Carve Out a Homestead in California's Redwoods.* Warner Books, 1992.

Copelan, Lewis, editor. *High School Subjects Self-Taught.* Halcyon House, 1940 (available through Brook Farm Books).

Dobson, Linda. *The Art of Education: Reclaiming Your Family, Community, and Self.* Holt Associates, 1997.

———. *Homeschooling the Early Years: Your Complete Guide to Successfully Homeschooling the 3- to 8-Year-Old*, Prima Publishing, 1999.

———. *Homeschoolers' Success Stories: 15 Adults and 12 Young People Share the Impact That Homeschooling Has Made on Their Lives*, Prima Publishing, 2000.

———. *The First Year of Homeschooling Your Child: Your Complete Guide to Getting Off to the Right Start*, Prima Publishing, 2001.

Dominguez, Joe, and Vicki Robin. *Your Money or Your Life: Transforming Your Relationship with Money and Achieving Financial Independence.* Penguin USA, 1993.

Gelner, Judy. *College Admissions: A Guide for Homeschoolers.* Poppyseed Press, 1988.

Griffith, Mary. *The Homeschooling Handbook.* Prima Publishing, revised 1999.

———. The Unschooling Handbook. Prima Publishing, 1998.

Guterson, David. *Family Matters: Why Homeschooling Makes Sense.* Harcourt Brace Jovanovich, 1992.

Healy, Jane M. *Endangered Minds: Why Our Children Don't Think and What We Can Do About It.* Touchstone Books, 1991.

Hegener, Mark and Helen, eds. *The Homeschool Reader: Perspectives on Homeschooling.* Home Education Press. 1995.

Heuer, Loretta. *The Homeschoolers Guide to Portfolios and Transcripts.* Arco, 2000.

Holt, John. *Teach Your Own: A Hopeful Path for Education.* Delacorte Press, 1989.

———. *How Children Fail.* Addison-Wesley Publishing Co., 1995.

———. *How Children Learn.* Addison-Wesley Publishing Co., 1995.

Illich, Ivan. *Deschooling Society.* HarperCollins, 1983.

Kaseman, Larry and Susan. *Taking Charge Through Homeschooling: Personal and Political Empowerment.* Koshkonong Press, 1990.

Kenyon, Mary Potter. *Home Schooling from Scratch: Simple Living—Super Learning.* Gazelle Publications, 1996.

Liedloff, Jean. *The Continuum Concept: In Search of Happiness Lost.* Addison-Wesley Publishing Co., 1986.

Llewellyn, Grace. *The Teenage Liberation Handbook: How to Quit School and Get a Real Life and Education.* Lowry House, 1998.

McKee, Alison. *From Homeschool to College and Work: Turning Your Homeschool Experiences into College and Job Portfolios.* Bittersweet House (WI), 1997.

Meighan, Roland. *The Next Learning System: And Why Homeschoolers Are Trailblazers.* Educational Heretics Press, 1997.

———. *Learning from Home-Based Education.* Education Now Publishing Cooperative, 1992.

Moore, Raymond and Dorothy. *The Successful Homeschooling Family Handbook.* Thomas Nelson Publishers, 1994.

———. *Home Built Discipline.* Thomas Nelson, 1990.

———. *Home Made Health.* Word Books, 1989.

Morgan, Melissa, and Judith Waite Allee. *Homeschooling on a Shoestring: A Jam-Packed Guide.* Harold Shaw, 2002.

———. *Educational Travel on a Shoestring.* Harold Shaw, 2001.

Pearce, Joseph Chilton. *Magical Child.* Dutton, 1974.

———. *Evolution's End: Claiming the Potential of Our Intelligence.* HarperSanFrancisco, 1993.

Rupp, Becky. *Getting Started on Home Learning: How and Why to Teach Your Kids at Home.* Three Rivers, 1998.

———. *Home Learning Year by Year: How to Design a Homeschool Curriculum from Preschool Through High School.* Three Rivers, 2000.

Sheffer, Susannah. *A Sense of Self: Listening to Homeschooled Adolescent Girls.* Boynton/Cook Heinemann, 1995.

Williams, Jane. *Home School Market Guide.* (Annual.) Bluestocking Press, 1998.

. . . And Books Teeming with Resources!

Buy these books, or check them out from your library, and you will *never* wonder where to get resources again!

Gold, Laura Maery and Joan M. Zielinski. *Homeschool Your Child for Free.* Prima Publishing, 2000.

Hubb, Don. *Home Education Resource Guide.* Blue Bird Publishing, 1994.

Reed, Donn. *The Home School Source Book.* Brook Farm Books, revised 2001.

Rupp, Becky. *Good Stuff: Learning Tools for All Ages.* Holt Associates, 1997.

———. *The Complete Home Learning Source Book.* Crown, 1998.

Homeschool Periodicals

Subscribing to homeschooling magazines is like insuring you'll receive a periodic booster shot of encouragement, inspiration, news, and practical advice. Go ahead, build another bookcase!

The Catholic Home Educator
PO Box 787
Montrose, AL 36559
Web site: www.nache.org/che.html

The Edgy-catin' Mama
903 Dyer Rd.
Sultan, WA 98294
E-mail: npackebush@aol.com

Home Educator's Family Times
PO Box 708
Gray, ME 04039
207-657-2800
E-mail: FamilyTimes@HomeEducator.com
Web site: http://www.HomeEducator.com
    /FamilyTimes

F.U.N. News
1688 Belhaven Woods Court
Pasadena, MD 21122-3727
Voice mail/fax: 410-360-7330
E-mail: FUN@unschooling.org
Web site: www.unschooling.org

Home Education Magazine
PO Box 1083
Tonasket, WA 98855
509-486-1351
Orders: 800-236-3278
E-mail: HEM-Info@home-ed-magazine.com
Web site: http://www.home-ed-magazine.com

Homefires (Homeschool Resource Network)
180 El Camino Real, Suite 10
Millbrae, CA 94030
888-4-HOME-ED
E-mail: Editor@Homefires.com
Web site: www.homefires.com

The Link
587 N Ventu Park Road
Suite F-911
Newbury Park, CA 91320
805-492-1373
E-mail: hompaper@gte.net
Web site: www.homeschoolnewslink.com

Moore Report International
Box 1
Camas, WA 98607
360-835-2736

E-mail: moorefnd@pacifier.com
Web site: www.moorefoundation.com

*Voices: The Journal of the National Home
    Education Network:* (online)
    www.nhen.org

Useful Non-Homeschool Periodicals

These periodicals address additional lifestyle aspects that may help you "tweak" your current circumstances enough to make room and opportunity for homeschooling. Most deal with the philosophy of simplifying, living a natural lifestyle, and parents at home.

Back Home Magazine
PO Box 70
Hendersonville, NC 28793
800-992-2546
E-mail: backhome@ioa.com
Web site: www.BackHomeMagazine.com

Full-Time Dads (online only)
Web site: http://www.fathering.com/ftd

Liedloff Continuum Network Newsletter
PO Box 1634
Sausalito, CA 94966
E-mail: LCN@continuum-concept.org
Web site: www.continuum-concept.org

Mothering
PO Box 1690
Santa Fe, NM 87504
505-984-8116
Web site: www.mothering.com

Natural Life Magazine
RR 1
St. George, Ontario
N0E 1N0 Canada
E-mail: altpress@netroute.net
Web site: http://www.life.ca

Paths of Learning
PO Box 328
Brandon, VT 05733
Web site: http://www.great-ideas.org/paths.htm

Simple Living—The Journal of Voluntary Simplicity
4509 Interlake Ave. N.
PO Box 149
Seattle, WA 98103
206-464-4800
Web site: www.simpleliving.net
E-mail: jluhrs@juno.com

Mothers at Home
9493-C Silverking Ct.
Fairfax, VA 22031
703-352-1072
E-mail: mah@mah.org
Web site: http://www.mah.org

Periodicals for Your Children

Children love to receive mail, and getting any of these magazines is sure to put a smile on their faces as you bring fun, up-to-the-minute learning materials into your home. Don't forget to search for magazines that cover any of their favorite hobbies and activities.

American Girl
800-845-0005
Web site: www.americangirl.com

Cobblestone Publishing
Cobblestone/Faces/Odyssey/Calliope/Ladybug, etc.
30 Grove St.
Peterborough, NH 03458
800-821-0115
Web site: www.cobblestonepub.com

Dragonfly
Web site: http://mizvx1.acs.muohio.edu
    /~dragnfly/index.html

Exploratorium Magazine Online
Web site: http://netra.exploratorium.ed
    /exploring/index.html

Highlights/Highlights Kids
1800 Watermark Dr.
Columbus, OH 43216
800-603-0349
Web site: www.highlights.com

Jack & Jill/Turtle/Humpty Dumpty
Web site: www.jackandjillmag.org

Junior Scholastic
800-631-1586
Web site: http://teacher.scholastic.com

Kids Discover
Web site: http://hallmags.com/title/kids
    _discover.shtml

Muse (from *Smithsonian*), *Ladybug, Cricket, Baby Cricket,* etc.
800-827-0227
Web site: www.musemag.com

National Geographic World
800-638-4077
Web site: www.nationalgeographic.com/world

New Moon
Web site: www.newmoon.org

Old News
400 Stackstown Road
Marietta, PA 17547
717-426-2212
Web site: http://www.oldnewspublishing.com

Ranger Rick/Your Big Backyard/Wild Animal Baby
8925 Leesburg Pike
Vienna, VA 22184
800-822-9919

Skipping Stones (by and for kids)
PO Box 3939
Eugene, OR 97403
541-342-4956
E-mail: skipping@efn.org
Web site: http://www.treelink.com/skipping
    /main.htm

Stone Soup (by and for kids)
PO Box 83
Santa Cruz, CA 95063
800-447-4569
E-mail: editor@stonesoup.com
Web site: www.stonesoup.com

Time for Kids
1271 6th Ave. 25th Floor
New York, NY 10020
800-777-8600
E-mail: emailbag@timeforkids.com

Zoobooks
800-992-5034
Web site: www.zoobooks.com

Curriculum Sources/Correspondence Schools/Potential Diplomas

There is a wide variety in cost, services, and expectations among the various providers. Thorough research into many options is recommended in order to decide whether or not you need a program. If you find that you do, your research will help you and your child decide which one best fits your needs.

Alger Learning Center and Independence
    High School
800-595-2630
Web site: www.independent-learning.com

Calvert School
105 Tuscany Road

Baltimore, MD 21210
888-487-4652
Web site: www.calvertschool.org

Cambridge Academy
3300 SW 34th Avenue #102
Ocala, FL 34474
800-252-3777

Child U
2400 N. Commerce Pkwy. #404
Weston, FL 33326
877-424-4538
Web site: www.childu.com

Clonlara School
1289 Jewett
Ann Arbor, MI 48104
734-769-4511
E-mail: info@clonlara.org
Web site: www.clonlara.org

Curriculum Services
26801 Pine Ave.
Bonita Springs, FL 34135
877-702-1419
E-mail: info@curriculumservices.com
Web site: www.curriculumservices.com

K12
866-968-7512
Web site: www.K12.com

Laurel Springs School
800-377-5890
www.laurelsprings.com

Oak Meadow
PO Box 740
Putney, VT 05346
802-387-2021
E-mail: oms@oakmeadow.com
Web site: www.oakmeadow.com

Phoenix Special Programs and Academics
1717 West Northern, #104
Phoenix, AZ 85021
602-674-5555
E-mail: e-mail@phoenixacademies.org
Web site: www.phoenixacademies.org

University of Missouri Distance and
    Independent Study
136 Clark Hall
Columbia, MO 65211
800-609-3727
Web site: http://cdis.missouri.edu/go/efh.asp

HCL Boston School
PO Box 2920
Big Bear City, CA 92314
909-585-7188
E-mail: bostonschool@bostonschool.org
Web site: www.bostonschool.org

Home Study International
12501 Old Columbia Pike
Silver Spring, MD 20914
301-680-6570
Web site: www.his.edu

Indiana University Distance High School
800-334-1011
Web site: http://scs.indiana.edu

Keystone National High School
School House Station
420 West 5th Street
Bloomsburg, PA 17815
800-255-4937
E-mail: info@keystonehighschool.com
Web site: http://www.keystonehighschool.com

Laurel Springs School
1002 E. Ojai Avenue
PO Box 1440
Ojai, CA 93024
800-377-5890
Web site: http://www.laurelsprings.com

Oak Meadow School
PO Box 740
Putney, VT 05346
802-387-2021
E-mail: oms@oakmeadow.com
Web site: http://www.oakmeadow.com

Seton Home Study School
1350 Progress Drive
Front Royal, VA 22630
540-636-9990
Web site: www.setonhome.org

Sonlight Curriculum, Ltd.
8042 South Grant Way
Littleton, CO 80127
303-730-6292
Web site: www.sonlight.com

The Sycamore Tree Center for Home Education
2179 Meyer Place
Costa Mesa, CA 92627
949-650-4466
Web site: www.sycamoretree.com

University of Missouri—Columbia High
    School (MU High School)
136 Clark Hall
Columbia, MO 65211
800-858-6413
Web site: http://cdis.missouri.edu/MU
    HighSchool/HShome.htm

University of Nebraska at Lincoln
Independent Study High School
33rd and Holdrege Street
Lincoln, NE 68653-0900
402-472-4321
Web site: http://cds.unl.edu/disted/ishs.html

University of Wisconsin—Extension
800-442-6460
Web site: http://learn.wisconsin.edu

Unschoolers Network
2 Smith Street

Farmingdale, NJ 07727
E-mail: UnNet@aol.com
Web site: http://www.castlemoyle.com
    /resources/state/plen1221.htm

West River Academy
2420 North First Street
Grand Junction, CO 81501
970-241-4137
E-mail: WRAcademy@aol.com

The Three R's, and More

Any resource worth its salt will cover more than
one "subject" area as your child learns. Such is the
case with the resources contained in this section.
Typical subject headings are used to serve as a
rough guide as you discover what is available.

Sample of Freebies Available on the Internet

Children's storybooks online: http://www
    .magickeys.com/books/index.html
Classified Ads:
    http://www.smalbizffa.net/ffa.pl?73403
For teachers: http://www.teacherfreebies.com
From the government: http://www.ed.gov/free/
ID those Insects: http://www.orkin.com/Main
    _Edu.htm
Library of Classics: http://www.information
    -resources.com/Library/library.html
McGruff Coloring Book:
    http://www.mcgruff.org/order.htm
Make your own word search and other puzzles:
    http://puzzlemaker.school.discovery.com
    /WordSearchSetupForm.html
Math tutorial (grades 6 to 10 California high
    school exit exam): http://www.etap.org
Nutrition and Fitness: http://www.sugar.org
    /resource/childdental.html
Peanuts: http://aboutpeanuts.com/eduorder.html

Perpetual Preschool Freebies, Messages, and
    Links: http://www.96.cyberhost.net
    /perpetualfree_internet.html
Sewing lessons: http://www.Sew-
    WhatsNew.com
Science and environmental resources:
    www.thegreenfrognews.com
Typing tutor: http://easytype.com/
Worksheets: www.freeworksheets.com
More worksheets: www.worksheetfactory.com
More worksheets: www.atozteacherstuff.com

Reading

Reading opens up the world for children. Here
are resources that will let them see the possibilities from the very first word.

Ball-Stick-Bird Publications (Learn to read)
PO Box 13
Colebrook, CT 06021
860-738-8871
E-mail: bsbpub@snet.net
Web site: www.ballstickbird.com

Book Links (Bimonthly information on books
    by themes)
434 W Downer Place
Aurora, IL 60506-9954
888-350-0950
E-mail: blnk@kable.com
Web site: http://www.ala.org/BookLinks

Chinaberry Book Service (Great books by read-
    ing level)
2780 Via Orange Way Suite B
Spring Valley, CA 91978
Web site: www.chinaberry.com

EDC Publishing (U.S. source of Usborne
    books)
PO Box 470663
Tulsa, OK 74147-0663
800-475-4522

E-mail: edc@edcpub.com
Web site: www.edcpub.com

Harper Trophy (Children's paperbacks)
10 E 53rd Street
New York, NY 10022
800-242-7737
Web site: http://www.harpercollins.com/hc
/aboutus/imprints/trophy.asp

Lost Classics
PO Box 3429
Lake Wales, FL 33859-3429
888-211-2665E-mail: mgeditor@lostclassics
books.com
Web site: www.lostclassicsbooks.com/

The Sonday System
800-321-7585
Web site: www.readabc.com

Internet
Adolescent Literature: http://www.adolescentlit
.com
Animal ABC's: http://www.janbrett.com
/alphabet/alphabet_main.htm
Bibliomania: http://www.bibliomania.com
Harvard Classics: http://www.bartleby.com/hc
Literature and more online: http://www
.knowledgerush.com
Literature Guides: http://www.literatureguides
.homestead.com/index.html
Phonics Pathways: http://www.dorbooks.com
Young children's stories (English and Spanish):
http://www.storyplace.org
Young Writers:
http://www.youngwritersnook.com

E-mail Newsletters
English Resources:
E-mail to ies@tradeplaza.co.nz (put "subscribe"
in subject box)

Mathematics

Child(ren) + homeschooling = ? A family that
discovers math together can embark on a
very interesting journey!

Academy for Economic Education
125 Nationsbank Center
Richmond, VA 23277
804-643-0071
Web site: http://www.alliedacademies.org
/econ-ed/aeee.html

All About My Money Kit
918 Hunt Dr.
West Chester, PA 19382
610-399-1510
E-mail: dweldon@dca.net
Web site: www.allaboutmymoney.com

Cuisenaire Company of America
500 Greenview Ct.
Vernon Hills, IL 60061
800-445-5985
Web site: http://www.etacuisenaire.com/index
.htm

Family Math
Lawrence Hall of Science
University of California
Berkeley, CA 94720
800-897-5036
E-mail: gcoates@uclink4.berkeley.edu
Web site: http://www.lhs.berkeley.edu/equals
/FMnetwork.htm

Gnarly Math
The SMP Company
PO Box 1563
Santa Fe, NM 87504
505-983-4138
E-mail: montyph@gnarlymath.com
Web site: www.gnarlymath.com

Hands-On Equations
Borenson & Associates
PO Box 3328
Allentown, PA 18106
800-993-6284
Web site: http://www.borenson .com

Math-U-See
888-854-6284
Web site: www.mathusee.com

Miquon Math materials
F.U.N. Books
1688 Belhaven Woods Court
Pasadena, MD 21122
410-360-7330
Web site: www.unschooling.org

Moving with Math
5100 Gamble Dr.
Minneapolis, MN 55416
800-852-2435
E-mail: mtpckp@aol.com
Web site: www.movingwithmath.com

Saxon Math
Saxon Publishers
2450 John Saxon Blvd.
Norman, OK 73071
800-284-7019
E-mail: info@saxonpub.com.
Web site: http://www1.saxonpub.com/

Singapore Math
19363 Willamette Dr.
West Linn, OR 97068
503-727-5473
E-mail: customerservice@singaporemath
     .com
Web site: www.singaporemath.com

Internet
Absurd Math Interactive: www.absurdmath-inter
     .net/abmath

Algebra Times Newsletter: http://mathkits.com
     /news.html
Boxermath: www.BoxerMath.com
Fractals: http://math.rice.edu/~lanius/frac
Highline Advanced Math:
     http://www.blarg.net/~math/index.html
Japanese Math Challenge: http://www
     .japanese-online.com/math/index.htm
Mega-Math: http://www.c3.lanl.gov
     /mega-math/menu.html
Natural Math: www.naturalmath.com
Pentominos: http://forum.swarthmore.edu/pom
     /project2.95.html
Tangrams: http://forum.swarthmore.edu
     /trscavo/tangrams.html
Tesselations: http://members.tripod.comm
     /~kateDC/tess.htm

Writing

Here are some resources that cover the physical act of writing, and others that explore the proper usage of the written word.

Grammar Songs
Audio Memory Publishing
800-365-7464
E-mail: h1@audiomemory.com
Web site: www.audiomemory.com

Italic Handwriting Series
Portland State University
School of Extended Studies
Box 1394
Portland, OR 97207
800-547-8887, ext. 4891
E-mail: press@ses.pdx.edu
Web site: http://extended.pdx.edu/press/italic
     /italic.htm

National Writing Institute
624 W. University #248

Denton, TX 76201
888-644-8686
Web site: www.writingstrands.com

Swansbury, Inc.
PO Box 117
Aberdeen, MD 21001
410-272-0836
E-mail: Swansbury@erols.com
Web site: www.BFHandwriting.com

Write Guide
835 Josh Dr.
Palmer, AK 99645
907-746-7052
E-mail: contact@writeguide.com
Web site: www.writeguide.com

Zaner-Bloser (workbooks)
2200 W Fifth Avenue
PO Box 16764
Columbus, OH 43216-6764
800-421-3018
Web site: www.zaner-bloser.com

Internet
Cursive Handwriting Rules: http://register
    .argonet.co.uk/users/quilljar/rules.htm
For Southpaws Only: http://register.argonet
    .co.uk/users/quilljar/rules.htm
Handwriting Practice: http://alex.edfac.usyd
    .edu.au/BLP/Sample%20lessons/writ_prac
Lesson Plans: http://www.edhelper.com/cat170
    .htm
Tips for Parents: http://www.hwtears.com
    /parents.htm
Write Guide, Inc: http://www.writeguide.com

Science

Did you know Thomas Edison was a home-schooler? With all these great science resources, you'll never know what your children will invent to join him in the history books!

Carolina Biological Supply Co.
800-334-5551
E-mail: carolina@carolina.com
Web site: www.carolina.com

Edmund Scientific Co.
60 Pearce Ave.
Tonawanda, NY 14150
800-728-6999
E-mail: info@edsci.com
Web site: http://www.edsci.com/Products
    /AdvancedSearch.cfm

Home Training Tools
2827 Buffalo Horn Drive
Laurel, MT 59044
800-860-6272
E-mail: customerservice@hometrainingtools.com
Web site: www.hometrainingtools.com/

MicroChem Kits, LLC
395 Flower Court
Platteville, WI 53818
608-348-3908
Web site: www.microchemkits.com

The Science Education Company
PO Box 60982
Jacksonville, FL 32236
904-388-6381
E-mail: krampf@aol.com
Web site: http://www.krampf.com/

Science Stuff
1104 Newport Ave.
Austin, TX 78753
800-795-7315
Web site: http://sciencestuff.com/nav/

ScienceWorks
800-478-8476
Web site: www.scienceclass.com

Tobin's Lab
PO Box 6503

Glendale, AZ 85312-6503
800-522-4776
E-mail: mike@tobinlab.com
Web site: http://www.tobinlab.com

TOPS Learning Systems
10970 S. Mulino Road
Canby, OR 97013
888-773-9755
E-mail: topsideas@yahoo.com
Web site: http://topscience.org

Internet
Bill Nye: www.billnye.com
Chemistry Quizzes: http://www.1001
    -periodic-table-quiz-questions.com
Children's Butterfly Site: http://www.mesc
    .usgs.gov/butterfly/Butterfly.html
Elementary and Preschool Science: http://www
    .sciencespiders.com/TheScienceSpiders
    /default.htm
Eureka! The Museum for Children: http://www
    .eureka.org.uk/
High School Ideas: http://www.stemnet.nf.ca
    /~jbarron/sh.html
High School Lessons: http://www.eecs.umich
    .edu/mathscience/funexperiments
    /agesubject/highschool.html
Rader's Kapili.com: www.kapili.com
Science Made Simple: http://www.science-
    madesimple.com/projects.html
Star Kids Astronomy Club: http://www.starclass
    .com.au/kids/kids.htmlHistory and Social
    Studies

History and Social Studies
The world's a big place. Bring it home, study its
past, and build hope for its future.

Bluestocking Press
PO Box 2030
Shingle Springs, CA 95682-2030
800-959-8586

E-mail: uncleric@jps.net
Web site: www.bluestockingpress.com

Clarion Books
215 Park Avenue South
New York, NY 10003
800-225-3362
Web site: http://www.houghtonmifflinbooks
    .com/clarion/

Dover Children's Books
31 E 2nd Street
Mineola, NY 11501
Fax: 516-742-6953
Web site: http://store.doverpublications.com/

Greenleaf Press
3761 Hwy. 109 N.
Lebanon, TN 37087
800-311-1408
E-mail: info@greenleafpress.com
Web site: www.greenleafpress.com

Jackdaw Publications
PO Box 503
Amawalk, NY 10501
800-789-0022
Web site: www.jackdaw.com

Smithsonian Shopping
Web site: http://www.si.edu/info/shop.htm

Wide World Books and Maps
4411A Wallingford Ave., N.
Seattle, WA 98103
888-534-3453
E-mail: travel@speakeasy.net
Web site: http://www.travelbooksandmaps.com
    /page.cgi?p=index&k=4

Internet
About Famous People: www.aboutfamous
    people.com
Biographies: http://www.yahooligans.com/School
    _Bell/Social_Studies/History/Biographies/

Civil War Timeline: http://www2.lhric.org
/pocantico/civilwar/timeline.htm

Explorers' Club: http://www.epa.gov/kids

Eye Witness: http://www.ibiscom.com/

Fun Social Studies: http://www.funsocial
studies.com/

Henry VIII and the Tudors: http://www.brims
.co.uk/tudors/index.html

History Channel Classroom: http://www
.historychannel.com/classroom/index.html

Kids' British History: http://www.kidsbritish
history.com/index.html

National Geographic Society: www
.nationalgeographic.com

Stories Past: www.storiespast.com

Vikings: http://home.freeuk.com/elloughton13
/vikings.htm

Foreign Language

In how many languages can you say "Yes!" to
homeschooling?

Audio Forum (carries "Living Language")
96 Broad Street
Guilford, CT 06437-2635
800-243-1234
E-mail: info@audioforum.com
Web site: www.audioforum.com

Bolchazy-Carducci Publishers, Inc. (Latin)
1000 Brown Street
Wauconda, IL 60084
800-392-6453
E-mail: info@bolchazy.com
Web site: http://www.bolchazy.com

International Linguistics Corporation
3505 East Red Bridge
Kansas City, MO 64137
800-237-1830 (816-765-8855)
Web site: www.learnables.com

Muzzy, The BBC Language Course for Children
270 Monroe Turnpike
Monroe, CT 06468

888-248-0480
Web site: http://www.early-advantage.com

Penton Overseas, Inc.
2470 Impala Drive
Carlsbad, CA 92008
800-748-5804
E-mail: info@pentonoverseas.com
Web site: www.pentonoverseas.com

Power-Glide
1682 West 820 North
Provo, UT 84601
800-596-0910
Web site: www.power-glide.com

Programs Abroad Travel Alternatives, Inc. (im-
mersion by travel for teens)
6200 Adel
Austin, TX 78749
888-777-PATA
E-mail: immerse@gopata.com
Web site: www.gopata.comInternet

Internet

American Sign Language Browser: http://comm
techlab.msu.edu/sites/aslweb/browser.htm

Basic Spanish for the Virtual Student: http://
www.itunisie.com/nihed/spanish.html

Ethnologue Page: http://www.sil.org/ethnologue/

French for Beginners: www.frenchforbeginners
.com

French, German, and Spanish for youngsters:
www.literacycenter.net

I Love Languages: http://www.ilovelanguages
.com/

List of Languages: www.tesarta.com/www
/resources/languages.html

World Lingo Translator: http://www
.worldlingo.com/products_services
/worldlingo_translator.html

Art

Start thinking about where you're going to display all the soon-to-be works of art your chil-

dren will present to you. Don't forget, they make great gifts too.

1001 Crafts by J & A
J & A Handy-Crafts, Inc.
165 S Pennsylvania Avenue
Lindenhurst, NY 11757
631-226-2400
Fax: 516-226-2564

Blitz Art Products, Inc.
Web site: www.bruceblitz.com

Curiosity Kits, Inc.
PO Box 811
Cockeysville, MD 21030
800-584-5487
Web site: www.curiositykits.com

Dick Blick Art Materials
PO Box 1267
Galesburg, IL 61402
800-447-8192
Web site: www.dickblick.com

KidsArt
Box 274
Mount Shasta, CA 96067
530-926-5076
E-mail: info@kidsart.com
Web site: http://www.kidsart.com/

Meet the Masters
331 W. Cristobal
San Clemente, CA 92672
949-492-1583
E-mail: Michael@meetTheMasters.com
Web site: www.MeetTheMasters.com

Music

Music can be appreciated on so many levels, whether your child plays an instrument or not. And with the wide variety of sources of instruments and methods for learning how to play, it's easy to fill your home with the sound of music.

Harps of Lorien
PO Box 77
Questa, NM 87556
877-273-8009
E-mail: raphael@kitcarson.net
Web site: http://www.taosnet.com/harpsof
lorien

Homespun Music Tapes
800-33TAPES
E-mail: homespun@hvi.net
Web site: www.homespuntapes.com

Lark in the Morning
PO Box 799
Fort Bragg, CA 95437
707-964-5569
Web site: www.larkinam.com

Mrs. Music Enterprises
310-472-6875

Music Masterworks
303-233-6791
E-mail: info@musicmasterworks.com
Web site: www.musicmasterworks.com

Sing & Learn
2626 Club Meadow
Garland, TX 75043
800-460-1973
Web site: www.singnlearn.com

Suzuki Musical Instruments
PO Box 261030
San Diego, CA 92196
800-854-1594
http://www.suzukimusic.com

Even More Ways to Learn

Stretch your thinking about education and see how many ways there are to learn with resources your children will think are just plain fun.

Audiotapes

Pop one of these companies' tapes into the car tape player, and the trip becomes more interesting than the destination!

A Gentle Wind
Box 3013
Albany, NY 12203
888-386-7664
Web site: www.gentlewind.com

Blackstone Audiobooks
PO Box 969
Ashland, OR 97520
800-729-2665
E-mail: admin@blackstoneaudio.com
Web site: www.blackstoneaudio.com

Bodkin, Odds
Rivertree Publications
PO Box 410
Bradford, NH 03221
800-554-1333
E-mail: odds@oddsbodkin.com
site: www.oddsbodkin.com

Boomerang!
The Children's Audiomagazine About Big Ideas
Box 261
La Honda, CA 94020
800-333-7858
E-mail: boomkids@aol.com
Web site: http://www.boomkids.com/About.html

Family Classics Library
Newport Publishers
912 E. Union St.
Pasadena, CA 91106
626-796-4027
Web site: http://www.audiobookclassics.com

Greathall Productions (Jim Weiss)
PO Box 5061
Charlottesville, VA 22905
Orders: 800-477-6234

E-mail: greathall@greathall.com
Web site: www.greathall.com

The Growler Tapes Audio Adventures
TNG/Earthling, Inc.
110 West 86th Street
New York, New York 10024
800-GROWLER
Web site: www.growler.com

Music for Little People
1144 Redway Road
PO Box 757
Greenland, NH 03840
800-346-4445
Web site: http://www.mflp.com

O'Callahan, Jay
Box 1054
Marshfield, MA 02050
800-626-5356
E-mail: jay@ocallahan.com
Web site: www.ocallahan.com

Yellow Moon Press
800-497-4385
E-mail: story@yellowmoon.com
Web site: www.yellowmoon.com

Games and Puzzles

Countless homeschoolers have found games and puzzles enlightening, fun ways to spend time together as families, learning as they play.

Ampersand Press
750 Lake Street
Port Townsend, WA 98368
800-624-4263
E-mail: info@ampersandpress.com
Web site: http://www.ampersandpress.com/

Animal Town Game Company
PO Box 757
Greenland, NH 03840
800-445-8642

E-mail: info@animaltown.com
Web site: www.animaltown.com

Aristoplay
8122 Main St.
Dexter, MI 48130
800-634-7738
Web site: www.aristoplay.com

Bits and Pieces
One Puzzle Place
Stevens Point, WI 54481
800-544-7297
Web site: www.bitsandpieces.com

Chatham Hill Games
PO Box 253
Chatham, NY 12037
800-554-3039
E-mail: info@chathamhillgames.com
Web site: www.chathamhillgames.com

Family Pastimes
RR 4
Perth, Ontario
Canada K7H 3C6
613-267-4819
E-mail: fp@superaje.com
Web site: www.familypastimes.com

HearthSong
1950 Waldorf NW
Grand Rapids, MI 49550
800-325-2502
Web site: www.hearthsong.com

MindWare
121 5th Avenue NW
New Brighton, MN 55112
800-999-0398
Web site: www.mindwareonline.com

Rex Games, Inc.
530 Howard Street #100
San Francisco, CA 94015-3007
800-542-6375

E-mail: folks@tangoes.com
Web site: http://www.rexgames.com

Software
The Information Age has come of age, and with it a virtual cornucopia of computer software to help children learn. Regardless of age, sex, interests, or needs, today there is something available for everyone.

CD Nation: www.cdnation.com
The Edutainment Catalog: http://www
.ShopMattel.com/education.htm
Educational Resources: www.edresources.com
Gandilab: http://ganilab.hypermart.net
Home Computer Market: www.home
computermarket.com
I.Q. Smart Educational Software:
888-612-4222
Knowledge Adventure: www.knowledge
adventure.com/home
The Learning Company: www.learningco.com
Purplus Software: http://store.yahoo.com
/purplus/
Wildridge Software: www.wildridge.com

Texts
Despite our warnings about textbooks, you may not feel comfortable unless you have a few on your shelves. This section is an attempt to at least keep your spending to a minimum by guiding you to sources of used books!

The Back Pack
PO Box 125
Ernul, NC 28527
252-244-0728
E-mail: backpack@thebackpack.com
Web site: www.thebackpack.com

The Book Cellar (used available)
100 Factory St.
Nashua, NH 03060

800-338-4257
E-mail: bookcellar@bookcellaronline.com
Web site: www.bookcellaronline.com

BUDGETexT Home Education
PO Box 1487
Fayetteville, AR 72702-1487
888-888-2272
Fax: 800-642-2665
E-mail: sales@homeschoolmall.com

Carty's Curriculum Corner
Web site: www.usedbookstore.net

Educators Exchange (used available)
10755 Midlothian Tpk., #308
Richmond, VA 23235
Order: 888-257-4159
Web site: www.edexbooks.com

Follett Home Education (used available)
1433 International Parkway
Woodridge, IL 60517
800-621-4272
E-mail: textbooks@fes.follett.com
Web site: http://www.fes.follett.com/Services
    /HomeEducation.htm

Homeschool Used Books
Web site: www.homeschoolusedbooks.com

Homestead Books
9422 West 58th Avenue
Arvada, CO 80002
303-421-7035
E-mail: books@homesteadbooks.com
Web site: www.homesteadbooks.com

Laurelwood Publications (used available)
82 Laurelwood Drive
Rochester, New York 14626-3758
540-554-2500, 1 to 5 P.M. EST
E-mail: Laurelwd01@aol.com
Web site: http://www.webster.monroe.edu
    /spry/laurelwood.html

Special Needs

If you would like to homeschool but your child has special needs, you don't have to feel alone. These resources are at your disposal for help, advice, and encouragement. If you need leads to more assistance, these folks can point the way.

Internet
Aut-2b-Home: http://home.earthlink.net
    /~tammyglaser79/authome.html
Autism: http://www.homestead.com/whole
    family/wholefamily1.html
Brightword Creations (gifted children with special needs): http://www.brightword.com
Deaf or Hard of Hearing: http://freepages
    .education.rootsweb.com/~maia/start.htm
Do 2 Learn: www.do2learn.com
Dyslexia: http://www.avko.org
Education by Design: http://www.edbydesign
    .com/specneedsres/index.html
Learning Disabilities Online: www.LDOnline.com
Power Learning Network: www.powerlearning
    network.com
Unschooling Special Needs: http://kidsactivities
    .homestead.com/Jacksonspage.html
WeMedia: http://wemedia.precision-email.com
Wright's Law: http://www.wrightslaw.com

E-mail lists
Attention Deficit Hyperactivity Disorder
    (ADHD)
Blank e-mail to: ADHDHomeschool-subscribe
    @topica.com

Autistic Spectrum Children
Blank e-mail to: ASLearningAtHome-subscribe
    @yahoogroups.com

Charlotte Mason for children with special needs
http://groups.Yahoo.com/group/CMspecialkids

Deaf Homeschooling
Blank e-mail to: deafhomeschool-subscribe
    @yahoogroups.com

Organizations
At Our Own Pace
Jean Kulczyk
102 Willow Drive
Waukegan, IL 60087

Gallaudet University Bookstore (American Sign
    Language material and more)
800 Florida Avenue NE
Washington, DC 20002-3695
202-651-5380

Greenwood Institute
RR 2, Box 270
Putney, VT 05346
802-387-4545
E-mail: homeschool@greenwoodinstitute.org
Web site: www.greenwoodinstitute.org

Hadley School for the Blind
PO Box 299
Winnetka, IL 60093
312-323-4238

National Association for the Deaf
814 Thayer Avenue
Silver Spring, MD 20910

National Handicapped Homeschoolers
    Association
PO Box 39
Porthill, ID 83853
208-267-6246
E-mail: nathanews@aol.com
Web site: http://www.nathhan.com

Parents Instructing Challenged Children
615 Utica St.
Fulton, NY 13069
315-592-7257
E-mail: picc@twcny.rr.com
Web site: http://www.amulvey.com/picc

Power Learning Network
E-mail: plnwebmaster@powerlearningnetwork
    .com
Web site: www.powerlearningnetwork.com

Utgnet: Uniqueness, Twice-Gifted
    & Gifted Network (Support network for
    parents and home educators of exceptional
    students—special needs to gifted)

Uni-Gift (Margaret Bradley-Simard)
10831 W Broad Street #231
Glen Allen, VA 23060
804-883-6757, mailbox #2
E-mail: UniGift@aol.com

Catalogs with a Little of This and That

As mentioned before, homeschooling resources
don't always fit into neat little categories, and
neither do the many catalogs that serve up a buf-
fet of items for different subjects and ages. These
catalogs offer wonderful examples of the choices
that await you.

The Book Peddler
PO Box 1960
Elyria, OH 44036-1960
800-928-1760
E-mail: TheBookPeddler@juno.com
Web site: www.the-book-peddler.com

The Education Connection
PO Box 910367
St. George, UT 84791
800-863-3828
E-mail: mailbag@educationconnection.com
Web site: www.educationconnection.com

Creative Teaching Association
562 E. Westover Ave.
Fresno, CA 93727
800-767-4282
E-mail: cta@psnw.com
Web site: www.mastercta.com

The Elijah Company
Rte. 2, Box 100-B
Crossville, TN 38555
888-235-4524
E-mail: elijahco@elijahco.com
Web site: www.elijahco.com

F.U.N. Books
1688 Belhaven Woods Court
Pasadena, MD 21122-3727
888-FUN-7020
E-mail: FUN@FUN-Books.com
Web site: www.FUN-Books.com

Home Again
888-666-0721
E-mail: gnome@home-again.com
Web site: www.home-again.com

Latter Day Family Resources
741 North State Rd. 198
Salem, UT 84653
800-290-2283
E-mail: CustomerService@ldfr.com
Web site: www.ldfr.com

Learning Resources
888-342-5381
Web site: www.learningresources.com

Michael Olaf Essential Montessori
65 Ericson Ct.
Arcata, CA 95521
888-880-9235
E-mail: michaelola@aol.com
Web site: www.michaelolaf.net

Shekinah Curriculum Cellar
101 Meador Road
Kilgore, TX 75662
903-643-2796
E-mail: customerservice@shekinahcc.com
Web site: www.shekinahcc.com

For Teens

Homeschooled teens face increased freedom and choices on their trip toward adulthood as the world continues to open up to them. Here are just a few of the many opportunities available to them, along with sources of inspiration to create even more.

Internet
Colleges that admit homeschoolers:
     http://learninfreedom.org/colleges_4
     _hmsc.html
Collegiate Choice Walking Tour Videos: www
     .collegiatechoice.com
Driver's guide for students: http://golocalnet.net
     /drive
Financial aid review: http://www.Financial
     aidreview.com
General Education Diploma (GED) Prepara-
     tion: www.free-ed.net/fr10/index.html
High School Hub: www.highschoolhub.org
Homeschool/Teens/College: www.homeschool
     teenscollege.net
International exchange program: www.afs.org
National Collegiate Athletic Association
     (NCAA): www.ncaa.org/cbsa/home
     _school.html
Older Kids: http://www.gomilpitas.com
     /homeschooling/olderkids/Transcripts.htm

Programs

AFS International Exchange Program
     (Be or host an exchange student)
313 E 43rd Street
New York, NY 10017
800-AFS-INFO

Apprenticeship Alliance (Be or take on an
     apprentice)
151 Potrero Avenue
San Francisco, CA 94103
415-863-8661

Center for INTERIM Programs
PO Box 2347
Cambridge, MA 02238
617-547-0980
E-mail: InterimCIP@aol.com

Hulbert Outdoor Center
2968 Lake Morey Road
Fairlee, VT 05045
802-333-3405
Web site: http://www.alohavt.org/hulbert
    /school.html

Not Back to School Camp
PO Box 1014
Eugene, OR 97440
541-686-2315
Web site: www.nbtsc.org

Student Conservation Association, Inc. (five
    weeks of work in nature for sixteen- to
    nineteen-year-olds)
PO Box 550
Charlestown, NH 03603-0550
603-543-1700
Web site: www.sca-inc.org

Pretty Neat Odds and Ends

Even more opportunities for your children who
defy even the loose categories we've already established. Enjoy!

Amateur Athletic Union (an alternative to gov-
    ernment school sports)
800-AAU-4USA
Web site: http://www.aausports.org/mytp/home
    /aau_index.js

Autodidactic Press
PO Box 872749
Wasilla, AK 99687
907-376-2932

E-mail: info@autodidactic.com
Web site: www.autodidactic.com

Barnes and Noble
Homeschoolers' discount—check local store for
    details

Clever Moms
http://www.clevermoms.com (save money!)

Computer books for visual learners
www.visibooks.com

Harrisville Designs (children's weaving
    products)
PO Box 806
Harrisville, NH 03450
800-338-9415
E-mail: info@harrisville.com
Web site: http://www.harrisville.com
Home Education Magazine's Free Information
    and Resource Guide
Web site: http://home-ed-magazine.com/ORD
    /frm_hrig.html

How to Start a Learning Cooperative
Houk, Katherine. *Creating a Cooperative Learn-
    ing Center: An Idea Book for Homeschooling
    Families.* Longview Publishing, 2000.

Insect Lore
PO Box 1535
Shafter, CA 93263
800-LIVE BUG
Web site: http://www.insectlore.com/index.html

Lego Mindstorm
Web site: www.legomindsotrms.com/fll/

Math Counts
1420 King St.
Alexandria, VA 22314
Web site: www.mathcounts.org

Nacel Open Door, Inc. (exchange students)
800-856-2411

E-mail: Loony2u@aol.com
Web site: www.nacelopendoor.org

Newsweek Education Program
800-526-2595
Web site: http://school.newsweek.com/

People to People Student Ambassador Program
(two- to three-week adventures for high
school and college age)
Dwight D. Eisenhower Building
110 S. Ferrall Street
Spokane, WA 99202
509-534-0430
E-mail: info@studentambassadors.org
Web site: http://www.studentambassadors.org

Pizza Hut's Book It! Reading Program
800-426-6548
Web site: www.bookitprogram.com

School Is Dead, Learn in Freedom:
http://learninfreedom.org

Think Quest
Advanced Network and Services, Inc.
200 Business Park Dr.
Armonk, NY 10504
Web site: www.thinkquest.org

Toshiba/NSTA Explore Vision Awards
(World's largest K through 12 student science
competition for teams of three to four.
Prizes to $10,000.)
800-EXPLOR-9
E-mail: exploravision@nsta.org
Web site: http://www.toshiba.com/tai
/exploravision/howtoenter.html

Staples
Now providing teacher discount to homeschoolers with "proof" (support group
membership card or something similar)

U. S. Chess Federation
3054 NYS Route 9W

New Windsor, NY 12553
800-388-5464
Web site: www.uschess.org

World of Science
Homeschoolers' discount—check local store for
details

Young Astronauts Council
202-682-1984
E-mail: YoungAstronauts@aol.com
Web site: http://www.yac.org/yac/index.asp

General Internet Sites for Parents

These sites are not necessarily homeschool specific, but they contain even more information that
will enrich your family's homeschool experience.

Aware Parenting
Web site: www.awareparenting.com

Building and Construction Books
Web site: http://www.b4ubuild.com

The Children's Book Council
Web site: http://www.cbcbooks.org

Consumer Information Catalog
Web site: http://www.pueblo.gsa.gov

Deschooling
Web site: http://www.deschooling.org

Educator's Guide to Free Video Tapes
Web site: www.freeteachingaids.com

Frugal Living Resources
Web site: http://www.igc.apc.org/frugal

Homeschooling Conferences
Web site: www.teach-at-
home.com/Lisevents.asp

Homeschooling History
Web site: http://www.americanhomeschool
association.org (click "information on
homeschooling")

Natural Learning Rhythms
Web site: http://www.encompass-nlr.org

Parent Soup
Web site: http://ww.parentsoup.com

Spare the Child
Web site: www.sparethechild.com

Study Web
Web site: www.studyweb.com

Teaching Is Easy
Web site: www.TeachingIsEasy.com

World Book Scope and Sequence
Web site: www.worldbook.com/ptrc/html
    /curr.htm

Site-Seeing for Kids

You're going to have to take a break once in a while from all your Net surfing and e-mail looping. Grab the children and check out these terrific sites they're sure to love. They'll lead you to other sites that will lead you to still more sites . . . you get the idea!

Africa Online
Web site: http://www.africaonline.com

A. Pintura, Art Detective
Web site: www.eduweb.com/pintura

Brain Pop
Web site: www.brainpop.com

Kids Carpentry
Web site: www.kidscarpentry.com

Children's Music Web
Web site: www.childrensmusic.org

The Concord Review
Web site: http://www.tcr.org

Exploratorium
Web site: http://www.exploratorium.edu

Franklin Institute of Science
Web site: http://sln.fi.edu

Kids Bank
Web site: http://www.kidsbank.com

Lego Site
Web site: www.lego.com

Little Explorers
Web site: http://www.EnchantedLearning.com
    / Dictionary.html

Louvre Museum
Web site: http://mistral.culture.fr/louvre/louvrea
    .htm

MEGA Mathematics
Web site: http://www.c3.lanl.gov/mega-math

NASA
Web site: http://www.nasa.gov

PBS OnLine
Web site: http://www.pbs.org

Scout School
Web site: http://www.cis.net/~cmmeyer
    /ScoutSchool

Seussville
Web site: www.randomhouse.com/seussville

Smithsonian Institute Homepage
Web site: http://www.si.edu

Terra Server Homepage
Web site: http://terraserver.microsoft.com

Things Useful to the Educated Reader
Web site: www.naciente.com/reader.htm

State Legislative Web Site Links

One of the best ways to preserve the freedom to homeschool is to *stay informed!* When rumors fly about legislation that could potentially bear on homeschoolers, it's best to go directly to the source. The Internet makes this easier than ever, as most states offer links to this information free for the taking.

Many thanks to Laura Derrick, an active homeschool advocate from Texas, for compiling the original list, updated for your use. The links are accurate at the time of publication.

Alabama State Legislature
Web site: http://www.legislature.state.al.us
    /ALISHome.html

Alaska State Legislature
Web site: http://www.legis.state.ak.us

ALIS Home Page (Arizona)
Web site: http://www.azleg.state.az.us

Arkansas General Assembly
Web site: http://www.arkleg.state.ar.us

Official California Legislative Information
Web site: http://www.leginfo.ca.gov

Colorado General Assembly
Web site: http://www.state.co.us/gov_dir
    /stateleg.html

Connecticut Legislative Guide
Web site: http://www.cga.state.ct.us/default.htm

State of Delaware General Assembly
Web site: http://www.state.de.us/research
    /assembly.htm

Online Sunshine—The Florida Legislature
Web site: http://www.leg.state.fl.us

Georgia General Assembly
Web site: http://www.state.ga.us/Legis

Hawaii Legislative Reference Bureau
Web site: http://www.hawaii.gov/lrb/lib.html

Idaho Legislature
Web site: http://www.state.id.us/legislat
    /legislat.html

State of Illinois Legislature
Web site: http://www.state.il.us/state/legis/

Indiana General Assembly
Web site: http://www.in.gov/legislative/

Iowa General Assembly
Web site: http://www.legis.state.ia.us

Kansas Legislative Services
Web site: http://www.ink.org/public/legislative

Kentucky Legislative Services
Web site: http://www.lrc.state.ky.us/home.htm

Louisiana State Legislature
Web site: http://www.legis.state.la.us/

State of Maine Legislative Home Page
Web site: http://www.state.me.us/legis

Maryland General Assembly Home Page
Web site: http://mlis.state.md.us

The General Court (Massachusetts)
Web site: http://www.magnet.state.ma.us
    /legis/legis.htm

Minnesota State Legislature
Web site: http://www.leg.state.mn.us

Michigan State Legislature
Web site: http://www.michiganlegislature.org/

Mississippi State Legislature
Web site: http://www.ls.state.ms.us

Missouri General Assembly
Web site: http://www.moga.state.mo.us

Montana Legislative Branch
Web site: http://leg.state.mt.us/

Nebraska Legislature
Web site: http://www.unicam.state.ne.us/

Nevada State Legislature Home Page
Web site: http://www.leg.state.nv.us

New Hampshire General Court
Web site: http://gencourt.state.nh.us/ns/

New Jersey State Legislature: Home Page
Web site: http://www.njleg.state.nj.us

New Mexico Legislature: Home Page
Web site: http://www.technet.nm.org/legislature

New York State Assembly—Welcome Page
Web site: http://assembly.state.ny.us

North Carolina General Assembly
Web site: http://ftp.legislature.state.nc.us

North Dakota Legislative Branch
Web site: http://www.state.nd.us/lr

State Front Page: Legislative Branch (Ohio)
Web site: http://www.ohio.gov/ohio/legislat
    .htm

Legislature (Oklahoma)
Web site: http://www.lsb.state.ok.us/

Oregon State Legislature
Web site: http://www.leg.state.or.us

Pennsylvania Senate WWW Server
Web site: http://www.pasen.gov

Rhode Island General Assembly
Web site: http://www.rilin.state.ri.us

South Carolina State House Network
Web site: http://www.lpitr.state.sc.us

South Dakota Legislature
Web site: http://legis.state.sd.us/index.cfm

Tennessee General Assembly
Web site: http://www.legislature.state.tn.us

Texas Legislature Online
Web site: http://www.capitol.state.tx.us

Utah State Legislature
Web site: http://www.le.state.ut.us/

Vermont Legislative Home Page
Web site: http://www.leg.state.vt.us

Virginia General Assembly
Web site: http://legis.state.va.us

Washington State Legislature
Web site: http://www.leg.wa.gov/wsladm
    /default.htm

West Virginia Legislature
Web site: http://www.legis.state.wv.us/

Wisconsin State Legislature
Web site: http://www.legis.state.wi.us

Wyoming State Legislature
Web site: http://legisweb.state.wy.us

APPENDIX B

State-by-State Information

Homeschooling Requirements in the United States*

	Statutory language describing nonschool options	Statutory requirements for the home teacher	Does statute give education officials discretion to judge and disallow program?	Does statute require standardized tests for pupil?	Home School or compulsory education law—citations
Alabama	(1) Instruction by tutor; or (2) Qualify as church school	Certification of tutor under option 1 only	Yes, under option 1 only	No	Alabama Code 16-28-3
Alaska	(1) Tutored by certified teacher; or (2) Enrolled in full-time approved correspondence course; or (3) Educational experience approved by LEA**; or (4) Meet requirements for private or religious schools (current SEA policy)	Teacher certificate under option 1	LEA approval under option 3 only	Yes, for options 2 and 4 only; testing at grades 4, 6, and 8	Alaska Statutes 14-30.010; 14.45-120(a)

*Adapted from Patricia Lines, "Homeschooling: An Overview for Education Policy Makers," Working Paper for the U.S. Department of Education, Office of Educational Research and Improvement (Rev. March 1997).

**Abbreviations: "LEA" means local education agency—either a designated official or board at the local level. "SEA" means state education agency and can mean either the state board or the state school chief. "Parent" includes guardians. "H.S." means high school. "NTE" means National Teachers Examination. The phrase "home can be a school" is consistently used to mean that some administrative or judicial authority in the state has ruled that a home can qualify as a private school under the requirements for private schools in the state. This may also be true in other states, but if there is no formal ruling on the matter, it is not included.

Arizona	Home instruction by parent or other tutor	None	No	No	Ariz. Rev. Stat. 15-802 through 805; 15-745
Arkansas	Home school	None (except for special needs students)	No (sec. 6-15-503(b): Reports to SEA are for statistical purposes only)	Yes. Children seven and older are to take a standardized test from an SBA list; children at age 14 also must take state's eighth-grade minimal competency test. Remediation required if below standard.	Ark. Stat. Ann. 6-18-201, 6-15-501
California	(1) Instruction by tutor; or (2) Independent study arranged through school; or (3) Submit documents as a private school	Tutor's certificate under option 1	No	No	Calif. Educ. Code sec. 48222; 48224; 51745
Colorado	(1) Instructed by certified teacher; or (2) "Home-based education"; or (3) Enrolled in private school that permits independent study at home (People in re D.B., 767 P.2d 801 (Colo. App. 1988)	Teacher certificate under option 1	No	Option 2 (which is structured as an exemption from compulsory requirements) depends on child testing above 13th percentile, at grades 3, 5, 7, 9, and 11. Child has opportunity for re-test before exemption is denied.	Col. Rev. Stat. 22-33-104 and 104.5
Connecticut	"Equivalent" instruction "elsewhere"	None	No	The SEA guidelines recommend a portfolio review; all LEAs require it	Conn. Gen. Stat. Ann. 10-184

continues

	Statutory language describing nonschool options	Statutory requirements for the home teacher	Does statute give education officials discretion to judge and disallow program?	Does statute require standardized tests for pupil?	Home School or compulsory education law—citations
Delaware	"Regular and thorough" instruction "elsewhere"	None	Law authorizes SEA to set approval standards, but it does not do so	Law authorizes SEA to require examinations, but SEA does not do so	Delaware Code 14-2702 through 2703
Florida	"Sequentially progressive instruction . . . by . . . parent"	None	No	Law requires an evaluation. It can be by means of testing, portfolio assessment, evaluation by trained third party, or any valid method authorized by the LEA.	Fla. Stat. Ann. 232.01
Georgia	"Home study"	Parent must have H.S. degree or GED; teacher who is not a parent must have college degree	No	Yes, but law specifies that parents are not required to submit test (§20-2-690[7]); reevaluation required if pupil does not show progress after one year of remediation at home	Official Code of Georgia Ann. 20-2-690
Hawaii	(1) "Appropriate alternate educational program"; or (2) "Home school" filing certain papers; or (3) Instruction by tutor	Under option 3, tutor must have B.A. degree	SEA approval required under option 1 only	Yes; standardized testing in grades 3, 6, 8, and 10	Hawaii Rev. Stat. 298-9
Idaho	"Comparably instructed"	None	No	No	Idaho Code 33-202

336

State					
Illinois	School attendance only, but home can be a school; People v. Levison, 404 Ill. 574, 90 N.E. 2d 213 (1950)	None	No	No	Ill. Rev. Stat. ch. 122, par. 26-1
Indiana	"Equivalent" instruction	None	No	No	Ind. Stat. Ann. 20-8.1-3-17 and 20-8.1-3-34
Iowa	"Competent private instruction," which the statute defines as instruction for 37 days per quarter, resulting in student progress	Teacher certificate unless parent enrolls child in a home school assistance program or otherwise offers "competent private instruction"	No	Yes, standardized test or other evaluation, including portfolio review. Must be above 30th percentile or make six months progress in year.	Iowa Code Ann. 299A.1
Kansas	School attendance only, but several unpublished court decisions have ruled that home can be a school	None	No	No	Kan. Stat. Ann. 72-1111 through 72-1113
Kentucky	School attendance only, but state board regs. allow home to be a school	None	No	No	Ky. Rev. Stat. 159-010 through 159.990
Louisiana	"Home study"	None	No, so long as parent certifies that the curriculum is equal in quality to that offered in the public schools	Yes, or evaluation by a certified teacher	LA. Rev. Stat. 17:221(A) and 17.236

continues

	Statutory language describing nonschool options	Statutory requirements for the home teacher	Does statute give education officials discretion to judge and disallow program?	Does statute require standardized tests for pupil?	Home School or compulsory education law—citations
Maine	"Equivalent instruction through home instruction"	None	SEA approval. Copy of application must go to LEA, which has opportunity to comment	Yes, or evaluation by a certified teacher, an LEA advisory panel, or a home school panel that includes a certified teacher	Me. Rev. Stat. Ann. 20A–5001A
Maryland	"Otherwise receiving regular, thorough instruction" in subjects usually taught in public school	None	No	No (voluntary testing at local public schools)	Ann. Code of Md., ch. 22, 7-301(a)
Massachusetts	"Otherwise instructed in a manner approved in advance by the superintendent or school committee"	None	LEA approval	Not by statute, but LEA may do so (several evaluation options available)	Mass. Gen. Laws 76-1
Michigan	Nonstatutory option: Attorney General opinion holds home can be a school. A.G. Op. 5579 9/27/79). New statutory option as of July, 1996: A child is in compliance with compulsory education laws if he or she is "being educated by his or her parent . . . at . . . home in an organized educational program that is appropriate" to the child's age and ability, and that covers specified subject areas.	None	No	No	S.B. 679, Amendment A, signed into Law Jan. 9, 1996 with effective date of July 1, 1996

State	Definition	Requirements		Statute
Minnesota	"Home-school" is included in definition of school	(1) Teacher certificate; or (2) Supervised by certified teacher; or (3) Pass teacher competency exam; or (4) Use of accredited program approved by board; or (5) College degree; or (6) Be a parent teaching a child who complies with pupil testing requirements	No	Yes, option 6 only; children below 30th percentile must be evaluated for learning problems	Minn. Stat. Ann. 120.101 and 127.20
Mississippi	Home instruction	None	No	No	Miss. Code Ann. 37-13-91
Missouri	"Home school"	None	No	No	Ann. Mo. Stat. 167-031 and 167.042
Montana	"Home school"	None	No	No	Mont. Code Ann. 20-5-102 and 20-5-109

continues

	Statutory language describing nonschool options	Statutory requirements for the home teacher	Does statute give education officials discretion to judge and disallow program?	Does statute require standardized tests for pupil?	Home School or compulsory education law—citations
Nebraska	School attendance only, but SEA allows home to qualify as (1) An "approved" private school; or (2) "Exempt" private school where parents have sincere religious objection	(1) Teacher certificate; or (2) Meet board standards for exempt private school	No, but SEA approval required for option 1	Statute gives board discretion to require tests but it does not require them	Neb. Rev. Stat. 79-201, 79-1701, 85-607
Nevada	"Equivalent instruction" at home	(1) Teacher certificate or (2) Parent must consult with certified teacher (requirement waived after one year of pupil progress); or (3) Use approved correspondence program; or (4) Board waiver	No. Statute requires "satisfactory written evidence" of kind approved by SEA, but SEA regs. leave no discretion if specified information is submitted	Not by statute, but SEA regs. requires testing at grades 2, 3, 4, 7, and 8 for options 1 and 2	Nev. Rev. Stat. 392.070
New Hampshire	"Home education," which consists of "planned and supervised instructional and related educational activities . . ."	None	SEA approval (sec. 193A)	Yes; or take a district test; or obtain a teacher evaluation or other valid evaluation of child's portfolio	N.H. Rev. Stat. Ann. 193:1 and 193-A

New Jersey	"Equivalent instruction elsewhere"	None	No. LEA limited to verifying subject matter coverage, Cf. State v. Massa, 95 N.J. Super. 382, 231 A.2d 252 (Morris County Ct. Law Div. 1967)	No	N.J. Stat. Ann. 18A.38-25
New Mexico	"A home study program that provides a basic academic educational program" operated by parent	High school diploma or equivalent	No	Yes	N.M. Stat. Ann. 22-1-2 and 21-1-2.1
New York	Attendance "elsewhere" and instruction that is "substantially equivalent" by "competent" teacher	Must be "competent"	LEA has authority to determine equivalency	Not by statute, but SEA requires taking test from list of SEA-approved tests	N.Y. Educ. Law 3204, 3205, 3210, 3212
North Carolina	"Home school" serving children from no more than two families	Must be parent or member of household of one of two families forming home school; and have high school degree or equivalent	No	Yes; annually	N.C. Gen. Stat. 115C-378, 115C-547, 115C-563 through 565

continues

	Statutory language describing nonschool options	Statutory requirements for the home teacher	Does statute give education officials discretion to judge and disallow program?	Does statute require standardized tests for pupil?	Home School or compulsory education law—citations
North Dakota	"Home-based instruction"	Parent must be (1) Certified; or (2) Have high school education and be supervised by certified teacher; or (3) Pass national teacher exam	Parent reports to LEA; may determine if child is making satisfactory progress for children testing below 30th percentile	Yes	N.D. Cent. Code 15-34.1-03 and 15-34.1-04
Ohio	"Instructed at home by a person qualified to teach the branches on which instruction is required . . ."	(1) H.S. degree or equivalent; or (2) Satisfactory test scores showing equivalence; or (3) Supervised by person with college degree until child shows proficiency on test	LEA approval, as delimited by State Board Regulations	Yes; or evaluation by a certified teacher; an agreed-upon person, or undergo alterna-tive assessment	Ohio Rev. Code 3301-34-04, 3321.03, and 3321.04
Oklahoma	"Other means of education . . . for the full term the schools of the district are in session"	None	No	No	Okla. Stat. Ann., Title 70 10-105(A) and (B)
Oregon	Instruction by a parent or other qualified person	None	No	Yes. Parents may choose among a list of standardized tests.	Oregon Rev. Stat 339.010, 339.030, and 339.035

State	Definition	Teacher Qualification	Approval	Testing/Evaluation	Citation
Pennsylvania	(1) "Regular daily instruction . . . by a properly qualified private tutor" and satisfactory to district superintendent; or (2) "Home education program"	Certificaton for option 1; H.S. degree or equivalent for option 2	LEA approval	Yes, at grades 3, 5, and 8, plus annual evaluation of portfolio by certified teacher or other specified professional	Pa. Stat. Ann., Title 24, 13-1326 and 13-1327
Rhode Island	"At-home instruction approved by the school committee . . ."	None	LEA approval	No, but SEA gives LEA authority to require an evaluation	R.I. Gen. Laws 16-19-1
South Carolina	Parents "may teach their children at home"; must meet specific requirements listed in statute	H.S. degree or equivalent	Approval by LEA, So. Carolina Ass'n. of Indep. Home Schools, or other association with 50 or more members and meets other requirements in statute (state reviews association standards periodically)	Yes	Code of Laws of S.C. Ann. 59-65-10, 40, 45, and 47
South Dakota	"Alternative instruction for an equivalent period of time . . . in the basic skills"	None	If probable cause exists to believe family is not in compliance, SEA may deny status	Yes. Parents may choose any nationally standardized test.	S.D. Comp. Law 13-27-2, 13-27-3 and 49-6-3001

continues

	Statutory language describing nonschool options	Statutory requirements for the home teacher	Does statute give education officials discretion to judge and disallow program?	Does statute require standardized tests for pupil?	Home School or compulsory education law—citations
Tennessee	(1) "Home school" "conducted by parents . . . for their own children . . ."; or (2) Affiliated with and supervised by church school	H.S. degree or GED required to teach grades K–8, and college degree for grades 7–12 under option 1; no requirement for option 2. SEA has authority to grant exemptions to requirements.	No	Yes; at grades 2, 5, 7, and 9. If child is 6 to 9 months behind in core subjects, parent must work with certified teacher to develop remedial course.	Tenn. Code Ann. 49-6-3001 and 49-6-3050
Texas	School attendance, "which includes home schools"	None	No	No	Tex. Educ. Code 4.25, 21.032 through 21.040
Utah	"Taught at home in the subjects prescribed by the state board . . ."	None	LEA approval	No	Utah Code Ann. 53A-11-1012
Vermont	A "home study program"	None	SEA approval	Yes; or other assessment among various options listed in statute	Vt. Stat. Ann. Title 16, 1121; 16(11); 166b

State	Definition		Testing	Citation
Virginia	(1) "Instruction of children by their parents in their home"; or (2) Child enrolled in approved correspondence course; or (3) Program approved by division superintendent; or (4) Bona fide religious objection to school attendance (§22.1–254.1D); or (5) Use of certified teacher	For option 1, parent must hold college degree, or qualify as teacher · Yes, under option 4	Yes (must achieve 4th stanine on test) or undergo alternative assessment approved by LEA. Law allows 1 year probation if test results are unsatisfactory.	Va. Code 22.1–254.1
Washington	"Home-based" instruction with "planned and supervised activities" and which covers basic skills provided by parent to their own children only	(1) Parent has 45 college credits or completes a course on home instruction at a postsecondary institution or a vocational technical institute; or (2) Parent teaches under supervision of state certified teacher; or (3) LEA deems parent qualified to teach · No	Yes; SEA-approved tests taken annually; or annual assessment by a certified person currently working in education	Wash. Rev. Code 28A.200.200; 28A.225.10

continues

345

	Statutory language describing nonschool options	Statutory requirements for the home teacher	Does statute give education officials discretion to judge and disallow program?	Does statute require standardized tests for pupil?	Home School or compulsory education law—citations
West Virginia	(1) "Instruction . . . in the home" or place approved by the LEA and by a "qualified" person; or (2) File report on home school program	Under option 1, home teacher must be qualified to teach publich elementary school. Under option 2, teacher must have H.S. degree and a) 4 years formal education above the pupil's; or b) achieve acceptable score on NTE. NOTE: The 4-year rule has been waived until June 1, 2003 pending a study on the effects of home instruction exemption by the oversight commission on education accountability.	Yes, under option 1; no, under option 2	Yes. In addition, SEA has authority to adopt guidelines for alternative assessments for special education students.	W. Va. 18-18-1
Wisconsin	"Homebased educational program provided . . . by the child's parents . . . or by a person designated by the parent . . ."	None	No	No	Wis. Stat. Ann. 118.15 and 118.165
Wyoming	"Basic academic education program" at home, and approved by LEA	None	Yes	No	Wyo. Stat. 21-4-101

Other Jurisdictions:

District of Columbia	"Equivalent" instruction	None	Yes	No	D.C. Code 31-401 and 402
American Samoa	No statutory provision	If qualifying as private school, certified teacher required	Yes, if qualifying as private school	No	American Samoa Code 16.0302 through 16.0308
Guam	Home instruction by parent or tutor	None quarterly	No, but Guam board rules require approval	No, but Guam board regulations require testing or other assessment	Guam Code Ann. Tit. 17, 6101 through 6109
Virgin Islands	Home instruction by parent teacher	None	Commissioner of Education must approve program	No, but Dept. of Education meets with parents and children	V.I. Code Ann. Tit. 17, 81 through 97
Puerto Rico	No statutory provision	None for private schools	None for private schools	No	P.R. laws Ann. Tit. 18, secs. 71–81
Northern Marianas	Home study	To be set by board	Yes	No	Mariana Code 3-1141

Author's Notes on Table

- The table is based on statutory analysis; check with your State Board of Education to verify information or to obtain updated information.

- Column three, "Does statute require approval" indicates that approval is needed if the SEA or LEA has authority to do something more than simply verify that the required documents are filed and provide the required information. Note all states except Texas and Oklahoma have mandatory or voluntary filing requirements. Typically, a parent must provide the name, age, grade of child instructed, and often material on the curriculum are part of information reported. Many states identify the form as a "notice of intent to home school."

- The table does not include information applicable to all children, whether in home school or other school, for example, age of compulsory education, and durational requirements for the school day and school year. Most states mandate the same requirements for all children, regardless of where they are educated.

- The table does not attempt to resolve legal ambiguities. Where a state or local education agency adopts rules that are not specifically authorized by the statute, there is always a question of the extent to which the rules are authorized. The table does attempt to indicate the situation where the agency is the source of a policy, if only to note the possibility of a legal challenge. Of course, a board with express authority to approve a home program will be in a better position to defend its more stringent requirements.

Index